Reading the Room

APPLE NAME: 4-PLAYER MODEL

The Kantor 4-Player Model Mini-Assessment will help individuals assess themselves to gain insight into the underlying drivers behind their most characteristic management and communications behaviors, which inform how they work with individuals, teams, and within organizations. With the app, users take a simple 11 question assessment to determine how they rate within Kantor's four "Action Modes" (introduced in Chapter 2 of the book), which can be described in one of four ways: Moving, Following, Opposing, or Bystanding. After taking the assessment, the app provides users with a report that includes their Action Mode profile, basic guidance, and tips specific to their profile, as well as the associated talents and traps of that profile.

Functionality and features include:

- An interactive in-app assessment with a graphic interface
- Personalized report generation based on your input
- The ability to share your report with others via email
- Sharing through your social media accounts including Facebook and Twitter

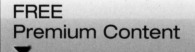

FREE
Premium Content
▼

JOSSEY-BASS™
An Imprint of
✪WILEY

This book includes premium content that can be accessed from our Web site when you register at **www.josseybass.com/go/davidkantor** using the password *professional*.

Reading the Room

GROUP DYNAMICS FOR
COACHES AND LEADERS

David Kantor

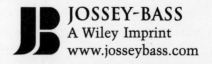

JOSSEY-BASS
A Wiley Imprint
www.josseybass.com

Published by Jossey-Bass
A Wiley Imprint
One Montgomery Street, Suite 1200, San Francisco, CA 94104-4594—www.josseybass.com

All figures originally created by David Kantor, The Monitor Group, and the Kantor Institute. Figures 6.1, 15.1, and 15.2 were illustrated by Kelly Alder.

Jossey-Bass books and products are available through most bookstores. To contact Jossey-Bass directly call our Customer Care Department within the U.S. at 800-956-7739, outside the U.S. at 317-572-3986, or fax 317-572-4002.

Wiley publishes in a variety of print and electronic formats and by print-on-demand. Some material included with standard print versions of this book may not be included in e-books or in print-on-demand. If this book refers to media such as a CD or DVD that is not included in the version you purchased, you may download this material at http://booksupport.wiley.com. For more information about Wiley products, visit www.wiley.com.

Library of Congress Cataloging-in-Publication Data
Kantor, David.
  Reading the room: group dynamics for coaches and leaders / David Kantor.—1st ed.
    p. cm.
  Includes bibliographical references and index.
  ISBN 978-0-470-90343-8 (cloth); ISBN 978-1-118-22120-4; ISBN 978-1-118-23504-1; ISBN 978-1-118-25960-3
  1. Communication in organizations. 2. Communication in management. 3. Small groups. 4. Leadership. I. Title.
  HD30.3.K364 2012
  658.4'092—dc23
                              2012008211

Printed in the United States of America

FIRST EDITION

HB Printing   10 9 8 7 6 5 4 3 2 1

CONTENTS

Preface   ix

ONE Reading the Room: Introduction and Framework   1

PART ONE A Complete Language for Understanding
Leader Behavior   21

TWO Level I: Action Stances: The Four-Player Model   23

THREE Level II: Domains of Communication: Affect,
Power, and Meaning   49

FOUR Level III: Systems in Control of Speech   79

FIVE The Behavioral Profile: A Synthesis of Levels
I, II, and III   109

PART TWO Identity and Leader Behavior in High Stakes   125

SIX Level IV: Stories, Identity, and Structured Behavior   127

SEVEN Narrative Purpose   151

EIGHT Leader Behavior in High-Stakes Situations   167

NINE The Heroic Leader in Crisis   193

TEN Sources and Signs of Moral Corruption in Leaders   231

PART THREE Models and the Ultimate Leader   263

ELEVEN From Personal Model to Leadership Model   265

TWELVE Building a Leadership Model   281

THIRTEEN A Model for Living   315

FOURTEEN Beyond the Behavioral Profile   339

FIFTEEN A Structural Dynamics Analysis of Barack Obama   361

AFTERWORD Where Structural Dynamics Goes from Here   385

Notes   387

Acknowledgments   399

About the Author   401

Index   403

To Meredith, my wife, my beacon, my muse, and my teacher in the ways of love

PREFACE
GETTING TO THE MODEL

There are communication problems, and then there are communication problems with billions of dollars and the careers of all involved hanging in the balance.

Reading the Room is a guide for coaches and leaders, designed to help untangle problems in communication in the office, at home, and in high-stakes situations. The text uses ClearFacts, a fast-growing green energy company, and the interactions of a credible cast of characters to unveil structural dynamics—a theory of communication that defines leadership behavior both in easy and hard times.

Following is an excerpt from Chapter Eight of the text, a typical testy interchange between Martha Curtis and Howard Green, two members of CEO Ralph Waterman's management team.

MARTHA: Ralph? Ian? This is a key procedural issue. This is about decision rights. I want to know whether Art or Ron or I have the authority Howard has assumed. Where the hell is our touted transparency? What he's done is irresponsible.

HOWARD: Don't ever talk to me about irresponsibility. I work hard and I produce. That's what leaders do.

MARTHA: You're no leader in my book. Leaders guide; they do not bullwhip.

HOWARD: Wrong, Martha. What leader of note has not taken a whip to a dumb mule?

RALPH: *(In a loud, cracked voice, almost shrieking)* Whoa! Hold that cursed tongue, Howard; you sound like a slave-master. Not

in this firm. Martha, you're not in control. *(Silence follows.)*
Sorry, I lost it. There is a blurry margin here. Why not put
a stop to the wrangling you two get into and let Ian look
into it?

Martha and Howard spar often, but generally manage to keep their underlying dislike and distrust under wraps when pressures on them are tolerably low. When the stakes sharply rise later, and the company faces a serious moral and financial crisis, they will clash violently, and their ability to make good decisions, the mark of good leadership in hard times, will suffer.

Notice in this exchange that Ralph stumbles into what I call the *communicative field.* In a session with his coach, Duncan Travis, we will learn what led him to temporarily lose control, what triggered him to take sides, and why, in that moment, he could not do what he'd learned he must do as a leader.

Utilizing both story and conceptual format, *Reading the Room* spells out the complete theory underlying the model of leadership Travis uses with CEO Ralph Waterman to speed his, Ralph's, journey: a quest to become a great leader with a leadership model of his own.

This model of leadership did not spring up overnight. Rather, it is the product of my nearly fifty years as a therapist, teacher, and coach. Getting to the model has been an informative journey, and the story of its evolution will help you develop your own.

STRUCTURAL DYNAMICS: EVOLUTION IN THREE CONTEXTS

Structural dynamics is a theory of how face-to-face communication works and does not work in human systems. Its roots lie in *systems theory,* the study of phenomena as systems of interrelated parts. Like other theories that apply systems thinking to human organizations, this theory has its own notion of structure. In *Reading the Room,* I delve into this structure of face-to-face communication, define its parts, and examine how these interdependent parts interact.

As an undergraduate, I balanced my major in psychology with an interest in its social applications and the individual aspects of behavior. These interests led me in turn to sociology, social psychology, and social anthropology.

By the mid-1960s, I had been drawn into the burgeoning field of family systems therapy and its origins in systems thinking. I was captivated by Ludwig von Bertalanffy and Norbert Wiener.

In those exciting, paradigm-shifting times, psychoanalytically oriented therapies were being challenged by newly conceived systems-oriented theories and methods that focused not on the individual patient but on the family as the client system. These methods were initially taught at free-standing institutes, academia only taking over years later. I, with colleagues, launched such an institute in Boston in 1967; another in Cambridge four years later; then a third, under my name, six years after that.

At the Kantor Family Institute, structural dynamics theory was taught alongside those introduced by the pioneers. Formerly known as "methods" or "approaches," I began to call them "models" instead, though my understanding of models would not fully mature until many years later when, in 1990, I formalized the idea of a "model of models."

What I sensed in the 1970s and 1980s was that the family systems pioneers were better at providing methods of intervention than they were at describing the theories that guided these treatment recommendations. Struck by this gap, I was determined to strengthen the links between my own theory and practice.

I was awarded an NIMH grant to study families in their own milieus.[1] My staff and I set out to study twenty-one families in all: one third were families with schizophrenics living at home at the time of the study, one third were families that had sought therapy to improve functioning, and one third were families that had never sought help and appeared to be well functioning. Our research purpose was to study the nature of communication across the three family categories and to discover differences, if any, between them.

No one before had studied families *in situ*. After testing the project's procedures in my own home, a special group of participant observers were brought aboard.[2] Each took up residence in one of the study households 24/7 for thirty days and nights. Tape recorders in every room ran nonstop, capturing every word and recognizable vocal sound. We saw everything.

The live-in observers kept notes and left the households daily at quiet times to report and record observations the machines could not capture. Both the taped and human observations were transcribed by a secretarial staff of fifteen. Both sets of transcriptions, filling a 15-by-18-by-20-foot room floor to ceiling, were analyzed by myself and Will Lehr with the help of four handpicked research assistants over a period of two years. The final results were published by Jossey-Bass in the book *Inside the Family* in 1977.

By the project's official end, the nascent theory with which we began had taken a big leap forward. Many of the concepts that appear in *Reading the Room* were established in the course of this research, notably the four-player model, the three domains of communication, and the three operating systems. Whereas we learned much about sequences and patterns of communication, yet to come was an explanation of why and how behavior changed when the people or the system itself was put under pressure.[3]

As you will see, it would take a closer look at couples to even begin to understand behavior change in high-stakes and crisis situations. I did this work in two steps: a study of one couple in their home and, several years later, a more elaborate study of twenty couples who had come to me for therapy and saw the value of simultaneously serving as subjects in research.

The First Step: The Friedmans

So, one year later, I moved tape recorders and cameras into the household of a young, recently married couple in a more limited but more focused study.[4] What could a young couple just starting out tell us about the more established patterns of communication we saw in the full-fledged family study? I was curious as to how these patterns, patterns of communication and miscommunication, got started.

Every other day, in the hours surrounding the couple's evening meal, a research assistant would visit, start the recordings, and leave. "The devices became mere parts of the landscape," the Friedmans said. So much so that the tapes were often forgotten until they ran out. After reviewing the tapes, I would follow up with a visit, in particular to explore the origins of the couple's fights.

They led me to the source, a very particular childhood story that was dramatically cathartic for both Friedmans in the telling, and eye-opening for the reflective researcher in me. Such stories, hinted at over and over by the couples in the family study, had a structure all their own. I set out to confirm or disconfirm what I had seen. I could do this informally on my own in my clinical work with individuals, but the training context offered a unique opportunity to do so in greater numbers.

At the Family Institute of Cambridge, which I cofounded with Carter Umbarger and Barry Dym in 1974, my class alone contained as many as fifteen systems therapists at any given time. In a training feature meant to deepen self-knowledge and clinical expertise, trainees took part in an exercise designed to elicit their childhood stories, and were asked to do the same with at least three of their clients. Jane Pilemer collated and readied these stories for my inspection.

The stories were found to contain four elements. I called them the affect structure; the mood structure; the role structure, or who took on which of the four player actions; and a "missing" element, a figure "whose actions would make the story of wrongful love come out right." The sample of over one hundred provided strong face evidence that another piece of the theoretical framework of structural dynamics was in place. I published the results in a paper called "Critical Identity Image" in 1980.[5]

The Second Step

The Friedmans helped establish a link between this critical childhood story and breakdowns in their communication, but the connection was vaguely defined. More research and a study that went deeper with greater numbers were required. The clinical context with couples seemed the best way to do this. Why? Because, whatever the reason couples first give for seeking therapy, sooner or later what it comes down to is, "Our communication sucks!" For many, these knockdown fights threatened the basic premises of their relationship. For an alarming number, they led to a breakdown in most sexual communication. "We've stopped making love!" It is plain to see that therapy with couples is an open introduction to one of the common forms that high-stakes situation take, and a key to examining it in other situations.

Twenty couples agreed to participate in this study. Their therapy went on as usual, but all session tapes over a period of at least six months were transcribed by my research assistant, Uli Detling. The couples received duplicate copies with the option to replay them as "homework." Using data gathered prior to launch from my nonresearch couples, categories for analysis were tentatively established and applied to the study-group data for coding and analysis. From this happy marriage of research and clinical goals, a typology of high-stakes behavior was born. A structural dynamics theory of face-to-face communication, though far from complete, had reached a new level of explanation.

Between the mid-1980s and mid-1990s at the Kantor Family Institute, which I'd launched in 1979, the theory received another boost. Still troubled by what I perceived as an unclear understanding of the relationship between theory and practice by those, myself included, who purportedly used systems theory to guide their practice, I dug in at the Institute. To meet accreditation standards, trainees were required to take at least a first stab at articulating their models in a paper they would submit to fellow students for discussion. I was determined to hone my own model, both intellectually and in practice.

Just as family therapy with a systems focus sparked a blaze of fresh thought in the 1960s, systems-oriented organizational consulting was taking off in the 1990s. Sensing that the former's firestorm of creativity was simmering down, I turned to the latter for new insight and inspiration for my restless quest to unify theory and practice.

The Culmination of the Model-Building Effort

My first stop on this new path, consulting with family businesses, was short lived. It was not simply that consulting for corporate leaders and their teams was more enticing. No, I was seduced by the quality of the thought of those who were writing the theories for practitioners, in particular Chris Argyris, Donald A. Schön, Ed Schein, and Peter Senge.[6] Perhaps, I thought, the gap that haunted me in the therapy world would be filled here.

Though far from abandoning the family therapy and training world, I noted a shift in context for theory building that had occurred in the decade 1990 to 2000. Employed over this period by three companies that consulted for big business, I was to use structural dynamics concepts in the service of their consulting models.[7] It was here that the art and science of model building took on shape and a new life. I could test, refine, and grow such concepts as the three phases of model building (imitation, constraint, and autonomy, introduced in Chapter Twelve), conceived at the Kantor Family Institute, in the organizational consulting context.

One other concept deserves special mention. It can be argued (and it is clear in my mind) that if structural dynamics concepts contribute anything of value to our understanding of face-to-face communication, *the model of models* stands out, along with the four-player model. The model of models (or meta-model) was conceived in a eureka moment in 1992, one late night after a session with a group of consultants I was coleading with Diana Smith. The idea then made its way into "Random Notes," an ongoing document into which scraps of ideas are cast for later retrieval, but also left to incubate in the back of my mind.

Three years later, the model emerged mature when I joined Dialogos, a company founded by Bill Isaacs in 1995, to promote the practice of dialogue for "strategic use at all levels of leadership within and across organizations."[8] In 1998,

I became part of a team along with Bill, B. C. Huselton, and Robert Hanig. We were to take dialogue, the core of the company's theory and practice, to new levels with my model of models as a template. Months later, Dialogos's Sea Change Model was born. It became for the company what we'd hoped, a far more powerful practice model that remains to this day the lynchpin of its consulting practices. For me personally and for structural dynamics, it was a climactic culmination of decades of singular concentration and credible support for my belief that it takes three theories, not one, to develop a formidable practice model with no end to its continuous growth.

EIGHT YEARS AT MONITOR GROUP

In 2000, Mark Fuller, chairman and president of Monitor Group, asked me to join the company as a thought leader and director of a business unit to be called Monitor Kantor Enterprises. A true visionary, Fuller saw my work as compatible with the groundbreaking ideas Chris Argyris had brought to the social sciences, to organizational theory and consulting, and, most important, to Monitor Group itself.[9]

My broad assignment, with much of its actual delivery left to my imagination, was to answer the challenging question, "How would you apply structural dynamics to leadership for use in the broad community, our competitive marketplace, with senior consulting staff and the clients they serve?" For the next eight years, I tried to carry this mandate forward. I am proud to say, much was accomplished.

WHERE FROM HERE?

This question is fully addressed in the Afterword, which forecasts where structural dynamics goes from here. What is left unanswered is a question that hangs heavy over any "theory of the thing," whether that thing is team leadership, coaching, or couples or family therapy: How does that theory apply in practice? How does the leader, coach, or therapist intervene?

Intervention is a vast subject. It raises a daunting question: Is there one underlying theory that serves all or many different practice models—models, for example, that are designed for intervening with two-person intimate relationships, teams, families, executives who lead, and the coaches who coach them?

There is one reason why structural dynamics, a structural theory of face-to-face relations, may fill the bill. All of these target systems (teams, families, and so on) involve a system of face-to-face relationships and a practitioner bent on helping them improve their functioning.

Reading the Room can be thought of as a presentation of a two-pronged theory of the thing, examining both how leaders lead and how best to coach them. This book, however, does not contain a full-fledged *practice model.* A workbook companion to *Reading the Room* that will present such a model is already under way. Titled *Making Change Happen,* the book attempts to lay out in full the principles and practices of structural intervention from a structural dynamics perspective. Following the theories laid out in *Reading the Room* chapter by chapter, *Making Change Happen* will help you identify the kinds of dysfunctional structures that typically occur at each of the four levels or domains of communication structure: action, language, system, and deep story.

chapter ONE

Reading the Room

Introduction and Framework

In the past decade, significant progress has been made in describing and finding good-to-great leaders and coaching them toward greater success, but both experts and high-placed leaders themselves still overlook this fundamental:

A leader falls short of greatness without great skill in face-to-face talk.

This is as true in the corporate world as it is in government, communities, and families. On some level, we "know" that effective talk in face-to-face relations and small group conversations lies at the heart of leading, but by and large, when we lead, we do not examine closely what dynamics are at work in a conversation, nor find ways to improve them.

The title of this book refers to a priceless leadership skill: the ability to *read the room* to understand what's going on as people communicate in small groups, including how the leader himself or herself is participating, when the conversation is moving forward, when it may be just about to leave the rails, and possibly even how to guide it back on course.

First, the leader is able to read the room; second, the leader knows how to contribute in the moment to keep the team talking on track.

What do you know right now about your own skills at reading the room? These skills can be learned at any age and any point in a coach's or leader's career. From penthouse to White House, no matter how high a leader has risen, becoming truly skilled at reading the room will elevate one's game.

A CEO CHANGES JOBS

Throughout this book I will trace the story of a CEO called **Ralph Waterman,** "the room" of the leadership team he directed, the members of his team, and a leadership coach called **Duncan Travis.** As the story begins, Ralph has already achieved much in his corporate leadership career.

At age forty-eight, Ralph was not the stereotypical CEO, but he had a glowing and well-earned reputation for turning around companies that had stalled or declined. In fact, he'd just done that before coming to ClearFacts. People joked about his love of quixotic slogans like "Think and ye shall find. Create and ye shall be given!" but they also considered him brilliant, visionary. Did they also notice how restless he was at how much his current company continued to rely on the status quo and how far it fell short of any great sense of moral purpose? Perhaps **Martha Curtis,** director of HR, could tell. Of the leadership team, she was closest to Ralph. He appreciated her warm and engaging way, the fact that she spoke out a lot, and her high emotional intelligence despite being only thirty-four. A short eight years before, right after college, she'd gone into management training and from there into human resources.

Of course, Ralph and Martha had personal lives as well. Ralph was married to **Sonia Waterman,** and for him the barometer of their relationship was the quality of lovemaking. By that standard, despite his working late many nights, he thought of his home life as "better than ever." Sonia, of a different nature, also loved Ralph and was committed to their marriage, but came at it from a different perspective. Martha Curtis's marriage was passionate, but also stormy at times. One tension was that her husband, **Lance Curtis**, was an artist, which made her the primary breadwinner. They had no children at this point.

At the outset of our story, Ralph had just left a company to take over the reins at ClearFacts, a fast-growing green tech company. The move was something of a pattern for him—tearing free of one organizational yoke whenever it got too tight, in favor of a new and looser one. His vision now was of "an organization every one of whose members would be treated with dignity, given meaningful work, and a place they could voice complaints and be heard." With that in mind, he convinced Martha to accompany him to ClearFacts, where she could head up a strong HR department "with a reach to every satellite office in the firm."

In addition to the dignity theme and Martha's coming with him, Ralph had made other stipulations to the ClearFacts board of directors about his entrance as CEO. One was that he would go about creating "a management team with a *model.*" He'd been introduced to this "models" concept at a training program in Cambridge, where he'd also met his new leadership coach, Duncan Travis.[1] Ralph had taken keen interest when Duncan said that if a company needed a model to achieve its profit-making and larger purposes, it also needed some sort of model of a strong leadership team with imaginative strategy and a willingness to change and grow individually.

A skilled sixty-year-old executive coach, Duncan Travis had spent much of his career in organizational consulting with a prominent firm, where he started at age thirty-five. Over time, the rewards of being paid as a star performer grew thin; troubled by the lack of fit between, as he put it, "who I am and what I'm asked to do," he'd searched out practices with a closer fit. At fifty, he'd gone his own way. In the course of his transition to independent consultant, Duncan became familiar with an approach called structural dynamics, and proficient with its methods. In this period, presenting at a conference Ralph attended, he and Ralph instantly clicked. Ralph, himself about to take a new position, hired Duncan as coach.

Ralph had made and been granted two last, large stipulations. One was that he be free to create and personally lead an R&D team to explore new green technologies that he knew ClearFacts needed and about which he was passionate. (I won't say much more about the actual business ClearFacts was in. For our purposes, as you will see, it matters fairly little.) The other was the creation within ClearFacts of a leadership training program, to be overseen by persons other than himself.

So far, our main characters are three newcomers to ClearFacts: CEO Ralph, coach Duncan, and HR director Martha. When Ralph arrived, he found three more who were to be part of his leadership team. The foremost, naturally, was the CFO and COO, **Ian Maxwell**, age fifty, a man admired for his clarity of purpose and unfailing precision, although many also called him "rule-fanatic" and "Sheriff Max" behind his back. At work, most subordinates kept a distance from him. Divorced, Ian hadn't a clue why he almost never saw his two grown children. Evenings, he exercised, ate lightly, and read military history and theory in honor of his high-ranking, career-soldier father.

Duncan got a clear sense of Ian right away at the first weekly meeting Duncan attended of the ClearFacts leadership team, which Ralph had asked Duncan to attend "to see me and our team in action."

"You know, Dr. Travis—" Ian began.

"I prefer Duncan," said Duncan.

"Okay . . . Duncan," Ian conceded. "Under Ralph's style of leading, our meetings are at times too freewheeling for my taste. As CEO it is his prerogative.

Yet we follow rules. Enforcing them here and throughout ClearFacts helps me, as chief financial officer, to keep things financially and culturally on track."

Also there at the table as Ian spoke were the final two members of the leadership team. Whereas Martha now reported directly to CEO Ralph, director of sales **Howard Green,** thirty-six and unmarried (except to the organization—he barely slept, and took his computer on Club Med vacations), and director of marketing **Arthur Saunders,** forty and married with children, both continued to report to Ian.

Ralph had already recognized Howard as a model worker in terms of quality and output, with a keen ambition (to become a CEO before age forty), and had mentioned these qualities to Duncan. What Duncan noticed now was Howard's nodding support of nearly everything Ian or Ralph might say. Colleagues at ClearFacts described Howard as a "must-win" guy, and Howard stayed closer to Ian than did Ian's other subordinates. Recent circumstances at ClearFacts had catapulted him and his sales crew into fierce competition with Art and marketing, and their sharing reports to Ian probably amplified the personal competition between them.

That is not to say that Howard and Art were equally competitive by nature, though Art's colleagues sometimes said he worked harder than he had to, and he and his marketing team consistently turned out great materials. At the same time, Art's subordinates loved and respected him and knew him as a great listener. In high gear at work, Art wrote sparkling prose, and his leadership bore fruit. He got more work done in less time because he knew when to break for walks and, until recently, when to call it a day. On the home front, Art felt deprived by his working late night after night. In two weeks, he hadn't once been home in time to put his three-year old, elder daughter to bed. She cried. His wife was furious and telling him, "I will save this marriage or bust." Her biological clock was ticking, and she wanted another child. Art was not so sure he agreed. He was also beginning to wonder whether he belonged in his ClearFacts job.

After the team meeting, the CEO and coach reconvened to debrief—a routine they would keep up every week from that point on. Part of it went like this:

RALPH: I imagine as a coach you got a pretty quick intuitive "read" on Ian, my redoubtable COO.

DUNCAN: A "read" yes. Intuitive? No. I'm using what I observe of him to begin to build a behavioral profile of Ian, and everyone else in the room.

RALPH: "Behavioral profile"?

DUNCAN: A systematic profile of how each of you communicate in the room.

RALPH: Some better than others.

DUNCAN: Yes. The behavioral profile isn't a value judgment; it comprises three objective characteristics. It's part of the model or theory of group communications that I've mentioned to you earlier, called structural dynamics. The behavioral profile lies at the core of what structural dynamics calls a leader's personal model, and the personal model lies at the core of his leadership model. The endpoint of the work we do together is your developing a leadership model.
(Duncan sits back in his seat and eyes Ralph.) But let's not get ahead of ourselves; the best times to begin to understand a person's basic profile are when the stakes are generally low.

RALPH: "Low." As far as I'm concerned, there's nothing *low stakes* about ClearFacts. This company can do great things.

DUNCAN: That's not what I mean by low stakes or high. In structural dynamics, the stakes are low or high depending on how high they feel, right at that moment, in a personal way, to the people who are communicating.

RALPH: Well, the meeting was fairly relaxed, even if Howard opposed my idea that you would facilitate our meetings.

DUNCAN: But overall, this is a fairly routine moment as your weekly meetings go, isn't it? Low stakes in that sense.

RALPH: Agreed.

So this book and the ClearFacts story begin in low-stakes situations, when "plain talk" seems easy. What makes that ease of communication evaporate when people feel stakes rising? How can we still make communication work in that future meeting, when everyone is "sick of talking" yet no decision has been reached? What is talk's connection not only to productivity but even to—dare I say it?—personal fulfillment?

As coaches and leaders inevitably learn, climbing higher in an organization does not mean that the conversation gets easier. As stakes rise, so do pressures. As this happens, every member of a team, no matter how experienced, falls back more and more on deeply ingrained behaviors and life patterns of action and defense. When stakes are really high, people also often act in ways that truly surprise them. This book does not leave off where matters grow truly complex, where formulas collapse, where talk degrades or flies out of hand, where tempers explode. Although it begins in the relatively "normal" atmosphere of a high-powered team, it continues beyond the point at which members are really at their best, even from their own perspectives.

STRUCTURAL DYNAMICS: A LENS ON THE NATURE OF HUMAN DISCOURSE

Structural dynamics is the broad term for a body of research that colleagues and I began in the 1970s in an effort to understand the nature of face-to-face human communication. As noted in the Preface, we first studied families and couples. Since then, for many years my own work has focused on corporate leaders and teams.

Structural dynamics is also a basic theory and model or tool, if you will, for *reading the room*. *Structural* connotes the idea that there is an underlying, largely unconscious *structure* to all human verbal exchange: when people converse, they construct and follow certain implicit understandings and patterns in which their conversation takes place. In turn, this structure—recognized or not—affects the outcome of the conversation. Those who want to be aware of this structure can become so, through the lens of structural dynamics. *Dynamics* connotes the idea that *ongoing patterns*, functional and dysfunctional, are inherent in all continuing talk, and that dysfunctional ones result from clashes between people and the structures they bring into conversation.

Structural dynamics is not a lens that most of us habitually wear. Mostly our attention is elsewhere: actively listening for and analyzing not the *structure* but the *content* and *style* of the communications in which we take part. We learn to frame our differences and conflicts in those latter terms. In a meeting of neuroscientists, a meeting of cardinals at the Vatican, a team in a workplace, or a family at the dining room table, we hear enormous differences in *style* (forms of etiquette, rules of order) and *content* (topics, opinions, and facts). But structural dynamics asserts that beneath style and content there exist deeper *universal struc-*

tures of how conversations proceed. I will argue that as the foundation on which all communications are built, these structures are the most significant predictors of the outcome of any verbal interaction.

Why make this invisible structure visible? *Because problems in face-to-face communication are often due to the unseen influence of this deeper, invisible structure.* So long as it remains unnoticed, the structure can violate and undermine people's communicative intentions. Without understanding why, people try to communicate and end up passing each other by, clashing and repeating old battles when they meant to connect and conciliate. Once the structure is made visible, individuals can learn to observe and even change it.

What is the structure? Let's begin with that part of it that we call the *behavioral profile,* which you will see Duncan teaching to Ralph as his main tool for reading the room and what each person in the room is doing to make communication more or less productive. Within the behavioral profile, let's begin with the basic unit of communication—an individual speech.

Speech as an Act

Structural dynamics regards speech as an **act,** so its basic unit of consideration (or measurement) is a personal utterance—for example, "Let's start the meeting, shall we?"

In structural dynamics research and in this book, we focus heavily on the actual *words* that people use. That may sound limiting, considering that context, body language, eye contact, and other evidence can enter into what a person's comment really means. In fact, we won't entirely overlook those nonverbal forms of communication; clearly much of what we say to each other is not exactly what we are thinking or even what we *mean* to say. Structural dynamics uses a concept it calls *voice* to capture these other forms of communication.

But a record of words is a powerful handle, allowing us to encode a speech act in measurable terms. After a contentious meeting, we can look back on the record and surmise what was going on down below. Being able to encode what goes on at the level of words also enables us to see when people's conversational practices actually change and improve.

Speech acts often follow one another in recognizable patterns. For example, you state an opinion, one listener disputes it, then another supports it, and eventually your opinion carries. We call such combinations of speech acts **sequences**; and when they keep occurring, we call them **patterns.**

Speech Acts and Four Levels of Structure

Figure 1.1 shows four interacting levels of structure that describe a speech act and help us describe the dynamics of a conversation. Three are visible and can be coded; the fourth, story, plays a major role but usually remains invisible.

Here follows a brief overview of the four levels of structural dynamics. Later chapters will explore them more deeply and show how the first three levels

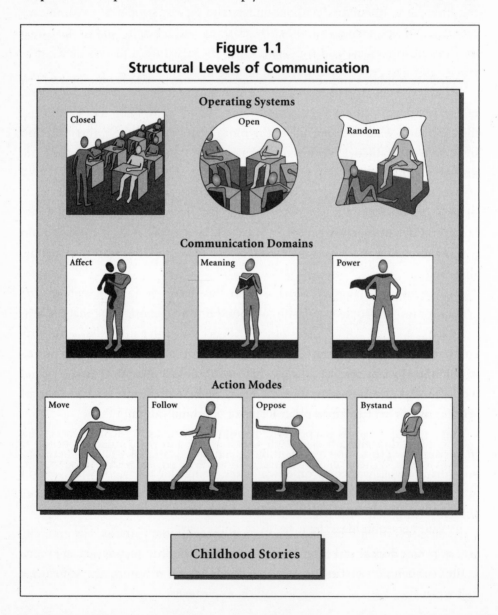

Figure 1.1
Structural Levels of Communication

Operating Systems

Closed   Open   Random

Communication Domains

Affect   Meaning   Power

Action Modes

Move   Follow   Oppose   Bystand

Childhood Stories

coalesce to make up one's behavioral profile (as summarized in Chapter Five). Other chapters will show how our stories have structures embedded in them that directly influence the more visible levels.

Level I: Action Stances   Most overtly, all speech takes one of four stances in relation to some action. We call this the **four-player model.** Each of the four **action stances** occupies the "interaction space" in a unique way:

- A **move** initiates action or suggests direction. It takes the center of the space: "Let's start the meeting, shall we?"

- A **follow** validates and completes an action. It closely adjoins the move: "I'm ready also."

- An **oppose** challenges and corrects the action. It blocks the way of moves and follows: "Hold on. Ralph's not here yet. We need our CEO."

- A **bystand** provides a perspective on the overall interaction, and attempts, in some way, to reconcile competing actions. It stands at the periphery where the speaker can view the entire interaction space: "It's no secret that he's typically late. Are there reasons you should not confront him directly?"

As we shall see, communication is effective when individuals move fluidly between different action stances, making full use of the interaction space. Frequently, however, speakers become "stuck" in one or more positions, constricting the conversational space.

Level II: Communication Domains   Every action stance also takes place within one of three **communication domains**. These domains or "fields" define the focus and direction of the speech. Incidentally, Ralph tends to arrive late to team meetings, which the rest of the team talks about now and then.

- The **affect domain** concerns itself with feelings and the connection between individuals: "Whenever Ralph forgets time, he leaves me with a sense that he doesn't care about how it affects me."

- The **meaning domain** attends to ideas and ways of understanding: "When he gets immersed in ideas, he forgets the whole world."

- The **power domain** takes on action and the issues of completion, achievement, and influence: "We can get things done while we're waiting. Let's do what we can."

As we will see in Chapter Three, an action stance in one domain is very different from the same stance in a different domain. For example, a move "in affect" ("Let's have a show of hands—how many of us really care if he's not here?") is different from a move "in power" ("For me it's about our agenda, so let's start anyway") and both differ from a move "in meaning" ("For me it's the ideas behind his inputs; we need them in this meeting").

As we shall see, talk frequently becomes confused when several individuals are unaware that they are speaking from different domains.

Level III: Operating Systems Structural dynamics applies what is called **systems thinking** to face-to-face relations. It takes two concepts from systems thinking: the concept of circularity, and the signature idea of positive and negative feedback loops. In circularity, Person A does something that has a controlling effect on Person B. Person B, reacting in turn, does something that has a controlling effect back on Person A. As this pattern repeats, A and B begin to anticipate each other's acts. This anticipation leads both parties to behave in ways that ultimately bring those acts about. Circularity, the absence of true cause and effect, is now in place. As for feedback loops: in brief, two kinds of feedback loops regulate behavior. Positive loops amplify, negative loops contract.

Structural dynamics applies these notions to three types of operating systems:

- In a **closed system,** where negative loops predominate, speakers are regulated by formal rules and orient themselves to the larger system.

- In an **open system,** governed by both positive and negative feedback loops, speakers are regulated by one another and orient themselves toward the collective.

- A **random system,** regulated by positive feedback loops, gives priority to individuals over any rules of the system; it encourages speakers to self-regulate.

Individuals and groups have preferences for different operating systems. A person's preferred system can cause him to interpret a second person's action stance or choice of communication domain in ways the second person did not intend. In other words, when we operate according to the rules of our own preferred or dominant operating system, we may unknowingly violate others' preferences and conventions.

Behavioral Profiles and Effective Communication Speech acts can be coded. Anyone can be taught to code the four Level I action stances (move, follow, oppose, and bystand). Levels II and III are more difficult to code rigorously, but my colleagues and I have verified that they, too, can be coded reliably.[2]

Teams develop different patterns of speech acts, and individuals make their own characteristic inputs to these patterns. For example, an individual who prefers a *closed* system, prefers the language domain of *power,* and is a frequent *opposer* will be recognizably distinct from someone who prefers an *open* system, uses the language of *meaning,* and is a frequent *bystander.* Repeated speech acts in sequence form what I refer to as patterns. These tendencies can be codified and described; they make up what I referred to as a person's behavioral profile, explored further in Chapter Five. Awareness of a person's profile greatly enhances our ability to predict and recognize what that person is likely to say—at our structural levels—in response to someone else's speech.

Because each person has her own profile, when communicating with others she is often attempting to do so across important differences. The ability to effectively do so distinguishes a good leader from a great one.

Level IV: Childhood Stories Level IV is not part of the systematic, speech-by-speech coding that make up a person's behavioral profile. It runs much deeper.

The power of story pervades modern culture. Its value is exploited in every aspect of life—in computer games, war games, entertainment, literature, and science. The Bible is a story, as is every theory. Storytelling is our age-old way of explaining where we've been and what we've experienced. In the personal sphere, story gathering, the act of creating a story from experience, is central to identity; and identity stories are central to our personal approaches to communication.

We all gather stories about ourselves. From the age when we are first able to observe ourselves as objects in the world, we form and store our own experiences and identities in narrative form. Our identity and its supporting stories shape what we say and how we react to what others say. To truly comprehend the structure of talk, we want to know as much as we can about our own underlying stories and those of others in the group.

The level of personal story and identity is not an easy one to enter, and most books on leadership avoid it. But the truth is, why a CEO like Ralph comes late to his own meetings and how his team reacts to that (and to his leadership in general) are hugely affected by their own identities, their self-told stories, and the state of their private lives.

Structural dynamics identifies a specific set of stories that determine how we communicate. This Level IV perspective helps explain why people's profiles differ and how the stories that form identity complicate or defeat communication. It attempts to fathom whom we select as lovers and spouses and why we partner most closely with certain colleagues at work. By recognizing our own stories, we enable ourselves not only to lead better but to live more fulfilling lives.

THE BASIC CHALLENGE OF ALL CONVERSATION

As I suggested earlier, each of us reflects a certain behavioral profile in how we speak with others; we also have certain expectations about how others will speak to us. All human communication is driven by *models*. Each person's communication is controlled in part by a model he or she carries around about how conversations ought to work.

The **model** is an explanatory system that includes how the person typically perceives and processes events outside himself, and how his inner stories prompt him to respond. We call this automatic and instantaneous screening mechanism one's *personal model*. Conversations succeed or fail based on the interaction of different personal models. Thus we are all often engaged in **cross-model conversations**—a pivotal concept in structural dynamics.

Inevitably, interpersonally, models sometimes clash, though even a repeated clash usually remains benign until some event raises the stakes for one or both parties. But significant **model clashes** between people in close and regular contact are more common than we like to think. Then communications can break down, and relationships get messy, even miserable. When a couple fights over the large amount of time one partner is away, they likely are in a model clash, an unsuccessful cross-model conversation. So is a team, often, when it erupts over different points of view about a key decision at a moment of crisis.

From the concept of the cross-model conversation, structural dynamics has built a number of principles and guidelines that can help you recognize model clash and take steps to ameliorate its problems. Among other things, structural dynamics is an invaluable way of decoding and understanding the model of conversation that is operating in the head of any individual, and how his or her model resembles or differs from your own and those of other members of the group.

LEADERS AND COMMUNICATIVE COMPETENCY

Communicative competency refers to understanding one's own behavioral profile and being able to expand one's own repertoire of choices as needed. Communicative competency is essential for successful cross-model conversation, which is central to effective communication and to leadership itself.

Structural roles are complementary. Movers need followers (and even opposers) and vice versa. Speech acts in the affect (emotional) domain need supporting acts spoken in terms of the power domain. All combinations are needed. Yet what often happens is that, because structural differences are also a source of confusion and conflict, individuals unknowingly surround themselves with others who have their same limited structural repertoire. This book can counter that and improve your interactions by expanding your behavioral profile—the range of such action stances you are comfortable taking in conversation. Expanding your own profile will also open more space for others to play a wider range of complementary roles.

In my view, communicative competency is the apex of leader development and thus difficult to summarize briefly. However, its full meaning will unfold in the course of this book.

REAL LIVES AND REAL LIFE STORIES

Most twentieth-century business organizations expected their leaders to achieve many difficult things at once: explore for and exploit new ideas *and* maintain focus on core business execution; keep a global perspective on the business *and* be open and accessible to employees; "delight" customers, motivate employees, be responsible "corporate citizens," *and* maintain a sizable bottom line . . . Little has changed in the past few decades.

The rewards offered are status and money. Rarely does a board ask whether the CEO has a happy and personally fulfilling life. Many top leaders are so focused on their work that they have little idea what the good life is.

In their hearts of hearts, next-in-line leaders see all this coming and, like their predecessors, settle for the status and money. But leaders are currently in transition in terms of their attitude toward this devil's bargain. Thankfully for them and us, increasingly they know that there is something better, something more. Increasingly they press for acknowledgment that *they have real lives*—partners, children, private pursuits—and expect to live them even while they lead.

My point is not only that leaders deserve to be able to pursue a life worth living. It is also that, insofar as they are leaders of teams, that pursuit is not contrary to but an indispensable additive for their teams' deepest success.

One conclusion of structural dynamics research is that this area of private relations (and personal histories) cannot be ignored, any more than most voters ignored the presence and influence of candidates' marriages and other love lives when they voted in 2008. The higher the stakes, the more these influences dog the events. This book gives both early personal history and adult intimate relationships the place they deserve in discussion of leadership.

As a coach, you probably understand that this line of thinking is true, but you may still resist addressing it in your coaching work. Few people are eager to look themselves squarely in the mirror, and leaders clearly don't want to talk with coaches or clients about these issues. In fact, they make sure the line stays firmly drawn so that the work world—and all its coaching and consulting—doesn't get involved with thorny subjects of love or private longing, except behind closed doors.

I ask you not to ignore the dark. We all have shadows. Unacknowledged and unattended, they do untold damage in our private and organizational lives, especially when stakes are high. *Reading the Room* will address these realities and can help you explore your awareness of them in your own life and among the leaders you coach. In turn, those leaders can expand their own awareness and become more effective in their leadership teams.

You may have noticed that I slipped in the dreaded four-letter word *love*. Our society has developed an unhealthy schism between work and love. *Reading the Room* is about the ways leaders learn how to think, how to talk, and, yes, how to love. I know my risk in confessing this. For decades, consulting practitioners have carefully observed the line between one's personal life and work life, and everyone in business is trained not to cross it. Anything that even remotely sounds like therapy or deals with one's personal life and early experiences is highly suspect.

But *Reading the Room* is about what is involved in a whole, unified, fully integrated life, and leaders want to be loved. That's why they do what they do, even when their motives may look simply material or power centered. Love is connection. Connection is the bridging of difference, and difference is bridged through words, language, talk.

THE COACHING PERSPECTIVE

This book takes the coach's perspective, but in a way that I believe will make valuable reading for leaders, too. I've included many illustrative dialogues like the short one shown earlier between CEO Ralph and his coach, Duncan. Throughout, we'll be seeing what the coach who is trained in structural dynamics looks for in group interactions and how he can train a leader in the same observational skills and enhance the leader's overall communicative competency. Many coaches already use the principles of structural dynamics as part of their work with leaders. I hope this book will be useful to them—for example, in showing how to pass on specific techniques. I hope also that leaders will gain a richer sense of what benefits are possible from structural dynamics coaching.

I am not suggesting that all coaches or coaches-in-training reading this book should necessarily take up all levels of intervention that the book presents, especially those that involve deep interpersonal techniques. Eliciting a "childhood story" *when appropriate* is a mainstay of my own, long coaching practice, as is talking to my executive clients about their life challenges wherever they appear. But this psychotherapeutic type of approach can cause much harm in the hands of untrained "helper" interventionists. Guiding another person in looking at his or her dark side does take a certain level of skill and experience not usually taught in business and coaching schools. My upcoming handbook of intervention technique, *Making Change Happen,* will explore ways to bridge this gap in greater detail.

Also keep in mind that coaching or consulting services in corporations are typically paid for by the company, usually with the tacit understanding that those services must help contribute to the goals of the organization in some way. If the individual needs personal "therapy" for other reasons, he or she should get it outside the corporate setting, regardless of its relation to performance. In the structural dynamics coaching model represented here, and in the Duncan-Ralph relationship, much work is done on the personal front without therapy.

In this book, a coach is teaching a leader how to incorporate structural dynamics into his repertoire of skills. The coach has in mind four stages of growth that I will introduce in the next sections. The first three stages fall within the coach's purview. In stage 4, the leader proceeds without further assistance from the coach regarding structural dynamics. Note that the same theory of face-to-face communication I am presenting here applies in both work and family settings.

Stage 1: Functional Awareness

In the **functional awareness** stage, the leader first comes to understand how the structure and patterns of communication in all his relationships play out in face-to-face relations, differently with each of his management team members and with his private partner or spouse.

Once the leader can recognize behavioral profiles in action and can read them in himself and in the room, the coach can take him to the origins of these behavioral patterns in himself. These are key stories gathered from childhood through young adulthood and determine his typical ways of interacting with key others.

Later in this stage, coaches round out leaders' discovery of the self in action by helping leaders see their *shadow behaviors* or, more dramatically, their *dark sides.* These too originate in stories, inconveniently and often destructively rising to the surface in high-stakes situations. The leader gains much in understanding what they are and where they come from.

Stage 2: System Awareness

Systems thinking relies on circular rather than linear ideas about cause and effect. No theory in my opinion has contributed more to our understanding of how organizations work. Many leaders have been exposed to it, but the greater part have yet to grasp it to any meaningful degree. Repeatedly the coach will focus the leader on system awareness. For example, he might point out circularities at the heart of a controlling system: "What is it in your behavior that causes X, whom you can't stand, to behave toward you in such a way that you can't stand him?"

A leader who fails to understand circularity in communication risks cutting off valuable feedback about goings-on in the organization. Poor insight into systems may be at the root of why his or her most valued close relationships fail. Without good systems thinking skills, the leader may also not understand how the organization works, how its parts interact—how, for example, if people in marketing fail to communicate effectively with people in sales or product design, the product may ultimately just sit on a shelf.

Stage 3: Moral Awareness

The moral dimension of leadership behavior has come to occupy a central place in structural dynamics theory. This stage of the process aims at promoting moral awareness in leaders, meaning basically an awareness of the forces that tempt fundamentally good people to do basically bad things.

Kilburg and others have begun calling attention to moral behavior and its corruption in leaders and their organizations.[3] Business schools, the most prolific generator of our future leaders and decision makers, are adding moral behavior to their curricula. If the fall from moral grace of some of their best and brightest graduates is indicative, however, that curriculum has a long way to go.

Stage 4: Responsible Self-Evolution

Advocates of structural dynamics insist that leaders and their coaches make the demanding but rewarding effort to develop and continue to "build their models." The advocates also hold themselves and their coach-trainees to this same standard.

The *capacity for responsible self-evolution* is my phrase for addressing the question, "When does the power to acquire skills and knowledge shift from 'others' to the self?" In this stage, when leaders have achieved functional and moral awareness and a high enough level of communicative competency, structural dynamics recommends that they take responsibility for developing two models of their own making: a leadership model that is uniquely theirs, and a model of a life worth living. This is the point of closure, ideally, when the coach can *leave*.

HOW THIS BOOK WILL WORK

In Part One, I elaborate the structural dynamics model at each of its four levels, including the behavioral profile that encapsulates Levels I through III. I point out ways that the model can be useful, and apply it, by way of example, to the weekly meetings of the ClearFacts executive team. For simplicity, Part One confines itself to communication in relatively low-stakes situations. Parts Two and Three up the ante. In these chapters, we see CEO Ralph and his team grapple with high-stakes problems, including and fueled by fraud within the team. The final chapter examines our current U.S. president, Barack Obama, in structural dynamics terms.

Reading the Room uses the story of a prototypical team to explain its concepts and to put them in a vivid, real-life context. This book covers a wide territory—conceptual, practical, and prescriptive—in three parts. Part One, Chapters Two through Five, lays out a conceptual framework for understanding why and how all people, with a special emphasis on leaders, act as they do under "relatively" low-stakes conditions. Our behavioral propensities, as measured in our instrument, the Behavioral Propensities Profile, determine how members of the Clear-Facts team act and speak to good and ill effects when conducting business and making key decisions. Provision is made at the end of these chapters for you to get a good estimate of your behavioral profile and to compare it with those of the team members.

Reading the Room offers critical insights into how and why behavior changes when there is a shift from low- to high-stakes situations. Part Two, Chapters Six through Ten, first provides a theoretical foundation for understanding the origins of leader behavior in high stakes, and then puts the theory in dramatic context as the ClearFacts management team is catapulted into crisis when one of its members is suspected of fraud, seriously threatening the integrity of the organization, and possible charges by the SEC.

Reading the Room has its own carefully articulated view of how to bring the development of future leaders to new heights of professional and moral behavior. In Part Three, Chapters Eleven through Fifteen, it lays out the course in detail. By following Ralph Waterman, ClearFacts CEO, as he does the hard work of building his own models under the direction of coach Duncan Travis, you will gain insights about your own leadership model and how to bring it to a higher level of development.

As you will see, the ClearFacts story delves into the private lives and histories of the members of the team, showing how those become part of the team's structural dynamics. You have already met most of the major characters. You will meet a few more, including **Ron Stuart,** who will join the team in a later chapter. I created the cast as composites of personalities and behaviors I have encountered in my consulting and counseling work. I believe you will find them real and familiar, if not classic types. The ClearFacts case will include few facts about the actual business or even about its product, but it tells you what you need to know.

As a start, these spare additional details should suffice: new CEO Ralph was brought in as part of a major restructuring of an organization that had plateaued. He was charged with putting together a strong executive team and with launching the company into Asian markets. The action takes place over a number of months. Figures 1.2 and 1.3 remind you who the various team members are at the outset. You will come to know them well.

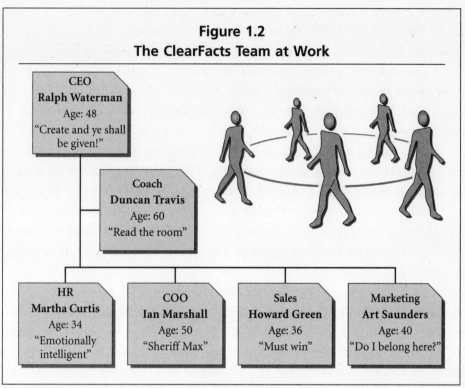

**Figure 1.2
The ClearFacts Team at Work**

CEO
Ralph Waterman
Age: 48
"Create and ye shall
be given!"

Coach
Duncan Travis
Age: 60
"Read the room"

HR
Martha Curtis
Age: 34
"Emotionally
intelligent"

COO
Ian Marshall
Age: 50
"Sheriff Max"

Sales
Howard Green
Age: 36
"Must win"

Marketing
Art Saunders
Age: 40
"Do I belong here?"

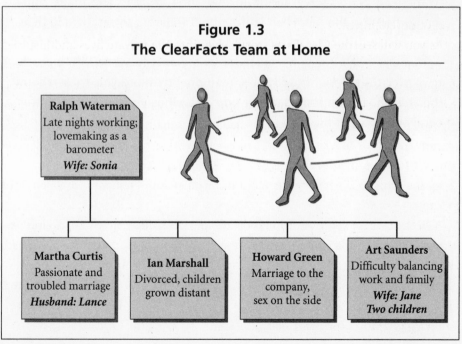

**Figure 1.3
The ClearFacts Team at Home**

Ralph Waterman
Late nights working;
lovemaking as a
barometer
Wife: Sonia

Martha Curtis
Passionate and
troubled marriage
Husband: Lance

Ian Marshall
Divorced, children
grown distant

Howard Green
Marriage to the
company,
sex on the side

Art Saunders
Difficulty balancing
work and family
*Wife: Jane
Two children*

From Insight to Action

If a book needs a mantra, let ours be this:

Great leaders are great in face-to-face talk.

Once you understand the theory of structural dynamics and learn how to use the four-level framework on which it is based, you will be able to understand the essence of verbal interactions and the underlying dynamics of communication between individuals and in teams and other small groups of people in close contact with each other. The room in which these interactions take place is not confined to a 20-by-30 conference room. Through policy statements and other means of communication, the room can grow beyond physical space. CEOs must go beyond their teams to communicate with an entire organization. In Chapter Fifteen, we apply everything we've learned about structural dynamics and individual behavioral profiles to the case of a sitting president, whose leadership is evidenced in his ability to communicate his model to a broad constituent base.

As a coach of leaders, you will be able to pass these same insights on to the leaders you serve and train them how to read and guide communications "in the room" and throughout their organization (and their lives outside it) for the rest of their careers.

If you're not a coach but a leader who wants to work with a coach to master these insights and skills, read on. The more you know about the challenge from the coaching side as well as your own, the better equipped you will be.

PART ONE

A Complete Language for Understanding Leader Behavior

Level I: Action Stances

L evel I of the structural dynamics model (see Chapter One, Figure 1.1) is the first of the three components of the behavioral profile. We call Level I the "four-player model." It describes two things: the four basic types of "players" individuals tend to be when they speak, and the actions associated with that player type. People possessing a high degree of communicative competency are versatile in taking any of the four player stances with ease as the need arises, and this is where coach Duncan Travis starts to focus CEO Ralph's attention during the team's Monday morning management meetings.

In Chapter One, Ralph Waterman took the reins at ClearFacts, and you learned a bit about his four-person management team: Ian (COO and CFO), Martha (HR), Howard (sales), and Arthur (marketing). Each of these hard-working people leads one or more teams of his or her own. Duncan had already told Ralph the following information about this level.

FOUR ACTION STANCES

Whether there are two people or twenty people in a room, each and every speech act they make can be categorized as either a move, follow, oppose, or bystand.[1] The terms employed by the four-player model are morally neutral and nonjudgmental. Saying that someone was "nasty" is a moral judgment. Saying that he "opposed" connotes neither good nor bad.

Move

A **move** is made by individuals to initiate action. It is an invitation for others to react and respond. A move may be in the form of an overt suggestion ("Let's look at our agenda") or a statement of advocacy or opinion ("We should celebrate the sales department for exceeding its goals").

The role of mover is paramount to any group. Without movers, a group usually doesn't last very long unless someone who doesn't generally tend to be a mover deliberately assumes the role for the group's survival. Although we typically think of the role of mover as positive, remember that *any* act can be helpful or detrimental to the group and its conversation.

Follow

A **follow** supports a stance that someone else has taken. The support may be partial or ambivalent, weak or strong, but a follow action always serves to perpetuate the action that is already on the table. Here are some examples of different follows in response to a move:

Speaker	Speech Act	Stance
Ian	We need to spend less time in these meetings.	Move
Martha	I agree.	Follow
Arthur	I have been concerned about the same thing for the past two weeks . . .	Follow
Howard	I'd be happy to serve as timekeeper.	Follow

Oppose

An **oppose** challenges the action on the table. Oppose behaviors can take many different forms and have very different impacts. Here are some possible opposes in response to the move I just introduced:

Speaker	Speech Act	Stance
Ian	We need to spend less time in these meetings.	Move
Martha	That will never happen. Can you imagine Ralph keeping a meeting to a half hour?	Oppose
Ralph	Sorry, Ian, but when we need longer meetings to address the issues on our agenda properly, we'll have them.	Oppose

Bystand

A **bystand** is an expression of reflection on the actions being made, without acknowledging agreement or disagreement. Here are several bystands, in among other stances:

Speaker	Speech Act	Stance
Arthur	Ian wants shorter meetings; Ralph notes that we need to complete our agenda properly. How do we reconcile those two goals?	Bystand
Howard	We all know that Ian is our team's conscience on efficiency.	A follow to Ian's earlier move
Martha	But let's not rush to a decision. If we need time, let's take it.	Oppose
Ralph	I agree, Martha; but what's your concern, Howard?	Follows Martha; moves to invite a move from Howard
Howard	Our agenda today has two loaded items that call for more time than we have today.	Oppose
Arthur	Step back and it's clear we all want the same thing: to do our work thoroughly and well.	Bystand bridging two opposing stances

Persons playing the role of bystander tend to place themselves on the periphery of an action field. From there they have four options: to remain a silent bystander; to enter the action as an opposer or a follower; to enter as a mover who bridges two opposing speakers; or to act as a mover to leave one field in order to initiate (move) a new sequence in a new field.

The Voice of a Speech Act

Note that *move, follow, oppose,* and *bystand* are structural descriptions of a speech act, and for the purposes of structural dynamics, we do not need to consider the actual *content* of what was said. For example, for structural understanding it doesn't matter whether my move is about, say, defining a topic for discussion or, say, ordering lunch. However, if we can, in practical situations, we should note the **voice** in which words are spoken for what it can tell us about what sort of stance is being taken. In an underlying manner, through pitch, rhythm, tone, and nuanced wording, voice helps define the structure of what we are saying and of what other people hear.

Try speaking aloud a few phrases you commonly hear (or say) in meetings, in differing tones and rhythms. As you do, you'll probably notice that, for example, an enthusiastic "Oh, sure!" is a follow, whereas a sarcastic "Oh, sure!" is an obvious oppose.

Pure, Compound, and Mixed Actions

Reading the room at Level I, one quickly becomes aware that there is more than one way to communicate actions: purely, in compound, or as a mixture of messages.

	Speech Act	Description
Pure action	I believe we should launch a new campaign.	A single message expressed unambiguously.
Compound action	I agree with Jane in launching a new campaign, and I think it should be focused on China.	A combination of two or more actions into an integrated sequence: a follow, then a new move.
Mixed action	Yeah, launch. Let's launch another new campaign.	Content and voice suggest competing stances: the statement sounds like a follow, but the voice has shades of oppose.
Mixed action	I don't know; maybe we should launch a new campaign.	Competing stances: the structure sounds like a move but is expressed in the uncertain voice of a follow.

Although mixed actions can be difficult to interpret, they are useful as a signal that further clarification may be warranted. Rather than make attributions of one's own about what the speaker intended, this is a good time to probe further with another question to make sure you know what that person is really trying to communicate with his or her mixed action.

Next we will see how the four-player model applies to the conversation at a ClearFacts Monday morning meeting.

ART'S UNEXPECTED OUTBURST AT CLEARFACTS

This ClearFacts two-hour Monday morning meeting started well, at the team's typical high level of communicative effectiveness. As usual, Ralph had planned two parts to the meeting: the first for "business plus strategy," the second for "culture plus people." Oddly, slowly, after about ninety minutes, the meeting drifted into tones of sarcasm, even shades of rancor, until suddenly a dig from Howard, the head of sales, triggered a surprising outburst from his rival Art, the famously even-tempered marketer and one of the team's most flexible, balanced communicators.

Speaker	Speech Act	Description
Howard	The issue I sometimes take with you, Art, and your team, is that you diddle too much with words and pictures. Your ads don't say to the market, *Buy now*.	A move against or oppose to Art
Art	Don't you talk to me like that, you freakin' tyrant!	A move in the voice of an opposer

The room fell silent, surprised by the force and evident pain of Art's outburst even though everyone had felt the atmosphere (to which they all were party, of course) turning poisonous. *This is a workplace, not a neighborhood bar*, said the looks on several faces. *Things aren't supposed to happen this way*. Privately, some team members wondered whether what had just occurred would shatter the infamously tense relationship between Art and Howard.

Ralph searched coach Duncan's eyes for direction, got nothing back. He looked to Ian, the team's usually steadying COO. Ian's noncommittal, cool composure—like a general surveying a field of battle?—did not surprise Ralph, but it wasn't much help, either. So Ralph elected to say the obvious in the form of a move: "We have serious disagreement here. Let's end the meeting and, when you've all had a chance to think about what happened, send me an e-mail."

As the room emptied, Ralph felt shaken, thinking, *Well, I make mistakes, but how often have I been* this *ineffectual at running a weekly meeting?*

Incidentally, recall my mention of Level IV in Chapter One—the deep level of personal background and story that influences what goes on in a room. Here's a brief, story-level foreshadowing about Martha, the only team member who actually sent Ralph an e-mail after the meeting. It read:

> CONFIDENTIAL! Art took a beating today at the meeting. I feel bad because I felt it coming, could have stepped in sooner but didn't. I've been thinking lately that I step in too much to protect Art. You know my story. In one way he's like my "big" sister. When we were kids, she would become very small when confronted by my ruthless mother. Dad was slow in stepping in. I was not. I took strong stands as sis's advocate, and when that failed I shot back at my mom. I would jab, jab, then throw an uppercut. I lost anyway, until later when I could at least fight her to a draw. But in the end, it did not help my sister. IT MAY HAVE HURT. I'm not asking you to do anything. In fact, I'm asking you to do nothing. I want to handle my issues by myself.

Our present interest in this note lies in what it says about Martha at Level I: she is describing herself as an advocate of free speech, and as a strong, strong mover fully prepared to oppose with equal force.

Both for coaches and for the leaders they advise, it's worth becoming familiar with the kinds of actual exchanges that often go on in the course of teaching how to recognize structural dynamics behavioral patterns. Here is the start of Ralph and Duncan's debriefing conversation a short while after the meeting:

DUNCAN: Now *that* certainly was arresting, wasn't it?

RALPH: It was. I don't think I've ever seen Art that way. You know how laid-back he is. Speaks only when he has to, and when he does, everyone listens. Oh, he has his moments with Howard. But he stuffs them for the most part. He lets Martha come to his rescue, which she loves.

DUNCAN: Yes, I saw all that and more.

RALPH: What do you mean—that you saw it coming?

DUNCAN: No. To understand the "more" I saw, you have to know what my mind is doing when I'm observer in the room, Ralph. I call it *reading the room*. You'll get to that, in time.

RALPH: Okay, I'll try to be patient. But what changes a guy like Art—calm, controlled—into this raging bull? Dunc, what did I miss?

DUNCAN: Well . . .

RALPH: That much? The ghost of Macbeth?

DUNCAN: Well, yeah.

RALPH: Come off it.

DUNCAN: *(Pulling back)* Look, for now, let's just go back to what was happening in the room before Art sounded off.

From there, Duncan and Ralph looked back on the meeting, considering several sequences of speech acts that Duncan thought might be revealing.

A First Sequence of Stances

In this sequence from fairly early in the meeting, during the "business plus strategy" part, notice who moves, who follows, who opposes. In the following sequences, too, begin to form an impression of the stances the team members often take in relation to the group and one another.

Speaker	Speech Act	Stance
Ian	Your report had much to say, Howard. I liked it overall.	Move
Howard	Thank you, sir. I set out with your guidelines and went from there.	Follow
Ralph	I fundamentally agree with Ian, but had trouble with section 3, where questionable opinions seeped into your otherwise rational arguments.	Follows Ian; opposes Howard
Art	*(Suppresses a grunt, nods, turns to his notes, and says nothing)*	Probably covertly following Ralph's oppose
Ralph	Let's put off further discussion on the report until Ian and I've reviewed it together.	Move

A Second Sequence

This sequence came later, nearing the point of transition from "business plus strategy" to "culture plus people."

Speaker	Speech Act	Stance
Ralph	You have been uncommonly quiet today, Martha. Something on your mind?	Move (by inviting a move). Facilitators and good leaders use this often.
Martha	Not really. Just thinking.	Oppose by declining.
Howard	When Martha goes a' thinking, beware.	Mixed stance: a move in the voice of an oppose (aimed at Martha).
		(Continued)

Speaker	Speech Act	Stance
Art	Pretty clumsy humor, Howard. I'd be interested if you have something to say, Martha.	Mixed stance: an oppose, followed by a faintly sarcastic move.
Ian	If you do and it is culture or people related, I'd ask you to hold it. We've got more business to conduct.	Compound action: an oppose followed by a move, spoken in a strong, pure voice—typical of Ian.

In this sequence, when Martha declines, Howard and everyone else knows something is up and that she will give voice to it. His response is a somewhat sarcastic, poorly disguised move-oppose against something Martha may be thinking of saying; correctly he suspects it has something to do with him.

This sequence clearly reveals tension in team dynamics. Coding gets easier once a coder, or anyone in the room, is familiar with the players and a history of their relationships.

A Third Sequence

This came later, during "culture plus people":

Speaker	Speech Act	Stance
Art	I must confess, Howard, I am irked by the veiled criticism in that e-mail you circulated of the ad my folks created. It is high quality and very effective in my view.	Opposes something Howard said in an earlier e-mail, then makes an advocacy move
Martha	I couldn't agree more. Perhaps the ad was too subtle for your concrete ways of judging things, Howard.	Follows Art's oppose

(Continued)

Speaker	Speech Act	Stance
Howard	What I meant in—*(cut off by Ralph)*	Probably about to move or oppose
Ralph	So, Martha, are you getting to what was on your mind earlier?	Moves (inviting a move)
Martha	I damn well am.	Follows Ralph
Howard	With your permission, Ralph, I'd like to speak for myself.	Follows Ralph by asking to speak (move) for himself
	The issue I sometimes take with you, Art, and your team, is that you diddle too much with words and pictures. Your ads don't say to the market, *Buy now.*	Moves against or opposes Art
Art	Don't you talk to me like that, you freakin' tyrant!	Opposes

BEHAVIORAL TENDENCIES AT LEVEL I

Most individuals have behavioral tendencies that skew their profiles in ways recognizable to others and to themselves, typically including at least one "strong," one "weak," and one "stuck" behavior: they characteristically overuse some options and underuse others.

- A **strong behavioral tendency** is an action we use often and well. People are known for and are associated with these behavioral tendencies. For example, in the sequences shown here, Ralph is a "strong mover," often coming up with a new idea or direction.

- A **weak behavioral tendency** is an action we fail or hesitate to use when the situation we are in calls for that action. For example, in the first two sequences here, Art looks like a "weak opposer."

- A **stuck behavioral tendency** is an action we use more often than necessary, limiting our wider ability to serve our team or family.

We would need to hear more to accurately characterize the action stance tendency of each team member. In the ClearFacts story, more evidence would lead us to conclude the following. (I mention official roles again here only to help you become more familiar with the characters, not because their roles in any way dictate what stances these individuals necessarily take.)

Ralph (CEO), as the team's nominal leader, has a lot to say and is a *strong mover*. People listen, not just because he is boss, but because he says much of interest. On every subject, however, he needs to "curb his enthusiasm" because the space he takes pushes others to the periphery and silence, even though he does want everyone to have his or her moment. Generally, he tries hard and succeeds in letting all speak and be heard.

Ian (COO) is another *strong mover*. He speaks with authority. His manner reeks of it. He picks his moments exquisitely, managing, when he has something to say, to find a wedge in the micro space between a question and its answer. A keen observer like Duncan also notices and will keep an eye on Ian's two-step tactic of first challenging (opposing), then proposing (moving). But Duncan hears others use this tactic, too, which makes him suspect that the tactic has something to do with Ralph, the leader.

Martha (HR) assumed the right to "freedom of speech" in the sequences shown here. More broadly, she's a *mover* with an *opposing* edge. At will, she playfully challenges (opposes) Ralph. She challenges others as well, not always playfully.

Howard (VP of sales) is the team's gunner, a third *strong mover*. He seems always to have an agenda that he can't wait to get on the table. At the same time, he defers to authority (a *follower* in that context). He scarcely takes his eyes off Ian, and when he does, he settles on Ralph. Toward his peers, Art and Martha, Howard precedes a testy *opposition* with a look of disdain. Once given the floor, however, he comes forth with smart, precise ideas (moves) that seem to please hierarchy more than his equals. Martha "manages" him, challenging him with impunity, but Art does not (usually) react.

Art (VP of marketing) speaks less than the others, but when he does, they listen. He owns the whole repertoire of stances. He *moves, follows,* and *opposes* with ease, and is clearly the team's best *bystander*. Back in the marketing department, he is correctly reputed as a creative and adored leader who actively leads (moves) his creative staff, but on an equal level with them.

Note in these descriptions that each person may show different tendencies when dealing with particular other members of the team, and specific dynamics may develop between them. These are nuances of voice that coach Duncan picks up quickly and will help Ralph learn to catch. For example, Martha fairly consistently challenges (opposes) Howard with a disapproving voice. She works differently with Ian, who does not appreciate her "playfully" challenging style. When she speaks, his red Aeron chair swivels, presenting his broad back and broad shoulders as he looks out the window. He seems to be sending a message (a silent but not very covert oppose), and Martha gets it. She stares back, shooting daggers into his back when they are clashing over some issue. These gestures readily translate into words (move-oppose) that Ian and Martha keep under polite control. Until they can't.

Our research shows that those individuals with more balanced profiles—who are able to shift their action stances when they want to—are natural facilitators. But they are often seen as weak leaders in some business cultures where exclusively strong or stuck movers are rewarded.

ACTION STRUCTURES, ACTION SEQUENCES, AND STRUCTURAL PATTERNS

Pivotal moments are often marked by repetitions. For example, coach Duncan noticed a pivotal point in the meeting that began when Howard asked for some time and got quite a bit of it. Recently, on Ralph's recommendation and pronouncement that Asia "is years ahead in green technology," ClearFacts had opened a new office there. Howard had fiercely lobbied for and won appointment as its director along with (against Ian's objection) an independent budget and full staff. In the current meeting, Howard had just shown computer slides about his investments in Asia, requesting still more budget for décor and for more professional and support staff. Above all, he wanted Art to travel to Asia to develop materials for the new marketing staff and to train them. In verbal interchanges about this big move, Duncan had noticed Art's body language begin to change to a mix of fear and moral disgust (a covert, unexpressed opposition). But silently bystanding, Art appeared increasingly disabled. (Later, we will learn more about his inner struggles.) Howard's big move also set off a repeating sequence of actions—

primarily involving Howard moving and Martha opposing. As the sequence repeated and heated up, Duncan noticed that Ian and Ralph also seemed disabled.

To probe the significance of the repetitions, we need to add a few more phrases to our descriptive language. In real conversation, actions are strung together very quickly into sequences called action structures. **Action structures** are identifiable pairs of related actions that occur within an interaction. For example, if someone says, "Let's order lunch now," and someone else says, "I think it would be better to wait til one o'clock," they would be exhibiting the action structure *move-oppose*. As you begin to notice such structural data, you will actually also get better at recognizing and retaining an interaction's content information as well.

Longer than an action structure, an **action sequence** is a string of three or more actions whose beginning and end can be reliably confirmed by observers. Here is an example of the action sequence *move-oppose-move-follow*:

Speaker	Speech Act	Stance
Ralph	Let's order lunch now.	Move
Ian	I think it would be better to wait til 1:00; we can finish item A.	Oppose
Art	Since we're all starving, how about breaking at 12:45 and doing as much as we can between now and then?	Move
Martha	Great idea!	Follow

When an action sequence repeats over and over again in a group, it becomes a **structural pattern.** Structural patterns tend to develop (one could say evolve), repeating often and embedding themselves within systems, recognizable to group members and observers as part of the group's culture. Patterns can be beneficial or destructive. Figure 2.1 illustrates the action structure, the action sequence, and the structural pattern.

Coach Duncan called Ralph's attention to another interaction during the meeting, saying it embodied a structural pattern in the team's dynamics. He also noted it as a telltale precursor to Art's blowup.

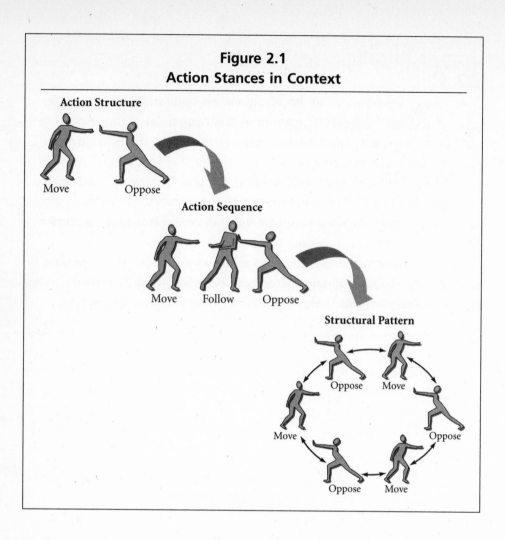

Figure 2.1
Action Stances in Context

Action Structure

Move   Oppose

Action Sequence

Move   Follow   Oppose

Structural Pattern

Oppose   Move

Move

Oppose

Oppose   Move

Speaker	Speech Act	Stance
Howard	I would like us to act soon on the group's recommendation.	Moves
Art	Not a good idea—we lack capacity to do it right.	Opposes
Howard	Nonsense. I have figures to say we can.	Opposes, then moves
		(Continued)

Speaker	Speech Act	Stance
Art	Your figures are based on ancient standards. I think there are better ones. Besides, I'd like to suggest an alternative to the group's recommendation.	Opposes, then moves
Martha	It would be my guess that if you two were to put your heads together outside the group, there'd be more agreement than we're seeing here.	Attempts to bystand
Ian	There you go again "making nice" and cooling dialogue down. Hey, a little heat may not be such a bad thing.	Opposes, then moves

It's a sequence that Ralph certainly knows, as he confesses to Duncan.

As an exercise, try labeling this last interaction between Ralph and Duncan in terms of action stances, without referring to the right-most column.

Speaker	Speech Act	Stance
Ralph	Yes, that sequence . . . I remember it, and I was thinking "Here we go again."	Follows, then moves
Duncan	The fact that you recognize it so easily is proof that it's a pattern.	Bystand, or bystander-type of move
Ralph	Seems like it happens often—Art and Howard going at it, Ian cutting Martha down.	Continues previous move; has bystand quality
		(Continued)

Speaker	Speech Act	Stance
Duncan	Let's keep it simple for now: any time two or more people who regularly engage in conversation get in trouble—as you and your team were when Art and Howard were going at it at the end of the meeting and Art killed the discourse . . .	Bystand with the quality of a move, a typical stance of coaches
Ralph	You're saying that was avoidable? But how? It came out of the blue!	Follows, then moves
Duncan	Not quite. Art and Howard were telegraphing it all meeting long.	Opposes (corrects), then moves
Ralph	So if I'd been reading the room, I would have seen it coming?	Follows
Duncan	You got it.	Follows

When structural patterns produce favorable outcomes, they are an important component of successful team process. For example, many strong mover leaders depend on one or more strong opposers in their groups to challenge their proposals and help lead the group to a better decision or plan. Recognizing structural patterns is essential because, uninterrupted, they can become self-sustaining and force certain, sometimes undesired outcomes.

Structural Patterns Mold Behaviors

Members of ongoing groups anticipate structural patterns and respond to them *in advance*. Individuals become so convinced that a certain structural pattern will play out, they limit their own choices for handling the interaction. For example, in the ClearFacts case, everyone expects that Ian will oppose Martha's attempts to shed light on a problem, so they get used to ignoring her contributions.

When the outcome is unproductive and the players become stuck in their roles in a sequence, we call this a **ritual impasse.** In such unsuccessful structural patterns, no one gets what he or she wants, the group feels stuck, and the positive possibilities of bystanding shrink or disappear. People respond to one another in line with past interactions rather than the current one. In these sequences, the structural pattern has begun to shape the content and to perpetuate the unproductive outcome.

Archetypal Structural Patterns

Certain structural patterns are so common in organizations that we call them **action archetypes.** These archetypes are easily identifiable in all types of group and couple communication. To train yourself to observe the invisible structures of structural dynamics, start by trying to notice action archetypes around you.

The most common action archetype is **point-counterpoint.** This move-oppose action structure is always at work in systems where groups face a challenge or are trying to change. When we are brought into conflict situations in families, in teams, or between partners, there is always a point-counterpoint structure at work. Mentally label the stances in these examples:

MOTHER: Time for bed, dear.
SON: No, I don't wanna.

BOSS: I'd like the product in my hands by the fifteenth.
MANAGER: Impossible; it can't be done.

HUSBAND: That boy should be grounded.
WIFE: I couldn't think of a worse solution.

Simple point-counterpoint structures provide opportunities for the group to learn and grow and are a catalyst for creativity and collaboration. But over time, when point-counterpoint predominates and becomes imbedded in the system, individuals stop hearing the content of what the other is saying and get locked into ritualistic argumentation, and follows and bystands become conspicuously absent. The result is volatility, conflict, and even escalating violence.

Look back at "A Third Sequence" for what we call a *point-counterpoint escalation*: assertion followed by attack followed by counterattack, in circular fashion. It is known to most teams. Art started the exchange with Howard, but faded in effectiveness and was replaced by Martha, who spoke for him. The pattern ended when the silenced Art blew up.

In contrast to point-counterpoint, there are several **compliance archetypes** that suggest agreement where there may be none. The **courteous compliance** archetype is common in traditional cultures or in teams that are just beginning to form. In the latter, someone (usually the designated leader) makes a move, and the team dutifully follows. The conversation is polite, with very little controversy or pushback.

Where a highly compatible team is making progress in nonchallenging areas, a courteous compliance structure sometimes takes hold. For example, the boss outlines the next steps of the project plan and reviews everyone's jobs for the next several weeks. Each team member agrees, and the meeting either moves to other items or is adjourned. When courteous compliance predominates, however, it lessens the appropriate and often needed correction that group input provides. Similarly, courteous compliance can reflect a mind-set that "any idea from George must be good" or that the action of following takes precedence over careful consideration of content. Group members turn on autopilot, silencing their own abilities to move or oppose and allowing George to be their sole initiator.

Covert opposition is a variation of courteous compliance. In this archetype, someone makes a move, and publicly everyone else either follows or bystands, but underneath these overt stances, they harbor skeptical or oppositional thoughts. Instead of openly confronting the moves being made, they revert to covert, closed-door blockage or sabotage. Meanwhile, the mover believes that the silence or acquiescence of the team signals its support. For example, in an organizational assessment interview, two team members express discontent with their boss, George, and the direction in which he is taking the team. When asked if they have talked to George about their concerns, they answer from a mind-set that "George never listens," "I couldn't possibly tell George how I feel," or "This place doesn't allow us to oppose." Here again we see how a repeating structure can totally overtake the content: follows and bystands (nonoppositional actions) overtake the ability to discuss content freely and openly.

BYSTANDING TO READ THE ROOM

Reading the room—taking note of what is occurring structurally within an interaction—is an intentional form of bystanding. Rather than moving, opposing, or following on the basis of your own subconscious behavioral hot buttons,

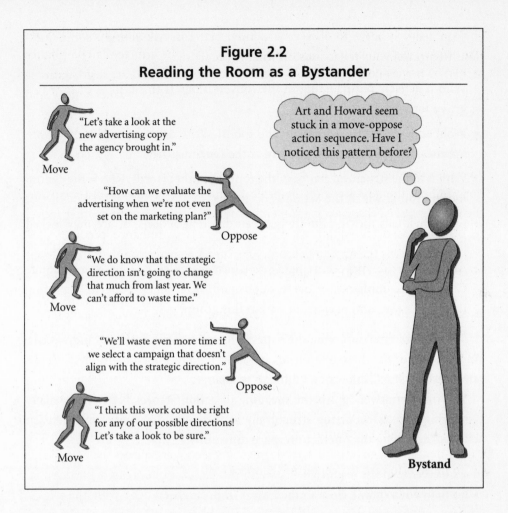

Figure 2.2
Reading the Room as a Bystander

"Let's take a look at the new advertising copy the agency brought in."

Move

"How can we evaluate the advertising when we're not even set on the marketing plan?"

Oppose

"We do know that the strategic direction isn't going to change that much from last year. We can't afford to waste time."

Move

"We'll waste even more time if we select a campaign that doesn't align with the strategic direction."

Oppose

"I think this work could be right for any of our possible directions! Let's take a look to be sure."

Move

Art and Howard seem stuck in a move-oppose action sequence. Have I noticed this pattern before?

Bystand

first learn to step back mentally and extract yourself from the action in order to see what is occurring. Figure 2.2 illustrates the concept.

Your first objective is to be able to identify the action structures, action sequences, and structural patterns at work and their impact on the group's productivity. A second skill objective will be figuring out which of these you want to encourage in your group and which ones you want to thwart.

These methods take practice. Especially when you are the leader of the group, with all eyes on you for direction, it can be difficult in the beginning to be able to step back from the action and reflect on the structures in the room. To start developing your skills, I recommend you find a committee, a meeting, or a group where you are not responsible for the agenda. Family settings can also be great environments to begin to observe structural patterns. Ask yourself some questions to prompt your reflections on what is occurring:

- Who is actively participating in the conversation? Is this typical of how this group interacts?
- What actions do you witness in the room? Write down examples of moves, opposes, follows, bystands. Are any of the four missing?
- Who is in the structural center of the room? In other words, who is the central mover around which the action is occurring?
- Are individuals moving fluidly between different actions, or are they locked into one?
- Are action archetypes occurring? Do you hear examples of point-counterpoint? Courteous compliance? Covert opposition? Are other patterns repeating themselves over and over again within this group?

Spend some time observing the patterns between various pairs of individuals. We have found that these one-on-one patterns tend to imbed themselves deeply, often become stuck, and can be difficult to change.

You may intuitively grasp the meaning of action stances better by spatially visualizing what is occurring structurally in the room. In your mind, see each action stance using the interaction space differently:

- To move is to take the center of the space.
- To follow is to come close to the mover in the center.
- To oppose is to challenge the mover from a position between the periphery and the center.
- To bystand is to position oneself on the periphery, whence all of the action can be observed.

Sometimes literal spatial relationships between participants can provide clues about the stances people are taking. When someone follows someone else, you can often see the two moving closer to one another. Similarly, you can often observe the body language of opposers and bystanders as they act.

When people in a high-functioning group engage each other over time, their structures typically include all four action stances. At some points, an individual may predominantly play one role—as mover, opposer, bystander, or follower. At other points, the same individual can fluidly change his or her stance as the discussion evolves. Generally in groups, if any two of the four stances are missing, communication will be impaired. Dysfunctional groups often have inadvertently silenced one or more of them (more on this in Chapter Ten).

GHOSTS AND OUTBURSTS AT CLEARFACTS

Obviously, Art's outburst against Howard was heavily emotional, and the next chapter will explore structural Level II, which brings emotion into the picture. In Parts Two and Three of this book, you will see extreme reactivity and volatility when people are under great pressure. At this point, however, by way of advancing the general story that's unfolding at ClearFacts, I'd like to let you know about two events that occurred on the Friday evening before the Monday meeting. This interlude will remind you that, in stressful moments, what actors say at the relatively obvious Level I (stances) and Level II (communication domains) at a meeting at work is likely to be affected by their own personal stories and relationships outside work. Other members of the team may know little or nothing about those influences.

A Prior Moment Between Art and Howard

Here's part of what had happened Friday evening:

Art leadenly left the office lost in troubled thought, making his way through the empty ninth-floor marketing corridors. A clock he glimpsed showed eleven, jolting him awake. Jane, his wife, would be furious. Why hadn't he phoned as he'd promised? *Why am I the only one still here?* he wondered as he stepped into the elevator. He'd begun to rehearse his excuse to Jane when the elevator stopped on seven, and Howard Green stepped on from the sales floor, along with someone Art did not recognize as belonging in the building. The man's long hair, a 1960s antique, made him stand out. If this dude was with Howard, the two were trying not to show it. Finally, Howard had no choice but to say, "Art Saunders, Template Jones. A Wall Street ex-pat." TJ, as he is called, will play a major role in ClearFacts's destiny.

Art acknowledged the stranger and exchanged a silent greeting with Howard. *Only seven more floors to freedom*, he thought, *followed by eight miles to hell, where a furious Jane awaits*. On the ground floor, they went their separate ways, the stranger following Howard.

Now what's he up to? Art wondered.

Art at Home with Jane

A while later:

Sounds of the garage door opening . . . Jane stirred and realized she had drifted off. The eleven o'clock news was over. Her thoughts churned sluggishly. *He said he'd be home at eight.* Wine and a little sleep had worn off the waves of anger she would have rolled over Art at nine-thirty. Now she was left with a deep sadness and little sense of hope. Last Saturday night, she had told him again so clearly, *You are a thinker, not an entrepreneur; this job is killing you and eating you up from the inside out.*

Art stepped quietly into the room. Which was greater—his fear of her and knowledge that he must engage her now, or his simple sheer exhaustion?

"Oh Jane, I'm so sorry . . . I don't know what to say . . ."

"Just say what's up. You look like you've seen a ghost. I'm furious, but I won't shoot you."

Art lowered his head and shrugged.

"Oh, that SOB Howard again?" she continued. "When he speaks, you hear your father's voice. Let's go to bed, Art."

From Insight to Action

The four action stances are the building blocks of communication. According to the theory of structural dynamics, they occupy the core of all verbal acts. Knowing how you use them and being able to recognize or code how others do are the first steps in developing communicative competency, a crucial skill for leaders and coaches.

Your Most Used Action Stances

1. Observe yourself in a group that meets regularly (ideally of six to eight members, but any number will do).

   • How often do you initiate topics (move)? When and why?

   • How often do you agree with or carry forward the direction others suggest (follow)? When and why?

- How often do you challenge directions others suggest (oppose)? When and why?

- How often do you stay back to observe others' actions without commenting much, if at all (silent bystander)?

- How often do you observe and then make comments about the nature of the conversation (active bystander)?

2. Estimate the percentage of time you use each of the four action stances (the total should amount to 100 percent).

Action	Percentage
Move	_____
Follow	_____
Oppose	_____
Bystand	_____
Total	100

3. Does your most often used action get *stuck*? (When and why?)

4. What is your least used action, your *weak* mode? How do you explain this?

Structures of Action Stances in Different Contexts

Identify the most common action structures (combinations of stances) that occur between you and key others in different relationship contexts. (For example, in your family you may follow a father who is a strong mover.)

- With your boss
- With your direct reports
- With your colleagues or peers
- With your spouse or partner
- With your children (or a particular child)
- With a particular sibling
- With . . . (name other very specific contexts)

Reading the Room

1. Observe others in group interaction (ideally the same group you used for the "Your Most Used Action Stances" exercise).

   - Try to name the sequences of actions others take in the conversation.

   - Identify sequences that "do not work."

   - Does the group have a stuck mover?

   - Does the group have a stuck opposer?

   - Does the group have too few or too many followers?

   - Does the group have no strong bystander?

2. Try identifying an action that is missing in a faulty sequence, and then make that action yourself. For example, if the discourse is dominated by serial moves, try bystanding, and then follow or oppose a previous action (in a pure voice).

3. Begin listening for how tone and voice negatively affect others and undermine the speaker's own message.

4. Look for common behavioral archetypes, such as point-counterpoint or courteous compliance. Try naming them, which is the simplest intervention; or call on the group's best bystander or opposer to "say what you think is going on here."

5. In an upcoming meeting when you are not the designated leader, pick a ten-minute segment when your primary focus is to read the room. After the meeting ends, ask yourself the following questions:

   - What did I notice in the meeting that I have not seen before?

   - How could that information be useful to me as a leader (or coach)?

   - Were there faulty sequences that emerged in the meeting?

   - Were these repetitive sequences that should be called patterns?

   - Were there actions that were overused or conspicuously absent?

   - How did the overuse or absence affect the dynamics in the room?

- How easy or difficult was it for me to start to see the room structurally? Why?

- Did I at any time consciously make the "right" but "missing" action? What were the results?

- Were there times when I sensed that a specific action was called for, yet I did not make it? Why? What were the results?

chapter THREE

Level II: Domains of Communication

Affect, Power, and Meaning

In Chapter Two, you began to learn how to read the room at Level I, the action stances (move, follow, oppose, bystand); Level I is the first component of the behavioral profile that will become useful when complete. This chapter explores Level II, **communication domains**: affect, power, and meaning.

We never just make a move, a follow, an oppose, or a bystand. We make it in the domain or language of *affect, power,* or *meaning*. Figure 1.1 located these domains in the context of our broader model of structural dynamics. I call this level "domains" to call attention to how the three terms describe both the *territory* where actions originate and their aim or purpose. One might also think of each domain as an orientation or "world" that preoccupies people as they communicate: some focus heavily on their and others' *feelings* (affect), others on *getting things done* (power), and others on what it all *means* (meaning).

The key to understanding what you hear lies in recognizing speech in each domain and combining that insight with your awareness of the speaker's action stance. Suppose you tell a friend that you are reading this book by Kantor. "It's about leadership," you say (thereby making a move). Your friend asks, "Why a book on leadership?" (inviting you to clarify your move). Three answers could follow:

Speech Act	Stance and Domain
I'm reading it because I *care about* the people around me, and I want to do my best to maximize the quality and depth of those interactions.	A move in the *affect* domain (intimacy, nurturance, relationships, social connection)
	(Continued)

Speech Act	Stance and Domain
I'm reading it because I believe that these *skills* will help me *get what I want* [for example, promotion, resolution of an existing group conflict, success].	A move in the *power* domain (what we want and how to achieve it)
I am reading it because I want to increase my *knowledge*; I want to expand my *understanding* of this model that I have heard so much about.	A move in the *meaning* domain (search for ideas, meaning, truth, correct understanding)

You can tell what domain speakers are occupying (coming from and pointing toward) by their use of specific words and phrases that typify the three areas, such as the ones I italicized in the left column of the table here. Notice also that the communication domains add not only *linguistic tone* and *context* but *purpose* to the four action stances. I like to speak of them as language domains, to indicate that they are languages through which each domain's purposes are realized.

The space in which we each focus our language is connected to a deep inner sense of what matters. Each of us has preferences about operating in one domain or another, despite the fact that each domain is indispensable to successful verbal interaction. From what you know already of COO Ian and HR director Martha, you can safely assume that they and other members of the ClearFacts team will differ not only in the stances they prefer but in which domains matter most to each—affect, power, or meaning. Ralph's challenge as CEO will be to combine his recognition of stances with a sense of domains. Only by being aware of conflicts at this level will he be able to effectively manage the speech of the group. Before we examine each domain more closely, let's get a sense of how they display themselves at ClearFacts.

THE LATEST CLEARFACTS WEEKLY MEETING

With Art's permission, Ralph opened the meeting by telling the group that he'd arranged a session between coach Duncan and Art, who'd exploded the previous week, and that Art wanted to "put the episode behind us and move on." Ralph endorsed that request, especially in light of today's big agenda.

Ralph proceeded by telling the team that ClearFacts was on target with its acquisitions and green energy investments, positioning itself well for the future. However, they needed to discuss how to handle excessive headcount totals since ClearFacts had acquired a start-up in Florida. The team noted that throughout ClearFacts, because times had been good, managers had been keeping poor performers on the payroll. Now the purchase of the start-up would flood the ClearFacts ranks to overflow in key departments. Pink slips were inevitable, the team agreed, but should they sweep the house quickly? Or should they try to preserve morale by holding costly meetings to explain their decision? At that point, the following exchange took place between Ian (COO) and Martha (VP of HR). Take a moment to fill in the action stance you see behind each of the statements. Leave the Domain column empty for now.

Speaker	Speech Act	Stance	Domain
Ian	These are grown men and women, not children. You don't use expensive perfume with slugs; you use disinfectant.		
Martha	They are not "slugs," Ian; they are persons. They are human beings and deserve to be treated humanely.		
Ian	When was the last time you calculated the costs incurred when a company coddles its workforce as you will no doubt be proposing? Ticking clocks versus beating hearts is how I see it.		
Martha	You are heartless, Ian. Heartless. Do you even have a heart?		

In a post-meeting analysis, Ralph told Duncan about the sequence he'd noted in these remarks: that Ian would oppose and Martha would move and oppose him, at which point Ian would oppose her and make a move of his own. Back and forth. Ralph was intrigued.

RALPH: I've never been able to figure out what is going on with them. They're running the Leadership Development Center together, training "high-potentials," yet they often quarrel like a couple divorcing in front of Judge Judy. They drive each other crazy—both of them *stuck*. It's like whenever things heat up, they seem to pass each other by. As if each is talking to someone else.

DUNCAN: Indeed. In fact, Ian and Martha speak different languages—Ian the language of power, Martha the language of affect. When they're running trainings together, they manage to keep their differences under wraps, though occasionally their very different answers to a trainee's question get confusing. Then, I've seen, Martha resentfully defers to Ian. In your weekly team meetings, when, as you say, "things heat up," her unhappiness erupts.

With that, Duncan explained the three domains of affect, power, and meaning.

THE DOMAIN OF AFFECT

Figure 3.1 briefly summarizes the **affect domain** in terms of its general orientation, the territory it covers, its broad goals, and what it amounts to at its best and worst.

The language of affect is the language of intimacy and nurturance, of being connected with others in the world. When we speak the language of affect, we are attending to the relationships between individuals and to each individual's sense of well-being. Affect is also the language of emotion, caring, and connection. Following are some statements in the affect domain. (Note that the interpretation of stance might differ depending on the sequence of speech acts in which each statement took place.)

Speech Act	Stance in Domain
Any time you feel sad or frightened, you can ask me to hold you.	Move in affect
I'm convinced that raising that issue will open an emotional can of worms that will license the ranks to act like children.	Oppose in affect
I'll do as you've asked. Since they both trust me, I'll try to get them to embrace and make up.	Follow in affect
It seems that whenever you two get too close, you have a fight that puts you at a "safer" emotional distance.	Bystand in affect

Figure 3.1
Affect Communication Domain

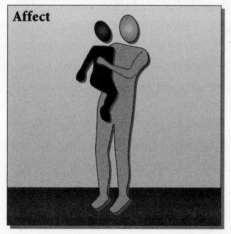

Orientation
Feelings and relationships

Territory
• How people are feeling
• Caring and being cared for

Goals
Nurturance and intimacy

Dysfunction
"Psychobabble"

Example
"How will people feel about the decision we're making?"

Metaphorically, to speak in affect is to speak from the heart. Individuals who are strong in the affect domain often value their relationships with others as much as or more than they value the tasks or outcomes at hand. In a conversation in the affect domain, you will hear them use such words as *empathize, sensitive, well-being, feel, care, love,* and *hate.*

Individuals who are tightly locked into one of the other two language domains and who are also intolerant of the language of affect may respond dismissively to these vocabularies openly or privately. "Insubstantial" or "irrelevant," a meaning advocate may think. A strict power advocate may think "shallow," "mediocre," or "expendable." They reflect the reality that the affect domain was formerly relegated primarily to the family arena. By the same token, strict advocates of affect may pejoratively judge those committed to the other domains: "detached" or "obtuse," they may say and think of fierce meaning advocates; they may consider strict power advocates "driven" or "heartless."

In corporations, affect is still the least commonly heard of the three language domains, although an affect revolution has been accelerating in business over the last thirty years. Because it is not the typical linguistic means for reaching the goals of a business organization, affect is often ascribed to "touchy-feely" types. In some highly competitive organizations, when the language of affect is used, it is often confined to pre- and post-meeting activity and to restaurants and bars where individuals are tacitly allowed to connect with one another on a more informal basis.

But evidence abounds that corporate groups now recognize the importance of affect. In large part due to Goleman's theory of emotional intelligence, leaders are now commonly evaluated on "how effectively [they] perceive and understand their own emotions and the emotions of others and how well they can manage their emotional behavior."[1] Developments in neuroscience validate a frequently held, but unsubstantiated, view that "we are wired to connect."[2]

Families do not always stress affect. Family systems deficient in affect and work systems abounding with affect are both more common than one might think.

THE DOMAIN OF POWER

Figure 3.2 briefly summarizes the **power domain** in several respects.

The domain of power involves the freedom to decide what we as individuals or organizations want and the ability to achieve it. However, people do associate

Figure 3.2
Power Communication Domain

Power

Orientation
Getting things done

Territory
- Action
- Productivity

Goals
Competence, efficacy, and completion

Dysfunction
"Steamrolling"

Example
"Who's going to make sure that there is follow-through here?"

the word "power" with force and with images of constraint, control, coercion, absolute authority, and tyranny; and there is also a place for these dark sides of power in our theory. Nowhere else than in the power domain is it more important to keep in mind the light and dark sides of our speech and other behavior. In this chapter, however, we will emphasize the light or positive face of power. Think of effectiveness, efficacy, competence, potency, skill, and productivity. These we distill down to *efficacy and a sense of competency* when identifying the basic goals and purposes of communication in the power domain.

Metaphorically, the power domain represents the muscle and sinew of an organization: few conditions are more pathetic than an awareness of what is wanted or needed combined with the lack of ability, freedom, or confidence to attain it.[3] Because of its focus on the completion of tasks to achieve objectives, power tends to be the dominant language in corporate life. In power we translate the ideas and theories of the meaning domain into real action in the world. One might say that in the corporate world, power language often reigns supreme, with meaning in a distant second place, and affect another twelve lengths back.

In manifestly intimate systems such as families, marriages, and other love-based partnerships, affect might appear to have no significant rival, but power and meaning also have major roles to play. The following are examples of statements in the power domain.

Speech Act	Stance in Domain
Folks, it's time to put all talk on the shelf and focus on action.	Move in power
Unless you add "putting the right people in place," my concerns about competitors catching up will continue to intensify.	Oppose in power
Your idea of investing heavily in training and skill building is spot-on. It serves both our short-term competitive concerns and our long-term growth goals.	Follow and then move in power
What you all seem to be saying is that our on-the-ground tactics are perfectly in sync with our best-case growth trajectory.	Bystand in power

At work, such words as *action, achieve, move forward, accountable, outcomes,* and *performance* signal the power domain.

THE DOMAIN OF MEANING

Figure 3.3 briefly summarizes the **meaning domain,** the space in which we seek understanding of the most difficult questions posed by the key worlds in which we live. It is the territory of ideas, purpose, high value, and an unfiltered access to information—all toward the coherent integration of thought. When we speak in the meaning domain, it is to test and cement our understanding of our identities, try out new theories, gather more information, and learn from those around us. Ultimately, the language of meaning is a search for truth in either of two veins, *analytic* and *philosophical.* The following table lists examples of statements in the meaning domain.

Speech Act	Stance in Domain
I'm concerned we're losing sight of our collective purpose.	Move in meaning
I find this department's dogmatic commitment to pluralism no different from so-called narrow fundamentalism.	Oppose in meaning
I support the idea of making sure we triple-check all the facts before including them in our report.	Follow in meaning
The ongoing discussions between philosophy and the social sciences could conceivably result in an entirely new field of knowledge.	Bystand in meaning

Figure 3.3
Meaning Communication Domain

Meaning

Orientation
Thinking, logic, and ideas

Territory
• Thought
• Searching for answers

Goals
Identity and integration

Dysfunction
"All talk, no action"

Example
"This campaign is the right one because of its consistency with our strategic direction."

Metaphorically, to speak in meaning is to speak from the mind. In meaning, we seek to develop a shared community of thought with others in conversation. In this domain you will hear such words as *ideas, purpose, integration, logic, understanding, theory, values,* and *patterns.*

Of the three domains, meaning is the most linked to context. Different kinds of organizations define their meaning differently. In the business world, conversations about vision, strategy, and purpose lie squarely in the domain of meaning. Many conversations in engineering, health care, R&D, and information systems departments also evolve in the meaning domain as individuals try to solve technical problems or seek out the appropriate information for decision making. In the family context, meaning conversations are those that deal with what we stand for and believe in as a family. In the church, meaning conversations attend to the highest theological levels.

Individuals who are most comfortable in the meaning domain often enjoy research and data gathering, and discussion of philosophy and theories. The pursuit of knowledge and information is a prime motivator.

For exercise, look back at the dialogues in this and the previous chapter. Try to ascribe one of the three domains to each speech act. (Be easy on yourself: some speech act wordings are difficult to interpret neatly when the context is unclear or mixed, or when a speaker changes the context.)

THE VALUE OF ALL THREE DOMAINS

As I said briefly earlier, structural dynamics asserts that a balance of all three domains is necessary over time for the effective functioning of any organizational system and for the highest functioning of good leaders, good parents, and thoughtful lovers. In some measure, the presence of all three domains is important because when one is overly dominant, it can have as much detrimental impact as when entirely absent.

Each domain has strengths and weaknesses, as Figure 3.4 suggests. For example, the affect domain creates a sense of safety and well-being and helps establish strong bonds between individuals. ("How are we all feeling about this? Honestly all on board?") These bonds can prove invaluable in organizational crisis. If a team can function only in affect, however, it is unlikely to perform up to organizational expectations. Meaning provides alignment between individuals through a shared sense of purpose and an understanding of the "why" behind actions.

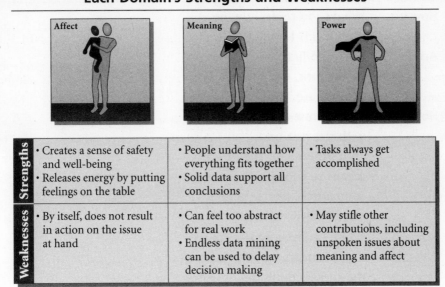

Figure 3.4
Each Domain's Strengths and Weaknesses

	Affect	Meaning	Power
Strengths	• Creates a sense of safety and well-being • Releases energy by putting feelings on the table	• People understand how everything fits together • Solid data support all conclusions	• Tasks always get accomplished
Weaknesses	• By itself, does not result in action on the issue at hand	• Can feel too abstract for real work • Endless data mining can be used to delay decision making	• May stifle other contributions, including unspoken issues about meaning and affect

("Does this plan serve your department's needs?") Overused, it can serve as a hiding place for those uncomfortable with taking action or with expressing concern about relationships or about speaking the language of love directly. The domain of power is critical to moving forward and making things happen. ("Okay, what's step one?") Focused on exclusively, it stifles other contributions and can turn thoughtful momentum into tyranny and reckless acts. And, of course, it too can cast a shadow of neglect on relationships at work and in love. ("Let's just vote and move on!")

STANCES AND DOMAINS ACROSS THE CLEARFACTS TEAM

Earlier in this chapter, I provided some dialogue between Martha (whose domain preference is affect) and Ian (whose is power) that showed how the clash sometimes gets them stuck. Try noting the stances and preferences also in this additional bit of dialogue from the meeting described in Chapter Two, in which Howard was criticizing Art's ads:

Speaker	Speech Act	Stance and Domain
Howard	What's the central theme in this TV ad? I don't get it.	
Arthur	Well, the first few seconds are metaphoric, not how things actually are.	
Howard	But the rest doesn't fit at all with the first part.	
Arthur	That's the point; the effect it means to convey is captured in comparison. Its message is intentionally nuanced.	
Howard	When I convey a message to big customers, I avoid nuance; the suckers don't get "nuance." They want profit, and ads that help them make it.	

As coach Duncan helped CEO Ralph learn to listen for the patterns of stances and domains among the members of the team (including Ralph himself), they had the following exchange.

DUNCAN: More than 50 percent of Ian's contributions challenge someone else's contributions. That's his opposer stance propensity. And when he opposes he is usually focusing on expediting solutions to make things happen. That's his propensity toward the power domain. On the other hand, more than 50 percent of Martha's contributions are moves laced in affect.

RALPH: Okay, but those two are so obviously different. How about Art and Martha?

DUNCAN: Art and Martha sound alike when discussing people issues, or any subject for that matter. But whereas she relies heavily on feelings and the language of affect, he balances his own propensity toward affect with the language of meaning.

RALPH: So those two could also generate storms?

DUNCAN: Yes, and if in general it can be said that storms develop from miscommunications, you, my dear friend Ralph, are making some worse.

RALPH: I think I've got you here, Dunc. I don't remember my being part of any storm. We've talked about the storms on my team . . . But I have consciously held myself back from stepping into the fray.

DUNCAN: *(After a dramatically enigmatic expression that tends to irritate Ralph)* I'm guessing you're annoyed. Even with me. Right now. When you are looking for explanations and they are withheld, you tend to react. Understanding things is important to you. In fact, when *anybody's* freedom to expound ideas is dismissed or systematically undermined or ruled out, you are capable of exploding. When you think you are consciously keeping a lid on your potentially stormy behavior, veins show up in your forehead and neck. Remember recently when Ian rather ruthlessly dismissed one of Art's poetic expostulations? Those veins in your neck and head seemed ready to burst.

RALPH: *(Feels his body tensing up; tries in vain to shut down memory of a violent confrontation with his father) (Muttering)* Son of a bitch. *(Aloud)* I know the moment well.

DUNCAN: *(Softly, muted)* Ralph, we both know that there is a story here. But we'll get to that later. For now, let this suffice: nothing is more important to you than *meaning*—your need to understand, your constant search for truth in all the worlds around you. When power is used to assault meaning, when the pursuit of understanding is shut down, you don't like it.

RALPH: *Meaning?* I'm hung up on meaning?

DUNCAN: When you are unobstructed, you gravitate to the land of meaning. But you can get stuck there. Oh, you are pretty trilingual, but you tend to drift into meaning.

Duncan takes note that Ralph's voice is softer than usual, Ralph's mind roaming, his energy subdued. Ralph doesn't say so, but now he's thinking of something he heard recently from Sonia, his wife. As I noted earlier, to Ralph, the quality of his marital sex life is his main measure of the ongoing quality of his marriage, and, as he'd been telling Sonia, that quality now is high—"as good as it gets." She wasn't disagreeing, but she did say to him, "Let's face it: it is a bit hard to get you out of your head and into your body."

Hmm, thinks Ralph. *From meaning to affect?*

PROPENSITIES TOWARD DIFFERENT DOMAINS

Most individuals choose one communication domain over the others, though many comfortably "speak" all three, assigning different weights to each while reserving their dominant choice for contexts that call forth their most representative self. Asked about this choice once they learn the concepts, they will say, "I haven't thought about it in these terms until now, but yes, you could say I have a preference for one language over the others."

When people come away from an important event—a heated conversation, let's say (in which, not incidentally, they are likely to have been overplaying their language of choice)—with different interpretations of what happened, their communication propensities may be implicated. Our dominant communication propensity makes us more likely to see, hear, attend to, and explain only portions of what those around us are saying. Think of it as a lens with two functions: a *sensor* that attunes us to hearing certain kinds of information, and a *filter* that screens out other kinds of information. If your language of choice is meaning, for example, you will notice and cull out issues in that domain, using the language of meaning to describe them. You will be less attuned to issues of power and affect.

COMMUNICATION AT THE INTERFACE

The general structural perspective works from the notion that much of the most vital action in any system takes place at the interface between two entities. When we talk about healthy organizations, we see that effective conversation is taking place more or less consistently at the interface of the organization's key subsystems—marketing and sales, for example, or R&D and finance. Similarly, individuals like Ian, Martha, Art, and Howard are also subsystems themselves, and their communication occurs at the interface as well: a common space created where they can listen and hear each other. In diagnosing failed communications between individuals and between groups, an understanding of the three communication domain preferences and their interfaces is key to establishing a place where meaningful communication can occur.

Communication Interface Between Two Individuals

Let's take a look at the interface between two *individuals* by eavesdropping on a typical exchange from a leadership training session co-led by Ian and Martha.

TRAINEE: *(To Ian)* Sir, I understand the logic of your explanation of what it takes to be a leader, but I have no appetite for your "warrior" metaphors. Does that mean I should give up trying?

IAN: You're damn right *(carefully timing an ironic pause)* . . . soldier.

MARTHA: *(Hurrying to catch up with Ian's barb)* Not in the least, if . . .

Ian and Martha stumble on to the end of the session doing their best to cover over the stark difference in their training models, which they had agreed not to make public. In their post-session debrief:

MARTHA: What you said to that—and, I might remind you, universally liked and respected—young manager was unnecessarily harsh, cruel, and simply wrong.

IAN: Catch your breath, Martha. I was simply using irony to test his mettle. I was saying that the life of a leader is, like Hobbes's view of the life of man, "solitary, poor, nasty, brutish, and short." You are no leader if you can't handle unnecessarily harsh and often cruel realities.

MARTHA: Let me breathe as I will, Ian. You've read his assessments. His staff loves him, they follow him, they produce for him.

An interface between any two components is where their outer boundaries touch. You are already familiar with our practice of spatializing system concepts. In Chapter Two I said that thinking spatially can shed light on and help unravel the complexities of relationships in human systems. Let's take this latter claim a step further.

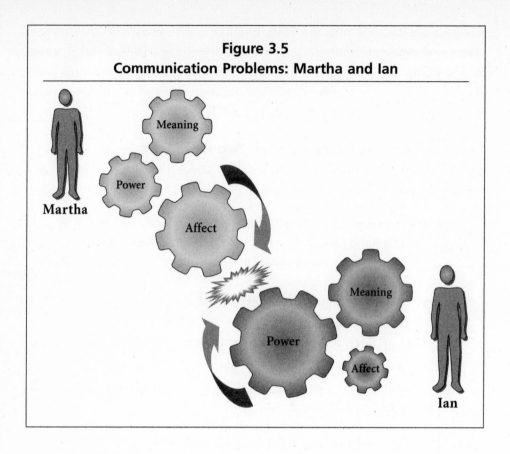

Figure 3.5
Communication Problems: Martha and Ian

Figure 3.5 illustrates Martha, who has a very strong propensity for affect and has preferences for meaning and power as well, and Ian, who has a very strong propensity for power, some for meaning, and no observable propensity for affect.

The figure represents Ian's and Martha's very different communicational realities. In fact, their primary preferences are so dominant that they have difficulty finding a communication domain where they can "truly talk" together. They are capable of meaningful conversation in meaning or power, but over time another obstacle has impeded their ability to get along. As people encounter repeated conflict, they build protective walls designed to reduce penetration and other forms of damage. Ian dreads any undermining of his commitment to efficiently getting things done. Martha dreads any undermining of her commitment to taking care of the people she's responsible for. Although she is by nature a strong mover, with Ian she is triggered to become a stuck opposer.

Let us look at an example of a more productive communication interface, that between Martha and Ralph, her boss (shown both in the following dialogue and in Figure 3.6):

Speaker	Speech Act	Domain
Martha	I am so emotionally drained from battling with Ian constantly—I don't know what to do with this relationship.	Clearly affect.
Ralph	I hear you. You are like a mother hen: fierce in protecting her brood.	Comfortable with the language, Ralph joins her in affect.
Martha	*(Laughs)* Thanks, but don't make me blush.	Still in affect.
Ralph	Let's get Ian in here and talk through your differences; if we lay the different viewpoints on the table, we should be able to reach some agreements. That done, let's all talk about what we can do to ensure that your shared goals are met on time.	Ralph first shifts to meaning, then to the power domain.

Martha is also able to move into the meaning and power domains, and is more open to doing so when others demonstrate that they are capable of valuing and acknowledging her communicative intents in the affect domain.

Trilingual Leaders

In structural dynamics terms, being trilingual means that you can *hear and speak* in all three communication domains, even if you prefer one domain. This capacity is essential for leaders who want to capture the full value of the differences among domains within their organizations. Being able to speak effectively across the communication domains allows leaders to be heard by their full constituency and to make people feel listened to and understood.

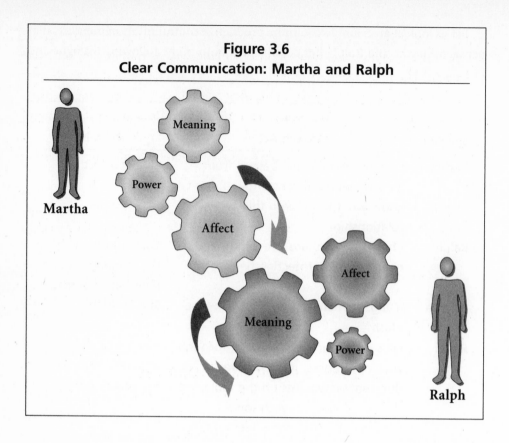

Figure 3.6
Clear Communication: Martha and Ralph

Leaders who do not understand the communication domains may unknowingly shut down the domains that differ either from their own propensities or from the organization's dominant domain. In their organizational systems, leaders occupy a special and extremely central position. When they repeatedly communicate their own ideas using one communication domain to the exclusion of the others, when they "hear" what others say primarily through the lens of that domain, they are sending a signal to the system about how to speak and how to be heard. Over time, those messages will silence the voices of the other domains.

Becoming Trilingual

A very few individuals speak all three languages with equal facility. For most leaders, the first insight is the realization that being able to expand their repertoire is a worthy and attainable desired state. Typically, they reach this conclusion by discovering that they are deficient in at least one domain, thus limiting their ability to successfully interact with key others in that language. The next step is recognizing the validity and value of the other language, even when they can't yet speak in it. The final stage of trilingual competency can take two distinct forms: when the leader is able to speak in all three communication domains at will; or when, as team leaders, individuals learn to call on others at the strategically optimal moment to execute language skills that they themselves lack.

As individuals develop their trilingual capacities, they should assume responsibility for

- Knowing when they are speaking in a language (that is, a communication domain) that is different from what is appropriate for the subject and the audience
- Recognizing the validity of another's preferred language system
- Learning to value the strengths and tolerate the limits of each team member's repertoire

AN INSIGHT INTO IAN'S CHOICE OF DOMAINS

Like choices of action stances, choices of domain, too, are influenced by Level IV of structural dynamics, the level of deep personal history and enduring identity stories, which I'll describe in Chapter Six. The following will show how this applies to Ian, who maintains his own personal stories and is clearly a mover in the domain of power, almost aversive to emotional expression.

Since youth, Ian has struggled between domains as a result of his parents' competition for most dominating influence. When Ian was born, his father, George Maxwell, was a recent West Point graduate from a Midwestern town. Two years before, George had married Ian's mother, Margaret Wells, a schoolteacher from the same town. Nineteen years later, the marriage ended badly after a sustained struggle over Ian.

The couple's war took place in two arenas: one was their bedroom, from which sounds of frightening anger and puzzling cries of pain led their son to close his ears in muted memory; the other was all the shared spaces where Ian was raised amid dual and dueling orders that forced him to choose sides.

"Strong boys never cry." When Ian was not yet five, his father declared him ready to ride his first two-wheeler solo—a ride to the corner, turn, and ride back, all on the sidewalk. Turning on a dime is too advanced for most kids, but George insisted he do it. "You are no ordinary kid. Do it. Just remember, control is in the back pedal." Too scared to disappoint, Ian set off, not taking a single breath until he managed shakily to navigate the turn. On the easy ride back to his father's arms, arms prematurely raised in triumph, a squirrel darted across the path. Instinctively Ian jerked the bike and tumbled hard, scraping wrist, knees, and forehead on the pavement.

His father, quickly at the scene, retrieved and inspected the bike, leaving the brokenhearted son to pick himself up. "Good," said the father, as if to the bike, "no damage. Not a scrape." He never glanced at Ian's wounds. Instead, he zeroed in on the tears in Ian's eyes. Even the four-year-old Ian knew that asking for solace in this way was a humiliation for him and a disappointment for his father. What he didn't expect and never forgot was what followed—no violent shaking this time, but the violence in his father's voice, through all but frothing teeth: "Don't *ever* let me see you cry about anything again. Hear me? *Never again.*" Ian heard.

By age seven, Ian knew who was in charge: Colonel George Maxwell. By that time, the only option—if there was one—was to please his father. When the father was away on military duty, Ian's mother cautiously tried to fill the parental vacuum in maneuvers designed to counter her husband's militant control. Ordinary comforting ("pampering," George called it) was out. Reading was not. It was her secret weapon, an attempt to guide his mind when cultivating his heart was out of line. No longer a schoolteacher, she now had Ian as her private student— their only connection. But she and her son soon learned that when his father returned home on leave, he would deliberately erase any mark of weakness "she'd" left on "my boy." Like an invocation to a god, the phrase "He is strong and she is weak" was drummed into Ian's psyche.

By age thirteen, George Maxwell had seeded in his receptive son a dream that boy would follow man by going to West Point. There, the son would also learn "character" (meaning honor, duty, and integrity), "discipline" (never cracking under pressure), and "strength" (the will to endure pain). In the father's view, these "virtues" were the precursors of leadership that would be instilled in Ian when—not *if*—he " rightly" chose the academy. Of the three virtues, strength was "most visible and susceptible to proper influence."

When Ian was fifteen, George—not one to leave things to chance—concocted a game ("our own Test of Strength") he insisted Ian not reveal to the mother, though she soon found out. In the game's first round, Ian was to tighten his stomach muscles to receive a fist-clenched blow, a full-strength punch from his six-foot, 180-pound father. Ian would be "fit" when he could "stomach" (a crude joke only the elder seemed to enjoy) ten such blows without flinching or giving ground. Stumbling on father and son conspiring at this ordeal and sensing her husband's insidious intentions, Margaret secretly vowed to steer her son out of the dangerous warrior path and onto a path of scholarship for her straight-A son, so uncommonly gifted in language, literature, and science.

Within six months, Ian could proudly stand ground through two punches, crying "uncle" only after the third. At age sixteen, a fat-free, steel-framed football star, he held out through seven and emphatically announced, "I will be fit in three months." And he launched a grueling, physically punishing bodybuilding regimen that included gradually increasing the weights he held at the back of his neck as he did more and more sit-ups.

On schedule, Ian took ten punches without a wince, and Colonel Maxwell, bursting with pride, declared Ian fit to be his son. Ian's "victory over pain" showed him to be someone who does what he sets out to do, "a reliable 'doer'" and a "future leader of men."

When Ian ultimately chose West Point over Princeton, Cornell, and MIT, Margaret covertly retreated into a mental courtroom she'd been devising in which she'd put her marriage on trial. Silently preparing enough beef stew to last for days, she disappeared into her locked room and came out changed. She embraced her son, congratulated him in morbid monotone, flashed a glance of disgust at her triumphant husband, and silently vowed to divorce him "at the right time." She never did, but she never entered the same bed with him again. "It was worse than divorce," Ian would later confess to coach Duncan. "The home to which I briefly returned after the Point was like a funeral parlor."

These and similar stories from Ian's childhood provide a context for the behavioral propensities he evidences in his relationships at ClearFacts, particularly with Martha and Ralph. His clashes with Martha mirror his parents' struggles of power versus affect. His relationship with Ralph, as you will see in Chapter Four, has shades of his relationship with his father.

SURPRISE AT THE MEETING'S END

The weekly meeting with which I opened this chapter went well through its business agenda, and the team felt good about its work. But at the close of it, Ralph said, "One last thing. I want to share with you a note from one of our employees that concerns me. This came through the mail from an anonymous source. It is clear the sender does not want to be traced." Ralph said this without fanfare, apparently aiming to leave the group to its own reactions without filtering them through his own. He read: "Office Asia is in danger of becoming a priapic, chauvinistic pigsty. Template Jones is a menace and a threat to the firm's image, purpose, and culture."

Silence followed, but expressions rioted. Ian took on the stern look of an inquisitor. Martha turned her hands upward with a questioning frown that asked, as if to some higher power, "What now?" Art nodded, *Of course.* Howard squinted, furrowed his brow, and stared into empty space. Ralph retained as blank a look as he could and held his tongue. (Among other things, he was trying to act on Duncan's suggestion that he learn to follow and bystand more, especially in difficult conversations.)

"Who in hell is Template Jones?" As usual, Martha broke the silence.

Howard dropped all facial affect. With admirable calm he explained that Template Jones was a Wall-Street ex-pat who, having left with millions and wanting to turn his mathematical genius to a noble cause "like ours," had sought out Howard, and Howard had hired him. "TJ" was now "taking the lead with investments and is doing spectacularly well. You must have noticed from my financials."

"With your permission, Martha," said Ian, without sarcasm and carefully trying not to antagonize, "I'd like to get some background on this from Howard. Howard, what more should we know about this Template Jones?"

From there, the discussion at the meeting had passed through three basic phases, which Duncan identified for Ralph afterward in their private debriefing. Throughout the three, Howard was naturally center stage, having to explain, react, and defend. But notably, it wasn't Ian from whom Howard needed to defend himself. Ian made it clear from the outset that what he wanted was information, not defense, justification, or rationalization; and remarkably he made no direct reference to the damaging allegation in the e-mail. Almost flaunting his fairness, he kept his infamous severity in matters of possible wrongdoing "out of the room."

Phase one centered around Ian and Howard. In a quiet, nonaccusing, information-seeking *voice*, Ian questioned Howard, who said that TJ was a bit odd, but brilliant. "But his private life is his own business—that's how I run my show." According to Howard, TJ kept to himself in their Asia office, except for the long hours the two spent together when Howard flew over, and on their daily phone calls when Howard was back in the States.

HOWARD: We work hard and well together. We set the bar high, and others jump.

IAN: Do people seem satisfied?

HOWARD: Well, I've seen nothing that would result in an e-mail like Ralph just quoted.

IAN: I didn't ask that. But tell me, when you are swamped with work, do people voluntarily stay on?

HOWARD: And no one has complained to me about anything.

IAN: I didn't imply anything like that either.

HOWARD: Besides, I've just hired two men and three pretty smart, self-composed women in marketing and sales.

IAN: Good. Tell me about them . . .

And so forth. In this phase, as Duncan pointed out in debriefing, Ralph, Martha, and Art had remained on the sidelines, per a request from Ralph. "Which was smart," Duncan added. "Then remember how, when Ian was satisfied he'd learned all he wanted, he sat back and nodded? And your onlookers were puzzled."

"Me, too," said Ralph. "I was also confused."

"Me, I thought Ian was masterful," said Duncan. "He followed an opposer stance with a clear move sequence. That's a surprising Ian we've not seen before. I suspect the maneuver caused Howard to reveal more than he intended. Structural dynamics would say that Ian was all active bystander, asking Howard to do all the talking, the moving."

The second, very different phase had featured Howard with Art and Martha. Martha had spoken with the opposer edge she customarily flashed when interacting with Howard—but in her favored language domain about caring, intimacy, and connection.

"And, Ralph, you must have noticed the distinct change in Arthur," said Duncan. "He was at his evenhanded best—at ease, more energy and spirit, but effectively in control of his balanced behavioral repertoire. When he had to, he would even oppose Martha, inoffensively getting her to back off so he himself could continue to engage Howard on his own terms. The language Art and Martha used—that's what I was tracking as well as the action structure—was distinct from Howard's and, if you listened carefully, from each other."

About the third phase of the inquiry as Duncan broke it down for Ralph, he said, "*You,* Ralph, were the person I noticed. In the first two phases you'd done your assignment well—following and bystanding. That was helpful to your team members who were probing in those first two phases. You added a useful sprinkling of your usual strong and frequent moving. (When you rain ideas down on them—oh, yes, you *do* that—they may feel more diminished than informed.) As for any of the scary opposing you sometimes do when one of your pet ideas is thwarted—you held that in check. In phases one and two, you were earning your A."

"Then I lost it a bit, at the end," said Ralph.

"Yes. When Martha steered the conversation to the 'alleged threat to your firm's purpose and image,' the *room* became a *ring,* and you leaped in swinging. You said, 'Things like that are never *local,* Howard. They are freakin' fodder for a voracious rumor machine. Our *purpose?* What do *you* know of it, really? It's the *money community that matters most?* What about the *moral* community?'

"Ralph, you were still throwing punches when Ian stepped in and refereed a stop to a one-sided fight."

"Okay," Ralph conceded, "you've got *me* on the ropes. And given me a lot to think about. Can we change the subject?"

So they did—to a brief recap of each team member's preferred domain and language.

Howard: Power. Used phrases like *the power of the street, brilliant at complex math, works hard, get things done, know one's place, stay on top of things, bottom line . . .*

Martha: Affect. Used such words as *heartless, compassion, not feeling safe, unprotected, emotional reactions, a sense of caring, connections, who can they call on.*

Arthur: Affect plus poetic meaning. In affect, he would say *hard-hearted.* In meaning he would add, *Who can feel with a three-inch peritoneum membrane encasing one's heart?* Of Wall Street he would say, *Hallowed be thy name.*

Ralph: Meaning. Used words like *moral sensitivity, higher purpose, pursuit of truth, values, community of ideas.*

DUNCAN: Ralph, I want you to focus now on the last ten minutes of
the meeting. You were rather strange, not your usual

direction-giving, optimistic self—more like a grand inquisitor. You seemed to be questioning each one's commitment to the firm's larger purposes—perhaps triggered by
Howard and the Asia affair. In any case, from the sour taste
it left, I'd say they felt diminished . . . that you were disappointed in them. What's going on?

RALPH: Do you think I have the right team? Sometimes I feel like
I carry too much of the load. Work, travel, Sonia's really
bugged about it, I know. She catches me getting out of bed
and says she feels abandoned, wants to know what I'm
doing getting up at 2:00 AM.

DUNCAN: What *are* you doing?

RALPH: Oh, sneaking in a little more reading on clean
energy science, Googling the competition, analyzing
portfolios . . .

RON STUART: NEW HELP FOR RALPH?

After that debriefing, Ralph began to think more seriously about a certain recent
contact he'd made with someone currently lower down in the ClearFacts ranks:
Ron Stuart, a lad of thirty-four who insisted he felt old, fearing we would "run
out of time before the earth either burns or drowns."

Ten years ago, Ron had finished both his Princeton liberal arts BA and an MS
in chemical engineering and quickly joined a Chicago-based solar energy firm,
which he soon left to join a start-up that was recently acquired by ClearFacts. At
the start-up he was known as a self-motivated, standout star going beyond the
call of duty to keep abreast of where "smart money" was being invested around
the world in green science and tech. His overriding goal was to make a contribution to the problem of global warming—a cause he would all but die for, according to Lani, his charming intimate partner and "bride in waiting." It was Lani
who'd suggested Ron go to the source and set his sights on headquarters. So Ron
had sent Ralph the following e-mail:

> . . . Investing in renewable energy is no longer a gamble.
> It's a necessity. Companies all over are hiring scientists to
> work on renewable technology. University scientists and
> green environment entrepreneurs are teaming up. I have
> contacts in an Arizona-based solar energy firm, still in the

start-up phase, that is interested in being bought up. They are receptive to some form of partnership with ClearFacts. They liked your *HBR* article. . . . With your reputation as a green energy visionary with impeccable moral standards, some form of marriage is a natural. May I request a meeting?

Ralph had been following the same developments and had been waiting for an opportunity to get into the act. In fact, Ralph's *Harvard Business Review* article, "Building a Green Economy Is the Most Alluring Challenge of the 21st Century," which Ron mentioned, was the same one that had drawn ClearFacts's board to take Ralph on as new CEO. As for Ron's words about marriage, Ralph smiled and wondered, *Who does this guy mean to stand at the altar, the solar firm or himself? Either way, I need to meet him.*

Their first actual meeting produced an instant professional bond. Ralph knew Ron at once for a passionate companion in arms. Both were committed to alternative energy in all its forms; both were information freaks; both sensed where the leading edges were; both were prescient and saw informed risk as the key to entrepreneurial success. Their conviction of a good match deepened over the course of two hours of talk.

That conviction soon became personal, too. Ron had earlier mentioned having been adopted. Now, when Ron complimented the company on the value it placed on diversity, thus opening the subject of his being African American and probing Ralph's level of color-blindness, Ralph came back with an unexpected question.

RALPH: And so, growing up, did you date white girls?
RON: *(Laughing)* I see you're no closet racist.
RALPH: *(Laughing)* No, just a competitive white guy. I had a black roommate at prep school—like you, better looking than me. Son of a bitch still is to this day. We go out for drinks and the best lookers size him up first. Tell me, Ron, *what do you want?*

Ron sensed that Ralph had carefully navigated this whole thing. When they parted, Ron felt a vague sense of warmth, of unfamiliar warmth—Ralph represented something in a father that Ron's legal father had never provided.

At home that same day, Ralph had recounted this meeting to Sonia. Sonia had learned from nasty experience that all too often whenever Ralph seized on some new venture, he was likely to go too far. Instinctively, she felt that this "Ron" was one of those times, and her realization led to one of their familiar scraps. The substance was new, but the ritual was old. Ralph had wanted praise for finding someone, as Sonia had suggested, who could relieve him of the burden of "leading the charge."

RALPH: But I've done just what you asked. Why aren't you pleased?
SONIA: What did you promise him?
RALPH: Nothing, only that I would raise with my team the terms he asked for.
SONIA Terms? Or do you mean demands? Sounds to me no different from your "not promising" anything when you proposed buying that start-up just one month into your term at Clear-Facts. Ian took you to task. He will again, I promise you.

And Sonia was right, as we shall see.

WHERE COACHES CAN GET STUCK

Often brought up in academic or therapeutic traditions, coaches (including Duncan and yours truly) always run the risk of getting stuck in or overusing the meaning domain. The academic environment prompts them to get hung up on theory, which might be called "ultimate meaning" because it attempts grand explanations. As a colleague once told me, "David, all of this stuff for you is like solving a tough detective story. Your mind never stops spinning its threads. Is that your notion of paradise?"

Maybe so. Coaches see great value in posing all kinds of questions and making potential connections that, through further discussion, might lead a leader to some urgent insight. They wonder what might be the origins of their clients' propensities for the different domains. Genetic? Environmental? Shaped by happenstance? Chapter Six will explore the stories that shape domain propensity.

In theorizing, other coaches may be drawn strongly to the power domain as well. But whether the coach's preference be affect, power, or meaning, the leader may be drawn to imitate the meaning preference of "the master." Both leaders and their coaches need to be wary of this. In the context of their leadership work, certainly leaders must have a very strong hold of the power domain, and the other domains often serve them as well. But the objective of coaching or being coached should steer clear of the leader's imitating the coach. Leaders need to develop all three languages, all three domains in ways that relate to their own direct experiences and awareness. In that way, skill in each domain will serve the leader's own unique needs. Whether he or she ultimately retains or can fluently talk about the theory behind them may not be relevant at all.

From Insight to Action

In real face-to-face communication, the four vocal acts (Level I) are not uttered in a vacuum; they are expressed in conjunction with one or another of three distinct language domains—affect, power, or meaning. Thus, a move in affect is distinct from a move in power, and when Jane makes a move in meaning and John opposes in power, they are speaking in different "languages" and are predisposed to miscommunication.

Understanding your use of the three language domains and being able to recognize and code how others use them is the second step by which you can further your development of communicative competency.

Your Use of the Communication Domains

1. Which of the three domains do you prefer? Do you know how you came to choose this and not one of the other languages? Is there a story behind this choice?

2. Rank the domains 1, 2, and 3, according to your preferences:

Domain	Rank
Affect	_____
Power	_____
Meaning	_____

3. Now rate them by circling High, Medium, and Low according to your comfort in using each language.

   Affect: High Medium Low
   Power: High Medium Low
   Meaning: High Medium Low

4. How challenging do you think it will be to broaden your repertoire beyond your current comfort zone?

5. Identify your use of the three language domains in two key relationship contexts:

   • In work relationships

   • In your most intimate personal relationships

   Are they the same or different? If different, how do you account for this?

6. Think of a time when communication between you and another failed because of different language preferences: (a) in your work relationships, and (b) in your closest personal relationships. Were the issues over different language preferences the same in both contexts? What do you conclude from that?

   Organizations generally rely on one domain or language system that is best suited to doing its work. What language does your organization expect of you? Does it match your strongest preference? If it doesn't, have there been consequences? How do they play out?

   Most intimate personal relationships employ a single language to enhance connection. What language domain governs yours? Does it match your personal preference? If it doesn't, have there been consequences?

Self-Assessment at Two Levels

After reviewing your answers to the previous questions, and combining the results with those of the exercises for Level I (Chapter Two), complete this statement: *I judge myself predominantly to be a . . .* (for example, a mover in power).

Check out this result with a close associate and an intimate partner or friend. What do you learn from this exercise?

Reading the Room

1. In an upcoming meeting, pay special attention to your use of the affect, power, and meaning languages in the conversation. After the meeting, consider these questions:

- What was your dominant language, the one you tended most often to use?

- Did it vary or remain constant?

2. Also listen to the prevailing language domain used by those present.

- Were there miscommunications or clashes between members based on different language preferences?

- When the group was most stuck, were competing speech acts in play—for example, between a move in meaning versus an oppose in power?

- How did your own preferences affect whom you supported and did not support?

chapter FOUR

Level III: Systems in Control of Speech

Ultimate conversational power rests not in individuals but in the systems they create and deploy to control speech behavior. This is Level III of the structural dynamics model in Figure 1.1. (For "system" you might also think loosely of the phrases "governance pattern" or "authority paradigm.") This level is the third and last we will need to create a behavioral profile.

Please remember that in continuing to focus on speech behavior, we neither ignore nor downgrade the importance of physical action and nonverbal behavior. We focus on speech behavior because that helps us lay out the theory of face-to-face communication as simply as possible.

Even if their formal learning about systems is minimal, most potentially effective leaders have a good intuitive sense of what makes people and organizations tick. They tend naturally to *think systemically.* Organizations often don't look for this quality, however, and instead choose leaders for their ability to get others to follow, for the results they get, and for other legitimate qualities (smarts, courage, power, expertise).

RALPH'S BOMB

During the evening following his meeting with Ron Stuart, CEO Ralph Waterman typed an e-mail to his team about him. Until that point, the team knew about Ron only as a fast-rising star in ClearFacts's Chicago office. He'd been picked up a year ago from a start-up. Beyond that, Ralph had told them Ron was of "tough mind and big heart, which he does not wear on his sleeve," and that he had an "unswerving" commitment to green energy.

> **Important announcement! My meeting with Ron Stuart this afternoon has exuberant possibilities for growth in a**

79

sector in which ClearFacts has, or should have, considerable interest—renewable energy. Ron has a lead on another start-up that is ready to be bought. More details at our Monday meeting.

To that he added in closing:

We'll leave for a later time Ron's outrageous ambition as expressed in the demands he is making. On Monday, let's just consider his case, while putting his demands on hold.

Then, on second thought, Ralph deleted those last lines.

Monday arrived, and the mood of the small talk before Ralph arrived (you could always count on his being late) was shamelessly celebratory. Howard Green had been boasting for weeks about what a good start he had gotten the Asia sales office off to, and continued while glossing lightly over the anonymous e-mail. Ralph had been right: Asia was years ahead in new green energy technology and was an untapped market for investment.

Ian Maxwell's news from operations was that the house had been swept clean of "dead wood," cutting costs; and company stock was soaring following its Floridian acquisition. But after fifteen minutes, a frustration set in that Howard was first to openly state: "I've a plane to catch; where in hell is he? I only delayed my flight because Ralph's e-mail said he had an important announcement to make."

Martha Curtis sighed out a reminder, "He really can't tell time. *And* refuses to wear a watch."

By the time Ralph showed up, the mood was foul. He'd intended to hold back about Ron Stuart's demands until he'd had time to measure the team's reaction to the initial e-mail. But he'd barely opened his mouth when Howard, although typically able to censor anything less than deferential to his bosses (Ralph and Ian), unleashed his fears unchecked: "What does that slithering, reptilian back-stabbing SOB *really* want?"

Unnerved, Ralph plunged in: "He wants a salary based on merit past and future and a promotion that includes his joining this team and reporting to me. I didn't say no."

As if on cue, Howard's elbow knocked a thick file onto the floor, scattering its contents underfoot. Howard swore, and they all started talking at once, basically siding with Howard.

MARTHA: With guys like Stuart, that "no" means "yes."

IAN: Being CEO, Ralph, doesn't license you to break the rules.

HOWARD: Ralph, I can't help saying this. You don't know that one of Ron Stuart's closest buddies in Chicago's marketing office is probably after my job? And here you are . . .

ART: *(No actual glance at Howard, but a look that says,* Good riddance!*)*

MARTHA: A rank betrayal, boss. I thought we all were guaranteed a voice in all major decisions.

IAN: The "rules," Mr. Waterman, rules. All top-level promotions start with operations—me. However they make their way to the team, they stop at *my* desk. *My desk.* Not in that chaotic heap on . . . well.

RALPH: *(Clenching his teeth, controlled but clearly angry)* Maxwell, you know nothing about what's being seeded in my "heap." Keep your *rules.* Keep your *order.* But keep your butt *out of my life!*

Before reading on, try to identify Levels I and II in each line of dialogue here. Do the same for the next exchange.

NOT JUST A BAD MEETING: A SYSTEM OUT OF CONTROL

For hours after the meeting, Ralph had no real idea what had gone so wrong. Later that day, he debriefed about it with Duncan.

DUNCAN: Well, you certainly stirred things up.

RALPH: *(Mumbling)* Yeah, I must have miscalculated. I hadn't expected such a violent reaction. Obviously I did something stupid.

DUNCAN: Not "stupid." *Random.*

RALPH: I don't know why, but I always felt a little, well, flattered when you've used that word on me before. Now it sounds a little dirty.

DUNCAN: No, no. I just mean to point out your random propensity. Not saying it's good or bad, but it's a pretty strong part of your profile. It has its upside, mainly creativity.

RALPH: And the downside?

DUNCAN: Chaos.

RALPH: Guess I dropped a bomb.

DUNCAN: Right. And not your first. But more than that, your system's bombing.

RALPH: My "system"? I'm imposing a system? By being "random"?

DUNCAN: Right. Oddly enough, random is a kind of system . . .

LEVEL III: OPERATING SYSTEMS

Concerned with human social systems—particularly with communication and information transfer—structural dynamics takes a "systems approach" to face-to-face relations. At Level III, *operating systems,* it looks at systems or norms of communication that persist both within and surrounding the individual and that shape her interactions in the room.

Systems Approaches in General

A systems approach is a great asset to any coach or leader. Such an approach to *any* subject views all entities (from microscopic cells to the vast cosmos) as *whole systems* whose parts are dynamically interdependent. Systems thinking has changed and continues to change our grasp of how the world works, taking us from simple paradigms to highly complex models in such disciplines as biology, economics, engineering, and so on. It has also touched most fields of application, including psychology.[1]

The following concepts are central to systems thinking:

- *The role of circular causal reasoning.* As noted in Chapter One, disquieting events are often regulated by circular causal reasoning in which, say, Person A influences Person B, and B influences A; they anticipate each other in ways that "prove" that their expectations are correct. The understanding of most relationship dynamics is more suited to systems logic than simple cause-and-effect linear thinking. For example, in the escalation between Ralph and his team, Ian did not "cause" Ralph's angry response, and Ralph's e-mail did not "cause" Ian's rage. Their encounter was structured by a system already in place between and around them, albeit quiescent up until then.

- *Positive feedback loops that increase or amplify a particular output.* For example, before Ralph entered the room, the angry team reinforced each other's feelings.

Positive feedback can be deliberately used to accelerate change, transformation, growth, or evolution in a system. But excessive use of positive feedback can send a system into runaway.

- *Negative feedback loops that reduce output.* Ian's insistence on making sure that all paperwork goes through him for approval is an example of a negative feedback loop. It is Ian's attempt to control Ralph's behavior. Negative feedback can be used to increase the stability and accuracy of a system, but excessive negative feedback can run down and stifle the system.

- *Control devices in feedback loops.*[2] One simple feedback device for controlling conversations is a meeting's agenda, which allows certain information into the conversation while screening out other information. In very complex systems (societies, financial markets, large business organizations), it is not always clear what the feedback loops and their controllers are, nor is it easy to know what to do about them when they get out of balance.[3] Moreover, multiple controllers may exist with multiple feedback loops operating at various levels of the organization. These elements operate with varying degrees of autonomy, can compete with one another, and are often changed by that competition.

Operating Systems: Open, Closed, or Random

In structural dynamics, an **operating system** is the implicit set of rules for how individuals govern boundaries, behavior, and relationships in groups. The operating system's role is to *control speech*—to enable, discourage, and monitor the types of speech acts that arise in a group conversation.

Growing up and living in such systems as families, classrooms, youth teams, and other organizations, individuals develop personal preferences for certain operating systems and manifest those preferences both in their own behavioral propensities (how they speak) and in the systems they choose to join or foster around themselves. Structural dynamics studies an individual's speech patterns for clues to his or her preferred operating system types, and studies a group for clues to how it is working, whether the group's system type is easily recognizable and shared, or whether, internally, the group may be conflicted with a mix of preferences and system types.

Our Level III model differentiates three operating systems—three alternative patterns of rules and expectations for how people should behave: open, closed, and random systems. None is inherently better or worse than the others; each has its value and limitations. As I will demonstrate using ClearFacts, we can tell whether a given system is open, closed, or random by looking into the following:

Orientation. Whose needs are given top priority?

Values. What do people care about?

Boundaries. Who enters the system, and how is entry regulated?

Access to information and people. To what information or other people do people within the system have access, and how is that access regulated?

Limits on speech. Who gets to speak and when?

Feedback mechanisms. How does the system change (for example, from closed to open as members sort out their preferences)? How is it influenced by entry of a new dominant type (for example, an open leader is replaced by a closed one)? How is it influenced by intervention (say of an outside consultant or therapist, who enters it intending to bring about change)?

Ways of managing deviation. How does the system respond to violation of its rules?

There is some overlap of features among open, closed, and random systems, and having a preference for a certain system does not mean that the individual promotes that system in all circumstances. For example, a leader who leans toward open systems may decide to take a more closed approach at times.

Recognizing Preferences for Systems

Organizations, teams, and individuals have preferences for one or another of these systems of control. Individuals know well the preference of the system in which they find themselves. That it may differ from his or her preference is a serious matter for individuals and for systems as well. In the following dialogue, watch for these preferences of the team members at ClearFacts:

• Art and Martha's general preference for open systems

• Ian and Howard's general preference for closed systems

• Ralph's preference for random systems

In describing an operating system, it is useful to make some judgment about how well the system is functioning with regard to its presumed social purpose.

And as individuals begin to recognize the various control mechanisms that dominate the different types of human systems of which they are a part, they can begin to learn when and how to shift the rules to fit the situation at hand. In other words, a skillful, influential member of a group may be able to temper and complement one system with another, depending on the occasion.

THE OPEN OPERATING SYSTEM

The best environment for me is one in which every individual voice can be heard in the interest of designing and meeting the group's goals.

Figure 4.1 outlines the open operating system. The following might be obvious indicators of a family operating under an open system: authority for decisions is shared and not held solely by the parent(s); children are free to verbally challenge the limits and decisions made by the parents, though the parents have ultimate authority when consensus can't be reached; outsiders or newcomers are invited in to special family gatherings or decisions frequently and without fanfare (also found in a random system); controversial topics can be discussed at the dinner table even if the opinions expressed are in conflict with those of the parents.

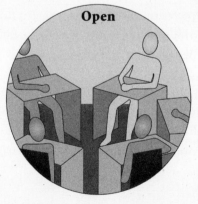

Figure 4.1
The Open Operating System

Orientation
Toward the collective

Territory
• Adaptation and participation
• Consensus and commitment

Characterized by
• Teamwork
• Rule by process rather than by formal leardship

Function
Leadership manages for balance of the good of the whole and the individual

Dysfunction
Tyranny of process

Characteristics of Open Systems

Open systems require communication. Work gets done by openly deliberating and exploring each individual's needs. In fact, in an open system, the needs of the individual are *initially* placed before the needs of the organization, with the assumption that by respecting all individuals and the challenges they face, the organization can develop shared responsibility, purpose, and leadership. Although it begins with focusing on individuals, the open system ultimately seeks a *collective decision arrived at by consensus.* Community grows out of deliberate respect for the individual, compromise, and reaching group goals.

Orientation   Because open systems lean toward balancing the good of the whole with the good of the individual, they are the darling of behavioral consultants, therapists, and similar practitioners. Organizational systems, too, advertise themselves as open. But what practitioners and organizations *espouse* may differ sharply from what they *do.* Often practitioners with strong open-system rhetoric retain a firm, closed-system underside that subverts open values. The result can be a cynical perception by employees that this "program of the month" shall pass like all the other new ideas proposed by management before they take root.

Values   The open operating system depends on people's valuing the process of learning and adaptation through participation. An individual's "right to be heard" is sacrosanct, but teamwork and discussion should ideally result in consensus decisions.

Boundaries   Typically, it is very easy to recognize an open system's permeable boundaries, where external inputs are accepted and often welcomed. A group operating as an open system or individuals with this propensity may invite newcomers and new ideas into their space in order to adapt and grow.

Access to Information and People   Because its boundaries are permeable, an open system's personalities often become known as the information sharers in the larger organization. They distribute FYI memos and reports, their office doors may always be "open," and they may walk in on others or blithely invite themselves to meetings.

Limits on Speech   No one person's views are assumed to be better than anyone else's, so challenges and new ideas are welcomed. Dissenting or contradicting voices are tolerated. At the same time, most open systems in organizations also have developed guidelines and procedures borrowed from closed systems for ending debate and ensuring that the group acts expeditiously.

Feedback Mechanisms   In the open system, there is balance between positive and negative feedback loops. At the individual level, positive loops predominate and serve to increase or amplify new behaviors. To reach consensus, the group and the nominal leader, who is responsible for keeping its rules, are empowered to step in with negative loops to end discourse.

At ClearFacts, Art has a strong propensity for the open system, using it to generate new ideas and solve problems in a thorough manner. During one of his marketing team meetings, after an unexpected development suddenly threatened their current project's outcome, his team went on for hours seeking solutions from all angles. In that open-system discussion, the expression of new information was invited, creating a positive feedback loop that amplified this behavior.

When he judged that the group's "positive loop" discussion had run dry, Art said, "We haven't heard a new idea in the last hour. It's time to vote on what you've agreed are the two best approaches." As leader, Art now wanted closure for the discussion. The open system had reaped its benefits, and it was time to move on.

But he was loudly interrupted by one of his people—a strong mover in meaning: "I'm not done yet. I have a new angle on an idea I shared earlier." The other teammates groaned, signaling Art to pursue closure, which, with gentle insistence, he did. Without further discussion, a vote was taken and the meeting adjourned. Art's use of a negative feedback loop had diminished the creative behavior and allowed the group to move to consensus.

Ways of Managing Deviation   At some point, every system will experience deviation: one or more individuals will violate its tacit rules. Deviation may come from the group's experience of carrying a good thing too far (say, the open-system discussion that goes on too long)—what we refer to as "tyranny of process." Even more common is deviation created by someone with strong propensities for a different system, for which he advocates at that moment. Such behaviors constitute a model clash with the currently operating system.

When a person preferring closed systems finds herself in an open one such as Art's creative session, she is likely to show impatience and ask for premature closure. The individual may demean other members who follow the group's open-system preference, may become even more confrontational, or may shut down entirely.

When a random-tendency person finds himself in an open system, he may seek to disrupt smooth conversation with the intention of finding more creative solutions. He may not only insist on sustaining someone else's right to talk but also challenge the group's titular leader from moving the group to premature closure.

Function Versus Dysfunction

In theory, if not in reality, a deliberative body like the U.S. Senate is an open system: it seeks to resolve differences through a process of open exchange. Often in dysfunctional open systems, process rules are supreme and pervasive, and individuals use them to avoid resolution and action. Closure is rare, and each individual is allowed full expression at all times, often limiting the collective ability to take quick action or meet critical deadlines. Thus, ironically, the total acceptance of all input to the process can also lead to the organization's demise, when individuals intent on destroying it have equal access to decision making and governance.

Open-System Preferences at ClearFacts

As I noted earlier, Art prefers an open system during some phases of leading his own team. Martha displays a strong, broader open-system preference. Martha's model clash with Ian in the leadership training program (illustrated in Chapter Three) was about both their language preferences (Martha for affect and Ian for power) and their system preferences (Martha for open and Ian for closed). Earlier in this chapter, we saw Martha admonish Ralph for violating the open-system rules he'd promised the team. Also in that heated interchange, Ian ("the 'rules,' Mr. Waterman, the rules") invoked his closed-system preference, and imposed it not only on Ralph's breaking his pledge but for doing so in a random way.

THE CLOSED OPERATING SYSTEM

I want to live in a world that is traditional, stable, orderly, and predictable.

Figure 4.2 briefly summarizes the closed operating system.

Figure 4.2
The Closed Operating System

Closed

Orientation
Toward the leader and the organization

Territory
• Order and hierarchy
• Security and stability

Characterized by
• Clearly defined roles
• Strong formal leaders
• Planning emphasis

Function
Leadership manages for the good of the whole

Dysfunction
Tyranny of monarchy

Characteristics of Closed Systems

The closed system is ultimately the backbone of most organizations. It is the most efficient means for getting work done. (Open systems do as well, but take longer, and the random system, though arguably inefficient, is the system of choice when creativity, rather than efficiency, is called for.)

Orientation   In open systems, leadership can be shared or diffuse, but in closed systems, strong, formal leadership is essential. Closed-system leaders typically have clearly defined roles and formal authority via job titles, rank, or seniority. It is *their* notion of needs that the closed system serves.

A closed system regulates the life of its members, particularly the time and space within which people work or live. For example, tracking individuals' time and activities during the workday, monitoring inclusion and exclusion at meetings and conferences, and strict adherence to corporate policy suggest that a closed operating system prevails.

Values   Closed systems value tradition, and place community and history over the needs of the individual. This leads to strong calls for loyalty and self-sacrifice for the group. Adherence to procedures and policies that facilitate day-to-day decision making in the organization is expected. In exchange for this adherence, the governed get stability, security, and predictability.

Boundaries   A closed system survives by creating a boundary around its members, for their safety and protection as well as to enhance group productivity. At the boundary, intruders or dissidents are screened before entering. Physically, people with closed-system propensities appreciate the need for closed meetings and closed doors. Metaphorically, they consciously or unconsciously create a circle identifying who is *in* and who is *out*.

Access to Information and People   With active screening boundaries and clear understandings regarding speech, the closed system carefully regards who receives what information and who needs to be involved in various doings. It is important to note that well-managed closed systems are capable of excellent communication and group participation; these activities are planned and executed carefully for the organization's benefit, within the leader's control.

Limits on Speech   Given the focus on inclusion and exclusion, on authority and hierarchy, in this type of system, it is important to be aware of protocols, traditions, and rules (spoken and unspoken) regarding who can speak and when, and what they are allowed to say.

Feedback Mechanisms   In closed systems, negative feedback loops predominate, producing homeostatic mechanisms that maintain stability and moderate change. Negative loops keep the system stable through close regulation and control. When change happens by intention, it is done gradually. When change is happening spontaneously, the closed system uses negative loops to moderate change, disabling threats to basic stability.

Ways of Managing Deviation   The closed system uses negative feedback to diminish behaviors deemed unacceptable.

The open-system individual living in a closed system typically insists on being heard and may challenge authority and group norms to do so. The open-system dissenter usually also understands and respects the need for the leader to shut down new inputs, and so will typically not escalate a challenge into full rebellion.

Random-system individuals not only *challenge* the authority of closed-system leaders but often will attempt to undermine it. Punishment of one kind or another is expected within the closed system when randoms carry challenges to the point of anarchy and chaos.

Function Versus Dysfunction

In families, closed systems display strong authority by one or both parents, higher degrees of scheduled organization, and clear and consistent rules and norms for all to follow. Parents who "run a tight ship" feel strongly about what their children should be exposed to and protected from, and believe that discipline and responsibility will help the family endure tough times.

Well-functioning closed systems are stable and highly structured. Their leaders manage for the good of the organization, and depend on their own vision and skills to continue to be responsive and effective. In high-achieving closed systems, leaders know how to delegate power in its best form, by handing over both accountability and authority for certain functions and decisions to qualified others in the organization.

Prior to divestiture in the 1980s, the corporate culture of Bell System phone company functioned very well as a closed system. As a monopoly in the market, the various corporations in the system managed customers, employees, and shareholders with a high degree of central authority and consistency. Policies, rules, training programs, and processes were highly valued and consistently maintained. Because the company was driven by strong values such as customer service, employee retention, and employee development, most constituents valued the security and stability that the phone companies provided.

When a closed system predominates for too long, performance may become mindlessly robotic. Although the search for maximal productivity through repetitive and efficient processing achieves outstanding results at first, over the long term, these results break down. A system committed to authority and ritual also becomes less receptive to new information, innovation, and change. In today's complex world driven by international and market demands, organizations that operate solely as closed systems are doomed because their workforce eventually loses its creative edge, their products imitate themselves, and competitors pass them by.

At its worst, the closed system has leaders who manage for their own benefit rather than for individuals and teams in the company. The organization experiences "tyranny of the monarch." Many closed-system leaders strongly believe in the "rightness" of their vision, and their only means of protecting that vision is to seal themselves off from a world filled with contradictory and radical beliefs. Over time, those in charge develop unchallengeable control, and the learning and growth capabilities of the organization become severely disabled.

Examples of such systems that have become corrupt or harmful to their members are easy to cite and remember, primarily because the nature of the dysfunction eventually results in dramatic change to the system. Revolution, internal fighting, and the exit of key individuals are signs that systemic clashes exist and that a closed system is involved.

Although closed-system families can be high-functioning and nurturing environments for all of their members, perturbation frequently occurs when children reach adolescence. For some teens, rebellion is a natural stage of development.

When a closed system is threatened, leaders tend to increase the number of negative feedback loops and tighten up more with increased rules and punishments. The result can be tragic for individuals seeking to connect with their own different needs and identity. Feeling that they have no power to influence the system and that the system is a source of repression, they can spiral into depression or even despair. The best strategy for a closed system when faced with this kind of predictable challenge is to borrow from another system type as it maneuvers through this stage, finding ways to provide freedoms and the ability to voice opposition. Random and open systems could take the same advice. Both random and open systems at times do well to tighten their rules by borrowing from those of the closed system.

Closed-System Preferences at ClearFacts

In the dialogue in the section "Ralph's Bomb" ("The 'rules,' Mr. Waterman, rules") and in Ian's statement to Martha, "When was the last time you calculated the costs incurred when a company coddles its workforce?" we can see evidence of Ian's assumption that all systems should always operate as closed. This assumption causes him to miss much of what is going on and to be frequently misunderstood and undervalued by people committed to open and random systems. At home, Ian adopted and modeled his father's closed-system tactics. Ian's son, however, fought the closed system every step of the way as he strove to assert his own random-system preference.

Howard also prefers a closed system. He is insistently "top down" deferential to a fault with his bosses Ian and Ralph; and, as we shall see, in Asia where he is in charge, he controls with an iron fist.

Martha's strong open-system preference could be enhanced by more closed-system tactics. In the dominantly open-system HR team she leads, Martha doesn't actually "coddle" (as Ian might allege), but she does let her staff lapse often enough into a "tyranny of process" mode. On such issues as pink slips, they can and do go on and on. In the leadership training program Martha leads with Ian, her unflagging support for trainees does almost fanatically favor the underdog.

THE RANDOM OPERATING SYSTEM

I prefer an unpredictable, inspirational, and improvisational world where others respect my creativity and autonomy.

The random operating system is the rarest in established organizations today. It is also the least understood and most feared because it is rare and because it basically threatens to undermine the rule of certainty and control. Figure 4.3 illustrates it in brief.

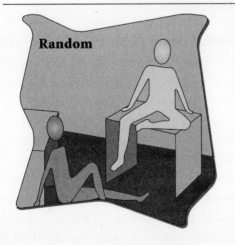

Figure 4.3
The Random Operating System

Random

Orientation
Toward the individual

Territory
• Exploration and improvisation
• Creativity and innovation

Characterized by
• Lack of formal structures, processes, and leadership
• High level of individuality

Function
Leadership manages for the good of the individual

Dysfunction
Tyranny of anarchy

Be careful not to conflate an individual's random-system preferences—which can be creative—with research into possibly genetically "right-brained" or "left-brained" people. Structural dynamics posits that randoms are that way as a result of choices stemming from their early experiences. We'll see this later on with Ralph.

Characteristics of Random Systems

Creative individuals who, rather than following traditional rules, make new ones, flourish in random systems. Start-ups are famous for creating something new and different, and random individuals are frequently the force that drives them.

Orientation   Random systems focus so strongly on the unique preferences of each individual that they are often viewed by outsiders as chaotic or out of control. Instead of lacking order, the random system represents a special kind of order of infinite possibilities.

It is not uncommon for individuals who prefer random systems to live their entire lives outside traditional organizational systems. During his most creative years, Picasso was surrounded by circle after circle of the newest and most creative minds. He pursued a multitude of diverse interests, from an untethered life of sexual expression to painting that mirrored his erratic and deep emotions.

Values   In random systems, individual autonomy and freedom are valued above all other organizational constraints or goals.

Boundaries and Access to Information and People   "Unfiltered" is the operative word for randoms: people as well as information are free to come in or travel out at any time. Day-to-day life unfolds with minimal constraint and formality. There are few standard procedures and structures; people are encouraged to "make it up" every time they tackle an issue. Naturally, randoms gravitate to innovative start-ups. They imagine new products that engineers (often closed-system types) make happen.

Limits on Speech   Random-system decisions can be made in numerous, very different ways; the process is based on ideas, not on status or structure. Input and leadership can come from anyone at any time, often from one or two individuals who happen to be dealing with the problem at hand. Who these individuals are is always subject to change.

Feedback Mechanisms   The rule in the random system is that individuals are not constrained but allowed to do as they will, moving, one hopes, toward some common goal articulated by the group. Positive loops predominate; negative loops (whose purpose is to close down change and bring about more stability) are rare.

Ways of Managing Deviation   Random-system individuals can find comfort in chaos. "Deviation" may be defined as "what gets in the way of a eureka moment." Yet when chaos is introduced for its own sake, without regard to its effects on others, a line is crossed. When rebellion becomes mandated and becomes the cultural norm, it has the power to undermine institutions and has a strong destructive influence.

Closed and open types trying to express themselves in a random-dominated system may feel inferior, uncreative, and undervalued, and may be driven out or shut down entirely.

Well-functioning random systems rely on intuition, the same mechanism used to create and innovate, to know when to manage down or end discourse.

Function Versus Dysfunction

Because of its high degree of freedom and personal expression, an excellent random operating system can innovate rapidly. Its lack of restraint and its freewheeling style stimulate innovative thinking and products. Many R&D organizations and academic institutions were founded by groups of individuals who were firm believers in the creative potential of life in a random system. Random individuals in start-ups often invent not only their own unique ideas and products but also their own style of working. The subculture that Steve Jobs—a quintessential random—was fledging at the start of Apple was responsible for some of the most significant innovations of the twentieth century.

Unfortunately, as a random system grows and begins to require maintenance and sustaining features, its leader must turn to negative loops and other operating systems' tactics. Earlier I cited Bell System as a high-functioning closed system; interestingly, during the same era, Bell Labs created a kind of "safe house" for a small group of unregulated randoms charged with developing innovations. In short, Bell maintained functionality by creating a small random system within its walls. In the 1960s, other organizations borrowed this practice.

At its worst, the random operating system provokes such rapid changes in direction and focus that no one has a clear sense of direction. People become confused and disoriented, experiencing the "tyranny of chaos."

RALPH'S RANDOM-SYSTEM PREFERENCE AT CLEARFACTS

As Duncan suggested, CEO Ralph, a random, prefers and has tried to maintain an open-system paradigm for his management team. The following portions of dialogue from Ralph's debriefing with Duncan convey Ralph's sometimes unconscious random-system gestures and how other open-system and closed-system members of his team can react to them. Duncan and Ralph have already talked about what's good about a random system and are looking at its darker side. Note that in this angrier realm, a random act by Ralph can also be arbitrary, autocratic, and effectively *closed*. I have witnessed leaders like this, who say, "Anything goes . . . Anything goes . . . Okay, you're fired!"

DUNCAN: Whether it was conscious or unconscious doesn't matter. You created chaos in that room. You dropped one bomb when you sent that e-mail announcing your dealings with Stuart. Chaos ensued at the meeting, and then you dropped another.

RALPH: I knew before I even mentioned them that Stuart's "demands" would set them off.

DUNCAN: And then something further happened. Something happened in the room that lit a fuse in you, and you exploded.

RALPH: You mean when I lost it with Howard?

DUNCAN: You're forgetting. The one you lost it with was Ian.

RALPH: That's strange. Why don't I remember it that way? Help me understand. What got Ian so ticked off?

DUNCAN: First off, you came late as usual. Many randoms can't tell time, and that irritates and insults some people—like Ian.

RALPH: Me, I think of it as an endowment. I'm no slave to the clock like him.

DUNCAN: Nor concerned about demoralizing those who *do* live by the clock?

RALPH: For me, open-ended time-space stimulates and sparks ideas.

DUNCAN: You are proving yourself a random and throwing me off the scent, and you know it. You asked for help. "Help me understand," you said. Remember? Look, Ralph, that RED you planted—sorry, that *Random Explosive Device*—you planted it there without warning, and it blew the system apart. Until then, the team you crafted worked fairly well because of a good spread of system types.

RALPH: Open, closed, and outright random me.

DUNCAN: Dealing with a pure, flawlessly true-to-type *closed*: Ian. Howard is less pure of a closed, if only because he is less mature.

RALPH: Martha and Art are both opens?

DUNCAN: Yes, and have flourished under your leadership. Randoms reward individuality, not obedience. That's how you've steered them through their clashes—clashes in speech behavior, clashes in language preference, and now, with you caught up in it, their clashes in system types. . . .

Let's look at the meeting again from scratch. What was the pivotal moment, when everything seemed to break down . . . who did what? Especially, what did *you* do to worsen the breakdown?

RALPH: I knew when I walked in that something was coming. The room reeked of anger. Funny, I don't usually have that much trouble with anger.

DUNCAN: So what set you off?

RALPH: *Bang.* Howard's voice. *Gotcha.* So I shot back.

DUNCAN: With what?

RALPH: What I said was . . . , I hadn't said no to Ron's demands, but I said it in a way that meant yes. Which Martha nailed in a flash. They got it, and boy, then, did they *give it* to me!

DUNCAN: Follow me in this, Ralph, but don't dwell on it. Like all humans you have a dark side. What you showed them was the dark side of the random—the impulsive, chaotic, anarchic rule breaker.

RALPH: Ha! Sonia says that!

DUNCAN: And what happened next?

RALPH: Mayhem.

DUNCAN: Tell me in slow motion. The highlights. Start with Martha.

RALPH: Right. Well, like I said, Martha nails me on the *not* saying no that means yes to a guy like Ron. She also said I was leaving her out on the decisions. And how she thought I'd brought her here to build a participatory, consensual team.

DUNCAN: Which is exactly what an open-system type would say.

RALPH: Howard almost seemed unnerved by the whole thing . . .

DUNCAN: Scared. He sees himself on a steady climb to stardom. Howard's a strong closed-system person who values predictability and the religious maintenance of order and due process. When order breaks down, he feels derailed and gets upset. What you did with Ron Stuart was a blatant sign of disorder and a threat to Howard's life plan. And Art?

RALPH: Art? I really have no idea what his reaction was.

DUNCAN: Because Art is your best bystander: open in affect and power, but random in meaning. You've used his marketer's image-making genius outside your meetings, but not his bystanding in the room.

RALPH: Art and I have never, not ever, clashed.

DUNCAN: That, I suspect, is because you are no different from the friends he hangs out with: artists, writers, poets, people who thrive on finding order in chaos. *(Probing)* So what about Ian?

RALPH: I lost it. Let's face it, Dunc: I lost it.

DUNCAN: *(Waits)*

RALPH: But I'm not ready to talk about it just yet.

Story Roots of Ralph's System Preference

Later, Ralph was sitting alone in his office when his thoughts went back to a memory that had triggered sudden anger in him in a previous discussion with Duncan.

His father's face loomed inches away. "Look at your desk! Now look at *my* desk. Order, son, not filthy mess."

"*Your* f—ing desk?" Ralph replied aloud. "*Your* desk is a graveyard: fresh-cut, two-inch grass on top, death underneath. *My* desk is a garden of exotic flowers the likes of which you can't even imagine."

Ralph's father was a retired minister, aging poorly—a bitter old man who had missed his opportunity to bring something important to the world. He read, walked, and demanded constant small attendances from Ralph's accommodating, uncomplaining mother. Growing up, Ralph dutifully loved but never respected his mother except in one respect that, even today, brought a smile to his face. Quietly enslaved, she secretly drank while playing out each day as the reverend's obedient, respectful spouse. Curiously, Ralph, also secretly, approved of this as a private act of rebellion.

Ralph's own rebelliousness—neither secret nor quiet—was one of their connections. He raised hell (with her nod of support) at every one of the six or more schools he attended between ages six and sixteen. At each, he established himself as king with his peers and court jester with authorities. When they depicted his playful infractions "as serious lapses in moral conduct," he invited his elders to join him in a level of moral discourse beyond his years. The usual result was that what he received from those required to judge him were smiles, and, as he got from his mother, nods of approbation instead of punishment.

Ralph had two answers to the question, "Why so many schools?" which the school officials asked at each new school where his mother placed him. The first was obvious. Ralph's reverend father was so difficult that it rarely took more than six months to a year for a congregation to turn out to be "incapable of making the changes I insisted on" and to ask him to leave. Ralph's second reason came from other sources—the looks on the faces of kids, children of families in his father's parish, as they left the reverend's study in the far reaches of the house, ostensibly there for private religious counsel.

When Ralph could imagine such a thing and give a name to it, he accused his father—not in words, but with looks informed and reinforced by those he saw on the faces of the child visitors, both boys and girls, when they left his father's sanctuary—of serial child molestation, an accusation that emboldened Ralph even more in the battle of words the two began to have.

How the Debriefing Ended

We can see the team meeting of this chapter as a sign of a suddenly destabilized system. What characterized the system before its slip into this state? It was a team whose leader very rarely interfered with its members' freedom to "be who they were." Ralph rarely asked for obedience. Any member could confront him as freely as they did one another. Order came not from Ralph, who cared little about it, but from Ian's presence. Ian knew better than Ralph that he was balancing Ralph's tendencies to let things go hither and yon. Ian also knew that he would never get credit for the sense of order he provided.

Ralph's debriefing with Duncan ended on this note:

DUNCAN: Ralph, do you think you should have handled the whole thing differently?

RALPH: Yes and . . . well, NO! New meanings, discovery—how else do they happen? Mainly after some sort of break-down . . . As time goes on, I feel like I can predict the position each person is going to take on an issue and how each of the rest will react. So what's the point? There's an excitement in the mayhem that happened. . . . Who knows? Maybe there *is* a method to my madness in even entertaining Ron's proposal. His becoming a member of the team would shake up the stalemate between Art and Howard. Martha would have a new target to size up: *Is Ron open like her and Art, or closed like Ian and Howard?* Ron is going to surprise them all. He will breathe life into the meetings. It certainly will get exciting again. For me, anyway.

DUNCAN: Organizations don't know what to do with types like you. They feed off of your energy, imagination, and vision, but all along they know you don't belong.

RALPH: It always comes back to that . . . me wondering whether this or any organization is the one for me.

DUNCAN: You think you're making a decision about your future, but in fact the organization is also making a decision. The system evolves all the time, and its ability to adapt is always a key factor. One thing about you, Ralph: in spite of your action, impulsive or not, you tend to intuitively know how big and small systems work, and you quickly learn the intricacies of the latter.

AS FOR RON . . .

Ralph survived the uprising. By the next meeting, the revolutionary dust had settled. Ralph stood by his decision to bring Ron on board, appealing for and getting a wait-and-see, with members meeting individually with Ron before Ron attended his first meeting, two weeks away. Backed by Ian, Martha asked Ralph not to "prepare" Ron for these meetings. Apparently, team equilibrium was restored.

Individual meetings went as expected. Martha smoothly slid from high to level ground. She liked Ron's complete candidness when, discussing his ambitions, he told her, "You push straight to the heart of the matter, Martha, but just know, some things are private." At home with her husband, Lance, Martha admitted to being a little jealous. She saw what Ralph valued in the newcomer: his greater commitment to green than hers, and his patient hanging back until he got the picture before stepping in.

Art and Ron talked only about literature and philosophy, also throwing in some Greek and Roman epics, from which they drew analogies to modern wars, business, and governments. Art learned all he needed to know about Ron's fit and lack of fit at ClearFacts.

Not unexpectedly, Howard and Ron did not "connect." By unspoken agreement, they kept circling around each other at a level of mutual suspicion that would not go away, not in this meeting and perhaps never. (*He's subtly seeking advantage by making me feel like a "black man,"* thought Ron. And Howard thought, *I've got to be ready. This guy has tricks up his sleeve.*) In fact, Ron hadn't mentioned the fact that his girlfriend, Lani, was a recent hire in Office Asia.

Ian's opening round surprised Ron: "If our country were in a 'just war,' would you volunteer to serve? . . . An 'unjust war'?" The ensuing conversations allowed each man equally to get a measure of the other. Ian clearly wanted it that way. Ian's second round (stepping up as "Sheriff Max" and COO-CFO) tilted the discourse: "How does all you've said affect how you deal with 'just' authority?" Ron heard the statement in the question. His answer, boldly honest and undefensive, didn't exactly please Ian, but it earned his respect.

HOW LEADERS BENEFIT FROM SYSTEMS THINKING

A significant number of today's most influential organizational and leadership theories have shifted into systems thinking. As one of the five core disciplines for learning organizations, systems thinking "helps us to see how to change systems more effectively, and to act more in tune with the larger processes of the natural and economic world."[4] In addition to the existing, well-articulated views of why systems thinking is so relevant and essential for organizations in today's complex world, I offer my own tally of the benefits of systems thinking for leaders today.

Guiding Development and Change

Organizations evolve and change because their external environment changes in response to new technologies, new competition, changing markets, and so forth. Internal forces—the introduction of new people, new processes, and ways of doing things and the evolution of the internal culture itself—also play a role in organization change.

Leaders and those with whom they surround themselves are responsible for steering their organizations through good times and bad. Leaders' understanding of external and internal forces needs to be *systemic, inclusive,* and *holistic* if there is to be effective strategic planning, management practices, and leadership development. It is a monstrous challenge to know how all the major parts—processes, teams, divisions, the rank and file, both formal and informal thought leaders—are functioning within themselves and among one another; but leaders who reflect on "how the system is working and might work better" are more likely to succeed.

Developing a "Leadership System" as Insurance Against Inevitable Crises

Organizational crises are inevitable. Most leaders surround themselves with handpicked lieutenants. If they have acquired systemic wisdom, they know better than to choose only like-minded bedfellows. Most cloned groups are poorly equipped to respond effectively and dynamically to crises.

By contrast, consider what I call a **leadership system.** In it, each leader is equal in mastery to the nominal leader but different in character from the other leaders in the group, and each is prepared to step up as virtual leader, bringing to bear capacities that are best suited for comprehending and managing the crisis at hand.

Solving Problems and Making Decisions with Fewer Mistakes

Referring to medical errors in hospital emergency and operating room systems, surgeon Atul Gawande has written, "Not only do all human beings err, but they err frequently and in predictable, patterned ways."[5] His point pertains to business systems, too: "Disasters do not simply occur; they evolve in systems." Faulty systems have built-in defense mechanisms that cover over faulty decision-making processes and structures.

Just as there are fatally bad doctors and good doctors who go bad, there are bad leaders and good leaders who go bad. A leadership system like the one I just described is an organization's corrective for the latter. Good leadership systems are specifically designed to catch (early, before they do damage) the corruption of moral values that leads to many mistakes in business judgment and decision making.

Increasing Capacity to Communicate with Multiple Audiences

Thinking systemically enhances a leader's capacity to communicate with multiple audiences. In the purest sense, thinking in terms of *system* means according "the other" a value equal to *self*. This is not to dispute the value of roles, status, hierarchy, and power differentials. But the ability to think neutrally about the system—and thereby identify the bigger picture and understand the relative importance or triviality of one's position and place at any given time—is as useful as it is humbling.

If your goal is artful, effective communication, then knowing how systems work is a good first step. Nurture an ability to step back to a systemically neutral place where you can view the whole, leaving yourself behind as one part of the system. Also nurture the ability to glide back in to engage as a participant.

Having a Life

It may seem odd to propose that maintaining a systems perspective is critical to "having a life."

Work systems are powerful. They put bread and butter on our plates. They define us as worthy or unworthy. They inflate or deflate our egos. For many, they are a home away from home, and for others they are the chief source of affection, intimacy, and love. As for work systems' harmful effects, leaders and would-be leaders are, curiously, more vulnerable than the rest. Workplaces can absorb, use up, even kill their leaders. Although having a systems perspective cannot promise immunity, it is a safeguard against the temporary losses of sanity that literally or metaphorically "kill" leaders. The endangered ones lose sight of the *whole*. The boundary between the self system and the work system dissolves; then intimate relationship systems and family can suffer, go unattended, or shrink in significance.

From Insight to Action

As human systems evolve, they tend to regulate the behavior of their members according to three types of control. In structural dynamics, these systems are referred to as open, closed, and random. These system preferences emerge in conversation, which can lead to minor miscommunications and to serious clashes. A move in open (system) affect is distinct from a closed (system) oppose in power, and when Jane makes a move in open meaning and John opposes in closed power, miscommunication can be off to the races.

Your Use of the Operating Systems

1. Which system do you prefer—open, closed, or random?

   - Do you know how you came to choose this system?

   - Is there a story behind this choice?

   - Were you raised in an open, closed, or random system?

   - Is your current personal choice the same or different from the one that prevailed in your childhood family?

2. Rank the operating systems 1, 2, or 3, according to your preferences.

   Operating System   Rank

   Open   _____

   Closed   _____

   Random   _____

3. Now rate them by circling High, Medium, or Low according to your comfort in using each system.

   Open: High   Medium   Low

   Closed: High   Medium   Low

   Random: High   Medium   Low

4. How challenging do you think it will be to broaden your repertoire beyond your current comfort zone?

5. In an upcoming meeting, pay special attention to the prevailing operating system—open, closed, or random—and listen for

   - The extent to which the nominal leader's preference influences how the group's work gets done

   - Clashes between members based on different system preferences

   - How your own preferences affected your inclinations in terms of whom you supported and did not support

6. Think of a time when communication between you and another failed because of different operating system preferences at work. Think of another in your personal relationships. Were the issues over system preferences the same in both contexts? What do you conclude from this observation?

7. Consider the following organizational contexts:

   - The military

   - An R&D department in a technology firm

   - A medical team in a hospital operating room

   - A pilot-copilot team

   - The Vatican

   - A university philosophy department

   What operating system tends to prevail in each context? Under what circumstance, in each context, could this be problematic?

8. Think back on leaders you have known in your life who reflected different operating systems. How did each leader's ways of operating hinder or enhance his or her abilities as a leader?

Self-Assessment at Three Levels

After reviewing your answers to the preceding questions, and combining the results with the results of the exercises for Levels I and II, complete this statement: *I judge myself predominantly to be a . . .* (for example, an opposer in closed meaning).

Check out this result with a close associate and with an intimate partner or friend. What do you learn from this exercise?

Reading the Room

1. In a group you currently are in, think of the relationship between the group's prevailing operating system, its prevailing language domain, and the "work" it is expected to do:

   • Are there any disconnects?

   • Is there a match or mismatch between your preferences and the group's?

   • How does this affect your performance and how it is perceived by others?

2. During a meeting of this group, listen for the prevailing language domain among those present. After the meeting, consider these questions:

   • Were there miscommunications or clashes between members based on different system preferences?

   • When the group was most stuck, were competing speech acts in play—for example, a move in open meaning versus an oppose in closed power?

   • How did your own preferences affect your inclinations in terms of whom you supported and did not support?

Operating Systems and Coaching

1. Consider a time when you had difficulty coaching a leader whose operating system differed from your preferred one:

   • What did you do about this?

   • How did it affect your relationship?

   • Did you openly discuss the issue?

   • Does your practice guide you in how to deal with this kind of issue?

2. Think back on the leaders with whom you have worked:

- Can you identify a leader who reflected each of the three operating systems?

- Describe each of these leaders in terms that highlight the way he or she tended to operate.

- As you consider your general opinion of these leaders, how did your rating of them reflect your own operating system preference?

Operating Systems and Leading

Consider a time when you had difficulty with a report whose operating system differed from your preferred one:

- What did you do about this?

- How did it affect your relationship?

- Did you openly discuss the issue?

- Did you downgrade your evaluation of the report strictly on this basis without knowing you did?

The Behavioral Profile

A Synthesis of Levels I, II, and III

In Chapter One, I introduced the concept of an individual's behavioral profile, which is a combination of his or her behavioral tendencies at the first three levels of the structural dynamics model of any speech act. In the previous three chapters you became familiar with each: Level I, *action stance*; Level II, *communication domain*; and Level III, *operating system*.

Any individual can be understood as having a certain behavioral profile (habitual pattern) when he or she speaks with others, especially in day-to-day, low-stakes situations. Recognizing one's own behavioral profile and those of others in the room is the foundation for learning how to *read the room*, which involves observing oneself in often challenging situations. By far the best way to learn to recognize profiles is to be assisted by someone who is also an excellent bystander in the room and can help you debrief about what's been going on, just as Duncan has been doing for Ralph. With sustained focus and the help of a coach who understands and has practiced the model, leaders can rapidly become more adept at reading the room.

As I will show in Chapter Eleven, individuals can develop great insights and skill through simply working with a coach, but there is also the possibility of using formal diagnostic instruments to aid in identifying any person's profile and to speed a leader's learning.

Understanding her own behavioral profile is the first step in a leader's conscious effort to evolve her ability to *act in the room*. Even in relatively easy contexts, when personal stakes are relatively normal and low, unawareness can limit or distort one's perceptions of what is taking place. For example, from the perspective of our general business culture, Ian's behavioral profile is indicative of a good leader; but because of it, Ian routinely distorts and only limitedly perceives someone with Martha's open affect profile or Ralph's random meaning profile. This compromises the strength, range, and quality of his performance as a leader.

As you have probably noticed, I haven't yet discussed the fourth and final level to the structural dynamics model: Level IV, the level of identity and personal story. I will come to that in Chapter Six as we move closer to more stressful, high-stakes situations in which people feel more personal pressures and risks. In high-stakes situations, behavioral patterns are often disrupted, which adds to the stress and communicative challenges of those high-pressure times. In those circumstances, Level IV can dramatically enter the room.

This chapter will get you into the swing of identifying behavioral profiles and should also further intimate the power of this skill. At times, context strongly determines an individual's behavior, but recall these general preferences on the part of the ClearFacts team (Table 5.1).

A CLEARFACTS MEETING IN RALPH'S ABSENCE

One Monday, Ralph was "on the road," site-visiting some interesting prospects for purchase or collaboration. He asked the team to meet in his absence and carry on with prepping for a later meeting when he returns. That later meeting will include representatives of an agency that does TV commercials, a big step in the firm's marketing plan. Ralph had asked the team to work together to come up with ideas for a video montage for the advertising pros to work with. Each team member was eager to get this done.

"Mind your manners," Ralph joked as he left. "On your oath, have fun with this. Don't waste your time or mine squabbling. Besides," he added in self-mocking allusion to his recent misstep, "I'll probably dismiss what you come up with anyway. I'll have the final word."

In effect, Ralph was asking them to keep their behavioral repertoires in the light zone with each other. As you follow the text, you will see that they almost get into their dark sides but are pulled back onto a productive path by a collective effort in which each individual's natural behavioral propensities are called into play in a timely way.

The following dialogue occurred before the team actually embarked on the formal agenda in Ralph's absence. They were shuffling about: Art mentally dabbling in the poets' realm, casually turning up his sleeves; Martha cooing a "see

Table 5.1
Context, Language, and Action

Actor	Action Stance	Language Domain	System	Effects of Context
Ralph	Mover, opposer	Meaning	Random	If his nearly obsessive fixation on his purpose is undermined, he can strike out with undue force.
Martha	Mover, opposer	Affect	Open	In her own HR team meetings, her leadership flourishes, unopposed. Not so her management team performance.
Ian	Mover, opposer	Power	Closed	He is uniquely consistent across contexts, except when, rarely, deeply personal matters threaten to break through his defenses.
Howard	Mover, opposer	Power	Closed	He plays to and follows his "bosses," but not his peers, whom he opposes. In his own work context, he is an authoritarian mover and opposer.
Art	Mover, bystander	Meaning, affect	Open	His varied repertoire can fall apart when types like Howard disable his bystander capacities.
Ron	Mover	Meaning	Open	This is his behavior when he trusts people. He can alter it in other contexts.

you in the lounge at six" to a friend, shutting her cell phone down and ceremoni-ously dropping it into her handbag; Ian straightening *his* agenda and two pads, one blank and ready, the other full of "concept maps" whose detail speaks to the care he gave to any assignment, but especially when he assumed he was in charge, as he did now; Ron casually doodling, cautiously surveying the climate of the room. Howard spoke up first, raising his voice just short of a shout to draw attention.

The dialogue in this opening scene has roughly forty speech acts, only enough to establish a pattern that, after a slightly bumpy start, will get corrected and roll smoothly toward the meeting's goal. Don't focus on the substance, subject matter, or issues that arise, but on the *structure* of discourse, the kinds of speech acts each team member typically utters having been asked to show his or her best self. What makes the dialogue work is the best-case use of each member's behavioral profile. I will provide more analysis following the exchange.

Speaker	Speech Act	Stance, Domain, System
Howard	I've thought long and hard about how to get this done.	A move in closed power.
Ian	*(Interrupting)* Not so fast, Howard; let's decide first how we want to proceed. I've done an agenda *(circulating copies)*. Nothing fancy . . .	An oppose and then a countering move, both in closed power.
Martha	*(Sarcastically)* As you always do . . .	Subversively opposing Ian, in power as she does often. She's driven here by her open-system preference.
		(Continued)

Speaker	Speech Act	Stance, Domain, System
Martha	*(Noticing Ian on alert)* Look, I love Ralph and his ways. He works on instinct, never seems to have an agenda. Yet somehow we "get there" and feel *heard.* You're never without *your* agenda. The question is, which way is the best way for this task?	A compound action: a move in affect and a bystand in power; open system.
Howard	Everyone here knows where I stand. I prefer working from an agenda. *(Looks at Ian's agenda)* I'm for moving on.	A move in power, then a follow in power, and then a move in power. Closed.
Martha	Good enough, Howard. But I'm just trying to get a sense of where everybody stands before moving ahead.	Follow, then move (in open power) to be more inclusive.
Howard	With due respect, Martha, your wish for "all voices to be heard" does often slow things down to a point where nothing real gets done.	Oppose in power; a closed power rebuttal to open power.
Martha	I take issue. It depends on how you define real work. To my mind the real work gets done when everyone is engaged and encouraged to freely contribute.	Oppose in power, move in meaning, continuing her open power stance.

Martha and Howard are beginning an all-too-familiar escalation—opposing each other's every move and making a countermove of his or her own.

Speaker	Speech Act	Stance, Domain, System
Art	*(Interrupting)* Let me make an observation, then a suggestion. Ralph's way and Ian's way both get us to where we want to go. Ian's is a kind of "let's go by land," which keeps us on solid ground; Ralph's is "let's go by sea," which is always an adventure that gets us there from a new direction. Let's do a route check every so often. If we get bogged down in detail, we can switch; if we get fogged out at sea, we can switch. And you, Ron, might want to be the one who calls the time-outs.	A compound bystander speech act: starting with a request to make a move, then a bridging bystand in power, and then a move in open power. A perfect example of the range of effective open-system bystanding—follow the action, then make a bridging move and then another move to include a newcomer.
Ian	Thanks, Art, that was helpful. Why don't you as our artist in residence start us off.	A rare (for Ian) follow in open power, then a move that invites a move in meaning (the creation of meaning being what the assignment is all about).
Art	Okay, if you all let me do it my way. I've got this oddly shaped stone *(sliding the object to the middle of the table)* that I carry around for inspiration. Hold it a few seconds, stare at it, feel it, search out its meaning.	Takes Ian up on the invitation and makes a quixotic, random-like move in meaning.

(Continued)

Speaker	Speech Act	Stance, Domain, System
Ron	*(Looking at Martha, then at Howard, then at Art; then, to Martha)* I'm still getting my "sea legs" on this team *(to Howard with disarming politeness),* so anything I say could sound like an intrusion. *(To Art)* Looks to me like an African sculpture, a woman with a bulbous belly, suggesting a "renewable" image.	Feeling his way, Ron covertly opposes Howard, then makes a move in meaning that follows Art.
Howard	*(Frowning, shaking his head, no, no, he stares, as if appealing to a judge, at Ian.)*	Oppose in closed meaning, then a move in power.
Ian	I see I've ignited a fuse. Howard?	A follow (honoring Howard's closed power), then inviting a move.
Howard	*(Loudly)* Damned if you haven't, sir. I feel betrayed, ugh, let down. I told you before we got to this room that I had some great ideas for how to do this assignment and do it quickly and effectively. So right off you turn the meeting over to *him* with his usual mumbo jumbo.	"Betrayed" is a word that can be anchored either in affect or in power. We can assume from history that for Howard, publicly at least, it belongs in the power domain. Upset, Howard has strayed from his closed-system respect for authority.

(Continued)

Speaker	Speech Act	Stance, Domain, System
Ian	Take it easy, Howard. I apologize. I made a mistake. I misread how invested you are in making this video a powerful statement. You've got a good case, but your outburst is out of line.	Like Art's, this is a critical speech act in a compound action sequence. Ian has decided to defuse Howard with a move-oppose in closed affect. Ian follows Howard, then effectively bystands before opposing Howard in power.
Ron	*(Interrupting Martha who is about to speak)* Excuse me, Martha; I have two things I need to say. I apologize for jumping in so quickly. I appreciate your investment in this exercise. And to you, Ian, I've something to learn about fairness.	A series of moves based on bystanding his previous act. Shows his strong preference for the open system here.
Martha	*(Continuing)* Let me help out, Ian. What you said might sound patronizing to someone as talented as Howard who's out there fighting the market wars to make us all rich. You haven't "heard" all of what I suspect he is saying.	A move in open power, then a bystand that supports Howard.
Howard	You're damned right, but I don't need your help.	Howard follows and then, true to the dictates of his profile, opposes. Closed power.

(Continued)

Speaker	Speech Act	Stance, Domain, System
Martha	Then indulge me, Howard, by just letting me say two things. How Art taps his creative juices does seem like mumbo jumbo to you. And it's a bit like Ralph.	Pressing on with a move in open meaning, then a bridging bystand.
Howard	*(Quieted down, listening now)* Right on both counts.	He follows Martha in meaning.
Martha	And you think Ralph doesn't "get" how creative you are and how you get there. Say something about that.	The essence of this two-part speech act is a bystand in open meaning and a move that invites a move in meaning.
Howard	I do a lot of research, taking lots of notes, which I organize, and when I'm ready to sit down at my computer, I expect that "it" and I will produce. And when it doesn't, I stare it down until the ideas begin to flow. And, to be truthful . . .	A move in closed meaning.

Howard is closed in power and also closed in meaning. He is explaining how someone with these behavioral characteristics creates meaning. I regard this as a perfectly legitimate route to creative thinking, though different from the random's route preferred by Ralph. People with Howard's profile often see meaning as power, which is different from the pursuit and use of meaning for its own sake. (Other individuals may be inclined to a different confusion—for example, seeing or reading affect as power.)

Speaker	Speech Act	Stance, Domain, System
Howard	I think that neither Ralph nor Art appreciates my method or what it produces. Ralph, anyway, appreciates the sales I manage, but not what's happening behind the scenes.	A move in power, with meaning as a subtext. Howard is lobbying the case of how closed power can make meaning. Note the irony: behind the curtain is a man who not only conflates meaning as power to good effect but also undercuts his case when he uses power to shut down affect, which can also generate meaning.
Ron	*(Neutral voice signaling a genuine inquiry)* And you think Ian does?	A move from Ron (a neutral bystander) to confirm or disconfirm another's move. Open like Martha, Ron makes purer moves with the closed Howard.
Howard	I know he does.	A follow in power and meaning.
Martha	And that leads to my second point. And I hesitate to say it, but I will. When Ian "appreciates" you, your methods, and what you produce, you feel . . . *(a long pause)* . . . cared for. *(What everyone in the room hears is "loved," a word Martha uses often, at times to gently provoke those like Ian and Howard who object to its use.)*	A move in open affect, whose subtle emphasis carries a touch of goading Howard into admitting he seeks love—that is, with a hint of challenge, or opposing.
		(Continued)

Speaker	Speech Act	Stance, Domain, System
Howard	Not quite; I prefer the word *appreciate*.	Howard, correcting her course, opposes Martha, insisting on staying on his own, a countermove in power as meaning.
Ian	I get your point, Martha, and yours, Howard. But this seems like a good time to move on. The air is clear. Does anyone have an idea how?	A constructive two-part action: a move from bystanding, within the bounds of the closed system. Follows Martha and Howard, then moves, and then moves again with an invitation for someone to step forward with an idea for getting on with the assignment.
Art	I do. Why don't you start us off with what you came in with, Howard? I for one will join you full-mindedly, as I'm sure everyone will. And when Ron calls for a check on how things are going, you decide whether it would help and be fun to turn the reins over to me for a while.	Art makes a series of actions: first a move, then a follow, then another move— all constructive, all apparently originating in his ability to bystand.

Howard likes the challenge and so agrees.

A FUNCTIONAL TEAM IN A LOW-STAKES CONTEXT

You've just read a fairly successful interaction, from which the team, after getting over some typical interpersonal tensions, goes forward with the assignment, their behavioral repertoires (stances, domains, and system preferences) aligning

Table 5.2
Behavioral Profiles Revealed in the Dialogue

Actor	Basic Behavioral Profile	Strong Area	Weak Area
Ian	Mover in closed power, opposer in open affect, opposer in random meaning	Power.	Follow is Ian's weakest stance, affect his weakest domain; open system affect barely exists.
Martha	Mover in open affect	Affect. Good at reading the room and acting on it.	Weak follower in closed power.
Howard	Mover and opposer in closed power	Power.	Weak follower in affect and meaning; put off by acts in open and random systems.
Art	Mover and follower in random meaning, open affect, and open power; also the team's best bystander	Meaning. Can regularly move in meaning, follow in affect, and bystand. Good at reading the room.	Oppose in power.

dynamically toward an end they know is good. The dialogue reflects strengths and weaknesses that those profiles include, summarized in Table 5.2. Behavioral profiles capture much of a person's level and style of communicative competency.

Note a few more things about *structure* in the team and its capacity to function when not under pressure:

1. Generally, all characters speak in their preferred action stances. Here, as would be demonstrated also in other conversations and contexts, Ian proves the team's "best" opposer, Art its "best" bystander.

2. Individuals express their "strongest" action propensities in their language of choice: Martha as a mover in affect, Ian and Howard as movers and opposers in power, Art as both bystander and mover in meaning.

3. Some have greater range and versatility than others. Art can regularly move in meaning, follow in affect, and bystand in all domains.

4. Like all of us, Art has a "weakest" speech act: he has difficulty opposing in power.

5. Like Martha, Art is good at reading the room. Using his ability to bystand, he recognizes structures (sequences, patterns, impasses, and archetypes) and can name them in a neutral voice. Martha's versatility can be compromised by certain closed types; following in power is her "weakest" speech act.

6. Newcomer Ron presents himself on his best behavior, with occasional slips. His first preference is for an open system, but meaning is his preferred domain, and he can support (follow) Ralph in random meaning.

7. *Acting in the room*—the ability to execute just the right speech act for advancing discourse smoothly toward a desired outcome—is less developed in Art's repertoire, in large part, again, because of his "story." This leaves a gap for Martha, his equal in communicative competency, to fill; and she fills it except when she is being hooked by Ian, something both she and Ian sidestep when the stakes are low.

Meanwhile, Ralph, a mover in random meaning, keeps working with his coach on expanding his repertoire.

THE VALUE OF BEHAVIORAL PROFILES

Here it's worth considering again the tremendous value of understanding behavioral profiles. As I said at the outset, a leader's understanding his own is the first step in his conscious effort to evolve his ability to *act* in the room. Unawareness can limit or distort one's perceptions of what is taking place. For example, as noted earlier, Ian's behavioral profile is what the business culture considers indicative of a good leader. Leaders with Martha's profile are not recognized or are relegated to divisions down in rank from those at the top, and leaders with Ralph's profile start out leading innovative start-ups, but are eventually replaced by those with more closed profiles.

In subsequent chapters, I will show how understanding profiles deepens and becomes even more powerful as a tool if one has some idea of their source. I've been suggesting already that personal history is the primary source of one's behavioral profile. Earlier, I introduced some backstory to suggest the origins of Ian's closed power preference. Here are two other critical life events that illuminate his aversion to affect. The first is a distant, buried memory.

Ian is eight years old. In the twilight zone before sleep, he is startled by sounds from behind his parents' closed bedroom door. "Controlling! Brutal! Cruel! Sadistic!" his mother screams. "You may have forgotten—not me. To spare you, fool that I was, I hid every bruise you gave me!"

Ian is bewildered. For years he'd never heard a harsh word spoken between them. But her screams have awakened another memory: from some dark chamber, he hears his own screams. Finally, the curtain comes down. His screams and the memory of them fade into darkness. Only silence from his parents' room.

The second event is reflected by Maura, Ian's ex-wife, describing their failed marriage:

"He never once touched me with affection in public—not my arm or my shoulder, no gently caressing intertwined fingers, no bold pat on my butt, no sniffing my body's aromas, no wink of sex to come. Oh, it did come on some schedule in his head. But more out of duty than desire. Yes, he was a good man. Duty. Honor. Tradition. And his ability to provide even after the tours ended when he quit the service? I never gave it a thought. But the intimate space between us was just too wide for me. Cross its outer rim without invitation? It left me feeling not odd, but alone."

From Insight to Action

Think of the six ClearFacts team members as prototypes that help in identifying a wide range of leader and potential leader types. Consider that how you relate with each type and how you judge the worthiness of each may have as much to do with matches and mismatches between your behavioral profile and that of the individual as with more objective criteria.

Who among the ClearFacts leaders is most like you in your work or personal life? Which is least like you?

Your Behavioral Profile

1. Your answers to the questions at the ends of Chapters Two, Three, and Four gave you a rough idea of your behavioral profile. (A more accurate and complete assessment of your profile is available at www.kantorinstitute.com. It includes a fourteen-page report on the implications for your work and personal life.) Summarize them in a paragraph beginning, "I am primarily a . . ." (for example, "an opposer in closed power"). Include such elements as

   • Your range of propensities at each structural level

   • What kinds of actions you might want to build into your behavioral repertoire

   • How difficult it will be to do this

   • What other profiles yours complements, fits well with

   • What profiles you recognizably clash with

   • The implications all this has for your leading or coaching

2. Knowing your behavioral profile allows you to understand which types match yours and which do not, with which you will feel a kindred spirit and with which you will not. Consider this statement: *A match-up in profiles is not always a good thing, and mismatches are not always bad.* Can you think of circumstances under which each part of the statement is true?

Team Profiles

Referring to the table at the beginning of this chapter summarizing the behavioral profiles of the ClearFacts team as a guide, construct a table of your own that describes the profiles of members of a team or group you are currently coaching.

Reading the Room

At an upcoming meeting, observe the group in low-stakes communication:

1. In your mind, silently, begin to code each member's verbal inputs as I have with ClearFacts in the first few chapters, focusing only on the four action stances—move, oppose, follow, and bystand.

2. When you have detected a dysfunctional sequence, try calling on the group member best equipped to supply the appropriate action. Clue: this could be any of the four actions—move, oppose, follow, or bystand.

3. The ability to code at two levels (for example, a move in affect, an oppose in power) comes soon, but coding in real time all three levels at once (for example, a closed move in power) takes time, practice, and training; but no harm is done in trying.

PART TWO

Identity and Leader Behavior in High Stakes

Level IV: Stories, Identity, and Structured Behavior

chapter
SIX

We move now below the behavioral profile to Level IV of the structural dynamics model. (Again see Figure 1.1.) The best way to describe the relationship between Level IV and the behavioral profile may be to say that Level IV takes us down to some major sources of the profile. No single concept is more ubiquitous in our lives, and none more difficult to unravel, particularly in close relationships, than what is commonly called *identity*; and no question is as great as *Who am I?*

Humans answer this question with stories—a surprisingly small set of them. These identity-forming stories are the essence of Level IV. The stories and what we make of them accomplish two fundamental human needs: first, they allow us to form a coherent sense of self that distinguishes us from other human entities; second, they give each of us a recognizable voice that allows us to be heard, understood, and responded to in human communication.

Preceded by much distinguished thought and research into identity, this book will limit itself to identity as it relates to communication in close, meaningful relationships. *Reading the Room* posits four stories as the bases of adult identity. This chapter focuses on two—the childhood stories of perfect and imperfect love, both typically conceived in early childhood. The young-adult hero myth, conceived between adolescence and young adulthood, is fully treated in Chapter Nine. The fourth story, the morals-shaping story, is cumulatively arrived at, originating in childhood, as Kolberg, Piaget, and Freud have established, but becomes vital, structural dynamics asserts, in mature adults, particularly those in positions of power.

Structural dynamics views leadership (which includes parents and others who model right and wrong behavior) as preeminently a test of moral character. On

127

a daily basis, leaders make decisions that have moral consequences for the lives of others. Part Two of this book exhaustively deals with prototypical leaders' moral sense and capacity for moral action.

However, with the possible exception of Howard Green and a summary of his adult, story-based character flaws (Chapter Ten), I do not posit the existence of a foundational story with structural offshoots as with the other three identity stories. This is because I've not completed the kind of live, out of the laboratory, empirical research I've done with the others.[1]

IDENTITY IS LINKED TO LOVE

Most experienced coaches have had training or experience that has led them to realize and acknowledge to some extent that love is vital to everyone, including leaders, and is an essential part of the human conversation. But many business leaders seem to regard love as the "L word"—irrelevant or inadmissible in questions about their working lives. Part of the challenge of Level IV is seeing how and why love is the one universal, the one thing everyone wants, indispensable to the deepest understanding of what happens even in the business "room." In this chapter, that challenge is on.

I will show how coaches and leaders greatly enhance their abilities by fathoming their own identity-forming stories. Although it is not always available to them, leaders and their work can also benefit dramatically from knowledge of the identity stories of others in the room, especially when individuals and groups enter the "high-stakes" territory we will explore from Chapter Eight onward. For the sake of your understanding of structural dynamics, the ClearFacts case will reveal more of the identity stories of the various characters than any one individual is usually likely to be privileged to know.

Being loved is the response all social and socialized human beings crave most. This desire, our theory claims, is derived from four questions that haunt us from childhood through maturity and beyond:

Was I loved?

Am I loved?

Do I know how to love?

Do I know how to be loved?

We work so hard to define and find love and to defend it against assault because identity demands it. I explored this issue in *My Lover, Myself*,[2] a book based on foundational study of families, as described in the preface of this book. No less than other mortals, great leaders seek to answer these questions; and the inseparable relationship of identity to love is crucial to understanding leaders and leadership. What distinguishes leaders from the pack is the special, often impossible tests to which their special responsibilities subject them. And unfortunately, many leaders give up on love at home and seek it in the workplace, where, in the form of rewards (money, power, and intramural or extramural sex), it abounds.

PERSONAL STORIES AND COACHING

When I first introduced structural dynamics to consultants over twenty years ago, some were skeptical about eliciting childhood stories outside therapeutic settings. Others thought CEOs would neither cooperate themselves nor approve the practice for other people under their supervision in the company. Both concerns proved overblown. Once trust was established, CEOs welcomed the insights their stories provided, and enthusiastically recommended the procedure for key people in their ranks.

As the field of executive coaching and its practitioner training has evolved, the use of stories and material from the past to inform and guide intervention has assumed a key role. Richard Kilburg at Johns Hopkins University has provided research and practical guidelines for using psychodynamic material in executive coaching, and has added supporting evidence to my earlier research:

> In short, unconscious material in the form of past experience, emotional responses, defensive reactions, underlying and unresolved conflicts, and dysfunctional patterns of thinking and behaving can contribute to poor leadership and consequently to decreased organizational effectiveness. . . . The nature and complexity of these structures, processes and contents have been widely explored both clinically and scientifically . . . and their ability to influence conscious behavior has been widely established. . . . Professionals who work with executives in organizations are foolhardy in the extreme to approach their work as if such forces did not exist and did not affect the people with whom they work.[3]

My experience as a practicing consultant, executive, coach, and trainer of consultants continues to confirm Kilburg's observations.

However, exploring a leader's past can lead underqualified "clinical consultants" into dark territory beyond their training to handle. The key word, of course, is "training." The methodology is detailed in a chapter in the *Casebook of Marital Therapy* called "Couples Therapy, Crisis Induction, and Change" and in *My Lover, Myself.* It has been successfully taught to scores of consultants. In our ClearFacts story, Duncan Travis is one of those.

Regardless of a coach's level of expertise, it is important to remember that a coaching intervention can be successful *without* delving into the story level of structural dynamics. As I mentioned earlier, stories are powerful factors in one's behavioral profile, but exploring them is not always warranted or appropriate. But where such exploration is the appropriate path, stories do provide a rich source of data for change and growth. From discovering one's own critical stories to diagnosing the unsuccessful interfaces in one's organization, storytelling experience is a means to more fully and deeply come to know oneself and express that knowledge with others.

STORIES

Stories are the primary means by which human beings make sense of the world and themselves in it. Each of us is a story gatherer—from birth observing and selecting images as basic references for our ideas about the world, what satisfies our hunger, makes us happy, brings us pain. We experience external events and, over time, contextualize them in narrative structures with themes, plotlines, and actors.

Story is the device that allows us to store, organize, and retrieve meaning from the images we choose to remember. Images are memories, pictorialized representations of events—thoughts in visual form. They involve the self and at least one other person. *Every individual's patterned behaviors, his or her characteristic tendencies in relationships, as in families and teams, are based on these images.*[4]

Our individual wealth of story (and image) not only shapes our behavior but also helps us share our impressions with others. Wherever people converse face-to-face, a story will ripen and unfold that defines and differentiates that gathering or group from other entities.

No one needs to be taught how to build a story; stories develop in us systemically over time. Story formation is an innate activity in our *connecting* with other human beings, sharing key experiences, and saying who we are—our identity. Of course, not all of our stories (or even all of our early ones) are identity forming. Starting at age five or six, and continuing into young adulthood (by which time our identities are well established), we gather, store, and tell our most formative stories.

STORIES BEHIND A BEHAVIORAL PROFILE

Once a leader, such as Ralph, is familiar with the language of structural dynamics, he can search his memory for the four stories that define him and his typical behaviors, including various expansions that account for whatever breadth of behavioral range he commands. Coached by Duncan, Ralph might explain his penchant for random systems with a story something like this:

My random leaning is at least in part a reaction to a rigidly closed father who was terrified of my status-quo-defying, creative instincts. My favorite professor as an undergraduate had long hair before it was fashionable. "Anything goes," he told us. "What you argue as true is okay, if you can make enough sense of it to stand up to me when I call on Socrates to challenge its structural logic."

Such a story from Ralph would also help account for his strong preference for meaning. Ralph could also identify and tell stories that affirm his affinity for Martha and Ron, his tolerance and respect for Ian, and his dislike of Howard. From your work in Chapter Five, you should also be able to identify, tentatively at least, the system preferences of people who begin stories with statements like those in Table 6.1.

TWO CHILDHOOD STORIES (PERSONAL MYTHS) OF LOVE

There are two basic **childhood stories of love**: a *story of perfect love* and a *story of imperfect love*. Each of us develops both stories in ourselves, with individual variations. The stories are as "true" as any of our vital childhood memories, but told with larger-than-life, rather fantastical characterizations. From hearing hundreds of these stories, I can attest that in certain dramatic moments of "telling,"

Table 6.1
Story Openers and the Preferred Systems They Suggest

Story Opener	System
What I prefer is a traditional, ordered world of a pope, over the chaotic world of a crazed artist. When I was an out-of-control teenager, my priest all but saved my life when . . .	Closed
My father was tighter than the nuns at the school I attended, and my mother was the family's atheist freedom fighter. They fought constantly. My wife and I set out to avoid the pitfalls of both those regimes. Our kids have a voice, but *we* have the final word.	Open
I remember with nostalgia my father's arrival precisely at six every night, and the comfort and sense of security it gave me. I want that same sense of order in our lives. Let me tell you what that was like.	Closed
I watched the calendar for my aunt's monthly visits like other kids watched it for Christmas. Every visit was a circus of fun. Her stories inspired mine. I learned from her what was possible for women who wanted freedom from all constraints, a willingness—no, a necessity—to break existing rules if it came to that.	Random

this is how they are reexperienced: extravagantly emotive, romantic, exaggerated, fairy tale, mythic.

The **story of perfect love** comes first. In the years immediately following birth, the expectation of pure, unending, unconditional, Edenic love persists in the growing child. The mother and those around her strive to meet all the child's needs and thus reinforce the expectation. This story that we will always have a source of perfect love is documented in a selection of positive memories that are both recollected by and told to the child.

In time, however, harsh reality inevitably serves up insults and injuries to this perfect environment. Eventually, contradictions—ordinary ones like illness, discipline, fears, and angers, and more serious ones like neglect, humiliation, and abuse—will conspire to challenge this story and inspire the child to come to terms with the imperfect nature of love by telling a second, competing story about love. This **story of imperfect love** may be even more poignant and compelling because of its almost mythic energy, its power to rekindle deep feelings of loss or pain, and a melancholic disappointment in a breach of the story of perfect love. Because it is created by a child—roughly between five and fourteen, we have learned—it has some of the character of fairy tale, with heroes and villains and themes of lost innocence, sudden awakening, betrayal, and disappointment.

When many stories of imperfect love are intelligently probed, the stories' universal character is strikingly revealed—they have the same *narrative structure*, by which I mean that they all tend to contain at least several of seven recurring features, which we will explore in detail later in the chapter. As adults we may have more choice, but as children we seem to have little choice but to see the world in moral terms. In our early striving to make sense of our family world, we assess ourselves and others with the belief that a behavior or person is good or bad, right or wrong, strong or weak.

To the child, even trivial affronts can be experienced as major assaults. Setting the stage for his or her own story of imperfect love, every child thinks,

---

I am weak and defenseless compared to my parents. I know that once, a long time ago, I was truly and perfectly loved, but it is only a memory. Am I loved now? How can I be sure? Why is it that, when I cry at night because I want to be with them longer, they get so impatient and angry? There! It's happened again. They hate me. They probably want me to go away or die.

Thus, as children we naturally dramatize our claims, and each offense—whether trivial, outrageous, or atrocious—is stockpiled in an archive of complaints against the stronger, more powerful family authorities, ready to be shaped into a story of betrayal. The stage is now set; the child, having absorbed the structure of story from stories read and told, is ready for her first creative act, writing a story of her own, the story of imperfect love, her personal myth. As mentioned, these mythically toned stories have seven recurring features:

1. The hurtful monarch
2. The silent conspirator

3. Resonant themes of guilt, disfavor, sadness, and deception

4. Melancholic disappointment

5. The truant hero

6. Longing and yearning for the ideal mate

7. The "When I Grow Up" hero

A story is ripest for telling when events in the present raise resonant themes from the past, which rise to just below consciousness. From there, on provocation, they make their way "into the room." When one partner says to the other, "That's not me you're describing; it's your mother," he or she is capturing this moment.

Anyone who has been in a key long-term and especially intimate relationship has probably experienced the typical repetitive, cyclical struggle, disagreement, or fight that results in an impasse, but to which both combatants return for yet another bout whenever a thematic trigger is pulled. I have described this cyclical pattern and the damage it does in several publications.[5] And there is no want of examples in my consulting and executive coaching experience, nor in those of colleagues.[6] You will see it in the following dialogue between Martha and her husband, Lance. When a coach (like Duncan) or a mate (like Lance) witnesses a ritually told tale spin round and round a repetitive theme, the story (Martha's) is ripe for the telling.

MARTHA AND LANCE—THE RITUAL FIGHT

I will use Martha's relationship with her husband, Lance, to illustrate the features I have just introduced. I will also bring in the concept of *ritual impasse* (noted in the section "Structural Patterns Mold Behaviors" in Chapter Two).

The Quarrel

Martha had gone to Asia on a business foray, one purpose of which was to do a little detective work about the anonymous e-mail that Ralph had revealed (Chapter Three). As we enter the scene, she had just flown home, disappointed. She and Lance settled in with a glass of wine, their usual routine after one of her trips and many times a prelude to "welcome home" lovemaking; but this time Martha was obviously tired and out of sorts.

"Lance, I was so *sure* something was going on there, or that people would talk," she said, "but not one peep. I feel so empty."

With this in mind, Lance hazarded something he intended as a means of lightening Martha's mood: "Well, maybe we need to freshen your tank."

Martha glared. "No stupid humor. I failed."

Missing a cue, Lance persisted, "Look, you've been obsessed with this thing. Let it go." But he knew as he said that it he'd made a mistake; he'd pulled a familiar trigger.

"You *know* my need to know," she replied. "Dammit, you sound like my sister."

Lance managed to duck and recover, sensing now that what she needed was not a muse but comfort. He listened, letting her talk until she cooled off, then, taking her hands, lifted her to her feet, embraced her with a tender touch, and led her to the bedroom.

On other occasions, the sex might have broken the tension of the skirmish. This time, the aftermath was an explosion into their own and all-too-familiar battle. Rising for another glass of wine, Martha caught the glow of Lance's computer, looked that way, and saw on his work table some sketches for his latest paintings and, next to them, photos of the nude in the sketches.

Suddenly beyond fury and outrage, she hurled her glass at the floor and cried, "You've gone too far! Again! And lying about it? The one thing we don't do is lie!"

"Again." "Too far." "Lying." The words began a speech that pressed every trigger Martha knew he possessed. In truth, Lance had written her an e-mail telling her of his need for a model, but anyhow she'd been away, so he hadn't actually sent it. *So, all right,* he thought, *technically I broke our pact. But never mind all that.* So Lance, too, entered the war zone. Resonant themes of his own ignited, the recycled argument ramped up.

Ever since that homecoming tiff—the "Asian affair," as they came to call it—the argument resumed now and then, each time leaving them exhausted with self-disgust, as happens at the end of most ritual battles. Judging by her performance at work and nearly everywhere else, one would have thought Martha, the master bystander, most capable of standing back, but on these occasions she couldn't.

At the close of one of those cyclones, however, Lance managed to step back and say to her, "Martha, please let me speak. Before, you haven't minded my using live models. What got to you this time was my not telling you in advance. Consciously? Unconsciously? Too lonely to admit? Okay, there's no excuse. No matter. I broke our sacred rule. But now, just let me make up for it."

To which she agreed. And when the conversation leveled to normal, she also admitted the keenness of his observation. Yes, he'd triggered her memories of disappointment and anger. But those guys at ClearFacts did, too! And it was this compounding of situations that turned her mind toward talking a few things over with Duncan, the team's ultimate, unofficial, and surely confidential bystander. *If that doesn't work*, she thought, *I'll call my old therapist!*

Lance's Past and Present

We are focusing on Martha, but Lance's stories matter also, as there are two people and thus two story sets present in every ritual fight. We sketch his here enough to provide a context for *his* behavior.

Lance's father had been an artist. A small circle of art aficionados considered him a modernist genius, breaking new ground on his own path. The rest of the art world disagreed, and in fact he didn't "make it." Lance's mother sided with that "rest of the world" and was ultimately even *less* sympathetic toward her husband. Lance, the son, an aspiring artist himself, revered his father's relentless perseverance and fully absorbed his deathbed advice:

It was worth it, Lance—every moment. The "rules" will strangle your creativity if you let them, son. Break those rules if you believe that doing so adds something to the world!

Breaking society's and "the academy's" rules for a higher purpose was Lance's personal and artistic slogan and mantra, and Martha admired him for it. Also, she was intrigued and aroused by Lance's defiant claims to *fun* ("Let's fly to Paris for a couple of days; we've been working too hard"). But the rules they shared about monogamy and telling the truth were clear, she thought: "No deceit: if ever there is reason to stray, we tell the truth and talk."

Some of Lance's peers considered his work pornographic and, from a purely artistic point of view, professional suicide, but Lance argued that it was an artist's responsibility to challenge the status quo; he must push the margins of taste in his work—yes, especially the boundaries of sex: "You see it in novels; I'm trying to do it on canvas."

Martha supported Lance in this, but with a caveat: "Yes, as you artists say, 'Eros animates the brush,' but that's also a sexual euphemism. It's an unacknowledged excuse for artists to screw their nude models."

"Not *this* artist," he pledged.

Martha's Childhood Story

When Martha met with Duncan, several of the previously mentioned features that show up in all childhood story narratives of imperfect love were revealed. Here is a portion of their conversation:

MARTHA: My mother? A year-round frost. She ran the help and my father with an iron fist. So for me, my father was more than charm and class; he was mother, uncle, brother, and best friend. He knew how to hold a child like a feather. If you're wondering, Duncan, it wasn't sexual, but deep, the way the best sex is . . . *(Later she told Duncan she was pulling his leg when she said that.)* . . . more like a snuggly. Sinatra, that's my dad—his touch. Lance is the only man who's ever come close to a touch like that. It's partly why I married him. But my dad betrayed my trust. He had a way of making a nauseating truth seem appetizing. Lance has that in spades, too, another reason I married him. But he's never lied until now.

DUNCAN: You seem to say you got through that scene with Lance all right, but let's look at the two themes it unearthed: truth telling and betrayal.

Taking steps he'd been trained in using, Duncan led Martha into telling her story. When telling their childhood stories in skilled hands, clients tend to reexperience emotions that drove the need to create the story in the first place. Duncan went slowly in taking Martha from her own strong feelings to new insights connecting the past and present with Lance.

Her story, which echoes the sounds of fairy tale and myth, is the birthplace of toxic themes that can unravel all humans facing extreme pressures and crises (see Chapters Eight and Nine). Like the sample illustration that I have also included (Figure 6.1, following the story), the voice in which I tell the story that follows conveys more accurately how the adult is *experiencing* the telling than any more "adult" and objective-sounding rendering would do. In the immediate moment of telling, grown men burst into tears, mature women tremble violently. When this moment passes, a trained consultant can help the storyteller tease out the critical themes, plot lines, and structures that are impacting their work and personal lives. These I interweave into the story.

My mother was a stately, powerful queen who married a rich and noble man, then ruled him like a child. She believed in the family, as devotedly as some do in God.

Whenever she saw me or my sister or brother in danger of leaving "the path," she'd remind us, "Build your house on high ground, on solid rock, and within its thick walls rule firmly, for the family is *the path, the source.*" I felt safe and secure in this big house—my mother's sacred realm—with its servants and familiar observances, ceremonies, and traditions.

Yet my gentler father was also a source of strength to the whole family, more than a pet! He was our guardian and the rock on which our house was built.

By age ten I had discovered a strange and at first frightening (because it glowed mainly at night) power in myself. If I surrendered to its magnetic pull, I could see the unseeable, know the unmentioned. I discovered not just worms and bugs buried under rocks, but dark truths and other "not to be's" with my power. When my mother often called me "too curious, child," she came close to exposing this secret to the light of day.

But then my power and I became friends. My curiosity was special because it beckoned from a life of its own inside me. At certain times—night mostly—it left my body and presented itself in a faceless, adventurous, and magnetic form I could not resist. When it said, "Come with me," I leaped to obey.

I kept knowledge of this power from my siblings until the day I had to share it. I was the middle child. My older sister was weak and afraid. As a young boy, my brother "Junior," four years younger than I, pretended he didn't exist. As a young child, he kept to himself a lot, and was all but raised by an au pair. Even later, he added little to the household. He was an "accident," or there was some mystery concerning his birth. I cannot say how I came to find these things out. Knowing would hurt people anyway. Did Junior know?

Sissy's never-strong will was crushed when she was severely punished for reading Mother's diary. Why? Was there something to hide? She was thirteen and I was ten and had just discovered my secret power, which made me even more inquisitive about Mother's private life. Mother intimidated Sissy. I was unafraid.

My mother and I loved each other but sparred a lot. She respected my spirit and decided to train me to be a strong woman, her successor. She tried to school me about "man's inherent and unconquerable weakness." I listened, watched, decided to make up my own mind, especially about my father, whom I worshipped. My nighttime intuition said she didn't love him as a man. Why did he not fight for his rights? What was wrong?

I became obsessed with championing my father, and Mother always firmly resisted: "Please don't sell him to me, dear. Your grandmother, my mother, did that before your father and I married, and she was dead wrong." But I wasn't so easily deterred. *Wicked queen!* I thought. In turn, Mother, reading my mind, reprimanded me for insolence. But I knew she had no intention of crushing my spirit, as she had Sissy's.

In my nightly wanderings, I knew in my bones that something was being concealed. I watched Father giving Mother plenty of room, especially on Wednesday nights when he stayed over at the club. I charged my mysterious power, *Lift the veil. Break the seal. Speak out.* When these incantations failed, I vowed one night to bring whatever it was into the light. It was Wednesday night, and Father had left for the club.

I went first to Sissy's room, announcing, "I'm going to Mother's room." Sissy was speechless, turned red as a beet: Mother's room was strictly off-limits, even to Father. "Come with me," I begged. Sissy turned white as a sheet. I waited. She shut her anguished eyes and silently rolled her head from side to side.

I left and tiptoed down the hall toward Mother's sanctuary, quiet as a hunter. I heard the man's voice, but did not see him. It was not Father's voice. I wanted to flee, but then the man's throaty sounds were joined by my mother's soft, honeyed sigh, and I could not tear myself away.

When I finally made my way to Sissy's room again, she lay there frozen, as before. Still gripped by terror, she whispered, "I dare not let you speak. Leave me. I beg you."

Next morning I rose early and put on a white and black skirt, as formal as Mother ever was at breakfast, and went straight to Sissy's room.

"Have you lost your mind?" she said when I revealed my plan.

"Do truth and injustice mean nothing to you?

"But do you know what you are getting into?" Sissy pleaded. She reminded me that Mother was renowned for her distaste for stealth, and how Sissy herself had been severely punished merely for "stealing a look" at Mother's diary.

I began to tell Sissy how much I needed her at my side, but she would hear no more and fled to school without breakfast. As usual, Father arrived home from the club in time for breakfast.

"I have something to say about what happened in our house last night," I gushed, as soon as Mother joined Father and me at the table.

Reading my mind, Mother slammed both palms down hard. "William!" she shouted. Father leaped up, as if in fear, or rage.

"Why are you angry, Father?" I said.

His voice quivered. "Please come with me. To the library. Now." Once we were alone, he demanded, "What are you about?"

"I've come to tell the truth. I want to restore you to your rightful place."

"No, no, my child . . . it is not for you to open the light that could harm us all. You should leave well enough alone. What's dead is dead."

"But Father, what is dead can be reborn. Where there is vinegar there is sweet honey. Where there is sorrow there can be hope."

"In the name of God, I must forbid you to go any further with this."

"But what I do, I do in the name of *love*."

"What I ask, I *ask* in the name of love."

I was seized by what I know now to be compassion. But I was deeply confused as we walked back to the dining room together, Father's arm resting lightly on my shoulder. I never felt more alone.

"Good," said Duncan when she was done. "My job is to help you explore how themes in your story carry over into themes at work. Here's one idea. Your distrust of Howard works two ways. Because of your sensitivity, you are probably on to something in your suspicions about what he might be up to. But oversensitivity can cause unnecessary trouble . . ."

Figure 6.1 is an artist's visualization of Martha's childhood story, which a coach like Duncan would give her to keep.

A CHILDHOOD STORY'S NARRATIVE STRUCTURE

Martha's story contained several of the common features of childhood stories, which we will now explore in greater detail.

Figure 6.1
Martha's Childhood Story

1. The Hurtful Monarch

Usually, the **hurtful monarch** (either the father or mother) is the dominant parent, the star protagonist in the storyteller's view of the family's dynamics. In some cases, some other adult (an uncle who perpetrates incest, for example) or a sibling plays this role. The child's "hurt" can result from cruelty or coldness or withholding, depending on the story maker's emphasis and interpretation. In Martha's story, her controlling (closed system) mother bids high for the part, but Martha's father shares the role because Martha is even more disappointed in love by her father's acceptance and "slavish" (Martha's word) support of his wife's deceit, and because of Martha's complete adoration of him as the more engaged parent.

2. The Silent Conspirator

Silent can also mean *silenced*—not "there" in time of need. Couple dynamics are most certainly at play in this most devastating of mover-follower structures. We saw these dynamics in Ian's story, and we will in Ralph's.

The **silent conspirator** in Martha's story, her father, speaks kindly, attentively, and lovingly, but he does not speak *the truth,* the truth of Martha's "discovery" at a crucial moment of confrontation. It is this resoundingly loud, unexplained silence that is too much for Martha, the object of his affections. Thus she adds "betrayal" to her litany of hurtful themes.

3. Resonant Themes of Guilt, Disfavor, Sadness, and Deception

In important interactions, **resonant themes** such as Martha's theme of betrayal are what animate partners and colleagues into cocreating ritual spirals. The childhood story, not truth or reality, names the resonant themes just as a playwright instructs a director and actors about the tone, mood, atmosphere, and thematic focus of a play.

Themes running through childhood stories range from universal to particular. At the universal level, we find broad themes of loss of innocence, sudden awakening, departures from paradise. At a deeper personal level, themes exist as emotional states that fall somewhere along the five continua shown in Figure 6.2.

Each of the five dimensions in the figure shows three terms along a continuum of greater intensity from left to right. My use of the term "greater intensity" is meant to suggest that adults telling their childhood stories speak of hurt or pain or harm that ranges from lesser to greater along the same continuum, and that the intensity of felt damage contributes to the depth of the shadow (discussed further in this chapter). The venom expressed in "love quarrels" can be traced to the anger-revenge-rage continuum, which interacts with each of the lower four sets of themes, adding fuel to burning fires that are ignited in close relationships over issues of identity, love, and reward. Thus the darkness of one's shadow is a factum of the intensity of the hurt-pain in each of the four continua conjoined with the intensity of the anger-revenge-rage continuum.

I do not suggest that the five dimensions in the figure are definitive or necessarily exhaustive. They are speculations based on my long experience in clinical

Figure 6.2
Birthplace of Themes: Four Thematic Continua as Influenced by Degree of Anger

	Anger	Revenge	Rage	
Less Shadows	Guilt	Stigmatization	Shame	**More Shadows**
	Disfavor	Rejection	Abandonment	
	Sadness	Sorrow	Grief	
	Deception	Fraud	Betrayal	

practice and on my habit of conceptualization. Their scope is intuitive, deductively constructed, and therefore imprecise. Besides, I am no match for the dramatic ingenuity of kids in inventing their own themes—being excluded or not being number one, for example. Could these clinical speculations be put to empirical test? Definitely, and they should be.

When we look at it from left to right, Figure 6.2 might suggest a continuum from health to pathology, but structural dynamics resists the unfortunate tendency of experts to define increasing numbers of behaviors as pathological. The shadow of our darker side, as much as we might deplore it, is universal, and we therefore cannot loosely view it as pathological. I suggest that rather than pathologize, apologize, or find excuses for your shadow, you get to know your own and take responsibility for it.

The themes at this personal level are particularly useful in understanding your shadow, a topic I'll discuss more thoroughly later in this chapter. Our shadow is a hidden expression of our fear that we are unloved or unlovable, which we turn on our self or on others. The strength of a person's shadow depends on where her psyche positions the self along each continuum in Figure 6.2.

Duncan had a good sense of Martha's vulnerability in the area of deception-fraud-betrayal. Martha's colleagues could trigger reactions of different strengths along the anger-revenge-rage continuum, for example: anger at Ralph and more at Ian; feelings of being defrauded by Howard, to the point of rage. It would seem natural to Duncan that the child in Martha felt betrayed by her acquiescent father, whose love she knew and valued, and by Lance, to whom she turned, as I think we all do in our choice of mates, to make up for the child's lost love.

4. Melancholic Disappointment

In nostalgia for the past, adults weave together remnants of the two childhood stories of love. Perhaps this is what accounts for the story's bittersweet quality: the "bitter" a reminder of betrayal, the "sweet" for the memory, or dream, of perfect love. For with the story of betrayal comes the child's first real disappointment in love. In childhood, it is experienced as a vague and for many an overbearing sense of melancholic loss of innocence. We carry this memory of disappointment with us throughout our lives. When our search for the ideal lover has at first paid off, but in erosive time fails or threatens to fail, we reexperience the child's sense of **melancholic disappointment** as another betrayal, doubly felt for the seeming fact that love has failed us twice. But then most of us gear up for another try, even after the ritual impasse has settled in.

5. The Truant Hero

The coconspirator's failure to challenge or balance the powerful monarch leads the storyteller to seek or, more likely, wish for the **truant hero**—that figure in the real or imagined life of the child who, if he or she would only appear, would do whatever it takes to make the story of love come out right in the end, as in most fairy tales and many myths. But alas, in the childhood story of imperfect love, this hero does not appear. Some children actively seek this hero as a real-life person. Most, however, rely on fantasy and fantasized rescue. Until! Until, older, they find themselves in two key relationships—one with an ideal lover and the other with an ideal partner in a close relationship at work (both of which, I insist, are about "love").

It is well known, to those of us who have attempted adult love, that we place an impossible burden on these partners. We expect them to bring closure to the story of imperfect love and, by the by, make it possible for us to reclaim our right to perfect love.

Thus the truant hero plays a prodigious role in our most significant relationships in adulthood. But in childhood, for all the child's wishing and imagining, the truant hero remains on the run. With his or her failure to appear, the child is left with a deep sense of longing and yearning.

6. Longing and Yearning for the Ideal Mate

As the previous discussion suggests, in adulthood, our longing for a truant hero turns into a keenly double-edged yearning and search for the ideal lover, someone with precisely those heroic qualities and characteristics that can do brave combat with and slay the monarch or any source of hurt. In the work arena, we seek a similarly close relationship. The love and work phenomena are different only in intensity, not in their basic nature.

7. The "When I Grow Up" Hero

In the period between the story's creation in childhood and our first serious sallies into the big world in young adulthood, we seek credible answers to two fundamental identity-forming questions: *Who am I?* and *Who will I be when I "grow up"?* Thus incubates the **heroic self** and the "perfect lover's" heroic type. *(Who will love me as I want to be loved?)*

Beginning with such vague queries as *Am I loved for who I am? Do I know who I am?* we gravitate to such questions as *How shall I shape my own adult identity? What kind of noble, heroic self will I bring to the world? What will the world love me and reward me for?* Roughly between ten and twenty years of age, we search the culture for prototypic figures we can emulate. But emulate is not exactly what we do. More precisely, we try on various figures like suits of clothes. We do this until we find one that fits our own behavioral propensities. Thus, what the childhood story contributes to the emerging sense of self is *identity,* the "who I am" in matters of love. With that in place, the evolving self searches further for "who I am in the world," the hero who will be rewarded for how he or she performs in high-stakes and crisis situations. Chapter Nine will say much more about the types of hero perceptions we adopt and how they shape our behaviors when the chips are down.

SHADOWS

Part of figuring out the "who I am" in matters of love involves seeking proof of love from those around you, though "seeking love" is not how most leaders would dare to put it. Your shadow "puts you in touch" with that disappointed child, eager to feel loved and "at the ready" to revisit the emotions you felt at the time your story was created, and reacting both to those who withheld perfect love then and those who are withholding it now.

The **shadow** is the buried memory of the betrayal—the sense of not being loved or of being unlovable—that cuts you off from your best (your loved and lovable) self and the natural impulses you had as a child and still have as an adult. In the puzzling ways of paradox, this is what causes you to *act in ways that are guaranteed to keep you from getting what you want most*—be it respect, admiration, freedom, fame, or whatever—from your bosses, peers, and subordinates at those times you need it most. Love, or the claim that one did not get enough of it, is the genesis of the shadow; and love, or the reclaiming of what is due, is the shadow's objective. However, the shadow goes about this in the wrong way.

Some shadows are darker and run deeper than others. The deeper the felt injury, the darker and less accessible the shadow. The strength of your shadow depends on where the psyche positions itself along each continuum suggested by Figure 6.2. In other words, a strong shadow equates to an extreme position—let's say on the guilt-stigmatization-shame continuum—combined with an extreme position on the continuum of anger to rage. Please remember, however, that the figure is only a framework for how we *think* about actual events. The story actually told is in the mind of the storyteller, as we know from siblings growing up in the same household and with the same parents who, when they each tell their stories of imperfect love, "cannot believe" each other's tales.

RON'S STORY AND SHADOW

So far, we have seen small parts of Lance's and Ian's story and Martha's in full. In later chapters, parts of Ralph's and Howard's will emerge. Here I summarize Ron's.

In recent weeks, Ron has firmed up his place on the team as a strong mover and bystander in meaning at the office, and as someone comfortable in affect outside it, having drinks with Martha, for example, and, perhaps ill-advisedly, at dinner at home with Ralph and Sonia. He has also informally built good, but different, relationships with Art and Ian. His relationship with Howard can best be described as cool. However, that will not last. The tension between Martha and Howard will soon increase around the meaning of the "anonymous e-mail," and in that context Ron's strengths as a neutral bystander will break down, revealing themes and the silhouette of his shadow hidden in his childhood story.

When Ron eventually puts his story together with Duncan, he will remember experiences when he was about five that have been haunting him, about how he felt when his father held him after a fall, or when the heat went off in a storm and his father wrapped him in a blanket. What he remembers feeling isn't warmth, but cold in his father's arms. *Maybe,* he will muse, *this coldness was my father's way of balancing power with his wife. Maybe it was because the poor guy didn't have it in him because I was a "mistake," a black child with white parents.*

Ron's Mother and Father

Adrianne Stuart, daughter of a white Episcopalian minister and wife, was an anthropologist settled in academe after doing fieldwork illustrious enough to earn a very busy tenure, keeping her ideas alive lecturing, attending conferences, serving on committees, and writing. In three words, "Busy and gone," said Ron.

When it was confirmed that she could not have children, Ron's mother pressed the idea of adoption on her distracted mate, a token executive in a long-surviving family business. The husband's mind was mostly on having used the wrong club in a golf tournament. "I need to act on my convictions," she argued. "I want us to take in a black child." Her husband did not share her convictions. Worse, he harbored prejudices he could voice post-martini at the club but not to his anthropologist wife. Finally, he sluggishly consented.

So, says Ron, "I was raised by a largely forgotten chain of caregivers, from nanny to au pairs to babysitters. And by an indifferent father left to oversee, reluctantly, the son he never wanted."

At six, Ron was already questioning, in a bright child's way, what love was about. He knew his mother was color blind. Also an ideologue, urging him to feel personally, as she did, the injustices against the weak and especially the racially oppressed. He knew *she* loved him from how he was held on her lap while being read to or being told exotic stories about tribal existence, and especially stories of tribal loyalties. That, to Ron, was what love was about: loyalty. Ron had never seen that motif in his father, but later saw it in Ralph, his "color-blind" boss.

Ron's mother exacted a pledge from Ronald Stuart senior to take their son along when walking the dog, on at least one of the days when she was away on travels. "He needs to know you love and care for him," she said.

On one of these walks, Ron experienced a disturbing revelation, his hand loosely held in his father's large, clammy one. A neighbor approached. Ron saw how the neighbor's eyes were fixed on those black-in-white hands, the white one seeming to be saying to the neighbor, *This is a mistake,* and to Ron, *and you are it.*

A Life-Changing Adolescent Trauma

Ron insists that in his social world growing up he never felt racially marginalized—until he did, painfully. He was attending the famously "right" and liberal secondary Friends School in famously liberal Cambridge, where no one stood out except by looks and brains. And he had both. Formal dating wasn't cool. But then came his year's year-end senior dance, the school's equivalent of a prom. Asked by Rene Saunders, one of his closest friends and confidants in those heavy discussions curious adolescents have about "the world out there," he accepted with casual grace. He liked the Saunders family, especially the mother.

Sitting with Rene's father while waiting for her to finish dressing would have been a trial for most adolescents. For Ron, what felt at first like an inconvenience surely became a trial and then an identity-challenging ordeal. The previously friendly elder, sensing sex on the horizon (it wasn't in Ron's mind—not yet, anyway), abruptly broke the rhythm of easy talk with, "Sex, Ron, is not an option. Nor is this anything but a *date.* A date to nowhere." In this stonily silent racial standoff, boy and man understood each other—relieved suddenly by Rene's flustered appearance, her beaming mother close behind. "Don't they make a handsome couple?" she said, but her comment couldn't reilluminate the darkness cast by the father's raw moment of truth.

Awakening of an Identity

What Ron did with this was not expected, except by his mother, who cheered him on. Accepted at Princeton, he took a year off and, guided by a black schoolmate who attended Harvard, made his way to one of Boston's black ghettos, ostensibly to work, but really to do a kind of anthropological research.

The results of this research amounted to an awakening. He saw the collapse of a future for young girls. But he also was impressed by the tough gentle strength of many single moms and by the role of grandmothers and great-grandmothers, women of previous generations who carried the burden of survival, of the "whole race," it seemed to him.

In this brief sojourn, he also learned firsthand about guns, drugs, and the perishing dreams of so many black males to become an entertainer or professional athlete. Firsthand he learned about the ubiquity of rage among black males and its self-destructive aspects. His conclusion? *Getting killed was a clever form of suicide.*

Ron knew that before leaving for college, he needed to cleanse himself—not of the rawness of his brief experience in the ghetto, but of his raw guilt over being able to escape. A counselor from his old high school helped him get in touch with his own anger—at the white world into which he was brought, at the contradictions and ambiguities of authentic love, and at his family. He concluded that the best way of passionately claiming his black identity was by "getting ahead, but not at the expense of the oppressed."

From Insight to Action

Two childhood stories, one of perfect love, the other of imperfect love, are the nuclear sources of behavior in our most meaningful relationships. They are also the forces that drive our "best" and "worst" selves. It is therefore crucial that leaders and coaches, for the sake of their practices and their lives, get to know their own stories and themes, and the stories and themes of those they lead and coach.

Your Stories

1. Spend a quiet half hour cataloguing the main childhood stories you tell yourself and others in defining who you are—that is, your identity.

2. Select three you consider closest to the core of who you are. Can you see correlations between key story themes and the issues that arise in key relationships?

3. Select the story you suspect is behind your struggle to preserve your sense of who you are in your most intimate relationship, past or present. This may be your childhood story of love. Reflect on this.

   • See if the chapter contains themes in your story that make their way into how you conduct yourself in this and other key relationships.

- Consider the possibility that your story and its themes are the source of what others and you yourself see as your worst behaviors—your shadow side.

- How easy or hard is it for you to take responsibility for your shadow?

- Think of a time or times when, under pressure, your shadow surfaced and took over, with untoward consequences. Was a theme from a past story involved?

- Who are the characters in this story from the past? Do they resemble key people in your present personal and work life? Would you consider that it is not the person but the structure of his or her behaviors that accounts for the resemblance?

4. Recall a recent event in your life at work in which your behavior or your reaction to another's behavior flew off the charts. First tell the story in moral terms; then step back and tell it in morally neutral structural terms.

Reading the Room

From time to time when you are leading or coaching, the conversation will take an unanticipated or dramatic turn where temperatures rise. As leader or coach you are called on to get things back on track. Being able to translate moral stories into structural ones, your own first of all and then those of others, is an essential skill. Absent this skill, you risk misreading what is going on in the room. With it, you take another step toward communicative competency.

1. Recall a time that meets the conditions I've just described in which you got hooked, perhaps losing control. Consider the moral story you probably told and reconstruct it in a neutral tone, as a purely structural story.

2. Do the same when two participants were taken over by shadows they brought into the room from their childhood stories. What did you do then to help reconcile their difficulties? What would you do differently or better now?

Narrative Purpose

In Chapter Six, I emphasized the importance of story in personal life. This chapter carries story to interpersonal and organizational levels. Doing this will prepare the way for our understanding some of CEO Ralph's perceptions and behavior when we move to high-stakes moments at ClearFacts. As individuals create, perpetuate, and alter their own essential unifying personal stories, in their ongoing social interactions they also weave the stories of others and of organizations in with their own. Recall that at the synthesized core of a person's stories lies the person's identity. So, too, shared stories are essential to forming and perpetuating the identity of a group.

For example, a married couple's unifying identity as a couple is based on the stories the pair accepts about how they each chose to enter the marriage, what commitments they worked out over the years, and what purpose their closeness continues to serve. Each partner might have his or her own way of telling and applying that story, but their versions share much common ground. The same applies to business partnerships, friendships, families, and other stable relationships, and continues to apply on up to larger organizations and institutions of which people feel they are part. In this chapter, our main interest lies at the team and corporate levels, but I will also go beyond that to, for example, a people's identity as a nation. National narrative purpose is defined and challenged in exciting times like ours.

In the workplace, at every level, one job of a leader is to articulate and defend the story that keeps the organization together and promotes its general success. Another job is to make sure that the story stays close to the truth. I refer to such a story maintained by a leader as an organization's **narrative purpose.** Narrative purpose is a group's or organization's reasons for being, particularly as understood and maintained by its leaders. It is a coherent articulation of what an organization "does"—its goals and relevant activities. Narrative purpose generally includes some conception of how the organization arose and what brings it to the current moment, in support of the narrative, not for the sake of chronology.

Like personal stories, a narrative purpose may be tinged with shadow in various quarters of any group as a whole. For a corporate leader like Ralph, the challenge is to keep the story of narrative purpose both bright and true enough to keep all groups in the organization directed, healthy, and productive.

Just as individuals gain by understanding their personal stories and seeing how those stories shape their behaviors, so a group of any size can strengthen its identity and gain in other ways by sharing a story and knowing what that unifying story is. By redirecting conversation to the level of narrative purpose, a stuck group can sometimes raise itself out of impasse and cycles of escalation to find commonalities and constructive links.

Learning about narrative purpose prepares you to understand the narrative challenge to Ralph and his leadership team when relationships at ClearFacts degenerate under high-stakes pressures. It will also prepare you to see what Ralph and Sonia Waterman can gain by handling, as a couple, the pressures of Ralph's working life.

ASPECTS OF NARRATIVE PURPOSE

In considering narrative purpose, it is useful to focus on how clear the purpose actually is, its social and moral dimension, ways in which the narrative can be shared, and the group's underlying model of practice.

Clarity of Purpose

The purpose ought to be clear. For example, Apple, named number one on *Fortune* magazine's 2010 list of the world's most admired companies, has maintained a clear narrative purpose: *innovation*. It is a "company that changed the way we do everything from buy music to design products to engage with the world around us," the magazine's Christopher Tkaczyk notes.[1]

At any point in time, an organization's leaders should be able to tell a story of where their organization has been, where it is at the time of telling, where it is heading (that is, its destination), and why it wants to reach this destination. In other words: Why was the organization started? What is it doing now? What will it do in the future? And what is the purpose of all of this? Like the plot of a good work of fiction, an organization's narrative purpose should be compelling—justifying the continued telling of its story, the organization's continuation. As Collins and Porras write in *Built to Last,* a good narrative purpose answers the question, "Why not just shut this organization down, cash out, and sell off the assets?"[2]

A Moral, Social Dimension

Among an organization's important reasons for being are what it wants to contribute to the world and how it wants to change the world into a better place—in other words, its social and moral purpose. To be effective, an organization's narrative purpose cannot be simply amassing profit or accruing power. Organizations need to be perceived as relevant and successful, and that requires a social and moral dimension.

How to define moral purpose? In *The Ascent of Money: A Financial History of the World,* historian Niall Ferguson says willingness to sacrifice money or profit is evidence of moral purpose.[3] Fundamentally I agree with this definition, although money is not the only possible "material" sacrifice. For example, legend has it that when President Johnson signed the Civil Rights Act of 1964, he whispered to an aide, "We have lost the South for a generation." LBJ was well aware that his party's support of civil rights for blacks would cost them thousands of votes.[4]

Of course, money *can* be sacrificed. In one of the most lauded handlings of a corporate crisis in history, Johnson & Johnson (J&J) in 1982, in response to a series of cyanide poisonings of Extra Strength Tylenol that killed seven people on Chicago's West Side, launched a major offensive. Its top executives decided to put customer safety ahead of profits and other financial concerns, and alerted customers across the nation, via the media, not to consume any type of Tylenol product. Along with stopping the production and advertising of Tylenol, J&J recalled all Tylenol capsules from the market. The recall included approximately thirty-one million bottles of Tylenol, at a retail value of more than $100 million. But the immediate sacrifice in cash also yielded some substantial long-term material return: thanks to the vision and responsibility—the moral purpose—of its leadership, J&J maintained a valuable part of its narrative purpose: its reputation for integrity and commitment to alleviating pain and suffering.

As J&J's example suggests, in order for an organization to serve a moral purpose, it must have moral *leadership*. An organization's narrative purpose must be carried out by leaders with moral character, whose individual or collective inclinations are to preserve a moral dimension of purpose. Not all firms have such leaders. In *The Rise and Fall of Bear Stearns*, Alan C. Greenberg, former chief executive of Bear Stearns, writes that his successor, James Cayne, led Bear Stearns during the time it "expanded recklessly into subprime mortgages and lost any semblance of a serious risk-management function,"[5] all, ostensibly, in the name of higher profits. Thus, Bear Stearns's reputation for risk management disappeared, and so did the firm itself; Cayne's failure of moral leadership lay in hiding risk from investors, losing sight of and damaging the firm's previous narrative purpose.

A Shareable Big Picture

Collectively, an organization's leadership must understand its narrative purpose. Although members of the leadership might have different day-to-day tasks and agendas—managing finances, developing products, handling legal issues, or tackling public relations, for example—they should all have a clear and consistent idea of the "big picture." They should be able to communicate this narrative purpose to the rank and file of the organization and to the general public (consumers, potential clients, and so on). In order to do this, an organization must have its own, often particular or unique language in which its key members are fluent.

Communicating narrative purpose to the rank and file of an organization— the secretaries; midlevel management; the workers answering the phones, tightening the bolts, filing the paperwork—is essential to an organization's success and the mark of a good leader. Not just the leaders of an organization but all its members must have a sense of purpose—an understanding that what they do is important and serves the organization's larger narrative purpose. In the best-selling *Leadership Is an Art,* Max De Pree discusses the importance of giving employees meaningful work—a strategy that De Pree practiced during his tenure as chairman and CEO of furniture maker Herman Miller.[6] The company's success must have been part of the reason that *Fortune* magazine has regularly named Herman Miller one of America's "best managed" and "most innovative," as well as one of the best to work for.

An Underlying Practice Model

Both in the telling and doing of "what it does," an organization should also rely on a model—a necessarily complex representation of how the organization works—in order to achieve its narrative purpose. This **practice model,** a studiously constructed set of guidelines (principles, steps, and practices) for reaching goals, should remain accessible on demand, in order to be ready for mindful change and adjustments as the organization evolves. Among other things, the model allows an organization's leaders to see its unified view. Lack of such a working model was a clear issue at Lehman Brothers, where betrayals and infighting among its leaders—the so-called Ponderosa Boys—brought down the firm and left it unable to cope when disaster struck.[7] Later in this chapter, I will discuss the idea of a practice model as it applies to our ClearFacts team.

When an organization commits to a narrative purpose, it provides itself an opportunity to serve a cause greater than its own self-interest, which becomes the means for its own success and for meaningful, purpose-driven lives for its employees. People who find broader narrative purposes to which they can commit, in their business or their personal lives, feel uplift, purpose, hope, and direction.

PRESENCE OR ABSENCE OF NARRATIVE PURPOSE

Thomas J. Watson Jr., former chief executive of IBM, summed up his view of corporate beliefs: "I firmly believe that any organization, in order to survive and achieve success, must have a sound set of beliefs on which it premises all its policies and actions. . . . [T]he most important single factor in corporate success is faithful adherence to those beliefs. . . . Beliefs must always come before policies, practices, and goals. The latter must always be altered if they are seen to violate fundamental beliefs."[8]

Of course every large organization's narrative purpose will differ from those of other organizations, but at its best, any organization and its narrative purpose might be represented by Figure 7.1. The multiple vertical columns suggest that the organizational narrative purpose needs the support of its various leaders. In turn, individual leaders need support and direction in the form of their own narrative purpose and their own individual model of leadership. While reviewing the figure, consider potential obstacles to sustaining narrative purpose that come from within and from without.

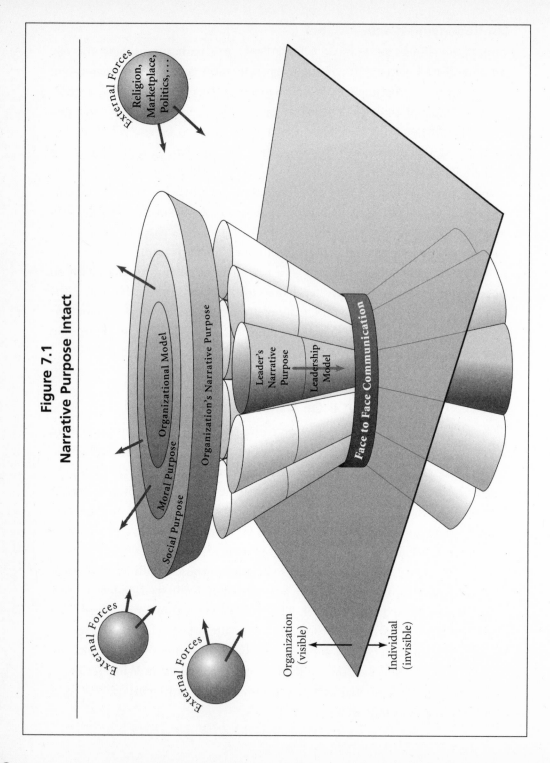

Figure 7.1
Narrative Purpose Intact

External Forces

Religion, Marketplace, Politics, ...

Organizational Model

Moral Purpose

Social Purpose

Organization's Narrative Purpose

Leader's Narrative Purpose

Leadership Model

Face to Face Communication

External Forces

External Forces

Organization (visible)

Individual (invisible)

Obstacles Without

Figure 7.1 includes forces outside the organization itself—in other words, the world we live in, with its many imperfections. These I refer to as *external forces*—such as outside social organizations, the marketplace, or politics. In that world, ideals are likely (or perhaps destined) to break down. This is one kind of obstacle to narrative purpose. Let me provide three examples:

- Planned Parenthood, whose narrative purpose undoubtedly involves securing for women various legal rights related to family planning, often encounters both political and religious opposition. Such opposition might occur at the ballot box or in pushback from such organizations as the National Right to Life Committee or the Catholic Church—whose own narrative purposes are at odds with that of Planned Parenthood.

- The Obama administration, in handling the Great Recession of 2008 and the Mideast uprisings in 2010–11, needed to weigh U.S. policies against the interests of other governments in achieving its narrative purpose.

- Google, whose narrative purpose might (more or less currently) be summed up as "making all the world's information available with a simple Web search," must deal with countless lawsuits, uncooperative or censorious governments (such as China's), and corporate rivals in fulfilling its narrative purpose.

Obstacles Within

Imperfections *within* an organization can also compromise its narrative purpose. One possible flaw might be that an organization doesn't have a strong narrative purpose or reason for being in the first place. More likely, its leaders don't understand the reason or strongly disagree on parts of it.

In the ClearFacts leadership team, for example, Ian finds meaning in Clear-Facts's narrative purpose, but emphasizes bottom-line policies as a means for getting there. Howard's commitment to ClearFacts's narrative purpose is questionable. His personal goals—power and wealth—basically supersede what Clear-Facts is trying to do in the world.

Often when organizations go through a period of change—such as a change in leadership—they lose sight of their narrative purpose or fail to modify and align it with a change in direction. One of the reasons many experts recommend that new leadership rise through the ranks, rather than be imported from outside the organization, is to sustain a company's purpose and moral foundations.

If a company's big story lacks key components (a practice model and moral purpose), its identity suffers, impairing its ability to achieve a fulfilling narrative purpose. This happens when leaders lose track of a company's big story, as happened at Bear Stearns. As I suggested in my earlier reference to Niall Ferguson's book, a narrative purpose without a social or moral dimension—thoughts beyond profit and material success—is unlikely to work in the first place.

Another possibility is that an organization has a coherent articulation of what it "does," but disallows competing models held by its leadership. For this reason, each organization must have internal mechanisms in place to reconcile differences between members of the leadership or to take advantage of these differences. For example, a company that provides medical care may have one leader focused on profits, another on innovation, and another on serving people. These goals are not necessarily mutually exclusive; however, they *can* be if not handled properly. In 2010, fighting in President Obama's inner circle over the Afghanistan war was made quite public, crippling its narrative purpose (which, in this case, was to present a united front against U.S. adversaries).[9]

Yet another problem might be that the organization lacks a "language," or its key members lack fluency in this language. Structural dynamics views failure in communication essentially as a failure of language. The breakdowns in communication it describes among members of a leadership team can be fatal to an organization's narrative purpose. Leaders must be able to communicate effectively with others with different views and profiles, especially in terms of power, affect, and meaning. If an organization does not have a model—a set of principles, steps, and practices—to deal with such language issues, or if its leaders do not have a dynamically unified view of the model, the organization will lack the diversity that must anchor unity of purpose.

Figure 7.2 illustrates how external forces and obstacles within can derail a narrative purpose.

Arthur Andersen: Rise and Fall with Change of Leadership

Not so long ago, the accounting firm Arthur Andersen LLP, cofounded in 1913 by Arthur Andersen, a former professor, was a legendary, ideal organization. In *Executive Wisdom,* Richard Kilburg notes that the historical cornerstones of Andersen's business were "to provide good client service, produce quality audits, manage staff well, and produce profits."[10] This strong narrative purpose, Kilburg writes, "rapidly earned [the firm] a reputation for both competence and ethical

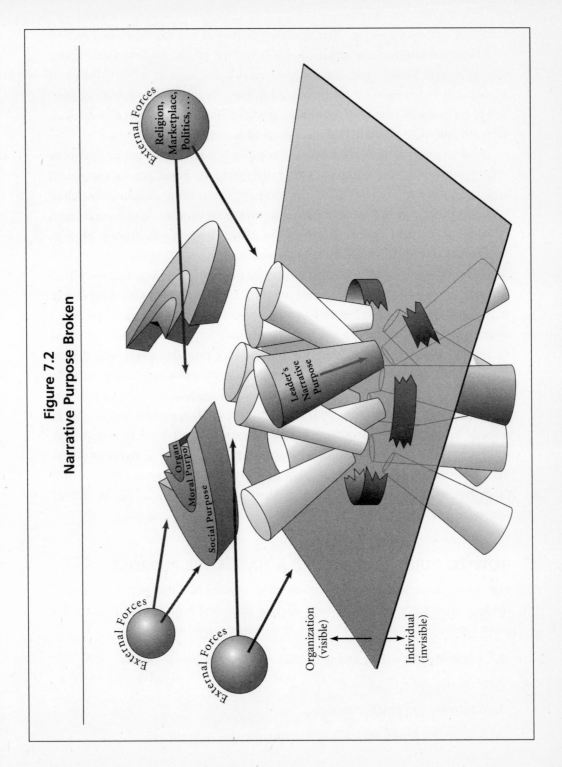

Figure 7.2
Narrative Purpose Broken

External Forces

Religion, Marketplace, Politics, . . .

Organ... Purpo...
Moral Purpo...
Social Purpose

External Forces

External Forces

Leader's Narrative Purpose

Organization (visible)

Individual (invisible)

behavior."[11] Most important here was that *profit* was not the be-all and end-all of Arthur Andersen. As a result of this brand of ethics, Andersen's company over the years became phenomenally successful and earned a "hard-won and generations-old reputation for professional integrity."[12] This reputation continued to serve it well even after Andersen's death in 1947; and Andersen's successor, Leonard Spacek, maintained its successes and growth.

However, after Andersen's death, the company began to expand its portfolio, thus transforming the company's narrative purpose based on its success in accounting, and by the mid-1980s, the company's consulting division, which had become far more profitable than its accounting services, split off to form its own company (eventually named Accenture) in 2000. This was a significant blow to the mother company, which had come to rely on its consulting practice for most of its profits. Joe Berardino, selected by over 90 percent of AA's seventeen hundred partners to head the firm, had gained a reputation for integrity and competence after implementing an agreement that required financial disclosure, but in an attempt to keep the firm's profits high, Berardino, despite his charge, continued to approve types of transactions that "its founder probably never would have authorized."[13] The reason was clear: money. Accounting disasters were eventually exposed, and led to over $300 billion in losses to investors, as well as a national outcry in late 2001 and early 2002. As a result of this scandal—and the inextricably linked loss of narrative purpose—Berardino lost his job, and Arthur Andersen surrendered its licenses to practice as Certified Public Accountants in the United States. Today, the once-great firm founded by the good professor still exists but only nominally—little more than a bad memory in the history of American business.

HOW TO BUILD AND SECURE A NARRATIVE PURPOSE

The Arthur Andersen story demonstrates that a strong narrative purpose is essential to a company's survival. I have already described four criteria to consider when creating or evaluating an ongoing narrative purpose:

1. A purpose that's clear and that reaches beyond financial success

2. A moral, social dimension

3. An underlying practice model

4. A shareable big picture

How to further ensure that your company acquires and maintains its narrative purpose? The primary keeper of a company's narrative purpose must be its executive leader. In line with this, as Coca-Cola CEO Muhtar Kent says, "There are two things . . . a CEO can never delegate. . . . The first is communicating your organization's vision for the future, and the second is ensuring that you are developing the right leaders to execute that vision. Everything about a company's reputation emanates from those two sources of influence."[14]

In times of crisis, a top leader's choices do not necessarily follow straight-line logic, but the goal—finding the right voices to articulate and carry his or her narrative forward—remains the same.

RALPH'S AND CLEARFACTS'S NARRATIVE PURPOSE

Well before coming to ClearFacts, but particularly after Al Gore brought the need for carbon-free fuel to popular attention, Ralph had been on a personal campaign to do something real about the "global energy crisis" and the need for a new national grid. "This is not political or ideological or even ecological alone. It is a matter of survival," he insisted.

Ralph had been in his third year as CEO in a company that, he concluded, profited from the energy status quo and had no interest in adding energy-saving features to the design of new facilities it was planning to build. His entreaties to his board to change direction fell on deaf ears. Around that time, he attended "Davos"—the World Economic Forum, an annual meeting of global political and business elites held in Davos, Switzerland—where he got the welcome ear of a member of the ClearFacts board.

At that moment, ClearFacts was in economic doldrums and desperate to put fresh wind in its sails. "As chairman," Ralph's new fan told Ralph at the end of the hiring process, "I had to twist a few arms, but I prevailed." High on the search firm's list of assessment criteria for a new CEO was that he or she "tell a good story." And Ralph was customarily forthright in his make-or-break, hire-me-or-not attitude when he finally met with ClearFacts's board. The next section is a brief account of what he said, including answers to some well-put questions. Although the rhetoric includes such terms as *mission, vision, plan,* and *strategy,* I will nudge Ralph's language toward our more layered terms, such as *narrative purpose, model, team diversity,* and *social purpose,* some of which were close to the words he used.

Ralph summed up his narrative purpose thus. (In it you will see mention of some of the stipulations he laid down when he was hired, as described in Chapter One):

A firm without a larger social purpose will eventually fail. I would support the long-range goal of carbon-free fuel, which means investing in all promising forms of alternative energy:

A smart grid. This is a short-term goal, not a long-term one. A more intelligent grid will protect the country's power sources from blackout or attack *and* deliver clean alternative forms of energy *and* save money. I think we should support this effort in every way we can.

Leading-edge technology. ClearFacts had been a product-manufacturing company that grew rapidly and then, after acquiring a rival that had been into a new alternative energy product, stalled, likely due to poor management and lack of vision. It hired me as a visionary. The best way to invest in the future is to invest in where the smart, new energy technology is taking place in the world. I would like to beef up that wing of what ClearFacts is doing in this arena. [He was thinking of a new office in Asia and his R&D strategy team.]

A firm without a moral purpose will fail. I point to cyclically predictable scandals in which great companies lose their way morally and fail. This is like building a house on piles of newspaper that will soon enough rot. In line with this goal, I seek

An organization every one of whose members would be treated with dignity, given meaningful work and a place they could voice complaints and be heard. [Ralph had in mind hiring Martha as head of a strong HR department with a reach to every satellite office in the firm.]

A management team with a model. About this I am emphatic. I was introduced to "models" attending training programs in Cambridge, where I also met Duncan. He said that if we needed a model to achieve our larger as well as our profit-making purposes, then we needed a strong leadership team with imaginative strategy, also willing to change and grow individually.

A strategy team. I am not against strategy consultants, whom I have used effectively. But without full knowledge of a firm's intimate culture and workings, strategies from without get lost on shelves or get mangled in internal politics. I am not against using a management team to decide on how to implement strategy, but such teams are often too caught up in managing to effectively do the research. [Ralph had in mind a separate team of imaginative, technically savvy academic ex-pats who, with his "big story" in mind, could help him see where the "action" was. Such a team needed autonomy. Ralph would lead it, bringing recommendations back to the management team for final decisions and implantation.]

Team member commitment to the firm's larger narrative. I recommend the board read an article by Clayton Christensen in a recent issue of the *Harvard Business Review* in which he advises students to find a "clear purpose" for *their own* lives and to commit to "a larger purpose and cause."[15]

The last is easier to do as a student, as Christensen himself was when he wrote the article, but harder when ensconced in the business world and subject to its pressures. However, if a firm's top leaders lack individual commitment to their firm's larger cause, or if their personal goals and models can't be reconciled with the firm's, both larger purpose and model will be at risk.

Ralph had gotten all he'd asked for: a new director of HR, with whom he'd worked before; a coach to help him and his team build their models; and an autonomous strategy investment team he would lead.

When he got his feet on the ground, Ralph felt that the management team he had inherited, plus Martha, functioned relatively well with the usual interpersonal glitches. Still, there were model clashes, which Duncan assured him he would learn how to manage. Duncan opined that these clashes were allowed, if not encouraged, by the open system Ralph sponsored, and that learning from them was far better than driving them underground.

The team's commitment to narrative purpose was another matter. Ralph discovered that individual team members' commitment to his and now the firm's larger purpose varied. Martha and Art were enthusiastic. Clearly, they were distracted by issues at work and home, but were committed nonetheless. Ian, admitting that he was a skeptic about the science of global warming, voiced an interest in principle; for now, his concern was more on the cost than the science.

Ralph sensed correctly that Howard viewed the new company emphasis as a career opportunity. Officially, he'd been given a director role in Office Asia with powers he would stretch beyond investment suggestions that had to be approved by Ian, Ralph, and the team, in that order. At this low-stakes stage, despite minor cracks, the team's purpose, model, and moral compass were more or less solidly in place.

In time, Ralph grew restive. Tired, over-driven, pressed to spend more time at home, but probably wanting more passionate commitment from his team on its green energy cause, he committed an impulsive act in bringing Ron aboard. Although this threw the team into temporary turmoil, they settled down, the foundations of their purpose and model pretty much in place.

The next chapter takes us beyond that point, to where Ralph and members of his team found themselves on high-stakes turf.

From Insight to Action

To maintain direction through the periodic storms they all face, organizations must be guided by a compelling, clearly formed and "tell-able" narrative, which explains the organization's meaning in terms other than financial success. An organization whose narrative purpose does not rest solidly on an equally compelling moral purpose that it demonstrates consistently in actions will fail in the long term, however spectacular its short-term results. A willingness to sacrifice something sacred—money or power in the business organization—is the truest test of an organization's moral purpose.

You, Your Organizations, and Their Narratives

Over time we develop three key narratives: our individual narrative, another for our intimate (couple, family, or other close) system, and one for work. They evolve unevenly in time. All are difficult to formulate and maintain. All are necessary for a full and examined life. Here, with a primary focus on work, are some actions you can take.

Using this chapter as guide, try telling the narrative for all three "organizations," no matter the current stage of evolution in which each narrative finds itself.

- What is or should be the moral purpose associated with each?

- Note gaps between the espoused and displayed narratives.

- What is the relationship between your personal narrative and moral purpose and those of the other two organizations?

Suggestions for Leaders

1. In the agendas of thrice-yearly off-sites, include a thorough review of the health of your organization's "dual" high-level purposes.

2. Conduct an open conversation that invites and gives voice to differences, both as to what the narrative is or should be and what its moral purpose is or should be.

3. If external realities or internal forces have blown the moral ship off course, do not leave the meeting without putting some structure in place to oversee recommended course corrections.

4. At the next off-site, review the success or failure of the recommended corrections.

5. Ask each leader to read, each year, at least one book or any piece of writing that is devoted to moral character and behavior and to reflect on its relevance to her own life and work.

6. In every individual annual review, check to see whether the leader "has a life" with goals in addition to or other than wealth and power.

7. Invite each leader to take one evening a month in which he turns attention away from all work concerns in order to conduct a private review of where he stands on these three questions:

- Is my organization on its avowed narrative track?

- What, if anything, am I doing to steer it off its true path?

- How willing am I to do what is necessary to get back on track even if there is risk in doing so?

Suggestions for Coaches

What applies to leaders applies to you as well. There is an obvious kinship between one's narrative purpose and one's practice model. The former is the story behind the latter. The task of formulating the narrative is easier if you are an independent like Duncan than if you are a member of an organization. It might be said that Duncan left an organization, despite its lavishly rewarding him, because of a disconnect between its narrative and model and his own.

Address the same questions posed for leaders and then ask yourself these questions:

- Does the concept of narrative purpose make sense? Resonate?
- Do I see its connection to models? My model?
- How prepared am I to help the leaders I coach develop their own narratives and models independent of my own?

chapter EIGHT

Leader Behavior in High-Stakes Situations

When stakes are raised, how does your behavior change from how you behave in ordinary times—that is, in low-stakes circumstances?

Chapter Six completed our basic tour of the four-level model of structural dynamics as the four elements appear when life seems relatively normal. In this chapter and the next, we will see what happens as the stakes climb in the minds of members of a team like the one at ClearFacts. We will also see how our behavioral profiles predispose us to fall into certain negative personal behaviors when high-stakes events and conditions *trigger* powerful personal themes. At some point, every leader or consultant has to deal with these high-stakes problems. Whether or not you have probed deeply into Level IV (the level of story and identity), knowing another person's behavioral profile will help you understand what that person is likely to do—and how you are likely to react.

"Stakes" lie within us. Although high-stakes situations can involve large amounts of money or even the fate of an organization, what makes the stakes high in structural dynamics is not the dollar amount or the magnitude of societal outcome. The "height" of *high stakes* is determined by what individuals are feeling and what powerful themes (originating in early childhood and late-adolescent stories) are triggered. Things that "push our buttons" can include *other* people's styles, the *voice* they use in conversation, and their domain or language preferences. (Remember that by *other* I mean persons with different profiles and personal stories.)

This chapter should put you in touch with your own high-stakes triggers and help you see how to enable others to reach that awareness. It should also reveal the kinds of people whose profiles pull those triggers, and the pairings with those "others" that can send you both into circular action and reaction. It should help you consider, when your own reactions go unproductively out of control, how your behaviors may originate in the dark side of your own behavioral profile. But don't be too quick to condemn yourself or others. Keep in mind that the drive and energy of our shadows are what mobilize, motivate, and drive both our best and worst selves in times of crisis—our light and dark sides.

MARTHA'S ERUPTION

Recall the two kinds of stories and themes to which Martha is particularly vulnerable: the undue use of power by others and others' failures to tell the truth. At the weekly team gathering a few weeks after her return from Asia, she sensed strange goings-on during the "business and strategy" part of the meeting. Ralph was showing predictable signs of support for a new acquisition that had been recommended by Ron; but Howard—usually irked by any "good idea" from Ron—was saying strangely little.

Also surprising at the meeting, the decision to sell an acquired company that had failed came up, but received only perfunctory attention. No one asked what due diligence had failed to notice when the decision was made to buy. At that time, Ian had wanted to kill the move, but Ralph's enthusiasm had eventually won the team's support. Contrary to custom, Ian, rather than taking his usual "analyze the situation and learn from it" approach, waved it off with a gesture. Rather than saying "Let's start with what I missed," which was Ralph's way of modeling the taking of responsibility, Ralph seemed distracted. Martha concluded that something other than what was on the table was going on.

To her it was as though they were all moving in slow motion yet tearing through business in record time. It was as if all present were gagged, unable to speak, or determined to say as little as possible. Something was in the air. By no coincidence, other rumblings sounded inside her, related to her own stories and themes: her continuing unease over Lance's broken pact; her now revisited childhood sadness over her father's mortifying protection of his wife's infidelity; and her history-driven, fanatical urge to nail someone who wasn't telling the truth. Right now that urge was aiming at Ian, though it would soon aim at Howard too.

At the shift to the "people and culture" part of the meeting, her inner smolder started to flare. At this point, she asked Ralph for a few minutes in the agenda, though she had not identified the subject. Ralph agreed.

MARTHA: Howard, I have a question: Who is this Template Jones?

HOWARD: He works with me, a kind of special assistant on development.

MARTHA: That's pretty vague. What does he do?

HOWARD: What is this, an investigation? I don't have to answer to you.

MARTHA: I'm afraid you do. I am HR director—

HOWARD: I went through your regional director.

MARTHA: That's okay for a lower-level person, not for a major hire. That comes through this team, and finally through Ian.

HOWARD: I resent this. The team and Ian approved my last budget request. A big item was personnel increase. My office is growing, and showing impressive profits. TJ is helping me make that happen.

MARTHA: Needless to say, I am pissed. Something smells. Ralph, since when does a member of this team or any office director have the power and authority to make a decision of this order without team approval?

HOWARD: I do have it; I have been given wide decision range to grow Office Asia, which is the fastest growing of any.

MARTHA: Ralph? Ian? This is a key procedural issue. This is about decision rights. I want to know whether Art or Ron or I have the authority Howard has assumed. Where the hell is our touted transparency? What he's done is irresponsible.

HOWARD: Don't ever talk to me about irresponsibility. I work hard and I produce. That's what leaders do.

MARTHA: You're no leader in my book. Leaders guide; they do not bullwhip.

HOWARD: Wrong, Martha. What leader of note has not taken a whip to a dumb mule?

RALPH: *(In a loud, cracked voice, almost shrieking)* Whoa! Hold that cursed tongue, Howard! You sound like a slave-master. Not in this firm. Martha, you're not in control. *(Silence follows.)* Sorry, I lost it. There is a blurry margin here. Why not put a stop to the wrangling you two get into and let Ian look into it?

RON: Martha, it's clear that you, and you, Howard, both care about this company, in your own ways.

Thus Ralph, with much needed help from Ron, who was establishing himself as the team's new best bystander, managed to quiet Martha down. At their post-meeting coaching session, Ralph aired his concern, and Duncan tried to explain what had happened.

RALPH: Martha's on a warpath. Her hatchet tongue is drawing blood. I've never seen or heard her like this. You'd think they were enemies she's determined to bury.

DUNCAN: You're thinking linearly again. As you know, neither Ian nor Martha nor Howard nor you is innocent. You have to think circularly about what's been happening in the recent past to understand what's provoking her. She's reacting and acting simultaneously. You're not seeing it all at once, but the whole is there—a vicious cycle spinning out of control.

The Martha-Ian imbroglios and the more recent Martha-Howard donny-brooks that I have covered so far are more common than the professional literature has discussed. I will attempt to give a new perspective on these high-stakes situations and the counterproductive behaviors they elicit.

VOICES, THEMES, AND TRIGGERS

As a trainer, to help my trainees recognize structures, I often say, "See with your ears, hear with your eyes." Earlier in this book I used mainly the metaphors of "seeing" or "reading" the room as a means of noting and naming structures. Now let's switch to the "hearing the room." Why? Because when stakes are high, hearing *voice* becomes central to diagnosing what's going on. That voice begins inside us.

Our High-Stakes Private Voices

Unproductive, out-of-control behaviors in high-stakes situations begin within our own private negative attitudes toward others of different profiles. Our poor behaviors begin with our own private voices, which in turn are influenced by our own behavioral profiles.

Only when pressed are most people willing to express "incorrect" social or political views. We are social animals, after all. Wishing to survive, we do not usually say aloud all we think. However, in high-stakes situations, we express these normally silenced thoughts involuntarily, against our conscious wills. Drawn into open discourse, they vex and incite others to respond in kind. Thus communication in high-stakes situations often turns destructive.

As our own private voices vary from those of others, behavioral profiles can help us sort out these differences. For example, the private voice of someone who is typically closed in affect differs from that of someone who is typically closed in power, and differs even more from, say, someone random in meaning. Table 8.1 briefly describes the differences among such private voices, ever present in

Table 8.1
Private Voices and Behavioral Profiles

The private voice of . . .	in . . .	says inwardly of people . . .	and thinks . . .
Closed	Affect	People drive me crazy when work needs to be done and they can't help talking about feelings.	I wouldn't choose to work in any organization that insists that I discover or express my personal feelings and affections.
Closed	Power	Poor performers should be weeded out early for the good of the whole.	If *I* ran the show, I would banish questionable, untestable, nonsensical slogans like "Real power comes up from the bottom."
Closed	Meaning	I have no patience for people who support endless, indulgent debate of ideas.	If I had unchallengeable authority, I would (hire, recruit) only those who understand and can come to share the ideas behind what we do. I would let go anyone who subverts or doesn't get them.

(Continued)

The private voice of . . .	in . . .	says inwardly of people . . .	and thinks . . .
Open	Affect	One of the best reasons to encourage communication of feelings is that they contribute to the best results in both the short and long runs.	If I called all the shots, I would devote as much training to helping people express relevant "feelings" as to developing relevant "skills."
Open	Power	We should not judge anyone a poor performer without also judging the judge and the environment.	If I held unchallengeable authority, my team at the top would be of diversely talented individuals, each of whom assumes the role of leader when his or her talents best serve the needs of the group.
Open	Meaning	I have little patience for those who dismiss extended dialogue as the best means for us to capitalize on different ideas.	In my ideal workplace, I would include the "radical thinker," who questions everything, and the "true believer," who doesn't question anything, so long as they let the group get its work done.

(Continued)

The private voice of . . .	in . . .	says inwardly of people . . .	and thinks . . .
Random	Affect	I don't care how emotionally wacky people in my unit are—if they do good work.	If I really ruled the roost here, I would collect and protect a small group of people who use their intense emotional range or so-called madness as a source of metaphor and analogy, from whence our best ideas grow.
Random	Power	People who can't tolerate chaos simply do not "get" how really effective work gets done.	"Who in the organization makes the key decisions?" That's a nonissue and the wrong question so far as I am concerned. If a culture rewarded people at every level for making their own decisions, most upper-level people would become superfluous.
Random	Meaning	I have little patience for both fixed ideas that invite no debate and for those endless debates that pass openness off as newness.	In my ideal workplace, I would hang out with people who know that how you get work done is not by "getting work done" but by coming up with new ideas, which may or may not get work done.

our minds. Read it over and think about the differences you hear. Then think about what irritations become uncorked when, under the pressures of rising stakes, we inadvertently loose them on people (in boardrooms or bedrooms) who are truly, inevitably "other."

Attitudes such as those shown in the table prevail in both team and couple systems. When the stakes are raised, those attitudes can migrate from the privacy of our minds to full-scale verbal assaults that are fueled by personal themes. Thus *theme* becomes a central concept in structural dynamics.

Themes

When I turned to discussing personal stories in Chapter Six, I described the source of an individual's resonant themes. By *theme* we generally mean a motif, topic, or subject that occurs in and brings life to various forms of communication— literature, theater, and film among others. In the context of structural dynamics, themes—especially our resonant themes—also bring life to verbal interaction in closely held groups of two or more people.

In structural dynamics, such themes predispose us to be catalyzed or triggered into strong reaction, often emotional in nature and negative in tone. The following is a list of ten more or less universal themes. When salient they can cause events to trigger most people into powerful actions or reactions.

Ten Universal Themes

- Fear of failure
- Fear of being unjustly seen as lacking character
- Fear of radical change
- Fear of poverty or loss of livelihood
- Fear of having one's basic identity questioned
- Fear of being unjustly accused of wrongdoing
- Fear of being publicly humiliated
- Fear of being denied fundamental rights and liberties
- Fear of dying before one's time
- Fear of being discovered as inauthentic—a fraud

Themes from the childhood stories (such as that of imperfect love, described in Chapter Six) accumulate and make their way innocently and more or less inconsequentially into everyday adult conversation, but in high-stakes discourse they erupt. What drives them to explode are the negative shadows we've attached to them (the hidden expressions of our fear that we are unloved or unlovable) and turn on ourselves or others.

I call the *very* high stakes themes that surface in live, high-pressure conversation **toxic themes** to emphasize both the extreme sensitivity individuals have to specific themes and the intensity of their reactions. Some thematic situations hit particularly close to home, often with deadly, venomous force and harmful or pernicious impact.

It is between couples and in closely held groups that toxic themes arise and do their greatest damage. In such groups, a toxic theme can escalate high-stakes behavior into disproportionately extreme attacks, sometimes physical, often with threats of divorce or rupture: "I want out." "I want a divorce." "Our professional relationship is over."

People know their toxic themes when they see them. And when they do, they can plunge into such depths of despair that they feel they can never climb out.

What Makes Situations Personally More High Stakes

As I've just suggested, within an individual, some themes have more power than others; not all are equally charged with energy to arouse, provoke, disturb, and cause the person to be upset. A person's high-stakes themes are strong in this regard. Look back at Figure 6.2, "Shades of Anger and Resulting Themes." This hypothetical but empirically testable figure allows us to assign greater force (potential for arousal in the anger continuum) as we move along each thematic continuum from left to right. From years of clinical and training experience, I suggest three factors that can be at work: the degree of meaning, the love factor, and the ritual factor.

The Degree of Meaning   Most people feel confident recognizing this factor, which involves distinguishing between what is and isn't low, high, or very high stakes for them. The issue here is identity: what matters; what "I" make meaning of; what touches "me"; and what triggers outsized reaction in me, toward the "other," toward my real enemy, or toward my lover-turned-enemy. The reaction to my **nemesis,** that despised polar opposite who, therefore, defines *me* as *his* opposite, is greater still. Identity formation is ultimately a meaning-making activity, and the meanings we make of most things are, crudely enough, a Me versus Not-Me phenomenon.

The Love Factor   Lovers and spouses, those to whom we look for love—in a real or symbolic sense—have more power to influence our behavior than, say, mere friends or less important colleagues. Similarly, if we have some psychological necessity to please a boss (because he is a symbolic stand-in for a parent's lost love), that boss will have more power than will, say, a peer. We burden these real or symbolically empowered figures with answers to the four crowning questions of love: *Was I loved? Am I loved? Do I know how to love? Do I know how to be loved?* When one or more of these questions are involved, the stakes invariably rise.

The Ritual Factor   Virtually all people in close relationships will quarrel. The inevitability of "difference" guarantees it. Of these quarrels, one will surpass all others in meaning because it crucially engages one or more of the four basic questions about love. With repetition, this often "vicious cycle" quarrel takes on a life of its own. In time, it "owns" us. In Chapter Two, I called it the ritual impasse, and in Chapter Six you saw it rise between Martha and her husband, Lance. With repetition and unsuccessful resolution of the conversational impasse, the reaction time it takes that couple to trigger each other has gotten close to zero, and the effect becomes more and more explosive.

We tracked the themes fueling Martha and Lance's ritual battle to two competing views of love (not the whole story, needless to say): for Martha, love's essence is *trust*; for Lance, love's essence is *permission to be creative in all ways.* In the heat of battle, such themes and the stories that contain them always seem irreconcilable. In fact, they can be reconciled, but the effort it takes to resolve them is great with couples, less so with coworkers.

The Relevance of Behavioral Profiles

Although structural dynamics Level IV (story) is where themes reside, Levels I through III are also useful in understanding how themes and situations become truly toxic. Consider impasses like these:

Level I, action stances: a stuck mover who leaves "no room" for a colleague who is slow on the uptake, because a sibling was quicker or more aggressive in the family's dinner-table conversation; or one spouse who, as a stuck bystander, bores the other, who feels disconnected.

Level II, communication domains: an HR director who evaluates recruits on the basis of the capacity to "connect" (affect) rather than on skill sets and competencies (power) when reporting to a boss with an aversion to the language of affect; also, the downsides of the three domains, which I described in Chapter Three.

Level III, operating systems: a division director who operates purely as a random, under the supervision of a closed-system boss. It could be that the director is in the wrong organization, or perhaps that his creative genius would be more useful in R&D than as the interface between a closed-system superior and a mixed team. Also, the downsides of the three system types, described in Chapter Four.

Note that these examples all involve communication between people with different behavioral profiles. All involve, as I put it in Chapter One, *model clashes* in *cross-model conversation.*

All of them also involve what I call negatively tainted *attitudes toward difference.* This is really the root of problems in high-stakes communication. Emotions twine themselves like spiked vines around a provocative word or phrase that someone utters "in the room." From his own behavioral fortress, someone fires a shot. If the situation is pressured, someone else (some "other," seeing and hearing things from a different behavioral profile) fires back from her own behavioral bastion. If the stakes are sufficiently high, an explosive point-counterpoint (move-oppose) sequence ensues. Friends, colleagues, and lovers who are "other"— formerly loved, liked, or tolerated—become enemies, targets of dislike, disdain, and contempt; and the room turns toxic.

Competing Themes and Their Shadows

As I suggested in Chapter Six, the story of imperfect love is the child's first creative act, a personal story of disappointment in love and a story that quantifies the kind and extent of perceived damage. I'll say more later about how the child reckons that *perfect* love will come in adulthood, in the joining of two heroic figures, the truant hero of the child story and a new, adult heroic self.

Experience tells most of us how difficult it is to achieve such an ideal, but that is no longer the problem. The problem henceforth is the "baggage" we carry forward along with our story—the things with which we encumber ourselves in various ways. To explore this, think of our limiting choices of language, how we express ourselves, our means of talking our way to life's two essential goals: love and achievement. In a deeper metaphorical sense, the baggage is also our shadow, especially our dark side, which not only slows us down but actively trips us up.

Here is another way of describing our high-stakes themes: in our pursuit of love and achievement, we carry also a highly charged sensor for words and phrases that, in high-stakes situations, offend our sense of the "right" and "wrong" way to be. Under the pressure of threatening events, individuals' insistence on their own "rightness" also requires that those who are "different" (or "other" in the sense that they perceive the threat differently and use different language in search of solutions) must be "wrong" and therefore deserving of disapproval and, in the extreme, attack. This tendency to attack falls within the dark side of our behavioral repertoire, the home of our shadow.

Through their competing behavioral profiles, paired individuals bring into their relationships competing themes with explosive potential. That potential derives from the shadow baggage that their thematic stories invariably lug along.

FROM HIGH-STAKES BEHAVIORS TO SYSTEMS IN CRISIS

High-stakes behaviors put stress on couples, teams, and other interpersonal systems. The framework in Figure 8.1 shows such behaviors circling out of control.

The rest of this chapter and the next deal with the structural dynamics view of high-stakes and crisis behavior. Six phenomena are at work here:

1. *A critical event takes place*—a catastrophe like the 2011 Japanese tsunami, an unexpected death of a child, the loss of a breadwinner's job, a new boss you are terrified to face. To a degree, "crisis" lies in the eyes of the beholder.

2. *A first continuum: the individual has a gradation of reactions that start internally and, in most cases, are outwardly expressed.* The individual reactions increase in intensity, say from threat to anxiety to fear to panic. Situation matters. Context matters, but so does the self's state of equilibrium, and personal history that results in different ways of handling crises (we address this in Chapter Nine).

3. *A subsequent continuum: relationships are affected between self and key others in one's relevant systems.* These, too, occur in gradations of increasing intensity, from accentuating the sense of others' differences, to discomfort (with

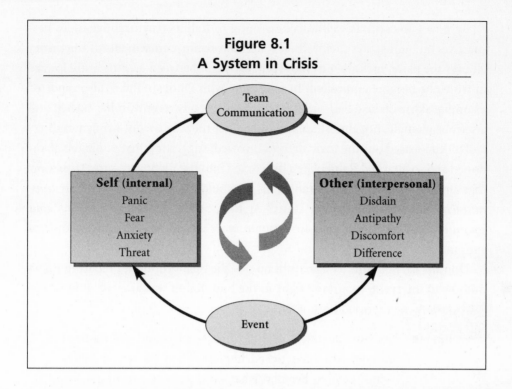

Figure 8.1
A System in Crisis

Team Communication

Self (internal)
Panic
Fear
Anxiety
Threat

Other (interpersonal)
Disdain
Antipathy
Discomfort
Difference

Event

"other") to antipathy to disdain. Seeking explanation of what happened to bring about the crisis prompts blame and moral judgment.

4. *Individuals in the system define an "enemy."* The boundaries between insider and outsider are more rigidly reinforced or are redefined, and the system sets out to address the crisis that threatens the group's identity and narrative purpose.

5. *Inevitably, the system enters a state of disequilibrium.* In well-functioning systems, this state is temporary; the system's leaders draw on their model to provide appropriate mechanisms for dealing with the issues; and eventually stability is restored.

6. *Poorly equipped systems (including those subject to moral desuetude) develop cracks, rupture, or break down completely.*

Work on Ralph's Awareness

The aforementioned framework of events underlies what we will see unfolding both at ClearFacts and in Ralph's marriage.

By now Duncan was well into describing to Ralph structural dynamics perspectives on high-stakes themes, and Ralph was seeing components of the theory all over the place, including in the recent skirmish between Martha and Howard in which he became embroiled. In a meeting with Duncan, Ralph also reported a familiar skirmish he'd had with his wife, Sonia. "Only recently it has turned into a serious wrangle, no, almost an armed conflict the way we got firing away."

Duncan teased out the toxic themes involved, suggesting that Sonia felt abandoned and so attacked Ralph when he worked into the night even after trips away that already exceeded her tolerance. Ralph would answer her saying, "My *commitments* are irrevocably who I am." At that, Sonia would erupt with, "*Your commitments!!* I thought your first *commitment* was to me." They were off and running.

Duncan advised him to wait until he saw the next eruption, preparing Ralph on how to intervene to nip the fight in the bud. Ralph was amazed at how well it worked. As he reported back later,

RALPH: As you suggested, all I did first was bystand, telling her I saw exactly what ticked her off. Then I made a follow action, telling her that what she'd pointed out in me was true, but it was also something *I* don't like about me, either. Then I *invited her to move.* Well, she had a lot to say. I learned a lot I didn't know about her history in relationships. Dunc, it can't always be that easy, can it?

DUNCAN: It *isn't* that easy, Ralph. You're luckier than most. Sonia is more self-aware than most people, including you.

RALPH: So give me the theory that was based on.

DUNCAN: Sorry—you have a way to go before we turn to any theory or model of intervention. For now, just practice what you know until you are more functionally aware.

In Duncan's model, the leader he coaches ideally achieves functional awareness (an understanding of how the structure and patterns of communications in all of his relationships play out in face-to-face relations) before developing his own leadership practice model. Without thorough awareness, the leader lacks adequate control over *the* key component of his practice model: the role of *self* in what he sees and how he acts on what he sees—be it "in the room," in larger rooms, or on the world stage.

In high-stakes situations, self-knowledge about one's low-stakes behavioral profile is still important but not sufficient. *In high-stakes situations,* a leader's best efforts can be foiled and miserably fail him. He therefore must be aware of his shadow and take responsibility for it; know the role behavioral propensities play in his and others' reactions in high-stakes situations; be able to grasp how different people with different profiles will react differently; and manage his team *system* and himself in that system even in the midst of crisis.

Learning to Listen to Voices

Uniquely, structural dynamics calls attention to a wide range of voices heard "in the room" that allow leaders and their coaches to recognize (diagnose) constructive and destructive communication structure.

Earlier in this chapter, I spoke of "seeing with one's ears." In Chapter Two, I noted that *voice* refers to the underlying manner, pitch, rhythm, tone, and other nuance speakers give to their words, and that voice can help us identify, for example, the speaker's action stance. Leaders should pay sharp attention to the voicings of others for what they tell of those people's meanings and intentions, and to their own voices for how those they intend to influence will hear them. Voice is subtle. It is also, as poet Jane Hirshfield says, "the underlying style of being that creates a poem's rounding presence, making it continuous, idiosyncratic, and recognizable."[1]

Is yours the voice of authenticity, of modest wisdom, of fertile curiosity? Or of disinterest, of skepticism, of elitism, or of bullying or disdain? At this point I would like to deepen your sense of voice with the concept of **vocal signature.** The structural dynamics model suggests essentially nine vocal signatures, each one deriving from the combination of one of the three basic operating systems and one of the three communication domains. So, for example, if you are functioning comfortably in an open system in affect, that preference strongly shapes the vocal signature you project.

In low-stakes situations, you may employ many different vocal signatures. In higher-pressure circumstances, however, your range of signatures narrows to conform with your basic behavioral profile. At high-stakes moments, your vocal signature also takes on the imprint of your shadow—the light and dark imprints of fear and desire that stem from your deepest stories. In short, in escalating, circularly caused miscommunications with "other(s)," your basic vocal-signature-plus-shadow takes over and becomes *how you are heard.*

"Get that report to me by the end of the day" is the unmistakable sound or vocal signature of closed power, even in low-stakes mode. But when you hear a closed-power person label a subordinate in public as "a complete incompetent," the subordinate hears the theme of "being publicly humiliated" (one of the ten universal themes listed earlier) and feels the moral tone and anger of the closed-power speaker's shadow.

Sender Voices, Receiver Reactions   Negative vocal signatures are likely to trigger anger in the person ("receiver") hearing any one of them. The following list is not exhaustive but offers a sampling of themes a sender may express that are likely to trigger strong reactions in receivers.

Themes That Trigger Reactions

- Having to interact with one's "fear opposite," one's nemesis
- Being degraded or humiliated when one can't strike back
- Seeing someone being degraded or humiliated in public
- Being suppressed or restrained in the freedom to act
- Having one's creativity stifled or squelched
- Being told one is a failure or incompetent
- Having to engage in pseudo-intimacy
- Living or working with someone who habitually lies or deliberately distorts the truth
- Witnessing violence, torture, or the rendering of physical harm
- Witnessing the unjust treatment of the powerless
- Witnessing cowardice or the fear of risk
- Betrayal of others for any personal gain
- Fear of loss of control
- Fear of chaos or anarchy
- Having one's feelings dismissed or belittled
- Witnessing or experiencing loss of emotional control
- Fear of displeasing a loved "other" or valued authority figure

- Being subjected to the exercise of absolute authority
- Having one's truths or ideas prohibited or revoked
- Being involved in or witnessing intense conflict with others
- Being called shallow or superficial
- Being with people who disguise ideology as ideas
- Being with people who are ambitious for financial gain only
- Being with people who evidence "eccentric," "bizarre," or "freaky" behavior
- Being with people who are inauthentic or phony, or who make false claims
- Being denied the right to be heard (feelings, ideas, solutions)

Watching Shadows   Structural dynamics seeks to separate itself from pathogenic explanations of behavior and to find a balanced view of the shadow's contribution to behavior, particularly in high-stakes circumstances, which typically *do* trigger verbal shadow behavior in the form of disapproval, attacks, criticism, censure, denigration, or blame. Remember that all of us have light and dark sides. Even "saints," stars, and cultural heroes, people whose light sides we exalt, have shadows, as do leaders and their consultants.

In my practice, I ask leaders to get to know *and* take responsibility for their own shadow and the impact their dark side may have on others. When they do so, their light side also emerges, flourishes, and is recognized. Only as the individual claims ownership and responsibility for his or her own behaviors can such change come about.

Escalation

In situations where the stakes are high for at least two players, **escalations** can occur in which someone "blows his top." What makes him "dangerous" is his potential for verbal and, at times, potentially physical violence. As the escalation spirals upward, energy and volume are driven upward by more and more debasing, denouncing, and intimidating moral judgments. What begins as *intolerance for difference* ends in the language of disdain and contempt, often accompanied by threats and other violent actions: "You're fired!" "I want a divorce!" "Get out of here before I . . . !"

Tops can blow in any context in which players are seriously invested in self, in other players, and in outcome; and, of course, these explosions are often triggered by themes transmitted by the "other." Such escalations are most common in intimate relationships where love and identity are directly at stake, but anyone who has been party to what happens in the "back room" knows that politics and business are not exempt. The principal driver of this escalation is one's **moral voice.** Its prevalence in high-stakes situations almost earns it the right to be called a fourth language territory in high-stakes settings: a "moral domain."

Noise An important attendant of escalation—its final phase, in a sense—is **noise.** By *noise* I mean the din that causes us no longer to hear the words of the "other." What we hear, if anything, is the roar and screech of our own voice. An escalation may begin with an exchange like, "What *you* said caused *me* to react as I did." "No, damn it, what *you* said caused it all!" But it ends in senseless threats of divorce or of being fired, or sometimes in physical violence between spouses or between parents and children. Or short of that, but no less tragic for communication, the noise level rises until someone cries uncle, or the resounding din itself silences all.

The most common "cause" of noise (cause is usually circular in origin, remember) is a mismatch in profiles, with their underlay of triggering themes and their shadows.

Mismatches in a Business Setting One of the most famous business mismatches in recent times ended in the "corporate divorce" between Steve Jobs and John Sculley at Apple computer in the 1980s, which began as an idolizing business romance but escalated to demonization in just two years.[2]

Some mismatches—like closed power versus random power—are so fundamental that clashes will occur in just about any context. In the context of a college philosophy department, meaning will be central to discourse and to communication clashes. In the military, power is at the center of discourse. Central to discourse in the Vatican, a rather special religious setting, is meaning as power, with closed-system features. From among many, each institution chooses its own battlegrounds.

From among more numerous possible mismatches, I will elaborate here on three that apply at ClearFacts and that occur often in other business settings and in organizations that consult to them, as well as other institutions (educational, for example) seeking fiscal savvy and profit:

- Closed power versus random power
- Closed meaning versus open meaning
- Closed affect versus open affect

One reason that all three mismatches I have chosen involve the closed-system preference is that the closed system is the backbone of most large business organizations and occupies the core of preferred leader characteristics. A second reason is that a mismatch between a closed system and any other system type most dramatically and visibly highlights differences.

Figures 8.2, 8.3, and 8.4 show language that each mismatched stance and domain uses to trigger the other's reactions, in escalating sequences. I focus here on words or phrases alone to encourage you to train your ear to listen for and recognize them in the room. Also note that in the heat of the moment, obscene, denigrating, and assaultive adjectives and nouns almost always accompany the triggering words.

Once sensitized to what triggers both one's own self and the self of some "other," our "hearing" becomes more acute. The very words people use are clues to their critical childhood stories and the typical preferred structures these stories

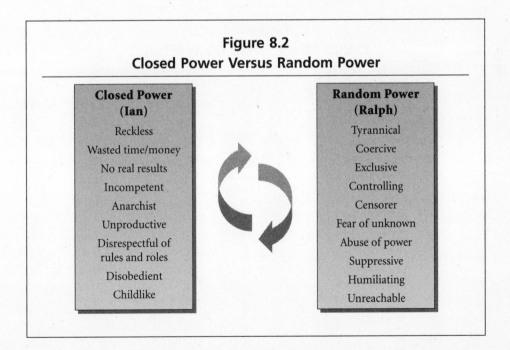

Figure 8.2
Closed Power Versus Random Power

Closed Power (Ian)	Random Power (Ralph)
Reckless	Tyrannical
Wasted time/money	Coercive
No real results	Exclusive
Incompetent	Controlling
Anarchist	Censorer
Unproductive	Fear of unknown
Disrespectful of rules and roles	Abuse of power
Disobedient	Suppressive
Childlike	Humiliating
	Unreachable

Figure 8.3
Closed Meaning Versus Open/Random Meaning

Closed Meaning (Howard)	**Open/Random Meaning (Arthur)**
Meaningless prattle	Shallow, superficial
Poetic nonsense	Narrow-minded
Reason in circles	Unimaginative
Lost in ambiguity	Without values
Irrational, illogical	Only one truth
Cognitive dissonance	Nothing but numbers
Mental chaos	Warped judgment
Space cadet	Sinister secrecy
Disconnected ideas	Constipated mind
Where's the data, stupid?	Idea killer
	Dishonest

Figure 8.4
Closed Affect Versus Open Affect

Closed Affect (Ian, Howard)	**Open Affect (Martha)**
Whining	Inhumane
Lunatic hysterics	No compassion
Pseudo-intimacy	Heartless
Out of control	Motherless
Heartthrob	Cold
Softness	Untouchable
Melodramatic	Insensitive
Thin-skinned	Thick-skinned
Insufferable victim	Emotional tormenter
Emotional invasion	Abuser

have promoted: their behavioral profiles and propensities; how these sound in low stakes; and, most important, how they trigger reaction when the stakes are raised, at which point the sounds (voicings) are unmistakable.

ANOTHER DONNYBROOK BETWEEN MARTHA AND HOWARD

Martha had been suffering from insomnia and had entered a period of drinking too much at home after work. She wasn't keeping up with her friends, a source of nurturance for her. She was angry at Ian; disappointed in Ralph, who had been on the road too much; and obsessed with Howard. Lance was relieved to be out of the line of fire. Wanting to make up for his faux pas, but knowing her touchiness at times like these, he tried to post himself at just the right distance, close enough to let her know he was "there," but outside her "fussiness zone," which he knows all too well. They squabbled, but he managed to keep the lid on.

In the meantime, Martha had her eye on Howard's every movement, her ear on every word, her senses open to every mood. Whenever he mentioned TJ, she was on him. How Howard managed to keep his cool impressed her. She meant to make him squirm, but was failing.

Martha decided to turn to Ron. Over time they'd gotten close; in fact, in this period of personal strife, he had replaced her friends as a source of outside connection and nurturance (affect).

"I see what Ralph sees in you, Ron," she told him. But it was reciprocal. Finding it easier to share his personal life with Martha than he expected, Ron let her elicit his childhood story and was grateful that she did.

"And I see what Ralph sees in *you*, Martha," he said.

Then Martha opened up further: "Let me speak the truth, Ron. I have an ulterior motive. I want your help in getting the truth about what's going on in Asia. When I was there I met your fiancée, Lani. She told me all she knew, but knows enough to mind her business. The whole atmosphere reeks of poison, worse than sulfuric acid. You won't believe this, but when I got to the hotel after my visit, I threw out the clothes I'd been wearing—my best dress, damn them. I want Lani's help."

Ron surprised her. "I spoke with Lani after your visit, and I have her permission to tell you what she told me. Lani was among the women who sent the anonymous e-mail. At the time, sexual predation on Howard's part was rampant.

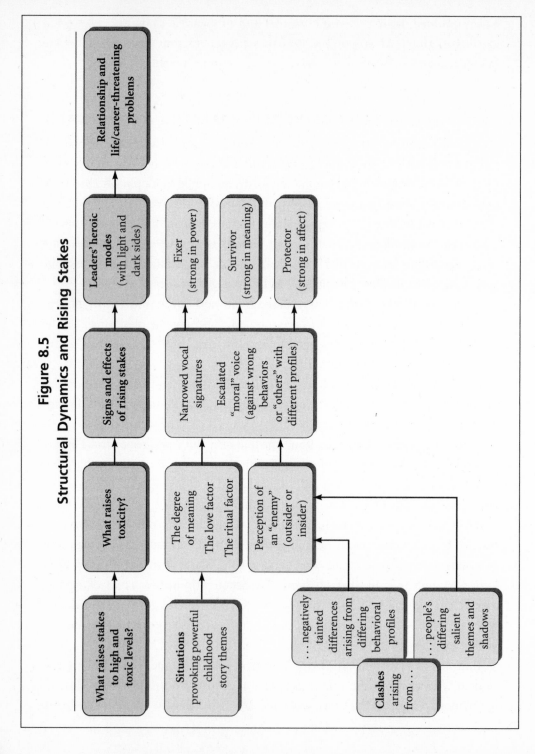

Figure 8.5
Structural Dynamics and Rising Stakes

Since your visit, Howard and TJ have been behind closed doors a lot more than usual. Also, Howard's added spikes to his iron fist. Both men and women feel and are acting like they're in police state."

Martha swore herself to keep from Howard what she now knew, until the appropriate time. But she couldn't keep the lid on her hatred of the man. During a private meeting to exchange views on a new hire, a chance remark by Howard released her pent-up emotion. Howard, finally showing his darkest side on the home front, was anything but a pushover. Here is a sample of the words each used in their explosive point-counterpoint confrontation: *outright liar–nosey sleuth; pleasure in causing pain–bleeding heart; ruthless ambition–emotional basket case; sexist con man–whiney bull-dyke; cruel prick–angry bitch.* Both knew a large explosion was coming, but for now they escalated together until they both were worn down in noise and stony silence.

Figure 8.5 serves as an overview of the preceding discussion and hints at where Chapter Nine will take us.

From Insight to Action

Few things are more important for leaders and coaches to know about themselves than what triggers their high-stakes behaviors and how they behave in these high-pressure times. For leaders, being deaf and blind to these forces and their impacts impairs their judgment, leads to poor or morally tainted decisions, and undermines or intimidates those whose very support they need in order to lead well.

For coaches, such deafness leads to misdirecting those they coach and burying truths leaders need to hear if they are to lead well. Without such knowledge, both leaders and coaches tend to mishandle the power given to them by their positions.

Your High-Stakes Behaviors

Knowing your high-stakes behaviors and what triggers them, through self-knowledge and feedback from others, is critical to managing others' high-stakes behavior.

What You Know About Yourself

1. Select from among the high-stakes themes cited in this chapter the ones that most apply to you. As a way to begin taking ownership, write them down and then reflect on the damage they do to you and others.

2. Identify a recent experience you would categorize as high stakes because of your strong overreaction. How would you describe your behavior? Was this reaction familiar to you?

   - What theme triggered your reaction?

   - Can you track your reaction to a story from the past?

   - What tone of "voice" got to you? Is this familiar?

   - Is there a story here, too?

3. Leaders must understand their darkest sides. What are yours?

4. Describe a recurring situation that triggers your darkest shadow behaviors. What is at stake for you? How does your behavior in this situation raise the stakes for others?

5. Just knowing your nemesis reduces the toll this figure exacts from you. What is your nemesis's behavioral profile? Would you consider that half the problem comes from one of your structure-forming stories?

What Others Say About You

Take as much time as you need to reflect on what you believe others say about you.

1. Discuss those beliefs with at least two peers who know you well and are not afraid to speak the truth. Listen openly when your view and theirs do not agree.

   - What do they say is your most horrendously objectionable behavior in high-stakes times?

   - Specifically ask, "Do I invite and welcome critical feedback? How hard is it for you as a peer to tell 'the truth'?"

2. Ask a subordinate or report, "What is it I do to make you behave in ways neither of us likes?"

3. Ask yourself, "How do I use hierarchy and my place in it to upend or undermine healthy power relations?"

Reading the Room

Skillfully reading the room and facilitating high-stakes behavior are enhanced when leaders and coaches have a sense of participants' profiles and the themes that trigger shadow and other high-stakes reactions. After establishing your "diagnosis," test it in a subsequent meeting.

For Leaders

1. The action exercise for Chapter Five asked you to chart the low-stakes behavioral profiles of group members. Very likely, you are now more aware of how behavioral profiles contribute to and detract from productive conversation and effective decision making.

   In high-stakes situations, people's behavioral profiles tend to detract, at times to breakdown, levels. Begin to pay attention to how *internal dynamics* influence high-stakes behavior. Chapter Nine will deal with *external* influences.

   - Are you able to predict, on the basis of mismatching profiles, who will clash with whom when the stakes are raised?
   - Are the dark sides of one or both players already in evidence?
   - Can you identify the themes each is sensitive to and the stuck actions that spur escalations? Can you "sense" childhood stories in play?

2. At upcoming meetings,
   - Try to predict and test your predictions. Did you see trouble looming before it happened?
   - The next time trouble does arise, step in. A strong bystand that seeks to bridge differences is your best bet. But do not be dismayed if the problem reappears.[3]

Knowing how to step into a volatile field with a precise *action* to defuse escalating sequences is integral to communicative competency, but to do this you must first learn to read the room with diagnostic and structural accuracy.

For Coaches

Everything said about leaders and high-stakes behavior applies to you, too, as it does to everyone else. But there is one additional high-stakes issue special to you as a coach: occasionally having to tell *uninvited truths* to a leader who has the power to ignore or fire you.

1. The issue raises questions about your *personal* model:

   • How comfortable are you with power in general?

   • Do certain profiles threaten you or put you off?

   • What about leaders who have unacknowledged shadows?

   • What do your own profile and formative stories have to do with these effects?

2. The issue also raises questions about your *practice* model:

   • Does your model include technical guidelines for dealing with resistance of various forms and intensities?

   • Have you ever knowingly compromised your model and its principles in the name of expediency? Out of fear?

   • Would you be willing to rewrite the compromising scenario in order to design a more desirable outcome?

chapter NINE

The Heroic Leader in Crisis

In Chapter Eight, I described how rising personal stakes and toxic themes escalate our voices into tense moral registers. This chapter continues that theme of moral voices, extending it to the heroic modes that leaders don when they see the stakes as very high. These are important dynamics for leaders to acknowledge in themselves and to recognize in other leaders with whom they interact.

When leaders perceive a state of crisis, they take on one of three mantles or postures of moral justice based on their own deep stories and behavioral profiles: *prosecutor, adjudicator,* or *advocate.* In concert with these postures, they also begin to express themselves in one of three distinctive *heroic* modes, based on the shadows of their strongest story themes and on the kind of hero who stands at the heart of resolving their own story of childhood loss. The basic types are *fixer, survivor,* and *protector,* illustrated in Figure 9.1.

Thus Ralph will perceive and project himself as a certain kind of moral agent and a certain style of hero; so will Martha, Ian, and the others. These transformations will generate specific chemistries between them—good or awful and largely unavoidable. Redemption comes from the fact that every actor can do her best to become more conscious of what she is doing and moderate the worst effects of these actions. Thus much can be gained by keen awareness of each actor's behavioral profile and his or her deepest story problem. Right now, let's catch up on events at ClearFacts.

THE CRISIS MOUNTS AT CLEARFACTS

At the end of Chapter Eight, we saw that Martha had unleashed her tongue on Howard, after Ron had substantiated the truth of the formerly anonymous e-mail that had mentioned morally outrageous doings at Office Asia. Now strong moral

Figure 9.1
Heroic Types in Crisis

stances were coming into play. From here on, the ClearFacts story would unfold dynamically, like a case coming to trial, with two enemies "in the dock"—one *insider* (Howard) and one *outsider* (TJ).

Apart from alarms that Martha was sounding now about the Asia office, Ian had had his own suspicions of wrongdoing there. He decided to turn to the books he himself oversaw, before examining the books that Howard's man, TJ, was keeping in Asia. *There must be a pattern here; there always is*, he thought.

Agitation: a new state for Ian. Out the window went his usual habit of finishing every last bit of work by six and taking nothing home. Instead, he began to return to the office after dinner. And the change of routine paid off; he did indeed sense something fishy in the accounts, though he wasn't sure what was wrong. The numbers added up, but their patterns were too pat. He saw enough to tell him that his next logical step was to go to Asia to look at TJ's books.

Ian discussed his findings and plans with Duncan as a sounding board, who suggested he take them to Ralph and, depending on the outcome of his trip, to the board. Duncan saw Ian's coming to him first as a gesture of trust and the beginnings of a change in Ian. In this talk with Duncan, Ian implied that until recently he had regarded Duncan as an outsider, but that had changed.

Duncan wisely brushed off the compliment: "Thank you. Ian. But in my experience, the insider-outsider complex is fragile, especially in tough times. I suspect you will see much more of this in Asia."

When Ian moved on to speaking with Ralph, his CEO approved the Asia trip but insisted that Duncan accompany Ian "to size up the system." In the meantime,

Ian asked for time to complete his own stateside inquiry before letting Ralph (with his commitment to transparency) announce the impending visit, not at the *next* ClearFacts weekly meeting, but at the one that followed. Thus Martha would know nothing about the trip until two weeks later, when it was announced.

In the interim, before the announcement and unaware of Ian's plans, Martha got into another ugly scuffle with Ian, continuing the escalating mutual frustration and clash between them of themes and shadows.

"Why are you letting Howard off the hook?" she demanded.

"I'm doing no such thing," said Ian. "I refuse to falsely accuse anybody."

Martha grabbed his lapels. "You're not telling all! I've been told you're coming back to the office at night. Why?"—which morphed into her accusation, "You won't speak the damn truth."

Now Ian was triggered. Here, like his mother, was another spineless woman pushing back emotionally with a form of blackmail (never mind that his view completely misunderstood his mother's form of protective love). "Fairness levied toughly" was the note he'd taken from his father. Slowly removing her hands, eyes beaming with disgust, he said, "Stop pestering me, damn you. I could swat you like a summer fly."

To that, Martha released an unbroken string of obscenities such as only Lance had heard until now.

Ian spat back. "You've got a dirty mouth, Martha. You're acting like an undisciplined, entitled, demanding, spoiled child."

Coming out of that encounter, both naturally muzzled their own behaviors at the next team meeting. Even regarding some vital people issues in the Canada office, Martha, the team's moral conscience, remained strangely quiet. Ian, too, seemed off his usual game. Where was Ian's usual slow, grinding logic that blew holes in reckless risk taking? Though guardian of the company's bottom line, he let slip by without comment another hint of reckless spending proposed by Howard and unchecked by Ralph. At Ralph's debriefing with Duncan, the coach called attention to these clues that Ralph had missed.

"Martha's and Ian's unusual behaviors raised eyebrows," he pointed out. "You might have said something."

Ralph didn't reply, but he knew that Duncan was reminding him of a lapse from a broader structural dynamic role that the coach had recommended: *Whenever speech patterns in the room take an unexpected turn, and no bystander names it, you, Ralph, as nominal leader, should name it.*

At the Monday meeting when the trip was finally announced, Howard showed no signs of alarm or culpability. About its prospects, Martha had mixed feelings, because hadn't she already gone to Asia and come back with nothing? But she held her tongue.

More Background on Template Jones

Beyond the thin description Howard gave of Template Jones that we saw in Chapter Three, Howard's assistant director of Office Asia can be seen as an inveterate "fraudster."

TJ, as he preferred being called, was formerly a Wall Street banker, already rich at thirty-seven, who, wanting to "give back," signed on with ClearFacts, a "company with a noble cause," and was willing to work "offshore," as he put it to Howard, who'd already wanted to hire him.

In order to clarify the dynamics, I next relate some information that TJ volunteered to Duncan later, after the fraud had been confirmed but prior to TJ's final separation from ClearFacts.

To begin with, TJ thought his mother was "weird, the most off-beat female, a mad scientist." As a result, he could not talk about his mother as other kids did. His father was, if anything, a worse-off figure, no hero for the son to emulate or boast about. Through years of domination under the weight of his wife's ceaseless "rata-tat-tat," the father grew catatonically silent and virtually invisible. No friends or peers of the father ever crossed the threshold of the family home. In the parents' frequent bouts, the father never came close to winning. Even the given name "Template," TJ was told, had resulted from an unfriendly prank by his mother after a parental battle, when she had declared, "I mean to shape him in *my* image."

In primary school, TJ stood out as a genius, a wizard in mathematics thanks to his mother's genetic gift and an encyclopedic memory that made every subject a breeze. As TJ put it, "My mother taught me math tricks that made me seem like an eight-year-old magician. My memory did the rest."

Would he share these gifts?

"Not on your life. At age twelve, I understood power."

Well, in secondary school, he did share—not freely but for sex. Avoiding girls as smart as he or who could give him a run for his money, he turned to beauties who struggled academically. For a "price," he would tutor, write papers, and even take exams when gender identity could get lost in a crowd. At UC

Berkeley, this same "no-brainer" strategy added a sexual surfeit to his straight-A average.

He greased his way into Harvard Business School with a carefully planned business apprenticeship. "Take me free," he'd told the company recruiter at the job that came before HBS. "It's your credentials I want." He scooted through Harvard Business, invisible in most respects, but getting the grades that next got him instantly onto Wall Street, riches, and then ClearFacts Asia.

Ian and Duncan in Asia

During the flight to Asia, Duncan and Ian coordinated their plans: Duncan was to get a reading on TJ's and Howard's sexual habits as were intimated in the anonymous e-mail; Ian was to investigate their financial practices.

Ian's encounter with TJ would not be easy, but something was wrong and he was determined to find it, if only through the stubbornness of the morally righteous. He sized up Jones as one of those people of infinite confidence who are unaware that they might have ever lost a battle. Ian knew those men. His books of military lives were full of such invincibles' eventual falls from power.

In the Asia office, Ian pored over Jones's books, met with him, went back to the books. Talked with him more. He noticed that Jones never bothered to ask the purpose of the visit—what, if anything, Ian was looking for—so self-assured he was. At one point Ian was tempted to plant his father's fist in TJ's smirking mouth when TJ told him mockingly, "Sir, I've got everything you'll find in those books right up here in my head. Every last detail. Just ask."

What TJ said to Ian, and what Ian heard in the flexing of TJ's intellectual muscle was, *It's there; find it if you can.* So Ian proceeded to ask. And ask. Not for number details, but in search of the cracks he sensed in Jones's armor of deception. (Experiencing waves of growing distrust, Ian thought of Martha, and smiled inwardly.)

And Ian did find it, by sheer persistence: TJ's new, amazingly sophisticated algorithm and code for creative bookkeeping. In Ian's opinion, Bernie Madoff's Ponzi scheme and bookkeeping sleight of hand were unsophisticated by comparison. After telling TJ he'd been found out, Ian sighed and added, "And you'll try this scheme or something even better wherever you go next, won't you?"

TJ smiled. "Bet your f—g ass. But, Maxwell, what you don't get is that it's all a game. Corporations aren't ruled by right or wrong. They're ruled by winners or losers. I play to win." TJ showed off the full-faced look of a fraudulent mind.

"Look closely at my books; look at my financial draws. I took nothing. ClearFacts gained until this one blip, when it didn't."

Ian lapsed into a deep silence. To TJ, he said nothing more. To himself he thought, *I'm looking for what is right about what this fraudster is saying. Fraud has become old news. Don't I, like many, read with interest about the next scandal, then turn to other things?*

Afterward, Ian began to see new meaning in who profits and who loses in the face of fraud. In fact, Howard was the only one who had "profited," and only in terms of possible future career, not money. ("Just let me loose," TJ had told Howard, "and I'll speed your race to CEO.") Ian noted that what Template Jones had tried to do was to prime Howard's pump of advancement. *And we let it happen. We reaped the benefits in the form of ill-gotten profits at our clients' expense.* And in Ian's view, it wasn't Howard but ClearFacts that would suffer the potential loss—not financially, so far as he knew yet—*but in its image, its narrative purpose, its moral purpose, its very reason for being.* Ian had a lot to think about.

Meanwhile, Duncan had been sleuthing elsewhere. Bypassing TJ and Howard entirely, he simply had allowed their assistant, Terry, to become his "guide" and unintentional informant. Duncan's most important agenda was finding out what the sexual innuendos in the now infamous e-mail amounted to.

"What are their lives here like?" he asked Terry. "Where do they go for entertainment? What kinds of entertainment?"

"So . . . you want to see the town?"

"Very much. Um, but as tourist, Terry, shall we say, not as participant, thank you."

By the end of that Dionysian evening, Duncan had learned more from a very drunk Terry than he could have from Howard and TJ themselves. Terry had been hoping to get some things off his chest about what "offshore" meant to TJ. It meant "off the radar screen," where TJ and the big boss Howard could "engage in serious play." At the end of the night, Duncan's head was filled with sexual matter even *Playboy* and *Hustler* would shy away from. For TJ and Howard, Asia was the perfect playground . . .

Back alone at his hotel he did not sleep well, not for conscience's sake, but for the inordinate amount of booze he'd shared in the course of loosening the young man's willing tongue. What would his wife say if she found out! What would Ralph say! What would *Ian* say! Never mind! Now he understood the import of that e-mail!

On the trip home, Duncan and Ian did not discuss what each had found, though Ian contemplated aloud, long and stirringly, on the might of the military mind.

Back Home: Proceedings

Back home, Ralph debriefed the pair and posted an e-mail to his team that set the stage for an internal inquiry into ClearFacts Office Asia:

> Like the rest of you, I am outraged by what happened, but want to share two concerns. First, that no one outside ClearFacts has been or will be hurt financially. I have instructed Ian to make amends in any client's favor wherever a question of loss exists. Cost is not at issue; our reputation is. Second, that we conduct the inquiry with grace. Having said that, however, I am not asking you to stuff your feelings. My own are profound. My entire sense of purpose has been put at risk.

The proceedings took three full days. The team (Ralph, Ian, Martha, Ron, and Arthur) and Duncan spent the first day reviewing Ian's and Duncan's experiences. Howard was not present. Informed by Ralph that he was not invited to this first meeting, Howard simply nodded inscrutably. "The man's cool; or whatever it is, it's impressive," Ralph mused. The questions were, What had Ian and Duncan found? What decisions should follow? and What could the firm learn for the future? In concluding his opening statement, Ralph said, "I don't mean to quash your feelings; it is hard to rein in my own. But ranting is not our primary purpose; reflection is."

On day two, TJ was required to attend in person, but Howard was not. Ralph wanted them treated separately, particularly because TJ had not yet directly implicated Howard—nor did TJ do so on that day. It wasn't clear whether his silence was a moral act, though it did protect Howard.

"Perhaps," Duncan reflected, "he just didn't want to share credit for the brilliant scheme he had concocted. That's not beyond his character as I now understand it."

Ian put it differently: "It is all about ego. He's still playing 'the game.'"

Day three was devoted to interviewing Howard.

"As for the purpose of this meeting," said Ralph, "it's not only about TJ and you, Howard. I suggest we see it as an opportunity for everyone in the room to learn something about the part we each played in bringing the company's reputation to the brink."

More or less successfully, the group focused on a systematic analysis of moral breeches in today's corporate culture, and on a thorough exploration of where, through their own fraud incident, ClearFacts stood on the issues. Remarkably, the emphasis here remained pretty much on the "case," though here and there tempers roiled against the individuals involved.

After the meeting, Duncan praised Ralph, saying, "I think you did the right thing in encouraging your team to keep a lid on their feelings. They won't be able to after today, of course—nor will you, I fear. The attempted fraud, as you said, puts the company's entire identity at risk. You and your team are in crisis."

ENEMY AND "OTHER"

Structural dynamics has much to say about how to understand what hit the team and how they were likely to react. The following summarizes what structural dynamics says about what leaders must *have* in such crisis situations, where individuals such as Howard or TJ are identified as "enemy." What happens will depend in part on whether the offending individual is perceived and treated as coming from inside or out.

America's response to 9/11 reflects how firmly embedded in our broader collective consciousness is the threat of an "enemy" doing catastrophic damage. Our instinctive reaction, unconscious and conscious, is to be ready for attack and revenge. Overall, the *leader in crisis* emerges as a response to the *enemy other*—inside or out.

The term *other* calls attention to the importance of structural dynamic differences and the language we use to achieve shared goals. I used it in showing how perception of difference turns to intolerance when the stakes are raised. Crisis deepens our sense of *other*; the reaction to the "other" evokes fear and hostility, acts of terrorism and counterterrorism, and morally motivated assassination.

Thinkers in literature, philosophy, anthropology, and other fields have long since explored notions of "otherness," particularly where the "other" is seen as the outsider, the stranger, the alien, the subversive, the radically different. What is unique to structural dynamics is a perspective on how otherness within close-knit groups in families and business organizations sometimes (in high-stakes situations) causes *insiders* to be transformed temporarily into *outsiders*. In all contexts, the outsider has the power to invoke fear and hostility, which results in our casting outsiders in severe morally judgmental terms.

Chapter Eight explored escalation, especially one between Martha and Ian, and a more volcanic one between Martha and Howard. In these pairings, each party temporarily became outsider to the other. In situations involving the outsider, there is often a quick escalation to high stakes.

Once people are labeled outsiders in time of crisis, how badly can they be treated? Sadly, history is rife with examples of extreme high-stakes reactions to the outsider. One of the most glaring modern examples is how events in Germany after World War I led ultimately to the Holocaust.

Sometimes the shift in how an insider is treated amounts to reclassifying him as an outsider. At the outset of our ClearFacts story, despite their differences, each member of the team was viewed by the others as essentially an insider— a member of the team. Yet they represented different departments. HR and finance, for example, might come to see each other as outsiders, with different goals and modi operandi in their approach to the business. For similar reasons, Martha and Howard often clashed over their competing visions as Martha focused on people, Howard on power and profit. In Chapter Eight we saw their perspectives shifting as they began to treat each other in more and more negative ways, tending toward extremes that one would otherwise adopt only toward outsiders.

Similar shifts take place in families. Like a firing, a divorce amounts to a literal redefinition of an individual from insider to outsider; but the perception of a change from insider to outsider does not require such official notice. Once, I had a pair of clients, a married couple, with deep-seated problems in their relationship. The wife analyzed their situation well, and quite eloquently, when she remarked, "I woke up one morning and found a stranger in my bed." The *intimate other*, her husband, had become the *alien other*.

Insider-outsider shifts happen because, at critical moments of need, two people are almost inevitably asking to be loved in different ways, depending on what they found missing in their childhoods; some of us might need honesty, for example, whereas others might need to feel protected. Usually these needs are incompatible. This is the logical dilemma at the center of the nature of love. The impasse can only be broken if one or another partner is willing to back off—for example, in the case of Martha and Lance, Martha needs honesty, so Lance surrenders his desire for privacy in his personal work.

Prior to Ian's Asia trip, Ian would have considered Template Jones as more or less an insider to ClearFacts and Ian's working life. But in the course of the trip, Ian inwardly redefined TJ as an outsider: alien to Ian's own moral makeup and profile-based behaviors. What sparked this redefinition wasn't just the discovery of TJ's misbehavior. To a great extent, it was sparked by opinions that TJ had voiced about business: *What you don't get is that it's all a game. You think business . . . is ruled by right or wrong? No, my friend, it's ruled by losing or winning—the ultimate prize . . .*

Ultimately, Ian was not the only one to redefine Template Jones. As Duncan had hinted earlier to Ian about the "fragility" of inside-outside status, apart from Template Jones's view and practice of business, his arrogance and blatant willingness to talk enthusiastically about sexual practices that mistreated women, very young women, were cause for one of the most volcanic eruptions ever to explode inside the company's walls.

"This 'outsider' must be punished!" Martha shouted at one point.

Ron snarled, "Jones is a sexist, and Howard is both a sexist and a racist. I felt it from the start."

Art wrapped his arms as though bound in a straitjacket, body twisting with pent-up rage; he sputtered, spewed, and shook his head in disbelief.

Eventually, after the smoke had cleared, more reasoned voices of *moral justice* could be heard.

This narrative and what it has said about "enemies" inside or out brings us back to the postures of moral justice and the heroic modes that are the focus of this chapter.

POSTURES OF MORAL JUSTICE: PROSECUTOR, ADJUDICATOR, ADVOCATE

Structural dynamics conceives three postures of moral justice: **prosecutor, adjudicator,** and **advocate**, illustrated in Figure 9.2. These terms describe how leaders can react when someone is being viewed as an outsider and when viewers feel pressured to pick out someone as an enemy. Table 9.1 summarizes a range of

Figure 9.2
The Moral Postures

Table 9.1
Three Types of Moral Posture in High Stakes

	Prosecutor	Adjudicator	Advocate
Light	Press hard for justice; do not waver. Correct misuse of the law. Enforce. Collect comprehensive data.	Conciliate. Try to see all sides of a situation. Deeply understand moral justice. Commit to order. Reserve judgment until all evidence is fairly presented. Mediate; reflect; admit mercy.	Defend the right to be heard. Preserve notions of fairness. Combat rules and practices that unnecessarily harm lives. Generate hope. Do all possible to see that the underdog gets a fair shake. Redeem.

(Continued)

	Prosecutor	Adjudicator	Advocate
Gray	Win at any cost. Be zealous. Detract (demonize, defame, impute, disparage, inveigh, express clear partisan bias). Introduce personal agenda.	Prejudge; be partial. Impose a habitual solution in place of correctness and fairness. Prefer familiar courses of action.	Ideologize. Trump law with empathy. Glorify the disadvantaged.
Dark	Manipulate truth. Act impetuously. Make no concessions; punish to the limit. Criminalize. Act by subterfuge. Harass and discriminate. Self-aggrandize. Incite with extreme language to attacks on the outsider.	Act with rigid impartiality. Allow oneself to be crippled by process. Falsely exonerate. Act with bias.	Show one-sidedness. Use emotion and meaning to outwit those in power. Justify. Vilify opponents.

behaviors associated with each posture, ranging from the lighter (more benign) to the darker. The dark range tends to be expressed where a leader perceives high stakes.

The moral postures add to our understanding of how different behavioral profiles may respond according to the continuum of perceived low, to high, to very high stakes. Thus a mover in closed power in low stakes will tend to become a prosecutor in high stakes, though I do not say this is *predictable*. Indeed, our focus on leaders' "expanding their repertoires" is tantamount to recommending that they defy such predictions. Still, knowing that people with certain behavioral profiles "tend" toward certain typal behaviors in high stakes, and that people on their own grow and change their range of behavioral options, gives hope for the training and coaching of leaders, helping them evolve their own individual leadership models.

One need not be a lawyer to wear the moral robe of prosecutor, adjudicator, or advocate, but easily recognizable examples naturally come from that field. One prosecutor type (and prosecutor by profession) is Eliot Spitzer, a classic mover-opposer, closed-system type in low stakes. He made his reputation from a ceaseless barrage of high-profile Wall Street prosecutions. As one colleague reported, "As attorney general, he could kill. He'd come up with the goods, bring suit, threaten to indict, and his opponents would cave." As another added, "He also bullied small fry." Spitzer even had government agents follow an opponent to discover any of that man's doings that might be exploited as political vulnerabilities.[1]

Louis D. Brandeis, justice of the Supreme Court, is a good example of the light side of adjudicator. He eloquently defended economic and moral justice, and thought that judges should begin with the text and the original understanding of the Constitution, then translate the framers' values in light of new technologies and political movements.

His slightly older contemporary on the court, Justice Oliver Wendell Holmes Jr., was also an adjudicator, but on the darker side, with overtones of prosecutor. Cold and brutally cynical, he had contempt for the masses *and* for the progressive laws he voted to uphold. Admired by progressives, he did not return the favor. A very restrained judge, he tried to stick to the letter of the law, what we would today call being a "strict constructionist," believing that judges should uphold virtually all laws, "even the ones they hate."

Holmes also played a critical role in the Supreme Court's decision to uphold the conviction of radical union and political leader Eugene Debs on a charge of espionage in 1919 for a speech the latter had made against the war.[2] He wrote the majority opinion. In it, he coined the phrase "clear and present danger"; it sealed Debs's fate, a ten-year prison sentence at age sixty-three.

For months afterward, Holmes was subjected to a barrage of criticism that, interestingly, eventually bore through his moral defensiveness; in fact, he changed his stance, at least in part moved by an article in the *Harvard Law Review*. Holmes later completely reversed his position on freedom of speech.

Of advocates, American trial lawyer Clarence Darrow was arguably quintessential. Even when Darrow knew or believed his clients were guilty, he worked hard to have them acquitted, convinced of the merits of a system of justice in which everyone's narrative has a right to be heard. In his long and illustrious career, Darrow defended not only the likes of the stubborn Ohio schoolteacher who violated the law by teaching evolution, but also people of questionable moral character, including Leopold and Loeb.

One can see glimmers of moral postures in what we now know of the ClearFacts team. Martha, driven by her adored father's failure of trust, has been preconditioned for a prosecutor stance, particularly when trust issues raise the stakes for her. That her profile would otherwise suggest a leaning toward advocate raises a question common with all typologies: How do we understand the conditions that lead to variance in type? Before he began to evidence change, Ian was a fairhanded prosecutor. In the crisis, he was a blend of this posture and adjudicator.

Howard's profile, too, presents interesting possibilities. It is hard to imagine him *not* being a prosecutor at the dark end of the spectrum if an underling in Office Asia violated a sacred rule. In other circumstances, let's say if he were to pursue a career in law, one could see him not only matching the alleged Elliot Spitzer image but surpassing it as a defense attorney of the type that vigorously defends (is an advocate for) known murderers, *if the price was right.*

HEROIC MODES OF LEADERS IN CRISIS: FIXER, SURVIVOR, PROTECTOR

As leaders can make themselves more aware of the moral postures they tend to assume as stakes become high, so they can also become more aware of the type of "hero" they tend to become in the midst of crisis. Although there are, of course, an unlimited number of personalities playing out their individual stories, our heroic natures distill into three basic types: the **fixer,** the **survivor,** and the **protector.** Although each of us carries parts of all three, we tend to express ourselves predominantly through one, or perhaps two, heroic modes. No one type is better, healthier, or more adaptive. Each is simply different, with a different way of relating to the world, processing experience, and giving value and love.

Here again we return to our childhood stories of imperfect love, from which we looked out into the world in search of a model for how to be as an adult woman or man, searching for a prototype to guide us. Driving this behavior is the expectation that we can earn the love we imperfectly received in childhood. Thus we write our **young-adult hero myth,** a story I mentioned briefly in Chapter Six. As adolescents, we declare, "When I grow up, the heroic person I become will earn love in the world and in intimate connection with others."

Many authors have addressed the "hero within," those deep and abiding models in the human psyche for "doing our best," in our own way, and being appreciated, rewarded, and even loved for these heroic qualities. Carl Jung's universal patterns, or archetypes, which help make order of these hopes for a meaningful life, are embedded in the most widely used current "typology" in the business community, the Myers-Briggs Type Indicator, as is Jung's concept of the shadow.[3] Joseph Campbell uncovered many ancient stories that provide the foundation for our inner heroes and role models.[4] Although the details differ from story to story, the theme is universal: the hero sets out on a journey, faces challenges, and gains insight from the experience.

Our approach here is more developmental. The search for a heroic model begins in early adolescence and continues through young adulthood, ending roughly between ages seventeen and twenty-five. The early twenties are a time of transition from direct dependence on parents to self-sufficiency and a time of freedom as we make choices about our career, lifestyle, and significant others. Around those years, our stories of an adult heroic self differentiate us from our parents and others and define our best aspirations for our inner selves. Starting with our family and then incorporating elements from pop celebrity culture, history, literature, and the arts, we form a picture of the best person we can be through grappling with fundamental questions:

How do I see myself in the world? How do I want to be known?

To what will I commit my life's work? And will my work and those in control reward or reject my way of being? Will I be loved for my heroic self?

Who is the best person I can be in the world?

Chance plays its part, but the search is not random. *This* celebrity (not *that* one) captures my attention; likewise *this* teacher, not *that* one; *this* parent, and so on. In short, the identity that the adolescent has been forming and the stories she has been making now begin to shape the world that shapes her.

As they do with the moral postures, certain behavioral profiles tend to direct individuals to certain heroic modes. For example, the mover in closed power in low stakes will *tend* (not predictably in everyone) to become both a prosecutor and a fixer at moments of crisis.

Our young-adult hero myth marches out to face the world when we begin to make our first commitments to work, career, and love.[5] It also determines our habitual reactions to critical events, how we define and cope with anxiety in these extreme situations, and what we do to make ourselves and those we care about feel safe in the world. The hero is not ever-present, but it is ever ready to show itself. Whenever it hears the alarms of threat or crisis, it steps forth and responds in its own characteristic way.

Like the moral postures, our heroic identities also have light, gray, and dark potentials. A "pure-type" heroic individual is one whose defining characteristics in all three zones—light, gray, and dark—tend to match those of one hero type—fixer, survivor, or protector. Most people are a mix, but when the stakes are highest as defined by the individuals themselves, most people tend to go into their **dominant heroic mode.** I refer to this dominant mode as one's *center of gravity* to capture how a person's two minor heroic types weigh in relation to the dominant type as the hero moves from one crisis to another.

In neither substance nor degree is there a difference between private and well-known public fixer, survivor, and protector heroes; if some saints and public heroes appear to have no gray or dark sides, that is to say only that their darker sides are not available to public scrutiny, but do show up in very close or meaningful relationships.

In the hero's light zone—his ascendant level—he shields others, performs great feats, and takes responsibilities that others decline. Experiencing our heroic characteristics in their light zone is a kind of peak experience. In it, we feel animated and capable of all that we want to do. When our hero is most recognized and applauded, it is the light side others are seeing and pointing out.

Leaving the light zone, we enter a gray zone where aspects of each heroic type are most awkwardly tainted. Although these aspects border the dark zone, people continue, at times reluctantly, to value them in the hero. But when gray-zone behaviors persist or go too far, they blacken our heroic image. Where the gray zone shades into the dark, we enter the vast, shadowy, inner domain that, no matter what hero type we embody, holds all our biases, doubts, and fears. This shadow, cast by our dark zone, causes us to project our own inner understandings onto people and situations, usually distorted by dark echoes from the past that are recalled in the present.

When thwarted, the energy that the shadow gives to inspire positive heroic exploits loops back into the dark realm, where it gathers resolve and force in a desperate effort to prove itself worthy and right and loveable. When the stakes are highest and when the shadow itself is very dark, these energies can turn demonic. But even when we cause harm from our darkest shadow, evoked by the presence of threat, we do so almost always unknowingly and without malicious intent.

THE FIXER

Figure 9.3 represents the fixer hero, who is strong in the domain of power. Keep in mind that we often postpone questioning these conquerors' means until, after victory, they are hanging all suspected collaborators. Three subtypes of the fixer are the warrior (wager of aggression), crusader (changer of social mores), and change maker (changer of broad ideas).

Warriors (male or female) are our instruments of defense and aggression, which are inseparable. On a national level, the military might be called the fixer arm of governments. Military heroes like Julius Caesar are famous for tremendous will. *Crusaders* also show great will—as did Elizabeth Cady Stanton, for example, when she boldly faced public ridicule for saying in 1848 that women

---

Figure 9.3
The Fixer

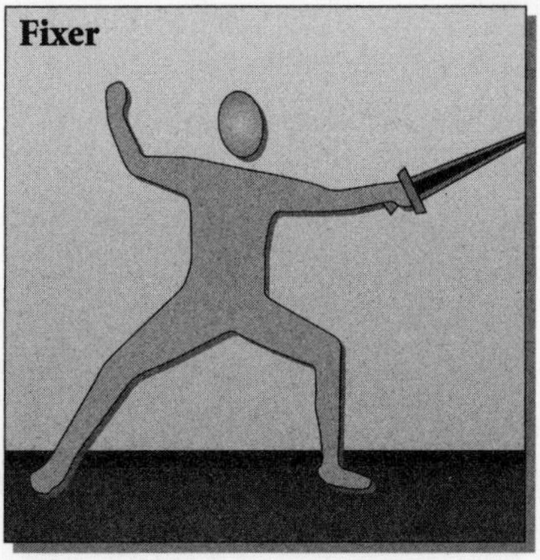

Fixer

Mantra
"I 'will' overcome, by sheer 'will' if necessary."

Source of Power
Muscular: aggressive energy

Duality
Beneficial force vs. malevolent damage

---

should fight for the right to vote. So did Ralph Nader beginning with his exposure of "designed-in dangers" of the American automobile. In the realm of ideas, *change makers* such as Thomas Jefferson and Sigmund Freud challenged and often offended established beliefs, overcoming powerful resistance as they broke new ground.

ClearFacts's Howard Green is a fixer, as Chapter Ten will show in detail.

Fixers in the Light Zone

Fixer characteristics in the light zone earn accolades and adoration because of the fixer's famous high energy and commitment.

Indomitable Will　All fixers have an indomitable *will* and are driven to *overcome* whatever gets in the way of their mission or their message—be it an enemy, a rival, or cultural norms.

Pablo Picasso generally avoided politics and disdained overtly political art. Yet his fixer (change maker) inner hero was aroused in 1937 when Generalissimo Franco's fascist forces threatened to destroy Spain's newly elected government. Picasso's depiction of the agony at Guernica broke from the artistic tradition of its time in not representing war in either romanticized or realistic terms. Initial reaction to it was overwhelmingly critical. But as Picasso himself commented, "painting is not done to decorate apartments. It is an instrument of war."[6]

Skillful Self-Presentation　Most fixers of all stripes are superb self-presenters, which tends to earn them rewards of recognition and adulation—and to attract followers. Throughout their lives, fixers tend to channel their energies into pursuit of their ambitions (and, in their shadows, into obsessive self-presentation). *Irrepressibly optimistic,* fixers believe in their powers to make things happen that others cannot. In the light zone, rewards flow naturally to them, particularly when these energies are directed to the common or corporate good. Followers become infused with their spirit.

Willingness to Lead from the Front with Formidable Energy　True fixer leaders do not hesitate to step into the breach when their judgment calls them to step forward, and they do so with formidable energy. This, paradoxically, only works or works best when they have infinite belief in their capacities or believe that there is no other choice and that they alone are left to make it.

Fixers think, *I know!! I know the right way.* They strongly believe that *they* can do it, and insist on free rein in taking the lead. When they carry this too far and when challengers insist there is another way, fixers are puzzled, or their ignited energies simply sweep these obstructions aside.

Fixers can be as hard on themselves as they are on others, including those they love. They typically have so high a capacity for driven self-assertion that it spills over onto others. As a conductor, change maker fixer Gustav Mahler, the nineteenth-century composer, ran roughshod over any display of slackness and lack of imagination. Musicians lived in terror.

An Appetite for Confrontation   Fixers also love to confront, as several of the aforementioned examples reflect.

Fixers in the Gray Zone

Behavior in the gray zone refers to characteristics that get mixed reviews. For example, high energy (being inexhaustible) is praiseworthy; aggression is not.

Inexhaustible Aggression   In soft or hard form, aggression is in the fixer's core. As they move into the gray zone, many fixers (especially warriors) have a seemingly *inexhaustible well of aggression* that satisfies the hero's thirst for competition and battle. Dick Cheney is cited as someone in favor of war and in support of torture, attributes we would assign to a fixer in the gray or dark zone.

Inflexible Zeal and Intolerance   What is seen as valiant crusading for a noble cause in the light zone, in the gray zone becomes inflexible zeal and intolerance. For example, Martha slipped into the gray zone in her dogged pursuit of Howard in the events leading up to the discovery of fraud.

Grandiosity   Fixers in the gray zone tend to be grandiose and unreal. They crave adulation and have a strong need to be worshipped. Combining this with their powers of self-presentation, they tend to attract many worshippers who reinforce these tendencies. They exhibit and often indulge in fanciful theories, their rich imaginations waxing far and wide. When they are "on" (like Einstein, Darwin, and Freud), they change the world. When they are "off," their visions seem impractical, wasteful, and self-indulgent. Thus fixer leaders should surround themselves with level-headed critics, not just ardent followers.

Blinding Focus   All fixer heroes can be so focused on their *missions* that they entirely absorb the lives and personalities of those their missions are meant to save or serve. At the same time they can misjudge their own powers and mislead others who are following behind.

In the light zone, many fixers exemplify the humane virtues of communication, negotiation, and collaboration. In the gray zone, the fixer reveals her blindness to contradictions. Whatever enemy she perceives, she carries the fight to it, eagerly making opportunities to wage an almost personal war.

Another blindness is that inevitably, at times, the fixer underestimates his enemy or misreads his circumstance. Worse, the *will to fight* will begin to supersede what the purpose of the fight was in the first place. The extreme fixer's battle cry is that the enemy must be eliminated if we are to survive and succeed. This was true of President Nixon, a political warrior, who, it has been said, was "born to fight," that he didn't need war; he made war.

Fixers in the Dark Zone

In the most dramatic moments of crisis, heroic behavior in the dark zone is forgiven. Later, when we look back, this same behavior is often subjected to criticism. However, it should be noted that the force and energy of this zone fuels the hero's behavior in the light zone.

Overcoming Whatever the Cost   Many fixer leaders are prone to overcome at any cost, and this can be a first step toward more extreme forms of fixer behavior. Because of fixers' contributions in the light zone, organizations turn their backs on this form of dark-zone behavior, continuing to interpret it in a positive light. Perhaps they ought not to. Howard is a case in point. It is even conceivable that, had he not been caught at fraud, he would have accompanied his demons down the ladder into an even darker space. Some of this became evident when he intensified his sometimes brutal control over his staff when he sensed danger.

Corruption of Power   At ClearFacts, Template Jones embodied corruption of power, and the nineteenth-century industrialist "robber barons" also exemplify this dark tendency in the business arena. The struggle between capital and labor in that era intensified to a level not known since. Armies of armed men on both sides were ready to shoot down one another in a climate of violence that persisted well into the twentieth century. Names of those on the industrialists' side—

J. P. Morgan, John D. Rockefeller, Cornelius Vanderbilt, and Jay Gould among them—are known today. Less known are the men on the labor side, leaders like Eugene Debs and union man "Big Bill" Hayward.

Hunger for Violence   It does not take much to identify Muammar Gaddafi as a fixer leader with a hunger for violence. His behavioral profile, as exemplified in his demonic threats against the rebels in the 2011 uprising in Libya, makes this characteristic evident. In Philip Gourevitch's *New Yorker* blog, Gaddafi was reported to have said, "If the world gets crazy with us, we will get crazy too. We will respond. We will make their lives hell."[7] Many brutal leaders share this characteristic. Few, however, have been so willing as he to put it on display and to follow his words with inhumane action.

Killing   In the extreme, the abuse of the fixer's shadow is bloodbath. Think of Slobodan Milošević's ethnic cleansing in Yugoslavia, Saddam Hussein's career in Iraq, and Joseph Stalin's rule seventy years ago, who actually killed more people *internally* than even Hitler.

THE SURVIVOR

Survivor heroes (Figure 9.4) are strong in the domain of meaning, which fuels their commitment to a perceived moral cause. Strong belief in their cause leads to a willingness to sacrifice themselves, often to the dismay of those they love. The survivor can *endure* any circumstance. Whereas the fixer uses the strength of physical power, the survivor relies on mind power—thoughts as a refuge from physical or emotional pain. The survivor is also viewed as a *martyr* when we experience his sacrifice or death as our own loss or loss to our shared common cause.

Common survivor variations are the *explorer* (Sir Ernest Shackleton, Sir Edmond Hillary), *marathoner* (Amelia Earhart and many professional athletes), and *pacifist* (Mahatma Gandhi, Martin Luther King Jr.). As we will see more clearly later, Ralph is a survivor.

Survivors in the Light Zone

All worthy causes and dangerous adventures—indeed, any project that requires unwavering physical or mental agility and commitment—do best with survivors who are strong in the light zone.

Figure 9.4
The Survivor

Survivor

Mantra
"I 'can' endure, at pain of death, if necessary."

Source of Power
Mind power: mental and physical discipline

Duality
Indefatigable commitment vs. abandonment

Extraordinary Perseverance and Endurance The survivor's greatest strengths are endurance and perseverance. Consider polar explorer Sir Ernest Shackleton who, after his icebound ship sank into the Weddell Sea, set off with four others in a lifeboat in miserably inhospitable seas to seek help eight hundred miles away and, though obviously doomed, somehow managed to succeed.

Shutting Out Negativity, Including Pain and Defeat Survivors frame reality by what is positive and good, schooling themselves to accept whatever comes their way without much complaint. To complain is to give in—to pain, tiredness, discouragement. Some survivors simply do not know the meaning of impossible. Nelson Mandela's autobiography (written clandestinely in prison over twenty-seven years) details his astonishing *forbearance* in his struggle against apartheid. Survivors are capable of waiting as long as necessary to realize their goals.

The survivor is one who has "yet to learn to want properly." Although they boast of their robust resistance to any form of vulnerability, they sometimes fail to see symptoms that should be addressed. A common boast: "I've never been sick a day in my life except for a common cold every once in a while. I just can't be bothered. I just don't have time. Being sick is a luxury."

Some survivors carry their pain as if it didn't exist. As Santiago, the enduring old fisherman in Ernest Hemingway's novella, *The Old Man and the Sea,* thinks, "Pain does not matter to a man. Man is not made for defeat. A man can be destroyed but not defeated."[8]

Preparedness and Confidence As quintessential *copers,* survivors privately turn to meaning to stay alive, literally in the case of Victor Frankl, a concentration camp survivor and author of the brief classic account *Man's Search for Meaning.* Separated from his wife and parents, who were killed at different camps, he came to his hallmark conclusion that even in the most absurd, painful, and dehumanized situation, life has potential meaning, and that therefore, even suffering is meaningful.

Resorting to meaning, survivors are keen observers who gather information, map forces that lie ahead, assess risks and possibilities, and learn to "keep cool" by knowing how to maintain distance from events that might otherwise swallow them up. This leads to a sense of preparedness that in turn breeds confidence in a better future.

Commitment to a Cause The cause can vary; what matters here is the survivor's power of commitment to it. Ralph was hired on this basis. When a leader brings such commitment into his organization, it becomes integral to his narrative purpose (Chapter Seven). Rarely do survivors panic morally. Their moral leadership has to do with a rock-bottom decency.

Survivors in the Gray Zone

In the gray zone, the survivor's light-zone assets begin to show their cracks, as absolute confidence based on such things as preparedness gives way to willfulness.

Dismissing Defeat Once a survivor has decided to commit to a cause, she willfully ignores any consequences of that commitment. Her conviction that she "can do" what she sets out to do leads to a unique relation to external power. Where fixers *use* power, survivors believe that *nothing has power over them.* They do not necessarily challenge external authority, but they deny any fear of it or its hold on them. Some survivors dismiss the power of authority out of hand, calling on the power of the mind to reframe reality when reality is too harsh. In the gray zone, this unwillingness to admit defeat can make survivors dismiss the possibility of defeat or even tactical retreat. The military leader who leads his men into certain death evidences this survivor characteristic.

The Cause Above All Else   Commitment, a good thing until now, can turn fanatical when the leader becomes obsessed with his cause and can speak of nothing else. The struggle involved (and there usually is one if the cause is worthy enough) defines his life, the struggle itself becoming addictive. Thus, after climbing a mountain, the survivor may look for a taller one. In war and revolution, survivors can be at the center of violent action in service of their cause.

Lashing Out   A survivor has a very hard time saying, "I've had enough." In the gray zone, when pushed over the edge, he doesn't say, "I quit." Instead, he turns into an angry beast. The anger takes two forms: a short-lived spurt of explosive wrath on a scale that often seems commensurate with the intensity of the survivor's commitment; and a chronic, erosive anger that festers just under the surface even while the survivor is performing at his best. Paradoxically, the beast's wrath is most often felt by those who are closest to him, often those for whom the survivor hero is sacrificing himself.

Choosing the Cause over Love   When the survivor has fully given himself to his cause, he takes himself away from those who love him. I have seen many clients who, like Ralph Waterman at ClearFacts, put their marriage at risk when they put the "cause above all else." Luckily for Ralph, Sonia, with the help of Duncan, will eventually rein him in.

Survivors in the Dark Zone

In the dark zone, the survivor's gray zone willfulness erects a wall that cuts him off from those he cares about and even from his own self-interests.

Sacrificing Self or Going Deaf   When the survivor has entered the dark zone, a pivotal psychological moment occurs in which she is convinced that the moral purpose behind her cause is more important than her *self*. It is this moment, for example, that organizations seek when recruiting the young to sacrifice their lives to a greater cause. Individuals like Ralph struggle with this because it is hard to turn back from abandonment of the self, another characteristic of the survivor in the dark zone. The psychological alternative to stepping back is digging in or "going deaf" to the importunate pleas of those who pay the price for the survivor's self-sacrifice.

Abandoning and Martyring   The *abandoner* is more complex than seems at first glance and is frequently misunderstood. People tend to think of a parent betraying a child through neglect or, in the extreme, leaving the child behind, or of a spouse walking out on a mate. I mean something different. Still immersed in his commitment, *while abandoning the self, the abandoner abandons the mate as well.* Think of John Proctor, the survivor hero in Arthur Miller's play *The Crucible,* who *chooses* death over a life that would mean betraying his beliefs and principles. And when he abandons himself—all the while basking in prideful delivery for his cause—Proctor unintentionally abandons his wife and children, the very same people for whom he is putting his life on the line.

Abandoning the self and martyring fuse in a final psychological decision. In most circumstances, self-sacrifice is mere punctuation to the abandoned self. Before Martin Luther King Jr.'s assassination, he had a premonition of death. His last speech in Memphis reflects this decision; he says that like anybody, he'd like to live a long life, but, as is the case for most martyrs, the strength of his cause diminishes the fear of death.

THE PROTECTOR

The mantra of the protector (Figure 9.5) is *I will not stand by idly pretending that our suffering doesn't exist.* Protectors punctuate this hymn in many ways, depending on the particular cause they vow to defend. They have a rare gift: the ability to identify areas of pain within themselves and others and to empathize with pain. Protector heroes are strong in the domain of affect. In personal relationships, they offer those close to them the care and intimacy they seem conditioned to give. In business relationships, such caring takes the form of concern and consideration, even when having to make hard decisions. Although we often seek their protection, we also squirm when the protector's suffering, upon entering the dark zone, becomes a relentless cry for revenge (Martha).

Protectors are legion and various, including many inconspicuous *philanthropists. Poet, writer,* and *philosopher* protectors (Tolstoy, Dickens, Hardy, Simone Weil, Steinbeck) go out of their way to consider or record the lives of unfortunate,

Figure 9.5
The Protector

Protector

Mantra
"I will not stand by idly pretending that our suffering doesn't exist."

Source of Power
Passion: commitment from the heart

Duality
Faith and hope vs. despair and gloom

vulnerable people. Among *naturalists,* John Muir saw and wanted to preserve the environment's utter beauty. Among mental and physical *healers,* Mother Teresa is the purest recent example. *Defender-advocates* are another subtype, stepping forward as spokespersons, supporters, and defenders of people who lack the power, resources, or information to represent themselves.

Protectors are often not seen as heroes on a par with the other two types. At best, they are considered "soft" heroes—people who merely admirably *shield* the environment from misuse or a child from a perpetrator. This diminished view is noticeably common in many competitive business organizations, where protectors are more likely to be thought of as healers and consigned to HR departments rather than strategic leadership roles. I wish to correct this flawed impression, because their role is essential in any relationship or group. Typically they are quicker than survivors in seeing problems and are able to provide information that fixers need to correct imbalances or disharmonies.

Protectors in the Light Zone

In the light zone, the protector is a fierce fighter against the doers of harm and a beacon warning of potential dangers not yet seen by other heroes.

Dedication to Caring and Shielding   Protectors are guardians and caretakers of the sick, the poor, the politically disadvantaged, the environment and its ecology, and relationships. They tend to speak fluently in affect, particularly when they are focused on their missions and causes. Protectors with healer inclinations go even further—they form very close relationships with clients, some even inclined to touch, physically and figuratively. The therapist's hug, once ethically verboten, is now acceptable professional behavior. (Duncan, a survivor, was slow to make this change.) Behavioral consultants of the protector type tend to join therapists in the practice of directly showing that they care about their clients' psychological as well as business well-being.

Anticipation of Danger   Protectors are *arch realists*: they see dangers and potential for disaster before others do and do not shy away from confronting them. This is the "upside" of their distorted perception of external power, about which more in the next section. This upside adds intense energy to the protector's *caring* and *shielding*; they forewarn with fiercely focused "calls to action" while others may sleep at the wheel. It is the protector who insists on packing only necessities and heads for safety when his neighbor *survivor* stubbornly hunkers down and the *fixer* froths with excitement at on oncoming hurricane; and who, like Martha, sensed danger before Ralph and Ian did.

Compassion for the Underdog   Protectors associate injustice with asymmetrical power and advocate *compassion* for the underdog as a means of redressing imbalance. They see a citizenry fed "false" or insufficient information about environmental and other dangers. Often turning social activist, they speak out for the "sick," "helpless" people who are "cast out," "cast off," or "unprotected."

Maintainer of Moral Standards   Like protectors, many fixers and survivors have a visceral sense of "being on the side of the good." What distinguishes protectors here is that they are driven by compassion and awareness of moral costs to society, organizations, and families. Protectors call on the rest of us to exercise our moral conscience alongside them. They are, in a sense, the self-appointed guardians of humanity's future, asking deep questions about human nature, good and evil: *Do we really care about the fate of "others"?* As *mirrors of empathy,* protectors ask, *How might we be more honorable and decent to others? What are we willing to risk to expose or stop something evil?* Protectors are also preservers of memory, in contrast with fixers, who tend to easily get beyond moral challenges like having to kill in war, and survivors, who tend to suppress memory.

Protectors in the Gray Zone

On the fringe of the protector's gray zone, we encounter her behavioral hallmark: the *ability to acknowledge feelings of vulnerability,* which fixers rarely possess, and survivors rarely express. *I feel weak or sad. This is not working—let's admit we are tired and lost. Let's wave the white flag if we must.* In short, the protector knows when to say, "I can't!"

Overly Sentimental and Emotional   In the gray zone, the protector carries the expression of affect beyond the point other heroes can tolerate. In male lore, women have been reputed to be more this way than men. And who does not know the woman who bursts into tears—or the man who chokes his tears off with a false cough—in a sentimental filmic moment? But recently more men have "come out" in this regard. Many more remain closet protectors who pay a price for this secrecy when least expected.

A classic protector in the gray zone is the mother who loves her child so much that when something goes wrong, she turns into the angry "mother bear" that may attack her child's teacher or trainer: "Why didn't you pick *my* child!?" In the darker zone, mother and father bears become accusers: "It's your fault! You never gave him a fair chance!"

Many protector poets and writers love the world too much and worry too much about it. Feeling the world's pain immobilizes them to such an extent that they can only write about it, which loops back to cause more pain.[9]

Shift from Realist to Pessimist   Valued as a realist in the light zone, the protector is seen as a pessimist in the gray. "Don't be such a Cassandra," we say of protectors, in memory of the mythological Cassandra of Troy, who saw disaster coming. This "Cassandra syndrome" lies behind much of Martha's dismay over what seemed to her a dismissal of her forebodings, or anyway, her sense of being boxed out by Ralph, a survivor, and Ian, a fixer.

Distorted Perception of External Power   Protectors are sensitive to all forms of violence and to the abuse (or in Martha's case, misuse) of power. The light-zone *anticipation of danger* and the gray-zone *shift from realist to pessimist* have apparent conceptual links to protectors' *perception of external power.* They generally feel that power exists outside the self (in contrast with the fixer's sense of power as an inner source and the survivor's sense of power as flowing from the inside out).

Protectors generally have neither the internal reserves nor the external resolve to sustain them in violent activity, except, paradoxically, when they plunge into the darkest of dark. Going there involves another gray-zone frailty of protectors, mentioned earlier: an *overwhelming sense of vulnerability.* The protector is distinguished among the heroes for her ability to express vulnerability.[10]

Protectors in the Dark Zone

Once in the dark zone, the protector can move rapidly from overwhelming vulnerability to abusive action—the violent action of the *victim avenger.* In this zone, he quickly becomes a maudlin victim. Blame and censure crowd out balanced perspective and reason. First, he experiences a sense of *victimization.* Obsessed with *vengeful* thoughts, the words of the victim accuser soon follow and can go on repetitively until the "other" piles on one more straw, the one that breaks the protector's psychological back. He resorts to a violently abusive action. In this mode, the protector's anger can be ferocious and incendiary, and no less ruthless than the fixer in the dark zone.

To understand the decision to avenge, consider Euripides' dramatic heroine, Medea. At the start of the play, Jason has abandoned her and their two children to marry the daughter of King Creon. Creon eventually banishes Medea and her children from the city, but she is granted one day before she must leave, during which she plans to achieve "justice" through the murder of Jason, Creon, Creon's daughter, and also her own children. Emotionally crushed by events, Medea focused her mind on revenge; the pain the loss of her children will cause does not outweigh the satisfaction she will feel in making Jason suffer.

HEROIC SQUARE-OFFS IN TIMES OF CRISIS

We define ourselves not only by *who we are* but by *who we are not,* and people often sense that true heroism only emerges in the face of a powerful enemy. At the farthest reach of who we are not stands our nemesis, or antihero, which James Carroll calls "the absolute other in relation to whom we define ourselves by opposition and rejection."[11] If people had no dark sides, any pairing of two different hero types could work. Because of dark sides, in times of crisis, some pairings come apart at their seams. Because we tend to define our polar opposite as evil, when contact cannot be avoided our hero dives into combat, insisting that "the evil one must be dealt with." Yet in demonizing the "other" as evil and thus defining ourselves as good, we are above all defining ourselves. In the next sections, we will look at each possible pairing.[12]

The Fixer-Protector Pairing

One of the most consequential of "mixes that don't match" is the pure fixer and the pure protector. In love, but not in war or work, many fixers choose protectors as their partners. Each type attracts and is attracted by the other's characteristics in the light zone. Trouble frequently plagues these partners if in times of crisis they trigger each other's shadow—*abuser* and *victim accuser*.

In war, signs of weakness drive fixers mad. In weakness they see or fear cowardice. Alleged cowardice is probably what was behind the famous World War II incident in which quintessential fixer General George S. Patton slapped two hospitalized soldiers. Abuses of this kind are uncommon in the world of work, but their less physical forms are not unheard of. In highly competitive business climates, or when an organization is in a "dogfight" with an "enemy"—that is, in times of crisis—the *shadow dance* between the dark sides of these two types can be just as volatile as it is in love and war (thus the earlier escalations between Ian and Martha and between Howard and Martha).

When, in times of crisis, organizations change their CEO, they commonly recruit someone they think will right what has gone wrong, looking at each candidate's heroic features. Depending on the context, any of the heroes is a possible choice, but fixers are the most popular choice. If the chosen one turns out to be a fixer with strong warrior characteristics who is unable or unwilling to keep his shadow where it belongs, protectors in the organization will rightly sense that they are endangered, particularly if they make the mistake of revealing their gray-zone or dark-zone characteristics in the fixer's presence at the wrong moment.

The Survivor-Protector Pairing

In love, this may be an even more common pairing than fixer and protector. Again, what attracts is each hero's characteristic behaviors in the light zone. This otherwise workable pairing goes bad in times of crisis when charged behaviors mount between the survivor *martyr who abandons* and the protective *sufferer who accuses.*

In war, the survivor-protector pairing has become more common as women and gays have entered the military and as straight protectors are freer to openly express their heroic qualities. Problems arise when the survivor—who is more likely to be in charge in combat—puts the protector at risk. For example, the survivor might refuse to retreat when retreat is wise. Or a survivor-martyr leader might show a courageous but wrongheaded willingness to sacrifice his own life, abandoning his leaderly responsibility and his protector comrade as well.

In the workplace also, the pure survivor is the one most likely to be in charge. Most competitive organizations in the past have filled their ranks with survivors who are willing to be led by fixers. Today protectors have also been let in, albeit gradually and with caution.

When shadows take over, the workplace conflict that arises between the pure survivor and the pure protector is easy to see. Imagine: huge project, much at stake. The survivor has just come off another project, also requiring seemingly round-the-clock effort. Sick from exhaustion, he presses on. The protector, famously more willing to say when he's reached his limits, begs off just when the survivor needs him most. When the survivor hears the protector's "I can't go on"—a "no-no" in the survivor's ears—the survivor's imperturbable, untiring, patient, and tolerant wall breaks down to reveal the gray-zone *angry martyr*—"Either I'm out of here or *you* are!"

The Fixer-Survivor Pairing

In my view, the fixer and the survivor can rival each other in intimacy and passion, though their forms of intimacy are different (and even more different from that of the protector). In love, the fixer-survivor pairing is special. It tends to occur when work, efficiency, and getting things done together are the primary basis for the connection. In this case, neither partner finds it necessary to lobby for love in the form of deep emotional connection. Lovemaking, most often with the fixer as initiator, can take on a functional quality. But survivors in lovemaking often take pride in sexual endurance, while their fixer partners add novelty and the fun of risk.

In warfare, a team of fixer-survivor is an ideal pairing, particularly when, as is most common, the fixer is in command. (But many survivors are given command over others in the context of war. Because their heroic virtues are so highly valued,

Table 9.2
ClearFacts Moral Postures and Heroic Modes

	Moral Posture	Heroic Mode
Ralph	Adjudicator	Survivor
Ian	Prosecutor-adjudicator	Light-zone fixer
Martha	Advocate	Protector
Art	Light-zone adjudicator	Protector
Howard	Dark-zone prosecutor	Fixer
Ron	Adjudicator	Survivor
Duncan	Adjudicator-advocate	Survivor-protector

they, too, can rise to high rank.) Still, problems can arise. In war, the fixer is a warrior type, the survivor often a battler or fighter (as in "freedom fighter"). The difference may seem slight but is not, particularly when the pair clash over strategy or how to face the enemy or how to treat subordinates. In crisis, with the shadows active, a survivor fighter's stubborn obsessions can butt thunderously against the warrior fixer's willful impetuosity, and if the survivor goes underground, in whatever way, he faces the charge of insubordination or expulsion.

In competitive enterprise, the fixer-survivor pairing is particularly valued when the work routinely calls for long hours of sustained output at a high level of competence. In the most common scenario—fixer in charge—a fixer can ask for nothing better than an army of highly developed, high-performing survivors. (Again, survivors are also sometimes in charge because their heroic virtues are valued.)

Table 9.2 summarizes the ClearFacts team members' moral postures and heroic modes.

SHADOW WORK AND WHY IT'S NEEDED

Although the hero story is the one we construct about ourselves latest in our development, it is also the most potent in its control over the self, its influence on how others know and regard us, and its potential for praise and scorn. Our greatest concern here is with the hero's shadow, particularly when he or she is in a position of official power and declared a leader. Once the shadow is triggered, it has the authority to bend all the leader's other stories to its will. Loaded with contradictions—one's very best and very worst selves—the shadow can suddenly shift between highly contrasting versions.

In crises, the unexamined shadow believes "beyond any shadow of a doubt" that it is *right*. Unchallenged, this moralistic certitude endangers the leader and all who would follow. Ultimately, the only remedy is the individual's willingness to assume full *responsibility* for his shadow's certainty.

Leaders who possess both enormous power over others in crisis and a strong but unacknowledged shadow are extremely volatile. The potential for these well-intended leaders to seriously damage others *and* their organization's mission is an overriding reason why leaders should engage in shadow work. It is an ethical responsibility for those whose job is to protect, guide, and lead others. Note that the objective of the work is not to eradicate the shadow. In certain circumstances, we need the fixer, shadow and all. War, for example, is bloody and painful. In the present culture, wars cannot be fought without fixers. Some enemies cannot be dealt with without necessary cruelty. But fixers who do not acknowledge their shadows may resort to unnecessary and spontaneous cruelty. They will not be able to exercise the judgment in knowing when cruelty is necessary and when they need to express it. Here are some general goals and benefits of shadow work:

- Discover the deepest sources of your most unproductive and ruinous behaviors in relationships with others

- Liberate the self and its creative energies from repeated wasteful behaviors

- Defuse the negative emotions that spoil your bid for love in intimate relationships

- Feel more and more free of the shame, fear, grief, or rage associated with your childhood experiences of disappointment and betrayal

- Recognize the projections that undermine your colleagues, partners, and others in close relationships as more your own responsibility than theirs

- Repair your most vital relationships through more honest self-examination and communication uncontaminated by your own demons

Leaders who commit themselves to discovering how shadow phenomena operate in themselves and others will be better able to appreciate the relationship between their most and least valued attributes. Here are ways to get them started:

- Shadow work begins with a nod: *Yes, I too have a dark side.*
- It follows with an oath of agency: *I will take responsibility for it.*
- It becomes an act of recognition: *I am willing to name my reputation-damaging ways and embrace them as shadow driven.*
- It requires getting help. It is not possible to do shadow work without engaging others. Like so much else that happens between and among people in work and love, the structures that count are cocreated.
- Therapy is a possibility. So is executive coaching.

If you are a fixer who resists the idea that you in any sense might abuse those you seek to aid or those at the periphery of your actions, think about this:

- Shadows are ubiquitous if not universal.
- The energy that fuels our shadow and the energy that fires our heroic achievements come from the same source.

Once an individual—citizen, lover, or corporate leader—takes responsibility for her or his shadow, the damage it does to the innocent can be mitigated if not eliminated, and more of its energy can be directed toward doing good.

From Insight to Action

When the world we know faces serious threat, its leaders are called to action. This chapter described two such threats and two kinds of leader actions by way of response. First there is the threat of the outsider. The leader's response is one of three positions on moral justice. She becomes a prosecutor, an adjudicator, or an advocate. Then there is the threat whose very scale (real or imagined) puts our world at risk. The leader's heroic response here is that of fixer, survivor, or protector. Structural dynamics alleges that there are direct, conceptual links between your typical behaviors in low-, medium-, high-, and very high–stakes situations and crises.

Origins of Your Moral and Heroic Choices

1. Think back to your adolescence and young adulthood, to the years between the ages of fourteen and twenty-five. Can you think of figures, either public or those close to you, whom you admired? What aspects of their character were most attractive to you? What moral and heroic aspects of these individuals' behaviors have you been able to capture as an adult?

2. In the stories you want people to tell about you, what traits match the heroic traits you ascribe to yourself, especially as these manifest during crises?

3. Next compare them with behaviors associated with the prototypical heroes cited in the chapter. Are there matches between the heroic traits you most admire about yourself and those associated with these figures?

Self-Assessment: Adding the Moral-Heroic Components to Your Behavioral Profile

Referring back to traits in the light, gray, and dark zones, apply a "me–not me" to each item, and simply compare each of these preferences to the three positions on moral justice. Do the same for the three heroic modes.

Your Positions on Moral Justice

1. Rank-order your preferences 1, 2, or 3 for each of the positions on moral justice:

Moral Stance	Rank
Adjudicator	_____
Advocate	_____
Prosecutor	_____

2. People who score high in power are drawn toward the prosecutor's moral stance; those high in meaning, toward the adjudicator's; and

those high in affect, toward the advocate's. To what extent do your results confirm or disconfirm these tendencies?

3. One could speculate that people who prefer open or random systems will score in the light and gray zones of each type's spectrum, and that people who prefer closed systems will drift from the gray to the dark zones. However, unaddressed shadows may account for the extent of this drift downward in each moral stance. To what extent do your results confirm or disconfirm a drift?

Your Preferred Heroic Mode

1. Rank-order your preferences 1, 2, or 3 for each of the heroic modes.

Heroic Mode	Rank
Protector	_____
Survivor	_____
Fixer	_____

2. Describe three situations that you would classify as "crises"—ones that you know as crises because they call forth your hero. Why do each of these constitute a crisis for you? If you were the designated leader at the time of the crisis and all eyes were on you, how would you be likely to respond

- In the public sphere?

- In the professional sphere?

- In the personal sphere?

3. Are there consistencies in your likely behaviors across all three spheres?

4. Have you had an experience in recent times during which the light-zone characteristics of your hero emerged? Were you rewarded by others? How? Did you reward yourself? How?

5. Now recall an experience during which your hero's gray- or dark-zone behaviors emerged. Were you criticized? How? With what descriptors?

The Leader's Shadows

The self-assessment questions here are meant to put you in touch with shadows that do damage to yourself and others. The shadows that surface in high-stakes and crisis situations tend to be darkest and most damaging. How ready are you to take up the challenge of assuming responsibility for your shadows, first in the privacy of your mind and then publicly?

chapter TEN

Sources and Signs of Moral Corruption in Leaders

A main point of Chapter Seven was the central place of morality in any group story. The last two chapters showed how moral voices, postures, and heroics take over when groups enter high-stakes territory. In such times, every beneficial group—be it a couple or a corporation—relies on the moral underpinnings that its members bring to its interactions to sustain the story. The leadership challenge at ClearFacts embodied in the deeds of Howard Green is basically a moral challenge—a challenge of moral corruption. ClearFacts can survive the crisis of fraud by Howard because other members of the team recognize and act on the situation in a moral way: they recognize the fraud in their midst and do their best to end it. In this way, they enable their company to carry forward its positive narrative purpose. This chapter explores Howard's signals to the ClearFacts team, as well as other more general signs of moral corruption in leaders.

Is there a way to foresee and ward off damaging immoral acts before an individual is able to commit them? Perhaps not entirely, but one way leaders can limit their occurrence is by building their own strong models of effective and moral leadership and by encouraging the same in their teammates and colleagues. Chapter Twelve will take us through a conscious process that coaches and leaders can follow to fashion a leadership model. Before we go there, let's see what we can learn about the various ways a leader's moral behavior can lapse and ways we can detect individual leaders who might in future go astray. We will do this by gleaning some structural dynamic insights into moral and immoral behavior, considering various real-world examples of corrupted leaders, and delving deeply into a structural dynamic assessment of Howard Green and his actions at ClearFacts. We won't need to go into the details of his actual firing, but rest assured he was fired! Once again, the behavioral profile will be useful.

First, we'll touch base again with Ralph, his progress toward building some kind of leadership model for himself, and some broad perspectives a counselor like Duncan would want him to appreciate about sources and abettors of moral corruption.

SONIA WATERMAN CALLS A SHOT

Wise coaches make an effort to know as much as they can about the spouses of the leaders they coach. Here we take up the story from the perspective of Ralph's wife, Sonia.

Sonia knew her husband, and now she knew he was exhausted, working long days reaching into nights on all fronts during those days of crisis and the firing of Howard Green. She didn't need to hear every confusing detail of his relentless search for new business opportunities, nor every painful resurrected childhood memory that was coming out in his work with Duncan on his own leadership model. When Ralph was *this* physically and psychologically weakened, she *knew* what the two of them needed to do, and made no bones about nor took excuses for it.

"We're going to Italy," she told him, and did not let him say no.

A good thing, too: after a week in Venice and some leisurely dinners alone, more restful solitude and slow love in an old country villa in Umbria, plus a tour of renovations at the Sistine Chapel in Rome, the two were solid and rested enough again that Ralph was able to reconnect in a positive way to challenges he'd left behind. On the long flight home, Ralph was looking forward to working again with Duncan on Ralph's own leadership model. As he told Sonia, in line with the moral narrative purpose that ClearFacts stood for in his mind, what Ralph envisioned now for himself was a leadership model he planned to call Moral Leadership. He also wanted to announce to the team a shift he desired in Duncan's role on the team, from observer to *facilitator*. And he planned to invite every member of his remaining team—Martha, Arthur, Ron, even Ian!—to have a coach who would take them through the process he'd gone through. From there Ralph himself would move on to something even closer to home that Duncan had recommended to him: a personal model for living. This was a massive step for both Ralph and ClearFacts.

"Sweetheart," Sonia replied. "You say that Duncan says no firm should be without a narrative. Then shouldn't couples do the same? If a company without a moral purpose is ultimately doomed to fail, then what's the fate of a marriage without one?"

Ralph nodded gravely. "That's why Duncan says we need a model for living."

"Did you say *we*? You'd better not mean you and Duncan! This has to be *our* model for living unless you plan on a life without me."

Her wisdom wasn't lost on Ralph. By the time they landed, he and Sonia had reached an important conclusion about what they wanted to do on the home front. They intended to create three narratives between them: Ralph's own personal story, Sonia's too, and a blend they would share as a couple. This would not be easy, but they both looked forward to managing it together.

Ralph's rapture over these vacation epiphanies carried him with a rush into his reunion with Duncan. "Coach," he began eagerly even before their handshake was over, "I've come to two resolves. First, I want to start working on my own leadership model—which, by the way, is going to focus on *moral* leadership—at the same time as my model for living, not consecutively. I want Sonia involved in my—no, *our*—model for living. And I've started my research, beginning with Confucius and the ancient Greeks and moving up from there to—"

"Yo, Ralph," Duncan interrupted. "Look, you want me to be impressed by your latest, deep-digging reading, and I am. But I am also concerned about a long-standing issue: Ralph the random; Ralph the visionary; speed-demon, fast-forward Ralph. You're painting the walls of a house before you've laid a foundation. Ralph, designing a life worth living isn't a lap of the Indy 500. It's about new ways to experience time—without the stopwatch or even a clock, or calendar time and schedules, deadlines, and getting more done. But there, you've done it again; sucked me into the future, when what we need to do right now still has more to do with understanding what just drove you off to Italy. You want to be a moral leader, and you're through with having people like Howard Green around who stand for something else. Well, Howard's gone, but what's going to keep another Howard from slipping in—or someone else on your team straying from the path?"

Ralph sighed. "So, it's back to that," he said. "Back to what always goes wrong."

"Not always." Duncan grinned.

MORAL CHALLENGES AND MEANS OF CORRECTION

We all recognize the tremendous challenge of making high-quality choices under high-stakes conditions. Many high-stakes choices have moral implications for the individuals within the organization and for the entity as a whole. The more pressured and difficult the decision, the more likely it is that the leader's moral judgment, or lack thereof, will be tested.

Some underlying forces tend to erode the foundations of ethical and moral decision making. In the following discussion, I demonstrate how a leader can apply a systems view to his or her own organization to assess its vulnerability to the types of moral "slips" that have become commonplace in businesses (and politics) today. This can give you a stronger sense of your own moral sensitivity and the role you allow it to play as you lead.

Prevention is possible. *Effective leaders can design mechanisms that help protect their organization from making decisions that lead to often unanticipated negative moral outcomes.* Communicational structures that help a system function well under pressure, or that can grease an organization's slide into corruption, can be identified and changed. Sadly, few leaders actively diagnose and correct such structures. In their own leadership models, our best future leaders will take on this central responsibility.

Feedback Loops: Protections and Perils

The central mechanism that protects an organization's moral integrity is the *feedback loop,* which I introduced in Chapter Four. In any human group—from couple to corporation—feedback loops exist and carry a continuous cycle of intended messages and subjective experiences that either amplify or constrain the behaviors of every person in the group.

Feedback loops give leaders critical information about the impact of their actions on the overall system. Loops are also how the system supports or constrains the moral decisions of the leader. When a leader is acting in a morally sound manner, feedback loops that reinforce, or amplify, the behavior will ensure that an organization stays on course. When a leader makes an unwise decision, a system with carefully crafted mechanisms of constraint can rein her in. When a leader moves into territory that is morally treacherous, negative feedback loops must constrain her.

Many organizations, particularly in times of crisis, unwittingly create mechanisms that corrupt collective moral judgment and prevent individuals from challenging its perilous course. Once such dangerous feedback loops get going, they can take on a life of their own. This truth lies at the heart of many seemingly incomprehensible acts of fraud, including the amazing and tragic recent fraud of Bernie Madoff.

Madoff's Ponzi

Outdoing even the legendary Charles Ponzi, Bernard L. Madoff is America's most recent and spectacular fraudster. In 2009 he was convicted on charges related to defrauding investors of over $65 billion. The judge who traced his fraudulent behaviors back thirty years called them "unprecedented" and "extraordinarily evil."[1]

Interestingly, Madoff's fraud was a direct product of his personal model—his basic way of being, perceiving, and acting. (Chapter Eleven will use Ralph to describe more rigorously what I mean by *personal model*.) It was not a deviation from a basically upstanding life. Although it is unclear how early the fraud began, it is indisputable that it permeated his model *long* before his wrongdoings were brought to light.

Notoriously secretive, Madoff refused to discuss investments substantively with any of his clients. He was also highly exclusive, allowing only high-powered investors to join his fund. He may even have hidden the most basic details of his fraud from his wife and children (several of whom worked with him at the firm he had founded in the 1960s and one of whom committed suicide after Madoff's conviction).[2]

How did Madoff acquire his fraudulent model? Mona Ackerman, writing for the *Huffington Post,* speculates that Madoff may have been a sociopath, but also offers another reason that might sound quite familiar: Madoff exhibited "all of the market's tendencies toward greed and a lack of aversion to high risk situations."[3] In other words, he found ideas for the model all around him and simply took them to the extreme. In the end, his fraud was so brilliant and well concealed that it consumed him beyond all other awareness.

I hardly excuse Madoff's disastrous crimes, but perhaps I can add something from a systems perspective to the explanatory mix: the self-reinforcing power of loops. Most of us know this power from personal experience. I mean the exculpatory stance we take to excuse the self for behavior we know to be "wrong." In child development we could call it the "cookie jar" loop. If nine-year-old Jane's small hand gets away with it once, the second time comes easier, the third time easier still as guilt fades in the face of repeated success, and a little "fraud" becomes as easy as a petty white lie. For adults with faulty character development, the cookie jar is a money-filled vault where the hand finds a means to slip in and out until, inevitably, the hand gets caught.

AN HOURGLASS OF MORAL CORRUPTORS

Spend a moment with Figure 10.1, which has many uses. The hourglass diagram represents influences that bear on the various interfaces in an organization. I use it in identifying morally corruptive influences or mechanisms throughout a system, at all three system levels: (1) the broader social structures, such as the

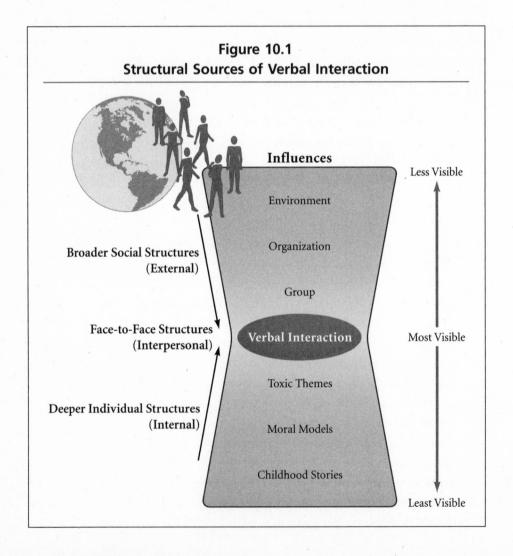

Figure 10.1
Structural Sources of Verbal Interaction

Influences

Less Visible

Environment

Organization

Group

Verbal Interaction

Most Visible

Toxic Themes

Moral Models

Childhood Stories

Least Visible

Broader Social Structures
(External)

Face-to-Face Structures
(Interpersonal)

Deeper Individual Structures
(Internal)

business environment and the overall organization; (2) the face-to-face structures, such as group dynamics and relationships; and (3) the individual structures, including personal models and stories. Let's look at each level's typical mechanisms of moral corruption and consider how they might be systematically corrected. By paying attention to and correcting these mechanisms, leaders can safeguard the moral health of their organizations.

Broader Social Structures—External Events

In the broader social structure, external events take place, such as changes in economic climate. Pressures often catalyze the creation of new mechanisms within the organization: the competition has come out with something bigger, better, faster than our industry-leading product; customer needs have evolved, and our best isn't good enough anymore; intense regulatory pressures require sweeping organizational change.

In our rapidly digitizing world, large companies seek advantage as the fastest, savviest, or most comprehensive purveyor of information on the Internet. In doing so, they cross ethical lines. For example, in digitizing the world's books, Google Books committed hundreds of copyright infringements, eliciting a successful lawsuit by the Authors Guild.

Shareholders and boards of directors place sometimes enormous and perilous pressures on organizations and their leaders to react to outside change. *Do something different! Fix the problem!* As stakes rise rapidly around and within them, leaders need to beware of broadcasting feedback that can undermine their organizational system's collective moral judgment.

Face-to-Face Structures

At the face-to-face structural level, five patterns can elicit and amplify moral corruption:

- The empowerment paradox
- Courteous compliance
- Co-opting the inner circle
- Silencing the witness
- Forgetting history

The Empowerment Paradox The **empowerment paradox** is common around powerful leaders. Wanting to "empower" subordinates, but not quite trusting their capacities, these leaders assign subordinates important tasks and then, paradoxically, systemically undermine what they produce. Subordinates are thus trapped. The following are three symptoms of an empowerment paradox:

- The formal leader is known primarily as the company's strongest performer.
- All of the organization's key decisions are made by the formal leader.
- Significant projects require multiple "approval" meetings from which the leader sends the team back out to do more work.

In their innocent form, strong-performing leaders genuinely want their followers to succeed, but their own behavioral propensities (as strong or stuck movers, for example) get in the way. When they "step in" to show how the task "should" be done, they are opposing. But in some organizations, the leader is far from innocent, and the paradox is insidious. In these cases, a leader systematically undermines her own team as a means of hanging on to the reins of organizational power.

In either case, the result is the same. The leader's team, once capable of employing the full range of actions, including opposes and moves, has been systematically reduced to follows and, through the process, has likely lost faith in the quality of its own actions. Thereafter, it willingly defers to an increasingly powerful leader.

Courteous Compliance I introduced this behavioral archetype in Chapter Two. **Courteous compliance** occurs in "polite cultures" that ostracize or cast out opposers. The following are three symptoms of insidious courteous compliance:

- There is an absence of debate, even around critical issues.
- All of the organization's key decisions are made by the formal leader.
- When the formal leader makes a suggestion, everyone promptly and without fail agrees.

Where courteous compliance prevails, disagreement is expressed only gently, in hushed tones, with apology. Opposers are ostracized or driven underground (creating its counterpart, covert opposition) so that the system can maintain its equilibrium. When the leader makes a move, everyone follows, making him the moral compass for the entire system. If he missteps, so will everyone else because all corrective feedback mechanisms have been silenced.

In these systems, leaders are prone to claim that they wish "someone would speak up." However, in practice, unless the leader does something to change the system, he is in fact reinforcing it.

On the path to corruption, courteous compliance often occurs in conjunction with covert opposition. The culture over time has cemented the propensities of stuck followers who subvert their opinions to powerful leaders. Perhaps in an attempt to correct itself, the system recruits strong opposers, then systematically shuts down their feedback loops to render them silent.

Co-Opting the Inner Circle   In 1937, President Roosevelt, tired of a conservative Supreme Court that found his New Deal programs unconstitutional, proposed a bill that became known as the "court-packing" plan. Essentially, he tried to appoint additional sympathetic justices to the court in order to favor his legislative agenda. The resulting conflict largely dissipated bipartisan support for the New Deal and significantly damaged Roosevelt's public reputation.

Co-opted inner circles are those that have been systematically disabled from seriously challenging the nominal leader. The following are three symptoms of co-opted inner circles:

- Absence of bystanding or opposition from a leader's closest counsel
- A small group of individuals tightly and jealously holding all of the organization's information and power
- Lack of change in the leader's core group over a long period of time

Many organizations' moral incorruptibility is based on well-functioning core groups whose members are chosen by nominal leaders for the diversity of perspective and voice that they bring to decision making. These inner circles of influence are not necessarily the same as those who hold top official positions; they may represent the leader's handpicked personal counsel.

In systems that are steering off course morally, corruption can derive from the nature and deployment of power. Being included in the leader's powerful inner circle of influence is a boon to one's own sense of belonging, entitlement, and power—power by association or vicarious power. In exchange for these obvious benefits, followers allow themselves to be co-opted, sometimes so subtly that they don't realize how vulnerable to corruption they have made themselves. Once they are in the inner sanctum, the risk of expulsion is terrifying.

Unless leaders include in their inner circle at least one scrappy opposer, they risk sacrificing one of their greatest assets—the pressures of moral correction. But to be most effective, this opposer must be joined by a bystander secure in her neutrality and free to present unwelcome viewpoints.

In recent American politics, the inner circle often includes a spouse. Many Americans who supported John Edwards's presidential campaigns were as excited by the woman at his side—Elizabeth Edwards—as they were by Edwards himself. Elizabeth won the admiration of millions with her dedication to her young children, her courage in the face of debilitating cancer, and her commitment to the causes célèbres of the American left—health care reform, gay marriage, withdrawal from Iraq. Oftentimes she would campaign alone, as big a crowd-pleaser as her husband. Undoubtedly, Elizabeth was an irreplaceable fixture of Edwards's campaigns. His Democratic nomination for vice president in 2004 and strong primary showings in 2004 and 2008 couldn't have happened without her. Much of the Edwards appeal related to their marriage and the background and values it symbolized.

Naturally, then, when it was revealed in mid-2008 (after Edwards had suspended his presidential campaign) that the candidate had carried on an affair with his campaign videographer, Rielle Hunter, Americans poured out their sympathy for Elizabeth. These feelings gave way to shock and anger, however, when it was revealed by various sources (including campaign aide Andrew Young, in the now-infamous book *The Politician*) that Elizabeth not only knew of but also helped conceal her husband's indiscretions. Once a media darling, Elizabeth Edwards was now plagued with questions of "What did she know and when did she know it?" Although she was not as pilloried as her husband (who later admitted fathering Hunter's child), Elizabeth undoubtedly suffered a huge loss of credibility and respect with the American public as a result of the scandal.

Certainly, Elizabeth did not create her husband's scandal, but she was implicated in it. By conducting the 2008 campaign as though nothing had happened, misleading the public as to the nature of her relationship with her husband, and risking the Democratic agenda with yet another sexual scandal (amid the Great Recession nonetheless), she defrauded the American people. Why did she eschew her own admired model—her espoused principles and values of fairness, equality, openness, and honesty—precisely when it was needed? Did she abandon it in support of the public good (perhaps truly thinking that Edwards, despite his flaws, was the best candidate to advance liberal causes) or personal benefit (the power and prestige of the White House)? Either way, she became deeply entangled, as so many spouses do. Her case exemplifies how temptations and trials permeate not only organizational inner circles but family inner circles as well.

Silencing Witnesses   Organizations and their leaders sometimes silence witnesses to limit power to a small and insular group. Symptoms of this dangerous practice include

- Ritualized excessive deference to the formal leader's perspective and opinion
- Prevalence of negative associations with "speaking up"
- Disappearance of iconoclasts who once challenged the leader's authority or perspectives

Silencing witnesses frequently accompanies co-optation of an inner circle. In fact, many of the mechanisms of moral corruption are mutually reinforcing and can develop a life of their own if left unchecked. Systems succeed in silencing witnesses in part by co-opting an insulated core group of insiders who, in exchange for being "in," do not challenge the nominal leader. They also systematically target and shut down iconoclasts who refuse to be co-opted.

Witnesses are arguably the most important voices in the system. Seeking out these perspectives is often the only way to give them an audience in a system on its way toward corruption.

Forgetting History   George Orwell wrote his classic dystopian fable, *Animal Farm*, to warn mid-twentieth-century leftists not to ignore a historical pattern of dictatorship that is traceable back at least as far as the French Revolution of 1789. It seems that some lessons are never learned.

When John Edwards began his torrid extramarital affair and then tried to cover it up, he seemed to forget the instructive fates of President Clinton and presidential hopeful Senator Gary Hart. Both of these men torpedoed themselves politically with extramarital affairs. Losing sight of past lessons learned makes organizations and their leaders vulnerable to repeating past mistakes or inventing new ones. Symptoms of forgetting history include

- Dismissal of organizational history as irrelevant or unnecessary; absence of historical relics or myths
- Obsessive focus on the future and the opportunities it holds
- Exclusion of "old-timers" from the leader's inner circle

Organizations and their leaders can have short memories. Failing to consider both past and present, they are capable of forgetting sordid history, both in the culture at large and within their own walls. With their sights trained on future victories, they lapse into what amounts to consensual moral blindness.

With the opening up of every new cycle of economic opportunity and promise, history suddenly seems far away and frankly irrelevant. At such times, thoughtful leaders must safeguard the lessons their organization has already learned. That doesn't mean playing the role of historian; it means keeping a feedback loop active between the organization's history, as retained and embodied by its elders, and the ears of its current leaders.

Individual Structures

It is easy to demonize public figures for their public moral lapses, but look back at Figure 10.1. At the individual level, structures within the behavioral profile render some leaders especially susceptible to moral corruption, but every profile carries with it moral vulnerabilities to which reflective leaders must continuously attend. By reflecting also on the mechanisms to which their behavioral profiles render them susceptible, leaders can prevent the harm those mechanisms can cause or at least minimize their effects. The following are examples of such problematic mechanisms or tendencies:

- "Not knowing"
- Unquestioning loyalty to the chief
- Reverence for power
- Not admitting error
- Absence of empathy
- Recklessness

"Not Knowing" Cardinal Bernard Law was forced to resign as Catholic archbishop of Boston in 2002, following news that he and the Boston archdiocese had covered up child sexual abuse by priests for decades. Rather than reporting allegations of molestation to the authorities, Law had simply referred the accused priests to psychiatrists or moved them to other parishes. This awful pattern of willful blindness and purposeful cover-ups left hundreds of children victim to predatory priests and devastated Boston's Catholic community. "I acknowledge my own responsibility for decisions which led to intense suffering. While that suffering was never intended, it could have been avoided, had I acted differently," Law later said.[4]

In a more recent book explaining the collapse of the "Celtic Tiger," Ireland's formerly roaring economy, "[Fintan] O'Toole uses the phrase 'unknown knowns' to describe a cast of mind that distances itself from facts it knows to be true but 'does not wish to process.'"[5] In *not knowing,* individuals actively engage in acts that they do know to be morally wrong but whose internal "meaning" they are able to alter in order to justify their choice. The human psyche is capable of extraordinary feats. In my opinion, of all the forces that contribute to the sacrifice of moral principles, this one has no rival. On the individual level, not knowing is roughly analogous to the face-to-face-level practice of forgetting history.

Martha Stewart, the lifestyle maven whose businesses include a syndicated talk show, a magazine, and countless other media and merchandise offerings, built her $650 million fortune and empire with her talents, ruthless ambition, and a shrewd air of public wisdom.[6] Talents notwithstanding, Stewart risked ruin in 2001, when her insider trading ultimately forced her to step down as chairman and CEO of her company, pay a $30,000 fine, and serve five months in federal prison.[7] What led Stewart to commit fraud for relatively petty gain? Not her usual business strategy, which emphasized work as pleasure, industry, commitment to good taste, and a beloved public persona. Whatever led her astray (the whiz and whirl of Wall Street life?), her failure lay in setting aside that successful approach.

Oftentimes, after the fact, a leader who has been involved in fraud will claim he was unaware of any misdeeds. "Martha Stewart has done nothing wrong," Stewart's lawyers said at the time of her indictment. "She knew Sam tried to trade [the ImClone stock], but she *didn't know* [my emphasis] why he was trading."[8] This excuse is frequently heard from elected officials accused of accepting bribes. Of course, this could be nothing more than willful blindness—conveniently ignoring what is obvious in order to shirk responsibility.

Leaders accustomed to adoration, praise, and success may convince themselves that what they're doing is right, even when it isn't. A leader who is certain she can "do no wrong" may indeed do wrong, especially if she also believes she is invincible or perfect. But I do not consider not knowing the same as denial, in either its dictionary or its psychiatric usage. In defining denial, the dictionary stresses active *rebuttal*; psychiatry, viewing it as a defense mechanism, stresses *suppression* in which a forbidden experience from the distant past is split off from conscious awareness. Thus, not knowing is not simply a "looking away" or a "turning one's back on" or "suppressing" a terrible reality. In not knowing, individuals are fully awake to what they are doing, but are able to play a trick on their consciousness in order to feed an appetite for wealth, sex, or power. While actively performing wrongful acts, they are also actively altering the meaning and presumed consequences of these acts in their own minds in order to preserve the belief that they are morally sound.

Not knowing is the most dangerous consequence of lack of self-awareness in a leader. Setting personal alarm bells and soliciting the scrutiny of others are the greatest defenses against it. The higher the degree to which the leader has explored her own behavioral profile, the greater the tickle of concern she is likely to feel about taking morally questionable actions.

Unquestioning Loyalty to the Chief   The individual and face-to-face mechanisms that lead to moral corruption tend to complement and reinforce one another. Leaders who demand unquestioning loyalty stunt the flow of critical, and therefore corrective, information within their organizations. Circularly, an organization with many individuals who display this loyalist tendency will create a system that values such face-to-face behaviors as courteous compliance.

Devout followers tend to derive their joy and their influence by following closely on the heels of a powerful leader. Likewise, many powerful leaders choose to surround themselves with devoted fans, yes-men whose primary purpose is to confirm the leader's authority. Deflecting critical feedback and boosting positive reinforcement, this reciprocal loop is emotionally satisfying and morally corrosive.

Rather than reward those who mindlessly obey, leaders need to unleash the voice of the opposer and actively solicit contrary opinions. Those leaders who find these tasks difficult will need to pay particular attention to this aspect of themselves as they examine and develop their leadership model (as described in the following chapters).

Reverence for Power   Power in some form—authority, hierarchy, or constraint of freedom—is inherent in social institutions, an inseparable aspect of making difficult decisions and hard choices. Individuals who tend to revere power can have difficulty opposing it and thereby lose their own power to help correct others' morally unsound choices. Reverence for power—or ambivalence about it or fear or hatred of it—takes shape originally in our childhood stories. As a mechanism of moral corruption, revering power is closely related to unquestioning loyalty to the chief.

As leaders, individuals must understand and take responsibility for the dilemmas that their hierarchical position may create for others and attempt, within reason, to free others from the constraint this authority imposes. This means releasing others to provide timely and difficult feedback without fear of retribution.

Not Admitting Error   It is naïve to think that people "in high places" with responsibility for the well-being if not the lives of others should always open their books, their files, or their minds to debate even inside their circles or to public scrutiny on the outside. They are understandably constrained by the reality of face-to-face communication. However, some in very high places do not admit error almost as a matter of policy or, worse, as a function of character. It is these latter who concern us here inasmuch as they discourage dissent, do not invite debate, and enforce secrecy, and are unable to admit major error without being forced to do so.

The greatest danger of not admitting error is its easy descent into cover-up and lying. A drift from little lies to big ones, from little transgressions to BIG ONES, is hard to stop. When people caught in moral confusion turn their heads from one corrupt decision, they become vulnerable to turning their heads from the next and the next.

Routinely shielding error from view opens the door for the types of mental contrivances that lead to not knowing. As a leader is convincing everyone else that "he has it under control," he may be convincing himself as well.

Absence of Empathy   When one is making difficult decisions that have an impact on others, empathy is critical to exercising good moral judgment. In its simplest sense, empathy is the ability to know the "other"—how the other feels and thinks and, in the best case, why the other acts or is likely to act as it does.

Although occurring naturally in some, empathy is as much a practice as it is a quality. In being open to the models of others and receptive to their perspectives, the leader takes a step away from a self-centered view and makes space for others to be present. Without empathy, our devotion to power can run roughshod over any moderating moral sense.

Recklessness   In Herman Melville's enduring novel *Moby-Dick,* Captain Ahab launches a maniacal pursuit of the white sperm whale that bit off his leg. Ahab continues to pursue the whale, despite widespread destruction, the death of every member of his crew but Ishmael, and early good advice from first mate Starbuck, who tells the captain, "Moby-Dick seeks thee not. It is thou, thou, that madly seekest him!" Eventually, the harpoon line that Ahab plants in Moby-Dick catches Ahab as well and drags him drowning into the depths of the sea.

For landlubbers, too, recklessness can easily set off a chain of morally corrupting events that lead an entire organization astray: a leader displays a thoughtless, rash, or indiscreet sense of license, and, when he succeeds in any capacity, the success bolsters an irrational belief that he is invincible and subject only to his own rules. When these rules are seriously challenged or a crisis descends, he feels greater need to control and makes increasingly unilateral decisions. To the extent that he relies on others, he manipulates them to serving his ever-narrowing ends. Those around him trying to help are infuriated by his inability to admit error, see the sources of his behavior, or apply his own checks and balances. More and more, he simply rationalizes, not even realizing that his acts are morally indefensible.

The Enron scandal, revealed in 2001, ranks near the top of many examples of reckless leadership practices. It destroyed the organization and resulted in the loss of billions in company pensions and stockholder value. With connivance from higher up, CFO Andrew Fastow created what were called "special purpose entities" that were hidden through the use of accounting loopholes. This tactic—applied to enterprises sometimes recklessly violating the law—hid billions in debt from failed deals and projects. Fastow and other executives not only misled Enron's board of directors and audit committee on their high-risk accounting practices but also pressured Arthur Andersen auditors to ignore the issues, thus bringing down that huge company, too.

At the root of recklessness is this leader's infatuation with his own power. He commands our attention because he is bullish under stress. He is willing to take on the toughest problems, ones from which others who are less purposeful and driven shy away. He is fearless about confronting anyone or anything thrown in his path. Yet those same traits that have won him such acclaim will become his Achilles' heel (his Moby-Dick) if they lead him over the edge into unjustifiable recklessness.

COMPREHENDING THE FRAUDSTER: SOME INSIGHTS INTO HOWARD GREEN

More study of Howard Green will lead us to a behavioral profile and other related dimensions that suggest a personal tendency toward fraud.

After Ralph's return from Italy, Duncan used an hourglass drawing like Figure 10.1 to work with Ralph on how systems promote or discourage corruption. Especially at the individual level, Duncan's guidance provided perspective on Howard Green—not only why he did what he did, nor only how Ralph might be able in the future to spot potential problems before he ever hired or promoted some similar potential leader, but also to prime Ralph's thinking about the morally cognizant leadership model that Ralph intended to build.

Duncan took an active part in discovering as much as they could about Howard's character and past in structural dynamic terms, including his childhood stories. One key "informant" was Howard himself, who'd let loose his own tipsy tongue at more than one prior company party. Another source of recall was Art, who had learned much about Howard in the course of past boasts and taunts that Howard had thrown at Art as a supposed rival. A third main source was Howard's younger brother, Sam, who had been Howard's childhood victim and witness and Howard's only known confidant. Spouses and partners were traditionally invited to the company's end-of-year parties. Sam, learning that Howard would not invite Vera, his "girlfriend," saw an opportunity. He asked to come along. In an effort to help out his older brother, Sam collared Duncan, revealing much about their childhood, in addition to what Howard had already shared.

Both Howard and Sam provided clues from Howard's preadult years. In his early years at home, he would seem to get pleasure in physically abusing Sam, his junior by three years. Parental lessons on "being kind to your brother" never had much effect.

To show their mettle in preadolescence, boys roughhouse with their peers. As a boy, Howard was an odd combination: a "nerd" who could fight hard, too hard at times, and resorted to outlawed physical tactics when fearing he would lose. It was not without reason that he was called "Who, me?" by other kids in the upper-middle-class, gated community in which he grew up.

In adolescence, Howard cultivated skills in exploitation and dirty tricks. In the elite coed boarding school he attended, most girls avoided him after a first date. A pattern that we see later in dealing with women was set early. He saw girls as sexual trophies and they "got it." Academically, he could only be number one, endlessly fretting or resorting to tricks to assure this coveted place. One boy capable of challenging Howard's place at the top of the class accused him of stealing and destroying a backpack containing the boy's final research report. Other incidents fit the same pattern.

A Primordial Sexual Story and Coalition Against the Father

It is not unusual for sexual themes to be central in childhood stories of imperfect love. Many of the stories involve outright sexual abuse. Some, like Howard's, fall short of abuse because of the way the child tells the story. Howard's childhood story is borderline in this regard. Around age eight, what began as ordinary bullying of Sam gradually turned into an erotic windfall for Howard that was arguably the genesis of his sexual habits as an adult.

When he was caught in a particularly serious act of bullying, his mother would drag him to her bedroom, the scene of punishment, where she had him drop his pants, "the better to show your bottom, young man"; and, "so's not to crease my skirt," she would tuck her skirt into her panties with the stern warning, "and don't you dare look." Understandably, Howard took this as an invitation.

This tantalizingly naked act of shared eroticism was not the end of the performance. His mother was strikingly beautiful and loved showing it off to her "three boys" at dinner, for which she elaborately primped. It did not take Howard long to suspect that his mother followed up the spanking episodes with such primping. If the synchronicity was not conscious on his mother's part, its routine predictability may well have made it seem so for the ever-curious (and easily aroused) Howard. At her door, with an audible sigh of pleasure, she would say, "Ah, and now dinner"—her conspiratorial signal for Howard to be ready, he thought, since the door was left just ajar enough for Howard, from his room across the hall, to see her nakedness as she dressed. When, at age ten, it became plain that what the punishment produced was not pain but an erect penis felt by both, his mother abruptly halted the practice.

His mother, who adored him—though more like a toy than a son she truly loved, more as a balm to her own narcissistic core—sucked him into a conspiracy that, for another child, would put him in an entrapping triangle and double bind. If he protects his father, he betrays his mother; if he protects his mother, he betrays his father. Unlike Martha, Howard offered no known protest about being drawn into such a trap. Far from resisting, he seemed to relish it. Is it going too far to say that he was titillated? Or was he a victim? That he freely told this and other self-condemning stories in a boastful manner says enough.

Aware of his mother's disdain for her spouse, Howard aped her in a coalition against his father, referring to the dad as a "thin-skinned, soft-bellied, second-rate doctor, more nurse than physician." His brother, Sam, painted an altogether different picture, saying, "Our father was a kind, deeply compassionate man," and explaining that his income suffered because he gave all his patients the time they needed, freely referred them to colleagues he thought could serve them better than he, and, in search of an elusive diagnosis, would work late into the night without demanding greater financial return. "We were far from poor, mind you," said Sam, "but not as rich as Mother and Howard would have it."

Howard's Choice of Hero

In the search for heroic models, the activity we think takes place seriously between adolescence and young adulthood, Howard dismissed his father for a different prototype close by: a rich, well-placed, ruthlessly competitive financier, his father's college roommate and a frequent dinner guest even when their father was working late.

With perverse pride, Howard had actually revealed a belief to Art, as a young man might brag of his own "first lay," that Howard's first real hero, "Uncle" Frank, was also his mother's lover. For this Howard in no part faulted *her*—the opposite if anything. In other matters, too, Frank became Howard's guru in the vile ways of "winning." The seeds of fraud had been sown.

About why Howard had told Art about this, Art thought it was meant to establish Howard's advantage in a rivalrous war that Art had no interest in fighting. Howard had fallen into a habit of taunting Art privately with his own erotic lifestyle, in contrast to Art's staid, "dull" relationship with Jane. Howard recollected his apprenticeship with Frank as an assurance of victory in his imaginary, one-sided war.

Sam also had insights into Howard's choice of Frank as a hero. From Sam's perspective, Howard had been entranced by the "uncle," sitting at his feet and taking in all that the fundamentally corrupt man had to offer. As Sam told Duncan, "Only later did *I* see how debased he was, but Howard was mesmerized from the beginning. I actually heard Frank once telling Howard about the thrill he got from making a sucker of someone. They deserved it, he said. If we only knew how most philanthropists get where they are—now *that* would be some surprise! He'd tell us there weren't any saints in business—just dummies who played by the rules and, here and there, men like himself who made up their own."

At another séance, Sam had watched as Frank showed Howard his credit card scheme. Frank had five cards at the time, each with a separate bank account, not all in the States, on which he'd run up large balances and which he regarded as "play money" in more senses than one. Staying below the radar, rotating credit from one account to cover payments on another, his scheme had already worked for a long time. As Frank would say, "It's all in the timing. You just need to know when to shut down one account and open up another."

What turned Sam's stomach most was how Frank had enlisted Howard in his secret liaison with their mother, getting Howard to put up the cover stories, which their father never saw through. Of the fact that Sam hadn't managed to do anything about all that, the best he could say was, "I was just a kid too scared to cross my brother."

Sex and Power in Howard's Adult Life

As a fixer, Howard is energized by crises, especially when they open up opportunity to exercise power in a contest of forces he can beat down, an "enemy" he can defeat. This fixer identity adds another twist: a relationship between sex and power.

Duncan was able to construct two stories from Howard's adulthood based on details provided by Sam. One involved Howard's sexual relationship with a young Russian woman, a writer named Vera, about whom Howard would boast to younger, "do-gooder" Sam. The second story was but one recent example of the kind of conversation Howard would initiate with Vera, then Sam, whenever Howard was under pressure.

Vera had her own reasons for putting up with Howard. Her U.S. visa would one day run out, and she needed him to hold to his promise to help her get her green card. In truth, she settled for very little, having intimated to Sam that her sex with Howard was "not that good," and she wondered, given that Howard was having as much additional, casual sex as he wanted, "Why me?"

She said she didn't love Howard, largely because she knew without a doubt that he didn't love her, despite his interrogations of what she did with whom when he was on the road or traveling. He treated her with "jealous contempt," but out of fear and loneliness she accepted him back into bed "on call." Prepared to compromise in order to survive, too afraid to lose him and his promise of rescue, she'd do anything he wanted; and what he wanted was always a bit of sadism framed in the form of play and playacting. His favorite sex with her was anal, her hands tied up with elastic exercise bands. In their playacting, Vera used her vulnerable persona to "bring him on." Her masochism aroused him. He despised her, his victim mistress, and was excited by his dominance over her and others like her.

Sam speculated further about Vera's relationship with Howard. Perhaps she'd been (and still was) attracted to him as a person of power. He was part of a world in which she needed protection from a man like that. He took pains to present himself as a man of power at his company and out in the world as the influential director of its Asia office.

Howard Under Pressure

Duncan and Ralph both wanted to know how it was that, throughout the inquiry that led to his final dismissal, Howard remained so apparently cool and unperturbed. According to Sam, in fact, Howard had been phoning Vera and him in turn. The ones to Vera could only run something like this:

VERA: (Picking up) Hello?
HOWARD: Vera? Good. I need a fix.
VERA: Hi, Howard. Right now isn't—
HOWARD: You didn't listen. I said "I need a fix." Big doings in Asia. Big! They're sniffing around. That f—g Martha. Asia is my territory. Mine. If those bastards catch on to my stuff, little lady—I have to be on a plane at dawn.
VERA: But Howard—

HOWARD: No "buts" except your pretty white round one. I'm late for a call with TJ. You'll see me as soon as it's over. Be ready. *(Hangs up)*

Immediately thereafter, Howard would call Sam:

HOWARD: Just cluing you in on something big. My baby, the Asia office, is under siege. I'll be on my way there tomorrow a.m. We'll see whether TJ's firewall holds up. They've sent their big guns, Ian and Duncan, so it's up to me again. You know my future hangs on this. My little Russki's standing by. I can't wait to get in the saddle. Ride *hard*—you know what I mean?

SAM: So orgy then war.

HOWARD: Kiddo, if the truth be told, for me they're one and the same.

SAM: Look, is that why you called?

HOWARD: Hey, you're my kid brother—"counselor"—remember? You know: "connection," that's what you always want, so I'm connecting.

SAM: Oh, Howie, when you picture all this in your mind, do you actually get hard?

HOWARD: No. Well, yes, but that's because I'm just about to see my—

SAM: Just call Vera, okay?

HOWARD: Hey, little man—

SAM: Please, Howard, let me go. Call when you get back so we can have a decent conversation. *(Hangs up)*

Howard as a Specimen Candidate for Fraud

I'm spending so many words on Howard because there is much to learn from him. Although he is a fictional character in my ClearFacts tale—the one most likely to tempt his fate in fraud—I assure you again that he has strong basis in history and fact. I created him from two main sources: articles, memoirs, and biographies from the public domain; and behind-the-scenes personal information to which only therapists and clinical consultants are regularly privy. I've done both of these jobs for decades, and, believe me, those experiences guided me in creating the character of Howard. From him let me distill for you now an informed portrait of likely candidates for committing fraud. I'll discuss the ten dimensions summarized in the following list.

Ten Dimensions Tending Toward Fraud

1. Behavioral profile: mover-opposer in closed power
2. Choice of hero: fixer
3. Proneness to insidious forms of courteous compliance
4. Absence of empathy and a denial of having a shadow
5. Narcissism
6. Evidence of moral compromise
7. Not knowing and admitting no error
8. Silencing witnesses
9. Excessive ambition and aggressive striving for competitive advantage
10. Weak intimate ties

1. Behavioral Profile—Only a Warning Sign   In low stakes, Howard is a mover in closed power, the core profile of many leaders who commit fraud, be it financial or sexual or both. However, I can't say often enough that profiles in low stakes tell little unless one steps back and assesses how the person's "up" and "down" sides compare, and how his behavior changes in high-stakes situations, including his dark sides and shadow. Howard's high-stakes behavior must be compared in two contexts. In his distant Asia office, his closed-power profile transmuted as one might expect, into the prosecutor and fixer modes, and was concentrated in the dark sides of both spectrums (as demonstrated by his tastes in sexual entertainment and by his underlings, terrorized into silence). Howard's duplicity, his behaving one way at home in the presence of authority and another in Asia when he was in charge, is a reminder that the profile of mover in closed power is only a warning that calls for alertness to behavior across contexts.

2. Choice of Hero   If Howard were one to scan culture and history for his choice of a hero (see Chapter Nine), figures like General Patton would be a logical selection. Rudolph Giuliani and Elliot Spitzer would be more current heroes Howard would model himself after. As it turns out, Howard chose someone closer by. He had no real contact with his cuckolded father, but he identified with Uncle Frank, a crassly boastful moral blackguard, a mentor in the erotic delights of "winning."

3. Proneness to Insidious Forms of Courteous Compliance

Howard's proneness to courteous compliance had unusual origins. Usually, courteous compliance comes from people who are afraid to speak up to a controlling or tyrannical figure in a position of power; it is typically a risk-aversive take on fearing to "speak truth to power." That was not the case with Howard. Ralph was a leader who, far from penalizing those who spoke truths difficult to hear, welcomed them. Howard's motive in not coming clean was more sinister. He, with TJ's help, was investing recklessly in order to prove himself a "winner," and when his judgments backfired, he turned to TJ to cover up their failures. Had he not failed, had he succeeded, not only would there be more reason for his bonuses and promotions, he would do Uncle Frank proud. In Howard's mind, courteous compliance was part of the game's excitement.

4. Absence of Empathy and a Denial of Having a Shadow

In Chapter Eleven, I will introduce an assessment instrument that measures and reports an individual's behavioral profile and its propensities. Experienced consultants like Duncan, familiar with structural dynamics, are able to make broad but fairly accurate judgments or assessments of how such an individual would score on this instrument from behavior observed in the room. Howard, Duncan would predict, would score low or near zero in the affect domain.

Howard's childhood stories are devoid of empathy. He had little for his brother or his father, or, incidentally, for his mother in her dying days and hours. He had no appetite for introspection, one of the best forms of constraint on moral excess. It is even possible that asking him to reflect on his dark sides and shadow might draw a blank.

I have made much of leaders' capacity and willingness to acknowledge and take responsibility for their shadow. Denial of the shadow both follows and is an extension of lack of empathy. If, on top of having neither empathy nor compassion for those damaged by our shadow, we deny we have one, we thereby remove virtually all hope of correction or redemption. In this respect, oddly, Howard comes closest as a fraudster to Bernie Madoff. Madoff snookered the SEC for years in what amounts to an attitude of courteous compliance.

Publicly, he expressed no genuine empathy for his victims' lost fortunes and broken lives, and his son's death suggests the stain he left on the lives of people closest to him.

5. Narcissism In public confession, John Edwards admitted to being narcissistic. Howard, at least as narcissistic as Edwards, would confess to no wrongdoing, and it seems safe to say that he would not have admitted to narcissism, either. Some people embedded in power simply do not have the word in their vocabulary.

6. Evidence of Moral Compromise Howard's record of moral compromise originates in his early history, as documented in his stories, which entailed sexual exploitation ("seeing girls as sexual trophies") and damage to competitors (his unfair fighting and a willingness to go to extreme lengths to be number one in his class). When moral compromise takes root in early character development, the fraudulence loop mentioned earlier takes on new meaning in adulthood. For Howard, conscious moral concern put up little resistance.

In the modern world of work, it is difficult if not impossible for any leader to hide the nature of his moral compass. Even if, as in Howard's case, an effort is made to hide it from superiors, those directly affected by his decisions and ways of leading will make their own informed judgment; eventually they will call him out. Thus Howard was unmasked by a cautionary e-mail.

7. Not Knowing and Admitting No Error Earlier in the chapter I acknowledged the moral ambiguity of some acts of *not knowing*. It isn't always possible to be certain the extent to which not knowing plays a part in fraud or how deliberately it enters into a fraudster's regular way of doing things. Some of the accused pedophile priests, though in fact guilty, were otherwise "good" people. Only in this sense was Howard a "good" person. He had high personal standards for achievement, pouring himself into tasks in search of perfection. These attributes can mislead those responsible for rewarding up-and-coming leaders like Howard, for behind this drive there was a need to succeed that bordered on the ruthless.

That he refused to admit any complicity, even when it was determined that he could not be proven guilty, does not bode well for his future either. Moral integrity is not his middle name. The boy who cried "Who, me?" lives on. Howard is not unique on this score. The band of CEOs and company officials who stood before Congress in January 2010 for questioning about their roles in the financial debacle of 2008 (Lloyd Blankfein of Goldman Sachs, James Dimon of JPMorgan Chase, John Mack of Morgan Stanley, and Brian Moynihan of Bank of America), and those CEOs implicated in the disastrous Gulf oil spill (BP's Tony Hayward most notably) were no more forthcoming than Howard. Perhaps that is why many Americans reacted so sympathetically to the late former secretary of defense Robert McNamara's admission of error related to policies surrounding the American war in Vietnam.

Coupling not admitting error with unquestioning loyalty to the chief can create a powerful, odd moral logic that pulls a person toward voluntary silence. But in Howard's case it is safe to say that his not admitting error was, if anything, driven more by loyalty to Uncle Frank than loyalty to the chief.

8. Silencing the Witnesses   At this, Howard did his best but failed. While he was free and ahead in his game in Asia, he used all available devices to clip the tongues of those he "led," developing a culture of fear, intimidating anyone who spoke up, firing those who tried. All this Duncan had learned during his night out with Howard's inebriated assistant, and later confirmed with others after the fraud was discovered. But before Asia—openly oppose? actively bystand? Howard didn't try them; he saw them as mistakes. During Asia, except for the early, end-run e-mail of unknown authorship about the fraud, he kept a tight inner circle, a party of two like-minded conspirators who we suspect eroticized the game of "beating the system."

9. Excessive Ambition and Aggressive Striving for Competitive Advantage   Howard made no effort to hide his ambition; he put it on display, at times with operatic grandiosity, and, as with many before him with similar behavioral profiles, he was rewarded for that display. The warning signs here are not so much the ambitions themselves nor his goals of achieving wealth, status, and power. The real tip-offs concerned his *means* for achieving these goals, his unsavory attitudes toward women and sex, and his unfortunate moral premise that winning is proof of having done "right."

Howard took pride not in work itself but in how work could serve his ambition to rise as quickly as possible to a position of real official power. He did good work, earning rapid promotion to director of sales.

10. Weak Intimate Ties   Where there is no home for empathy, intimate relationships are homeless too. Howard had few close ties beyond his brother, Sam, from whom he took but gave back nothing of quality in quick teaser phone calls that flaunted his sexual or warrior prowess. He had one friend whom he'd not seen in years, but only Vera showed up on his dance card, and his relationship with her was exploitative, at best. Oh, he had many business contacts, but knew no one capable of calling him out on wrongful acts out of concern or love. His hidden, nefarious partnership in fraud with Template Jones cannot possibly count here as an intimate relationship.

You know by now how much weight I place on intimate ties; indeed, they are the heaviest counterweight and external check on any candidate's vulnerability to fraud, if intimates are able and willing to bystand and oppose in the service of a shared moral purpose. Jane provided this service for Art, as Sonia did for Ralph in high style. Neither of these men, I venture, would be likely candidates for fraud, sexual or financial.

THE LITTLE WE KNOW

We need to learn more about how to understand and assess the development of moral character in leaders and potential leaders.

- What clues might ignoble morals-shaping stories like Howard's offer?
- Can morally exalting stories, once elicited, be relied on to hold firm under pressure or temptation?
- Is it possible to assess a leader's moral character before he does damage to himself and those around him?
- Can an organization build into its culture practices that attenuate individual tendencies to succumb to egregious moral lapses?
- Is immunization from the fraud virus possible?
- What role does an organization's incentive system play?

GOOD MODELS THAT GO BAD

At this stage in his career, from all we know about him, Howard does not have an even indirectly expressed leadership model, and certainly not a "good" one. Most good models rest on a sound moral foundation. Chapters Eleven and Twelve will argue that a leader who builds his model seriously and systematically will be a better leader. Before going there, it must be said that a proven good model can go morally wrong if one absolute requirement of model building, responding to a legitimate constraint, has been ignored. A **legitimate constraint** is a properly delivered challenge to some aspect of one's model.

The example of Alan Greenspan, chairman of the Federal Reserve for eighteen years, is particularly useful here because a chink in his model, a dismissal of a legitimate constraint, had serious moral consequences with direct links to fraud. Here, briefly, is the relevant part of his story, that of a "great" leader's fall due to a flawed moral decision. In Chapter Twelve, we look at Greenspan's model itself.

Alan Greenspan tells of his assiduously built economic model in his charmingly candid memoir *The Age of Turbulence.* In a word, free-market capitalism without regulation lay at its core. Throughout Greenspan's long service, his model helped the market survive down cycles and spawned a period of continuous growth. A PBS Frontline documentary, *The Warning,* picks up on his story. It depicts a models clash between Greenspan and Brooksley Born, a securities law enforcer appointed to an obscure bureaucratic agency charged with monitoring arcane instruments known as derivatives, or "swaps," by Wall Street because only the parties in the transaction knew what was happening. The only detailed records had been buried in the filing cabinets of the immediate players. In them, Born saw recklessness and a probability of fraud. When Born confronted Greenspan, she was flummoxed by his model's dedication to deregulation. "Even when there is fraud?" she is reported to have asked. "Yes, even fraud," he is said to have answered.

When Born refused to back off, the documentary continues, Greenspan set his notable disciples (Robert Rubin and Larry Summers in particular) on her like guard dogs in what was judged intimidation calculated to silence the witness. And when she still wouldn't back down, she faced them and a one-sided congressional committee, which stripped Born's agency of its powers. Not long afterward, she resigned.

SUMMING UP AT CLEARFACTS

I began this chapter with interactions between Ralph and Sonia Waterman leading up to Ralph's resolve to make morality a central part of his leadership model and his recognition that the same concern about moral rightness must inform the models for living he and Sonia would work on together.

Ultimately, Ralph and his team recognized that only a multicausal account can make sense of failures in moral behavior. The larger environment is implicated. Wall Street is implicated along with Congress. The immediate organizational context is implicated and so are an organization's leaders, individually and as a group. But the team was willing to pledge to do whatever was called for to insure itself against a repeat of the Howard-TJ misadventure. For example, ClearFacts would support external regulation of the financial industry, which seems to many to foster the culture of greed that morally vulnerable organizations and leader types buy into. But will these steps be enough? No. External controls are not the best and only source of control. Unless individual leaders, in whose hands final responsibility rests, act consistently and forcefully, external controls are unlikely to stem the tide.

In Chapters Eleven and Twelve we move on to Ralph's experience creating his own models, partly in collaboration with his wife, and extending resources to his team so that they can work on useful models for themselves.

From Insight to Action

Many of the mechanisms discussed in this chapter are created out of an individual's attraction to power—not power as I've defined it herein, as competency and efficacy, but in an unsavory sense of the word, as "influence over" others and control over scarce resources. Power in this sense is recognized in high status and great wealth. That the need for power in this latter sense is likely related to moral corruption—which is, if anything, but a shortcut to status and wealth—is a reasonable assumption that should be closely examined.

Your Relationship to Power

You can begin with some self-examination: What is your relationship to power in its darker sense? In what ways are you attracted to it? In what ways are you repulsed by it? What is the role of power—not in your espoused leadership model but in the model you display?

1. Describe the last time you faced and had to deal with an ethical issue in your organization. What was the issue? Were you inclined to avoid it? Why did you get involved? What actions did you take? How satisfied were you with the outcome?

2. Can you see any of the mechanisms described in this chapter at play in the profiles of those involved in this situation? In your own profile?

3. Describe a decision that you have seen another leader make (preferably within your own organization) that caused you moral discomfort. What was the issue? What, from your perspective, were the available options? What would you have chosen to do on that occasion and why? Can you identify any systemic or individual mechanisms that contributed to the choice that was made?

4. What do you see as the most difficult moral decisions that you as a leader may be asked to make? What advice do you give yourself about how to approach these issues? Do you have a different way of thinking about these decisions than the other kinds of choices you make as a leader? If so, what is different?

5. Determine whether any of the following mechanisms that can lead to moral corruption are present in your organization today. If so, describe how they came to be and what keeps them in place.

    - Unquestioning loyalty to the chief

    - Silencing the witnesses

    - Co-opting the inner circle

    - Insidious forms of courteous compliance

    - Forgetting history

    - Not knowing

    - Reverence for power

    Of these, which ones cause you the most concern? In what ways are they especially endangering the moral health of your organization? If you, as a leader, were going to target these mechanisms for change, how would you go about it?

Moral Intelligence

1. Reflect on the following questions:

   • Is there such a thing as moral intelligence?

   • How would you define it?

   • As a leader, how would you help those you lead develop and build on it?

2. Reflect on this statement: The moral intelligence of a leader should be a precondition for the position, because it is this kind of leader who earns the trust of followers. An organization's hiring mechanism should find a way to assess it.

PART THREE

Models and the Ultimate Leader

chapter ELEVEN

From Personal Model to Leadership Model

At the weekly meeting shortly after Ralph's return from vacation, the team was "businesslike" in tackling the serious issue of reporting ClearFacts's internal problems to the SEC. It ended up choosing Ian and Ralph as the logical spokespersons for the report.

"We must stand by our policy of transparency, as much for our loyal workers as for the financial community," declared Ralph.

"More so!" Martha rejoined, "This team needs to know that we will not sacrifice transparency for expediency."

In the "people" portion of the meeting, Ralph introduced a new "Duncan project." Months before, when Duncan had first been allowed into the meetings, Ralph had suggested he facilitate them to some extent, but Howard had objected strongly, saying that the team "must focus on business, not people and relationships," and Duncan had remained an observer. Now Ralph again suggested greater participation.

First, Duncan would work directly with the team for a limited, specified time, his purpose being to help all team members achieve greater communicative competency and thereby raise the team's "collective intelligence" and functioning. Team members would also carry what they were learning into their own teams. What was great in all this, Ralph excitedly told the team, was that Duncan would be using a process model called Accelerating Team Performance (described further in Chapter Twelve) that would ensure clearly defined goals, a process of monitoring progress, and (rare from consultants) a means of actually measuring results.[1]

Second, as Duncan worked with Ralph on Ralph's next phase of growth as a leader—"articulating my own leadership model"—other team members could

265

also begin to work with a coach toward *their own* leadership models as well. At this second proposal, the arrows flew:

"What's the cost?"

"Cost *effectiveness*—can we measure that?"

"What's the commitment in time?"

"Can we test it before we commit?"

"What happens to me if I say no?"

In the end, consensus was reached to move forward. Ron and Ian had reservations, but everyone noticed that Ian did not block the project. He seemed to make a conscious effort not to dilute Martha's open and expected enthusiasm. Then Ralph asked each member to schedule a private meeting with Duncan, in which to learn more about the project and the key idea of communicative competency and to express his or her level of interest.

RALPH'S PERSONAL MODEL AND CURRENT FUNCTIONAL AWARENESS

After the meeting, Duncan handed Ralph a summary of what Ralph had confronted and learned about himself in the past several months. Its roughly ten items basically captured what Ralph had done to understand his own *personal model*, which in turn shaped the way Ralph interpreted, perceived, and "read" the structures he encountered and then acted on in repetitive ways. Ralph's future *leadership model*—how he would lead in practice—would need to incorporate on a behavioral level the main features of his personal model. The roughly ten items could also be regarded as steps or junctures through which Ralph had passed in the course of achieving considerable functional awareness: awareness of how he currently led, of how he impacted and was impacted by others, and of his shadow and what triggered it intensively in high-stakes situations. Keep in mind that, given the unpredictable realities of leading and coaching, the list here is not an exact prescription of tasks or the order in which they must occur in every case. Still, they reflect the natural general nature of what Duncan helped Ralph learn up to this point in his growth. Here we will briefly review Ralph's experience at each juncture.

Discovering Your Personal Model: Ten Junctures for Maximal Learning

1. Taking the Behavioral Propensities Profile instrument
2. Consciously expanding your behavioral repertoire
3. Recognizing and taking responsibility for your impacts on others
4. Recognizing model clashes and their repetitive patterns
5. Disclosing your childhood stories and their themes
6. Linking childhood story and structure-forming stories
7. Knowing your behavior in high stakes and crises
8. Identifying and taking responsibility for your shadow
9. Expanding your tolerance for difference
10. Linking work and personal relationships (optional)

1. Taking the Behavioral Propensities Profile Instrument

As you have seen, individuals can discover their behavioral profile without using any formal instrument, but Duncan has all coaching clients like Ralph take the Behavioral Propensities Profile (BPP), an online assessment instrument.[2] The instrument, which on a click gives users a fifteen-page report, was developed at Monitor Group and is available through the Kantor Institute. The returned report provides one's behavioral profile and one's distributions of scores across all structural levels; one's strong, weak, and stuck tendencies; the kinds of traps one tends to step into, with tips for how to avoid them; and implications of the results for one's leadership and personal life. His full report is available as Premium Web Content at www.josseybass.com/go/davidkantor. Although Ralph looked very much the mover in the corporate meeting room (Chapter Two), we saw bystander tendencies in him, too. Overall, Ralph's report characterized him as a bystander in random meaning.

2. Consciously Expanding Your Behavioral Profile Repertoire

From Duncan, Ralph had learned to ask,

"What happened?"

"What did I miss?"

"What did I do to make that happen?"

Further, Duncan had helped him expand his awareness with questions like these:

"Why do you oppose more with Ian than with Art?"

"Where did you learn that behavior?"

"Why, besides because you're the boss, do you so seldom follow?"

"What did you see; what was the context for you?"

"You do at times become a stuck mover. How do you explain these tendencies to yourself?"

Eventually Duncan asked,

"Can you tell me a story about its possible origins?"

And when Ralph was ready, Duncan would go on to suggest that Ralph expand:

"How about experimenting with a new action the next time that same structure is in the room?"

For example, Ralph came to see himself as a strong bystander, but he saw also how he too often left this stance too soon when swept up in his own new excitements. Beginning in Chapter Five, we continuously saw Duncan trying to help Ralph slow down and curb this stuck mover tendency. Expanding one's repertoire does not happen in one fell swoop. It is an ongoing process of learning that bores deeper each time an old behavior reappears.

3. Recognizing and Taking Responsibility for Your Impacts on Others

Helping people accept feedback has long been a part of therapy and clinical consulting. The systems perspective of structural dynamics extends the practice from the passive "taking information in" to *actively soliciting information we do not usually want to hear.*

This is done through an exercise I call *circular causal inquiry.* In it, leaders actively seek feedback by asking, "What is it I do that makes you behave toward me in the way that you do?" The aim is to discover any hurtful, harmful impact you, the asker, may have. The question signals a willingness to take responsibility for your own part in circular, looping patterns of interaction. Ralph's mastery of this exercise helped him recognize and take responsibility for the impacts of his personal model on others, including Sonia, his wife.

Circular causal inquiry could well have been part of how Duncan helped Ralph recognize his impacts in team meetings as well—recognizing, for example, how his enthusiastic waxings

- Tested the patience of CFO-COO Ian, who tried to stick to already full agendas, and even that of the ever fair-handed Art
- Sparked Ron, a comrade in meaning, to additional speculative imagination
- Elicited courteous compliance from Howard, ever waiting to get on with a private agenda
- Evoked censure from Martha, who typically took it on herself to close out her random boss's meanderings

Duncan would have alerted Ralph to the fact that having a generally trusting relationship with someone does not mean that a circular causal inquiry with him or her will be a piece of cake. *Everyone has invisible structures.* For example,

- *With Art:* Ralph might not have easy going even with Art, who trusted him fully. Art's volcanic reaction to Howard (Chapter Two) was a sign of *something* problematic (the manipulative, meddling father whom Art did not trust). Art could be sensitive to the context of the "inquiry" itself and to any "voice" that resembled that of his father's. But even if these sensitivities were aroused in Art, most likely he and Ralph would have completed the exercise productively.

- *With Martha and Ron:* Similar challenges to those faced with Art could arise with Martha and Ron, whose trust Ralph had already gained and with whom productive, open, two-way conversations were possible even over testy issues, but generally they would manage because their profiles matched Ralph's own in most significant dimensions, and the themes they provoked were rarely toxic to one another.

- *With Howard:* Circular causal inquiry would have been much more challenging for Ralph in relation to Howard, whose possibilities for mutual trust were weaker and whose profile and invisible structures clashed more with Ralph's. Ralph would have been well advised not to take his eyes off the deceptively self-serving Howard. Between them when stakes were low, courteous compliance would likely have shut down any real inquiry; in high stakes, too, untrustworthy Howard could well have outmaneuvered Ralph.

- *With Ian:* To conduct a circular causal inquiry with Ian would have required much nuance from Ralph. Each man tended to impact the other—not unexpectedly, considering their profiles. Clashes between Ralph's penchant for meaning (and his running away with any subject that interested him) and Ian's penchant for power, including meaning as power (getting business done posthaste) and other predictable clashes between the closed and the random, leave them rife for mutual structural impacts. Consider Ralph's impacts on Ian: Ralph was a connoisseur of chaos, which Ian dreaded; Ralph tolerated and displayed disrespect for authority, which angered Ian; Ralph's random-like tendencies toward lateness and wasting time would habitually upset Ian; and so on. Consider Ian's impacts on Ralph: "hearing" his critical father in Ian's voice under pressure, Ralph tended to explode in a voice of rebellion, in turn leaving Ian feeling that he was dealing with a crazy. Ralph needed and received a lot of help from Duncan with this "ghost in the room," Ian's harsh tones when *Ian* felt under pressure. Ralph never put this issue entirely behind him, but he brought it under control. He reached a point where he could say to Ian, "There I go, hallucinating again."

4. Recognizing Model Clashes and Their Repetitive Patterns

When a leader has enough distance, learning how to defuse patterns that get in the way of a team's effective discourse is relatively easy. Ralph had gotten a handle quickly on one repetitive pattern: the often hot exchanges apparently started by Howard that triggered Art and signaled Martha to step in. In their course, unprovoked except in his own mind, Howard critically undermined Art (opposed Art's move); feeling attacked, Art faltered in some way, becoming a disabled bystander or mover, let's say; then Martha came to Art's rescue by moving to oppose Howard. Urged by Duncan to correct his random tendency to let things happen, Ralph had learned to take such actions as saying, "Art may not be asking for your help, Martha," or "You can find better ways than that to make your point, Howard," or "You two, if you dared, could take a time out, openly discuss your differences, and get help from the rest of us in bridging them."

More difficult had been dysfunctional patterns in which Ralph himself was more invested in the outcome or harbored a bias for one player over another.

Then, stepping in could be treacherous. But whenever a work-stopping pattern made its way into the room, he could use his knowledge of behavioral profiles to look for some form of failed cross-model conversation. Thus grasping the conflict, he could master practice skills to defuse and constructively redirect its force.

Ralph had also noticed failed cross-model conversations in his life at home and, commendably, brought the relevant principles home to share with a receptive Sonia. Both agreed to take responsibility for recalling those principles when either one violated them or when they faltered at addressing something in their relationship.

5. Disclosing Your Childhood Stories and Their Themes

Chapter Six described how Duncan helped Martha explore key childhood stories and themes when she consulted him about problems of anger and triggered memories. With her permission, Duncan subsequently reported some of that process and story to Ralph. This had helped Duncan and Ralph—when Ralph insisted he was ready—to pursue a somewhat shorter route to get to Ralph's own stories. To start that process, Duncan focused Ralph on the interchange we saw in Chapter Four, in which Ralph had burst out heatedly at Ian ("Keep your *rules*. Keep your *order*. But keep your butt *out of my life!*").

With Ralph, Duncan took the short route, the one most likely to be used in business consulting and in training coaches. I have used it effectively in both contexts.[3]

Through this process, Ralph discovered that Ian was a structural doppelgänger for Ralph's father. The realization helped ease his gut reactions to echoes of his father's harsh *voice*, which he heard again in Ian's firm reactions to chaos or incompetence. The presence of Ralph's father in Ralph's dark shadow zone was something with which he would always need to grapple whenever he perceived abuse of power.

6. Linking Childhood Story and Structure-Forming Stories

When we are causing *or* solving problems, most of our typical behaviors are fueled by structure-forming stories, themselves springing from the nuclear childhood stories of love. Many of Ralph's post-team-meeting dialogues with Duncan had explored these connections. Let's consider Ralph's relations with women and with men; male-female relations is a subject all leaders must come to terms with despite major changes in recent decades for women and their place in positions of power.

Ralph with Women   As an unexpected benefit of revisiting his childhood family story (see Chapter Four), Ralph discovered the role his mother played in the family drama and emerged with more compassion for her than he had previously allowed. Recall how Ralph, a blossoming random, had clashed violently with his religiously austere, taskmaster father, a closed with a dark shadow, while his intimidated, undone mother sat helplessly by. The story made clear that she had been politically silenced (in the power domain) by her husband and also denied the right to express her emotions (in affect) without invoking the husband's cold and at times fierce putdowns.

As Ralph's childhood waned, his mother, "weak, bullied, and an accomplice in betrayal," was at best a dismally disappointing model. Thenceforth as a young and then not-so-young man, he'd stumbled blindly into and out of romantic relationships. Eventually an experience had opened his eyes: doing research for a tenured professor—a woman young but married and a mother of three—he saw someone at ease with her own power, a power that allowed her easily to hold her own in a department dominated by men. After Ralph finally recalled this old story, he was able to connect the professor with Sonia, then also with Martha. In their own ways, each fitted the mold.

Ralph with Men   Recall from Chapter Four Ralph's discovery that his father was a morally fraudulent pedophile. This may have added force to his disgust with Howard and led to his decision to call his model Moral Leadership. This brings us to consider the structures of Ralph's relations with *men* in closed power.

Unlike many CEOs, Ralph's lowest score on the BPP had been in *power*: 17 percent, in contrast with a much higher affect score (37 percent) and a very high meaning score (46 percent). But he respected, hired, and skillfully deployed other men in closed power, then was troubled when their dark sides damaged others, generally women inclined to exercise their own forms of power—open-system women, strong mover-opposers like Martha.

The structure-forming story behind his liking for strong, "un-baggaged" men began the day he met his college freshman roommate, Chad, an African American. As Ralph told Duncan: "Chad liked what he saw when he looked in the mirror. I did not at the time. In a most curious way, he helped me, as no one before or after, to know and like myself—the criteria for this, anyway. I hate the term, but the guy 'stood tall'—it never occurred to him that he needed a weapon other than his basically secure, self-directed self."

7. Knowing Your Behavior in High Stakes and Crises

A leader with a strong tendency in low stakes toward, for example, closed power, will likely tend even more strongly so in high stakes. A leader with a more balanced repertoire in low stakes has more options in high-stakes situations as well.[4]

Ralph's BPP results placed him in the latter group. In low stakes, he scored highest by far in meaning but was moderately high in affect; only his score in power was remarkably low. Still, the imbalance was important and limiting to some degree. As Duncan told him from observation:

"You tend to make your strongest and most frequent moves in meaning, turning moves in power over to Ian and Howard. Wise, on one level, but dangerous on another, as you painfully discovered. I want to alert you to some telling ways you've behaved in high stakes, as I've observed you under pressure.

"When you privately felt that your team lacked purpose and drive (high stakes for you), you were probably seduced by a convenient matchup in profiles between you and Ron, so you impulsively, unilaterally hired him, which violated your alleged commitment to an open system. In this way, you undermined your team's authority and brought them to riot. What saved your neck is that Ron on his own earned his right to be on the team.

"The failure of government to convert to green energy has been a soul-stirring issue for you, but this passion has at times enervated your team, insulting them by implying that something is wrong with them because they don't share your commitment. For you, the fact that 'the world is frying,' as you say, is a high-stakes matter. Unfortunately, it isn't for most. That drives you nuts. You go into high gear and constant motion, exhausting physical reserves, threatening your marriage, and then relying on Sonia to rein you back in, with (your words) 'wile, wit, and sex.'

"When these have not worked, her patience runs thin, and *her* themes are triggered (abandonment, I would guess from what you say the two of you fight about). Then she either becomes a fixer-like terrorist or scares you into thinking she's romantically involved elsewhere. *Your* survivor mode, triggered by anything or anyone who blocks the momentum of your moral crusade, renders you completely unaware that you have abandoned not only yourself but those you leave behind.

"In heroic mode, you're a survivor. Survivors tend to be cool in high stakes and crises, but when the right button is pushed, they can blow their tops. When Howard pushed one of your most sensitive buttons, moral integrity, you blew up publicly and fired him. You came apart, unlocking new, concealed resentments toward your father."

Arriving home one night during the internal inquiry into the fraud discovery, Ralph was so upset, it scared Sonia. She did her usual best to quell his rage, but at one point he turned on her, and she in turn screamed, "I'm not your mother, damn it!" Confused as to how their talk got to this moment, she demanded a time-out and called Duncan. "It's as if I'm not here; he's somewhere else." To which Duncan said softly, "Yes, he's in his family space. It has nothing to do with you. So step back; give him time and space to spend his rage. Then be sure to tell him you called me. He'll quiet down." These instructions helped, and Duncan's forecast was accurate.

The next day, Ralph told Duncan the whole story. Back to his usual self, avidly curious, eager to learn by putting to work all he'd done in recognizing the relationship between his childhood story and his reaction to company fraud helped this temporarily frazzled leader and his coach make short work of recovery, with new insights. "But," Ralph said at one point, "you've told me I'd achieved a fair level of functional awareness. Where did all *that* go? I've regressed horribly."

To which Duncan said: "This won't be the last time you slip. Regression is not the point; what you do with it is. You are discovering the persisting power of the childhood story. Just keep in mind that each time an event evokes the story and you revisit it, you can learn something brand new about yourself. Now don't forget to thank Sonia for keeping her cool. You could easily have made her into an enemy."

8. Identifying and Taking Responsibility for Your Shadow

One often charming aspect of Ralph's random style is his apparent openness to the discovery of shadow behavior in his own repertoire and in those of others. In one session with Duncan, somewhat boastfully, he said, "'Randoms' like me are at ease with chaos and extreme behavior. I'm really okay with shadows."

Those words came back to haunt him when Howard and TJ's Asia caper brought forth Ralph's own darkest shadows from his childhood story—anger at a controlling and unloving father—and from his young-adult hero myth, the survivor's confidence in his ability to withstand almost any challenge to a cause to which he commits. His survivor mantras—"If necessary, I can endure on pain of death," "I can persevere," "I'm invulnerable," "I can shut out negativity," "Little can hurt me"—gave way. Howard's insidious fraud and Ralph's father's pernicious lie joined forces, undoing Ralph's customary poise and triumphal optimism.

What Duncan tried to bring home to Ralph was the relationship between one's light and shadow sides in high stakes. As a rule, the dark side of the hero beneficently fuels the light side, in Ralph's case the obsessively good work he does in connection with his commitment to green energy. But ghosts from a powerful childhood story can undo all this. Once or twice at work, and even more forcefully at home, he'd lost control in blasts of vitriol toward Howard.

9. Expanding Your Tolerance for Difference

Ralph's head start on tolerance for differences in how people with different behavioral profiles see and act in the world can be attributed to a random's natural leaning to openness to many things, such as new art forms and content that transgress convention and taboos, and other attempts to shed new light on things by challenging what exists. This had been Ralph's learning edge, enabling him to tolerate Ian and Howard's closed-system preference and Martha's open-system preference until, in high stakes, his shadows locked horns with theirs. But Duncan warned Ralph that as he dug into his leadership model, he would face new challenges in this regard.

10. Linking Work and Personal Relationships (Optional)

Structural dynamics strongly suggests that leaders make connections between their work and personal relationships. Of all the characters I've depicted, Ralph found this easiest to manage. In this sense he was a true random. The "other," the outsider different from one's own self, one's class, race, category, or behavioral profile, was a welcome addition, and from the start he had no problem deciding to examine the links between what he did at work and what happened in his relationship at home with Sonia. One of the reasons their relationship had worked in the past was that Ralph shared a lot with her about his work life, and even more about what he was gaining from his coach. In response, Sonia was more than curious, insisting on knowing what he was learning, probing detective-like when he gave lazy responses, pushing for detail even when he claimed exhaustion, puncturing the bubbles of silent thought, and relishing the shared delights of new learning that made *their* lives better.

Whenever he lapsed into serious reflection, Ralph even suspected that when he told Duncan of relevant events at home, he might be delivering messages that Sonia had intended him to carry back to Duncan. She was a scrupulous custodian of the relationship, and when it was threatened in any way by work, Ralph heard about it in no uncertain terms—and so did Duncan.

DUNCAN: I venture that your Sonia is a rare combination of fixer and protector who functions primarily in the light zones.

RALPH: She had good therapy before we married. And she *is* a force.

DUNCAN: You mean her power's internal, built in by some previous relationship.

RALPH: A gift from her father.

DUNCAN: What attracted her to you?

RALPH: Not "what I was" but "what I could become." She's fought for me, stood by me so long as I don't do stupid things that squander my best stuff.

DUNCAN: Could be. A survivor—that's with a small *s*—who saw the Survivor in you as a threat to you both.

RALPH: She nails it. She can look me in the eye and say something like "Ralph, the pride you feel in your capacity to endure is nothing but Narcissus admiring his own lovely face in the pond."

Ralph's late father remained a figure with the power to stun and immobilize him in certain contexts. With this in mind, Ralph pledged with Duncan to continue detoxifying people who, innocently or not so innocently, replicated his father's hold on him.

Structural dynamics allows people like Ian to choose to opt out of linking work and personal relationships. When Duncan was new at ClearFacts, it would have been unrealistic to think Ian would consent to sharing his childhood story or the story of his marriage—not, certainly, if these were to be made public, as would be the case with the model Ralph presented to the team at the start of this chapter. But structural dynamics does encourage people like Ian to move in that direction, and Duncan raised the possibility in Ian's private meeting with him; when Ian predictably demurred, Duncan mentally exempted him until Ian himself was ready.

Actually, though Ian wouldn't yet share his most important childhood stories, a few months earlier he had turned to Duncan briefly when he feared that his son, a random in rebellion against a closed father, would act on a veiled suicide threat. Before that talk, Duncan had already sensed that although publicly Ian was all power, privately he was strong in meaning (his fascination with military history suggested as much), so Duncan and Ian had made some connection in meaning. The conference about Ian's son had enhanced that with some connection in affect—a rare thing for Ian. The latter connection was likely the beginning of changes taking place in a heretofore much bounded-off Ian, changes that became visible to other team members during the firm's crisis. Of course, Duncan and Ian's effective collaborative mission to Asia had also strengthened their connections.

When Ian left their private meeting about working toward a leadership model, Duncan was cautiously optimistic that in time Ian would join the effort, but on his own terms. We would predict that one of Ian's terms for agreement would be that he work with Duncan only, in a sense chaining Duncan to the job. Such developments are not unusual.

ONWARD

At this juncture, Ralph has achieved functional awareness: he knows enough about how his personal model plays out in his relationships with each of his team members and with his wife, Sonia. He knows the upsides and downsides of his profile—a bystander and mover in random meaning. He knows what the light side of his survivor heroic mode contributes to ClearFacts, how its dark side affects his relationship with Sonia, and the conditions under which this dark side undermines his best heroic self. But he also knows that all of this is only the beginning of self-knowledge; some of what he thinks he knows will be challenged as he consciously moves on to the next phase.

"The next phase," said Duncan, "is deliberately building the leadership model you'll try to follow in the future. We'll launch that phase together, but after I leave, you'll be developing it on your own for as long as you remain in an active role as leader."

At first, building one's model seems impossibly demanding, but once begun it is an astonishingly rewarding process, in the long run saving more time by far than time spent. Model building with a coach who has done so already, a coach with a model he is willing to put on display, increases efficiency and power. Ralph was a willing enlistee to model building. Duncan, his coach, had built his model with me.

From Insight to Action

Ralph is a random strong in meaning. He is automatically a good candidate for team leadership. Martha is a multilingual open. Her profile type is, arguably, even more receptive than Ralph's, making her thereby a perfect leader for HR. Ian is a classic closed, with this caveat: he can be reached through meaning. In short, a leader's behavioral profile strongly influences his or her receptivity to model building.

1. Revisit what you earlier judged to be your behavioral profile. Now revisit any thoughts you had about your receptivity to model building as you read this chapter. Is there a link, obvious or not?

2. Discuss this question with a colleague who has read the chapter. What implications do you draw as leader or coach from your conversation?

3. How ready are you at this time to undertake a model-building program?

In his coaching model (structural dynamics), Duncan identified ten junctures of maximal learning, steps he took Ralph through to help him discover his personal model and to acquire functional awareness, a requirement for understanding how he manages relationships with specific colleagues and *their* personal models.

For Coaches

1. Which, if any, of the ten junctures resonates with your coaching model?

2. Are there some steps you would *constrain*, either because you think they are inappropriate or because your model covers the same territory, but better than the structural dynamics model?

3. What would that cross-model conversation look and sound like? What would you ask Duncan to reconsider? What might you reconsider in your model?

4. Structural dynamics takes a strong stand: for maximal performance, leaders should have a leadership model of their own creation, and knowing their personal model is a prerequisite for developing their leadership model. Do you find this extreme? Does your model already cover this territory, but in its own way? Have you articulated your model?

For Leaders

1. Duncan helps Ralph look at patterns in his routine dealings with each team member, and attempts to show connections between these patterns and his personal model. Is any of this familiar to you in your key relationships?

2. Do the suggestions I make in "For Coaches," question 4, seem too extreme?

3. Is doing some variation of what Ralph is doing on your professional development horizon?

Building a Leadership Model <small>chapter</small>
TWELVE

"No rest for the weary," Duncan liked to say to leaders like Ralph who have done the equivalent of the personal model work described in Chapter Eleven and are ready for the next big phase: developing a *leadership model.*[1]

First I present the rough overview Duncan provided for Ralph for this phase, followed by a description of how he and Ralph proceeded with the work.

AN OVERVIEW

Models underlie how we think, what we see, and how we act on what we see when we interact with the world. They are, in the broadest sense, our picture of the world and our map of how we intend to go about working in that world. As master modeler, master architect Frank Lloyd Wright once said, "The thing always happens that you really believe in; and the belief in the thing makes it happen."[2] Wright's distinct buildings have different functions and exist in different environments, and yet are all easily recognizable manifestations of Wright's architectural model. In it, he captured the essence of what he believed to be true about good architecture and how that could be expressed through the buildings themselves.

Models arise intuitively, often outside our day-to-day conscious awareness. Spurred by the need to grasp the social world, we start building our social models of that world at a very early age. The process becomes second nature and almost entirely automatic as our models take in a constant stream of new information, incorporating it into our maps of the social world and telling us how to respond. These models are expressions of each person's unique identity.

Anyone can *deliberately build* a model, but few people do much of it. Instead, they remain dependent on their unconsciously developed models, missing opportunities to increase the reliability, efficiency, and effectiveness of those models in guiding their lives. Conscious model building is a disciplined process and encompasses the discovery of *what* it is we think we do, *how* we actually do what we say we do, *why* we do what we do, *who* we are when we are taking these actions, and what we *hope* to achieve with the actions we take. In building a model, we can systematically examine our *implicit* models in order to choose which of their aspects to keep, which to reshape, and which to discard altogether in the face of a demanding future. The process lets us become deliberate about how we, in this case, choose to lead.

Being aware of and being able to articulate one's own models inevitably increase their strength and influence. This awareness and ability also provide the recognition that *everyone* operates from models, making us more open and interested in learning about the models and logics of others. It is essential to be able to recognize one's own and others' models because of an implicit paradox, which is that every model brings both clarity and distortion to one's perceptions of the world: clarity in that we would be unable to make *any* sense of the world (circumstances, facts, data, problems, opportunities, people) without some sort of model or template; distortion in that *every* model reduces the complexity of what we can see. One of the greatest benefits of consciously examining our models is the realization that "truth" is in some ways a construct of our model. This awareness opens us up to the possibilities of others' model-defined truth.

Social Models and Cross-Model Conversation

The ideas here should sound familiar from Chapter One, in which I introduced the concepts of cross-model conversation and model clash. One person's model varies inevitably from that of someone else, and some degree of tension is always present in social interaction stretching between our "truth" and the "truth" as the "other's" model defines it. Potentially, these tensions (and even outright model clashes) provide important developmental opportunities: the interplay between your model and those of others leads to an increase of the reliability, efficiency, and effectiveness of your own. Too often, however, in the course of a clash, we interpret the pushback from others as mere "noise" and continue on without acknowledging or learning from it.

The Use of Cross-Model Conversation

Any time people express their differences, they do so through the lens of their models. A closed parent will have a different view from a random parent about whether a child of ten can set his own bedtime hour and about how to handle a seventeen-year-old's experiments with alcohol. At home and at work, our profiles, in all their component parts, lead to such clashes. In a sense, these are all cross model-conversations.

Cross-model conversation is a very specific process for dialogue, grounded in the idea that the difference between the ways two people view the world is not a problem if they have a way to constructively explore these differences. Cross-model conversation is a two-way reflective conversation dominated by sincere inquiry into how the other views the world. It aims at deepening the discourse by offering the other an opportunity to substantiate or supplement his or her model and by doing the same with one's own. Two principles underlie the process:

- Difference is a key source of learning about ourselves and our models.

- It is pointless to assert that one model is "better" than another. Every model has its limits, which we must face in order to be able to grow. The only "bad" model is one that does not recognize its own limits, wrongly assumes it is complete, and presumes itself better than other models.

When you have become adept at the cross-model conversation process, you will be able to more effectively capitalize on the value of the diverse models around you—ready to compare and improve your own.

MODEL BUILDING AND THE MODEL OF MODELS

Model building is the discipline of reflecting on and systematically enhancing our deeply embedded views of the world, of ourselves, and of our work. It begins with standing outside ourselves to observe our interactions in the world, noticing how our behaviors come together with the behaviors of others to produce both good and bad results, then incorporating those reflections back into our underlying belief systems.

In Figure 12.1, note the term *displayed model*. In exploring our models, we typically start with our observable *practices* and behaviors, the most tangible and accessible aspect of our implicit models. Our practices are what we actually say and do in response to the world. Too often we try to change these practices at the

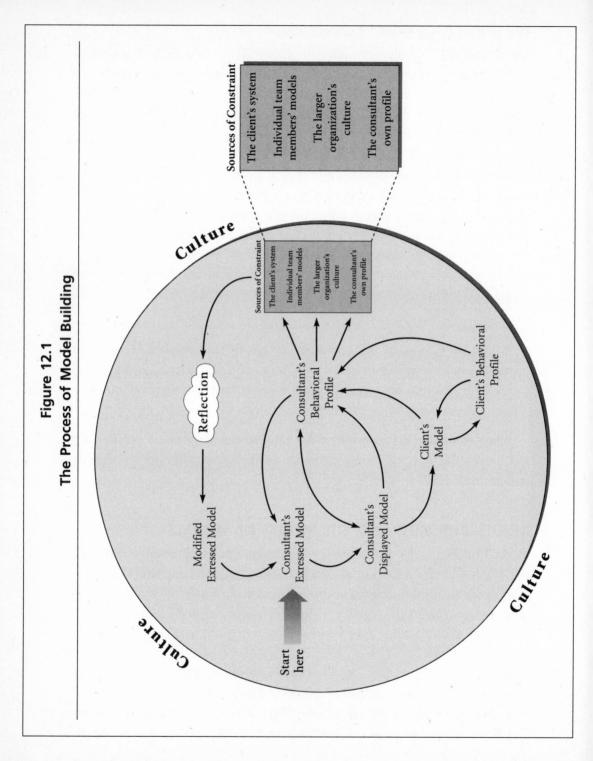

Figure 12.1
The Process of Model Building

surface level, trying to just "do something different." This approach ignores the fact that practices are merely expressions of an underlying belief system. In order to change what we do, as is often the goal of model building, we must have a greater sense of where our behaviors originate and why our model instructs us to use the practices we follow. Without knowledge of the *what* and *why* of our model, we cannot change the *how*.

Steps in the Process of Model Building

Model building on the ground is dynamic and interactive, but it also relies on reflection, from which continuous change and growth take place. To simplify a complex but altogether manageable process, I will describe it in steps:

1. A practitioner enters a field of practice with a practice model, a template for how she plans on proceeding with a client. This is her expressed model, what she intends to do.

2. No expressed model is ever delivered in its pure form. Both the practitioner and her model are constrained by forces not entirely in her control. The result is her displayed model, what she actually says and does, not what she intended at the outset.

3. Reacting to constraint, which I will describe more fully in the next section, the practitioner automatically adjusts and adapts her plans, if only in small ways at first.

4. Over time, more serious push-back or the mere accumulation of constraints from four sources result in more serious change in those aspects of her model that are being challenged. These are

   • The nature (for example, the dominant profiles) of the client system itself

   • Models held by individual members of the system that compete with the practitioner's model

   • The larger organizational context (for example, its culture)

   • The way the practitioner's own behavioral profile unavoidably modifies both her expressed and displayed models, particularly in the face of personal challenge

5. When a model is constrained, producing unanticipated results, the practitioner faces three choices: she can decide that they are mere "noise" and dismiss

them; she can realize that her model has failed in some way and has gaps that must be filled; or she can respond spontaneously, coming up with a new concept or technique she can add to her model.

6. Finally, at this time, the practitioner engages in reflection that results in a change in her expressed model. The circular nature of this process is, in effect, the crux of model building. Its core mechanism is constraint.

Constraint Defined

Constraint is the creative tension that is generated when proponents of two or more different theories, methods, approaches, or models engage in conversation or other face-to-face transactions. It has been proposed in these pages as the core principle behind the practice of cross-model conversation. It is, as noted in the previous section, just as critical to the process of model building. Indeed, model building can be seen as an ongoing cross-model conversation between a practitioner and her clients, session by session, throughout her career.

In the room, constraint—challenge or push-back from one or more of the sources cited in the previous list—can have either disappointing or exciting new results. Postsession reflection out of the room, the appropriate response to constraint, should implicitly be seen as ever present in the discussion of the model of models that follows.

Model building may sound dauntingly abstract. How do we know which of our countless beliefs, memories, and so on are influencing our behaviors at any given time? To think about what to look for as you unearth and organize your model, it is useful to have an overarching set of theories (or requirements) that I call a *meta-model.* This is not hard to grasp. The **meta-model** (or "model of models") is a framework that defines the aspects of a fully formed and robust model. Within it we can organize and interrelate the pieces of our models. Any social meta-model needs to propose three kinds of theories: theories of the *thing,* of *change,* and of *practice.*[3]

A Theory of the Thing

A **theory of the thing** names and describes the entity on which your model focuses:

- What is it? For example, this book presents a systems-oriented theory and examines the skill of *leadership.*

- What are the underpinnings of that skill? This book singles out communicative skill, beginning with communication in face-to-face relations.
- What assumptions does the thing (leadership here) depend on? One assumption in this book is that leadership often entails leading high-performing teams.
- What are the component parts from which the thing (leadership) is built? Or how is it supposed to work? Charisma? Knowledge of the behavioral profile?
- Can a set of principles define the thing (leadership)? Or can a set of linked concepts present a coherent picture of the whole?

Approach these questions through specific ones like these:

- What *is* "high team performance"?
- How would you define leadership to someone who has never heard of it?
- What (moral) values must a leader possess?
- How do you identify good leadership in others? How do you know it when you see it?
- What specific characteristics, actions, and beliefs define a leader?
- How does leadership fit into the landscape of your personal model of how the world works?
- What kinds of leaders do you admire and why?
- What experiences have shaped your definition of leadership?

A Theory of Change

The **theory of change** says how to bring about change for that *thing* on which your model focuses. It describes the nature of change and how change happens within or for the entity:

- What are the prerequisites of change (in our case, the changing of a person to become a better leader)?
- How does change happen? What brings it about?
- Is there a consistent process that leads to change?
- How does context—time, place, and person—affect change?

- Does change occur the same way in an intimate human system versus a larger, more impersonal one? Specifically, if *someone* wanted to change some entity, how would that person bring change about?

- How can change be sustained?

For the thing called leadership, you may need to consider these questions:

- Specifically how do leaders bring about the changes they desire in themselves and in others?

- If leadership's goal is better team performance, what is the baseline, and what is the standard (in this book "communicative competency") at the other end?

- What is it that brings about change in a leader?

- Through what stages does a leader evolve?

- What contextual factors affect an effort to change a leader?

- How can a leader sustain newly developed characteristics?

A Theory of Practice

A **theory of practice** suggests what actions should occur based on your under-standing of the *thing* and how it changes:

- What actions must be taken in order for the thing (leadership) to change?

- What is the goal of our practices?

- What tools, techniques, and methods can be used?

- What are the practices acting on? For example, Duncan's practice "acted on" Ralph's profile and his tacit model.

- Must practices follow a certain sequence? In principle, yes; Duncan saw ten "critical junctures" Ralph needed to work through to reach functional self-awareness (Chapter Eleven), and there was some order to the ten. At the same time, those ten practices did tend to advance in a spiral produced under reality's circular influence.

- Is the theory of practice consistent with the theories of the thing and of change?

Guidelines for Leaders: Some Key Questions

- What are your leadership goals?
- What characteristic actions or practices do you want others to associate with your leadership?
- What specific tools, techniques, and methods do you use as part of your leadership?
- What new behaviors are you capable of incorporating into your leadership? How do you want these behaviors to evolve throughout your leadership life?

The theory of practice of leadership unites your theory of leadership ("effective leaders tend to do X or Y") with your own behavior as a leader.

When we have done the work of articulating our current model's theories of the thing, of change, and of practice, we can then critically examine each to determine how they are meeting our needs. A key task of model building is choosing which aspects of our current models we will keep, which we will reshape, and which we will discard altogether. Because our models to date have mostly formed unconsciously, they may contain outdated beliefs and unproductive practices, and may even lack a theory of change. No model is ever perfect or complete. Any model can be improved through a conscious model-building effort.

Three Stages of Building

As we progress from discovering our implicit models to actively enhancing them, we tend to seek out other models from which to learn. This proactive exploration represents the first of the three stages of model building, visualized in Figure 12.2. I call the stages *imitation, constraint,* and *autonomy.*

In stage one, **imitation,** we read about other models, seek out mentors, or enter a program where we are being coached by someone whose model we want to explore. We try to temporarily surrender our own model in order to more fully understand the model of the other. Often clumsily, we try to imitate that other's model to see how it fits, complements, and contradicts the one we currently have.

In stage two, **constraint,** we begin to test the limits of the other's model and restore possession of our own. This is done by productively "constraining" the model of the other: exploring ways in which it is incomplete or breaks down in some circumstances. *All models, when put to the test, will occasionally fail.* The

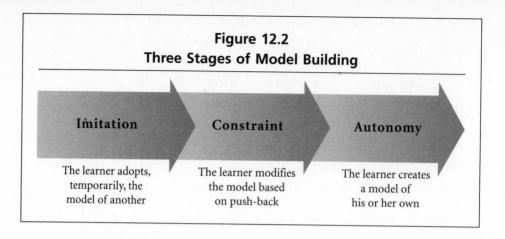

Figure 12.2
Three Stages of Model Building

Imitation → Constraint → Autonomy

The learner adopts, temporarily, the model of another

The learner modifies the model based on push-back

The learner creates a model of his or her own

best models are simply those that recognize their limitations and continue to evolve.

In the stage of constraint, model building becomes two-way. The constraint we offer to the other's imitated model, if reflected on and incorporated, can expand both the other's model *and* the one we are building as we say yes to *that* but not to *this*. The process is, in effect, a special form of cross-model conversation, a process essential in this phase of building one's own model. As will be discussed in the companion workbook to *Reading the Room, Making Change Happen,* cross-model conversation can proceed when your model is constrained, let's say, by another leader's model.

In the third and final stage, **autonomy,** we evolve our own practice model (and, for the well advised, the theories of the thing and of change that drive it) into a more developed and mature version of its former self by adopting those aspects of the imitated model that are most critical to us and rejecting the rest. At this point we have moved from wholesale "borrowing" to a more independent focus on our own model, developed enough for others to imitate.

Model building is really a lifelong pursuit. When we cannot find, deeper within our model, an answer to a legitimate constraint, the cycle can begin again.

Articulating our models signals that we are ready to begin enhancing them. For a model to be imitated or constrained by others, we first have to find a way to share it with them. Without a statement of our models, other people are left to simply interpret and judge our *behaviors.* These interpretations are filtered through their own models; therefore, they are more a statement about *their* models than ours. If we want others to see and understand our model, we should be able to say, for example, "In my model, leadership is . . . " Once we are truly clear about the model, we will find clarity about how to express it.

Model building is not easy. Organizations wanting to develop their high-potentials into future leaders will have to decide whether the investment seems worth it. It is no secret that I am trying to make a case for it as a wise investment that will pay off. Business schools, the dominant training field for business leaders, also must decide whether what they do to prepare leaders could be significantly enhanced by incorporating into their programs something of what is being offered here.

Greenspan: A Good Model That Failed

Alan Greenspan is one leader who did the hard work of building a model on the ground—and did it well until circumstances demanded an appropriate response to legitimate constraint. Ralph and all model builders will encounter this same barrier as they build on the ground.

I reiterate, Greenspan was exceptionally conscientious in how he chose his theoretical sources and built his model step-by-step, according to the meta-model. His theory of the thing (the financial market) was clear, as was his theory of change about how that market evolves, if left alone, on a steady gradually rising slope; and in his theory of practice, he was attentive in his use of empirical methods—data gathering and analysis—as a basis for decision making.

Starting by imitation, he drew initially from the models of established econo-mists like Milton Friedman. Later, like many in his youthful generation, he also came under the influence of the novelist and social thinker Ayn Rand, adopting and subsequently for many years holding fast to one of her major assumptions: faith in the individual's wisdom to do the right thing in both the rational and moral sense. But the obvious constraining question neither Rand nor Greenspan apparently posed or answered: "Why, then, *do* individuals act irrationally and immorally?" In the end, his and his model's downfall was prepared by his refusal to give proper due to constraints.

In Chapter Ten, I discussed the moral necessity of explicit constraints and of an openness to consider new constraints as they become apparent. Every model when watched closely over time develops contradictions and qualifications. Greenspan had sensed the key constraint earlier when he had questioned Rand on a different but similar fundamental issue: "Would an individual who saw a need for government voluntarily pay taxes?"

"They would," she had argued with persuasive power. At that moment, he writes, he bought into her model, then carried her philosophical banner until the model failed with near disastrous consequences. Only years later did he acknowledge the "flaw" in his model, long after Brooksley Born, the government regulator, had confronted him and his belief that the market, left on its own, would regulate against fraud. Continue the story from there to the 2008 financial crisis and the subsequent 2010 congressional hearing in which legislators examined the role of federal regulators in 2008. Pressed as to whether his fundamental economic policy was "wrong," Greenspan said, "Yes. I found a flaw."

Congressman: "You found a flaw in the reality."

Greenspan: "Flaw in the model that I perceived as the critical functioning structure that defines how the world works, so to speak."

What he doesn't say is that his flaw was not only in how he mishandled Born's legitimate constraints on his model and its core assumptions but also in his longtime refusal to engage in an effective cross-model conversation.

As I said earlier, put to the test, all models will occasionally fail. The best models are simply those that recognize their limitations as revealed by legitimate constraints, and continue to endlessly evolve.

FINDING RALPH "ON THE GROUND"

Before we begin this model-building journey "on the ground" with Ralph, let's look at how he reacted to Duncan's introduction:

RALPH: *That* was a lot to digest. How in hell does anyone learn it all?

DUNCAN: You learn as you go along in your practice. It seems overwhelming, but you have a personal handle on the language system of structural dynamics, and you are motivated to think theory in concert with practice, unlike most executives.

RALPH: Right. "Too damn busy."

DUNCAN: It may surprise you that many coaches are much the same. They've studied under someone else, and therefore they already "have a theory," even though in fact they have no model that truly fits them. Executives, coaches: for differ-

RALPH: ent reasons, neither tear themselves away from whatever their practices are. Nor do they need to.

RALPH: Hold on. You're saying they're fine as they are? Then why am I jumping through all these—

DUNCAN: Hoops? Yes, in the short run their models suffice, but not in the long. People are ritualists; they do the same things over and over, repeating the same mistakes, trying harder with solutions that do not work. When you live in a hurricane zone, you try to build your house to stand up to hurricanes. You don't consider that it might be better, long term, to pick up and build somewhere else. Leaders and coaches see themselves living in hurricane zones, in constant threat of the unexpected—"If I could just make these windows thicker!" Once they build well enough to *survive* in high stakes, once they build that model, they have no inclination to give it up for something that might be better.

RALPH: But the short run is real; my time right now is real and objective. And limited: twenty-four hours in a day. How do you convince "busy people," as Sonia describes me and others like me, to think otherwise and find time to ever look much ahead?

DUNCAN: First, when a model in process passes a certain threshold, it begins to *save* time. You make fewer mistakes, you spend less time making amends and picking up the debris the wind blew in, you lose less talent to avoidable personal storms, and you act sooner to open the exit door to those who do not belong. The net time gain in the long term far exceeds the time, in the short term, that you put into passing the threshold.

Second, when you get around to designing a life worth living, you may revise your thinking about measured time. Measured time is the only kind of time busy people know. They live by the clock and calendar. When you and Sonia design a life worth living, you will discover that there are other kinds of time.

From here we follow Ralph well into the three stages of building his model: imitation, constraint, and autonomy. Keep the Greenspan story in mind as you notice Ralph's attention to the moral dimension and his honoring of constraints. Of course, life at ClearFacts did not stop while Ralph took up his model.

ART'S DEPARTURE AND A NEW APPROACH TO HIRING FOR THE TEAM

In the continuing aftermath of the Asia office crisis, marketing director Art Saunders resigned in spite of generous offers from Ralph aimed at getting him to stay. His departure and Howard's firing left two seats vacant on the leadership team. In addition, a decision had been reached to add two additional members to the team, for a total of eight.

When Art's moment had come to decide whether to stay or to leave the firm, Duncan had been commissioned to offer him a package (no travel, no long days into night except by necessity, paid leave when his next child was born, and so forth). Art's refusal of the offer led to a meeting between Art and Ralph to finalize his departure.

ART: Just so you know, Duncan did a great job in presenting your kind offer to help me stay. It touched me deeply how well he understood my dilemma. Even Jane, when I told her, was impressed with the new terms.

RALPH: They still stand. They represent our regard for your creative genius. But more, Art, they represent the affection I and others have for you as a human being.

ART: *(Silently allows a tear)*

RALPH: *(Graciously extends the silence, merely nodding, mumbling something like, "good man"; then, to lighten the mood)* Just don't let Jane talk to Sonia, or I may be following you out the door. She doesn't like the ugly side of this warlike world any more than Jane.

ART: Again, just so you know. Duncan's the culprit, not Jane. She has wanted me out of the business world from the day I started. The moment I really decided to leave was when Duncan helped me see that the decision to stay or leave was mine, not hers.

RALPH: And how did Duncan help you come to that moment?

ART: By helping me end my fight with my father. I discovered I was here, not because of him, but because I did not have the stuff to take him to the mat. In that moment of insight, I could stay or leave. I chose to leave.

RALPH Whew! A lot to think about. I see you're giving me the green light to get on with the business of managing the transition. We'll need your help in choosing your replacement.

One of the issues that Art's departure raises for CEOs and organizations is what to do with people who, for the sake of making a living, become performance leaders, when their natural, profile-based inclinations are different from what a career of "performing" requires of them. Often they stay on and become more miserable. (To this problem, structural dynamics has proposed a radical but viable solution called Five Leadership Pathways. Briefly, it proposes that at a key juncture in a long career, leaders be afforded the opportunity to remain vibrant in their organizations by choosing from among five different leadership pathways: the performance leader, the vision leader, the citizen leader, the wisdom leader, and the exit leader. Ralph took great interest in this model.[4])

Turning to the problem of rebuilding the team, Ralph worked in concert with his leadership team to round out the eight positions. Duncan assisted him with some guidelines like the ones listed here. Notice that this list introduces an entirely new way of choosing high-level people, including ensuring balance based on a distribution of behavioral profiles. Art's and Howard's positions were filled from within; so was the first new position, by a high-performing leader with many years' service; an external search filled the remaining new position.

Guidelines for Hiring onto a Leadership Team

- Hire for skill set, but even more important, choose people whose profiles match the job and fit in with the team's individual and group profile.

- Choose for a diversity of profiles to balance openness, getting business done, and creativity.

- Make a determined effort to identify the recruit's dark-side behavior, inquiring into how he or she behaves or misbehaves in high-stakes situations.

- Create an interview format that reveals what the candidate does in the room rather than what she and others say she has done elsewhere. For fairness in this game, the interviewer should, before ending, explain the intention and what was found; not incidentally, this discussion can elicit even more valuable information.

- The team should be aware of each interviewer's behavioral profile and how it might distort or bias the findings of candidate interviews. (We saw this bias when Ralph hired Ron.)

Within weeks, the team was reconstructed, and Duncan began working with it toward a level of communicative competency required for the achievement of **collective intelligence**—a level of team performance measurably superior to the sum of individual performances. In this effort he used his own adaptation of a process or model called Accelerating Team Performance (ATP), which I'll describe in detail in this chapter. As you will see, Ralph would decide to imitate this ATP model in the course of building his own leadership model.

Duncan also began individual coaching with Martha and Ron. Martha had already indicated that she saw herself both as participant and apprentice trainer, and, once having earned the right, she was bent on developing an individual coaching model and on using the ATP process with her own team and elsewhere in the company where specific teams made critical decisions. Ron also moved forward with determination, though less eagerly than Martha because he had yet to deal with his childhood theme of "being cautious about whom you trust."

Duncan also began to coach Ian, but only after much soul searching on Ian's part, two intense private talks between them, and an agreement that Ian could opt out of the coaching after a certain number of sessions. (He would later decide to continue, but with reservations about personal disclosures. Ian would also confirm Duncan's hunch that disclosure would be an act of disloyalty to his father, who may have physically abused his mother.)

The team had thrown a send-off party for Art to celebrate his future. At moments tearful, the event had triggered some deep soul searching in Ron and Martha about what it meant to be on the firing line for "the most vigorously precious period in one's life." Ralph, too, had thoughts on the subject, particularly as he and Sonia had begun "designing a life worth living," as you will read in Chapter Thirteen. Recognizing Ron's and Martha's personal struggles, Ralph was considering how to design a workplace worth living in for loyal and talented people who work so hard and long that their once-green and energetic spirits dissolve or rust in tedium or exhaustion. For the time being, he decided to trust Duncan's claim that a leader who commits to the never-ending process of building his model will neither get bored nor burn out, and that designing a life worth living would keep work life and personal life in balance.

RALPH BUILDS HIS LEADERSHIP MODEL

Recall the three phases of building a model: imitation, constraint, and autonomy. The following describes Ralph's work mainly in the first two phases.

Ralph's Imitation Phase of Model Building

Beginning by imitation means trying out someone else's basic model on a problem of one's own—in other words, learning by doing. Ralph chose to start by imitating an existing model: Duncan's version of the one called ATP. Learning by doing is implicit in that model.

Learning by Doing   Duncan has recommended learning by doing to other clients who have come to him for coaching, be they freelance consultants who seek training in how to consult better or forward-thinking executives who want to lead better. When the client arrives, as most of them do, with a problem that has stumped his or her present resources, the best learning will come from actually working on the problem, partly because progress in solving the problem will be a good measure of whether the learning is valuable and effective.

Here are examples of two other clients that Duncan shared with Ralph to illustrate the range of clients seeking help with their models. Initially, he said, their circumstances might look quite different from Ralph's, but the basic techniques Duncan used were not.

The first client was a physician who came to Duncan for executive coaching. "Dr. J. is a department head in a hospital with a record of high numbers of 'preventable mistakes' and unnecessary fatalities." He was in transition to a new job in another state, where he would lead a key decision-making team.

"Most doctors are arrogant," Dr. J. told Duncan. "They have the same mentality as those guys on Wall Street who cause us to lose money. Arrogant doctors lead to loss of life. They intimidate subordinates and don't listen. And they make decisions in their own, not in patients', interests."

Dr. J. had taken the Behavioral Propensities Profile (BPP)and was arranging for his new team members to do the same. In current practice, interns learn in part from simulations of live medical procedures. The stakes are high because their superiors are present. The stakes are further raised by the sudden introduction of an emergency in which the simulated patient's life is endangered. These routinely videotaped situations are perfect for analysis of behavior change under pressure. In addition, Dr. J.'s team of high-level decision makers would, like Ralph's, participate in the Accelerated Team Performance program. The hypothesis was that if this team could achieve communicative competency, they would positively influence that part of the hospital's interactional culture that tended to put patient safety at risk.

When he came to Duncan, Dr. J. was already under the pressure of fast-moving events. For Duncan's second coaching client, Lisa, an independent consultant, the urgency was even greater: she was already in a firestorm. When she began with Duncan, she had just been hired to help a CEO and the CEO's poorly functioning team; and in one-on-one interviews with team members, Lisa had learned that the CEO was regarded by the team as a "tyrant," largely unaware of how her "controlling," "dismissive," and "humiliating" behavior was demoralizing the team and undercutting its performance. She had had the CEO take the BPP and met with her to discuss the results and how these would likely impact team members with different profiles. The CEO had then asked Lisa to facilitate a team meeting, the outcome of which, the CEO implied, would affect the prospect of Lisa's being hired as executive coach and continuing as team facilitator.

RALPH: So this doctor and the consultant both faced challenges to whatever model they had been using up to that point.

DUNCAN: Right. Which is your situation, too. Both also presented a challenge to *me* as the one who was just about to start helping them build their models.

RALPH: But, unlike me, both were already seriously under the gun, so they needed the speeded-up version of what the two of us have been doing.

DUNCAN: Ralph, you had problems, too, when we first started working together. The dynamite was there; only, Howard hadn't yet lit the fuse.

RALPH: So you were asking them to sit back and ponder models when the fuses were already burning?

DUNCAN: Well . . . All right, it's fair to ask whether they and I could possibly do justice to the complex, demanding task of model building while simultaneously facing immediate problems on the scale of theirs. But I say unequivocally yes: *simultaneously learning while doing makes the doing go better.*

RALPH: Too bad, then; we've already dealt with Howard *(laughs).* But now that you mention ongoing problems, I have one with my R&D group.

DUNCAN: Okay. Out with it.

RALPH: And I must confess I'm worried, even nervous, and I'm admitting that to you though it's something I've not said many times in my life, except to Sonia. And not just nervous from the thought of my being under your microscope. I've recently discovered that two of my best R&D guys are in a serious fight. Najjar favors our decision to invest more in Asia than here in the States. Beresford insists on making the case for U.S. investments, and—

DUNCAN: *(Gently interrupting)* Okay, that's "content," so set all that aside for now. What is going on *structurally?*

RALPH: Well, Beresford is a bit of a p—k: arrogant until challenged, then a bully.

DUNCAN: Now you're into structure, kind of, but you're coating it in moralistic language. A bias against this guy Beresford?

RALPH: Okay, I'll wash my mouth with soap. Beresford seems to be one of those movers in power who moves, moves, moves, effectively silencing opposers and leaving no space for other movers.

DUNCAN: That's better. Your next task is to diagnose what happens in the room, what structures are created around Beresford's profile, and so forth. What matters for the moment is that we've reached the main point of our work together: *building your model from watching yourself lead* your R&D team.

Ralph's Meta-Models   In this early, imitation phase, in the midst of all that Ralph was doing, he needed also to be thinking, "What is the theory of the thing and of change that instructs one's theory of practice, and the particular practice— in this case, a team model that asks its members to monitor their moral integrity?" At the same time, Duncan recommended that he focus on the *practice* aspect of the model and its theory. Structural dynamics recommends that the other two components remain on a shelf, in view, but off to the side while the task of imitating a practice model gathers momentum. Still unable to restrain himself in matters of new learning, Ralph would charge ahead and Duncan would need to rein him in. Let's take a look at where Ralph's unstoppable curiosity led him.

Recall that the theory of the thing describes the entity on which a model focuses—in this case effective leadership. In true random fashion, Ralph surprised Duncan with some of the sources he chose for his theory of the thing. Happening upon an article in the *New York Times* (September 23, 2010), Ralph fixated on the work of Dr. Giulio Tononi:

DUNCAN: The *New York Times*? Just like a random.

RALPH: It's a new theory of consciousness, what Tononi calls an Integrated Information Theory. It is based on the study of brain networks and how when parts of the networks are wired together, they have a big effect on what he calls phi.

DUNCAN: Interesting stuff, but . . .

RALPH: . . . but what does it have to do with teams? I don't know. I don't pretend to understand this thing called phi. But he does go on to say that his theory applies to human networks like teams.

DUNCAN: A big leap, that, and a bit loopy, but interesting.

RALPH: (*Ignoring "loopy"*) Yes, a big leap. But what are leadership teams but a network of specialists who talk with each other with the purpose of maintaining a firm's moral purpose? This in turn depends on their maintaining a consciousness of moral integrity that is relentlessly vigilant.

DUNCAN: I think I see where you are taking this.

RALPH: Without conscious vigilance, the "not knowing" phenomenon you speak of in your model is given moral license.

DUNCAN: I confess, the leap you are taking is not as large as I thought.

RALPH: And I might add that the collective intelligence your model sees as the desired effect of communicative competency is analogous to Tononi's phi.

Recall that a theory of change says how to bring about change for the thing the model is about—in other words, how leadership changes or, better, how it evolves. Ralph knew that Duncan was demonstrating how his consulting practice made change happen, but Duncan had revealed little about the theory of change behind it. So Ralph asked Duncan about it.

DUNCAN: I think it is too soon to get into this. Had you asked, I also would have discouraged you from leaping so soon into the theory of the thing.

RALPH: You've been working on this habit of mine from day one. I've obliged where I thought you were right . . .

DUNCAN: . . . and resisted when you thought I was wrong. Look, I admire your curiosity, and sense that you will not let up in this matter, so here is a clue. Go back and bone up on Charles Darwin. His theory of evolution is, to my mind, a breakthrough theory of change.

RALPH: And what does structural dynamics have to say about change?

DUNCAN: Since you ask, I'll send you a paper by Kantor.[5] You won't initially recognize the connection to Darwin in it, but there is one. What you will recognize is Kantor's design for bringing about change in couple systems over three stages, just like with ATP. Now, can we get on with it? You are well along in your imitation phase.

Ralph's Main Source for Imitation: Duncan's Version of Accelerating Team Performance (ATP) Structural dynamics alleges that a good model can be described in three stages, each with its own goals and steps that a consultant or leader can follow to achieve them. I briefly describe ATP here because it is the model Ralph was imitating to a large extent, but also, of course, because it is a model that coaches other than Duncan might explore and eventually, in some form, pass on to a leader. Please note that the ATP process is not as linear as the following simplification might suggest. There are always loops and overlaps.

Stage 1 of ATP is *laying foundations*. It can be broken down into ten steps for the team:

1. Take the Behavioral Propensities Profile (BPP) and review individual and team results.

2. Establish a new culture of learning. Briefly, this involves substituting being rewarded for being right with actively acknowledging gaps and flaws in order to grow and change.

3. Teach the structural dynamics language system.

4. Identify and explain ATP goals. In essence they are communicative competency and collective intelligence.

5. Receive and discuss the first feedback from off-site structural dynamics analysis of the team's behavioral patterns in meetings. Here the team is looking at its structures and dysfunctional patterns, individual stuck behaviors and gaps, and ways to reinforce a culture of learning.

6. Identify team goals and ideal structural discourse for reaching them.

7. Teach basic intervention skills.

8. Identify current high-stakes issues and begin applying intervention skills.

9. Receive and discuss the second set of feedback from off-site structural dynamics analysis. Here the team is looking at how high-stakes issues change behaviors.

10. Set goals for individual and team behavior change.

Stage 2 of ATP is *deepening skills in high stakes*. This is done by cycling through the following three steps, three times on average, more if necessary:

1. Review feedback results from off-site analysis, including trends and evidence of change or lack thereof, and collectively diagnose reasons in structural terms.

2. Introduce new structural dynamics concepts that deepen understanding of high-stakes behavior.

3. Identify the most pressing current issues; diagnose how they are contributing to team dysfunction; establish how gaps in each individual's repertoire, including his or her shadow, are implicated; and, using structural dynamics principles of intervention, deal with these in the room.

When consultant and team conclude that the program is approaching completion (that is, when the team is demonstrating communicative competency and collective intelligence that is backed by structural dynamics metrics data, and also is reaching desired results as specified in stage 1), more and more responsibility for managing the change process starts to shift to the team. This occurs in two ways. The team is reminded at the start of each session that all members must take responsibility for reading the room and entering it; and members begin rotating as **primary mover**: the person responsible for stepping in with the "right" speech act when others fail to do so.

Stage 3 is *transferring capacities from "us" to "them" and ending.* Its three "steps" are all of a piece:

1. Summing up and anticipating future vulnerabilities

2. Transferring capacity for continuing growth

3. Celebrating a new beginning

At this point, the team should know its strengths and limitations and be able to estimate its vulnerability to future perilous, high-stakes events. In session they will anticipate what scenarios could happen in the future and design strategies for responding. A credible final test of the program's ability to transfer capacity from "us" to "them" is *Do team members have the confidence to run the program on their own, with their own teams?* If the answer is yes, the team is ready to celebrate a new beginning.

Ralph's Constraint Phase of Model Building

There is no clear-cut boundary between imitating and constraining a model because all imitators will constrain the model they are imitating, even when they think they are following it faithfully; the individuality of their profiles will see to that. Also, a consultant's clients or a leader's team members will push back. Then, too, external forces will have an effect. As I've maintained here, all this is to the good if the model builder knows what to do next. We've been charting that course already somewhat, but still on the surface. Here, I will first discuss the constraint theme in Ralph's model building while he is still basically imitating. Then I will go on to later matters of constraint.

How a Leader's Profile Constrains   The ATP model is not biased toward any one behavioral profile; for example, it expects a mover in closed power to take it in a rather different direction from, say, a mover in open affect, and so on with other profiles. So Ralph, a mover in random meaning, would constrain it in line with his own profile.

We would therefore not expect Ralph to strictly follow the model's linear look as literally as other leaders might attempt to do. Ralph's innovative inclinations would most assuredly give a new fresh look to the practice. He might drop an infatuation with brain researchers like Tononi, or it might take root; but if dropped, other "loopy" ideas (Duncan's word) would take its place. Duncan might want to warn Ralph not to let his curiosity so distract him that he failed to firm up a theory of the thing that effectively *instructed* his practice as leader, as CEO, and as a team leader.

That Ralph is no prisoner of rigid form, routine, or sequence can be good or bad, depending on the task. In Ralph's R&D team situation, ATP is less time bound than it would be for a consultant with a similar profile who is contracted to effect measurable change by some specific deadline. But in general, randoms like Ralph—who often do not wear a watch and, as Martha would say, "don't know *how* to tell time"—will surely constrain the ATP model in line with that preference. In contrast, if Ian chose to deploy the model, he would certainly bend it more toward a routine sequence and stricter limits in time.

How the Systems of Clients or Team Also Constrain the Leader and His or Her Model   In model building, one is well advised not only to know thy self, but to know the system you are "treating," the people in it, and you as a special member in it with responsibility for managing your place. As part of the random aspects of the overall system Ralph tended to promote, Ralph would tend to have looser boundaries than someone in a more closed system and frame of mind. He, but not Ian, might invite team members home for dinner or out for a drink. He might also give special attention to a team member like Martha, Ron, or Art. Team members who are more different (like Ian or Howard) and the system elements they bring could also push his buttons in ways that ultimately cause him to constrain his model. Knowing the client team's dominant model (ClearFacts is open) and the profiles of individual members (Ian and Howard are closed; Martha is an open who tends to oppose those in closed power; and so forth) informs team leaders about predictable internal conflicts and visible or invisible sources of constraint on the model. If the leader knows how his or her own profile may lead to biased perceptions and unconscious side-taking, all the better. As it turned out, Ralph's new and largely handpicked team of eight was loaded toward open and random types, though one closed legacy (Ian) remains—again, not a bad thing, except that in this instance he is locked in conflict with another member (Martha). Our broader conceptual point is that the system you are leading will constrain you and your model.

Moral Integrity as Ralph's Main Constraint on the Model He Is Imitating In its current stage of evolution, structural dynamics does focus on moral behavior and decision making, but it leaves to Ralph the work of showing first steps in how that can be built into a practice model. Let's fast-forward to a later conversation with Duncan:

RALPH: I did as you suggested and read Gardner, Goleman, and some others, but I found Coles, Kilburg, and Toffler particularly relevant to my bringing to leadership the importance of moral integrity.

DUNCAN: Who was most relevant?

RALPH: Hard to say. Each was relevant in a different way. Coles's *Lives of Moral Leadership* brings social issues to life. It turns up the ground with examples of well-known moral leaders.[6] Kilburg's *Executive Wisdom* . . . well, he's a clean-cut, professional, objective psychologist, who definitely takes off his gloves.[7] You can feel his passion on the subject of leadership and failed moral behavior. I liked that. Toffler's *Tough Choices* was really practical, and her *Final Accounting* came close to home. She wrote as an "insider" at Arthur Andersen.

DUNCAN: Yes. I recommended Toffler because she describes firsthand how some "bad" guys can disassemble a "good" firm's narrative purpose. A subject that interests you. But how are you planning to use all this in your model building?

RALPH: I'm still sorting that out. By the way, I've decided to rename my model Monitoring Moral Integrity—for now, anyway.

DUNCAN: That puts you in phase three, autonomy. Let's first look over the ATP model again, and how you and the model you bring to the group will be subject to constraint.

RALPH: OK, OK, I feel your reins. But that won't stop me from reading ahead. Not even Sonia succeeds in doing that.

DUNCAN: So! You are a *very* stuck mover in meaning. So be it. A good thing til it isn't. And when I think it isn't, I will not stop pulling back on the reins, not until you fire me or I quit.

Ralph is fully aware that moral crises come and go, that the public has a short memory, and that among leaders moral sensitivity quickly fades from consciousness under the demands of current realities. As Ralph was struggling with how to keep moral sensitivity alive, Duncan passed on to him an unpublished paper focused on what the author calls the *audience effect*.[8]

The notion of audience effect feeds off the simple observation that you are more likely to act "good" when others are present, and that admitting your "bad" actions in a safe environment has an even stronger effect of maintaining a true moral course of action. Parents are more likely to avoid fighting when their children are around. Empowered regulatory agencies are intended to keep a lid on the moral infringement Wall Street exercises in the name of market freedom. The ancient Greek philosophers required their students to record daily breaches in their moral behavior, reflect on these, and then share their reflections with other students. In all these instances, audience, by which is meant "those who bear witness," is key; this sharing empowers the witness, the opposite of silencing the witness (discussed in Chapter Ten).

So, as one of his constraints to the ATP model, Ralph would provide contexts for his leaders to speak openly about past and possible future moral lapses and to be audience for each other.

Ralph's Autonomy Phase of Model Building

As Duncan suggested earlier, Ralph was pushing on into autonomy even before he'd really completed as much work on constraints as Duncan would have preferred. Inevitably, Ralph, with his keen interest in leaders and moral integrity, will put a special stamp on ATP, perhaps even taking it in a direction that no longer looks like the original. And that will be a good thing indeed, as Ralph is a leader who has both moral and intellectual integrity, as we have seen, and will take few shortcuts along his journey toward building a model of his own making, one suited to his profile, one reflecting his narrative and moral purpose.

Imagine now that Ralph has led his R&D team through ATP's three stages and feels satisfied with the team's progress toward greater collective intelligence. Imagine also that Duncan agrees!

From here, Ralph wants to progress further toward his own leadership model, Monitoring Moral Integrity, and at the same time to "get on with" his model for living. Duncan agrees that that is a good way to go, but once again tries to rein Ralph in:

RALPH: Let's get shakin'!

DUNCAN: Still a man in a hurry to learn *(Ralph laughs.)* Designing a life is no cakewalk. Many assumptions you've never questioned will come up for scrutiny.

RALPH: You sound like Sonia. She's chafing at the bit to get on with *our* models for living, but seems more serious about it than I am.

DUNCAN: About things like this you are more naïve than she. Besides, you're not listening. Some of those assumptions will break down.

RALPH: Again you sound like Sonia. How long will the model-for-living part take?

DUNCAN: That's a question only time will answer, but try this on for now: you never will be done, and *that* is the excitement and the power of model building. You've heard me say this often: its goal is not to know it all, nor ever to achieve complete mastery; its goal is to always *pursue* greater mastery. When we think we know it all, we feast on praise and then begin imitating ourselves. A better way is not ever to let up on welcoming constraint on your model; welcoming challenges from others that may reveal the model's flaws in the real world of practice; keeping an open mind to what you don't know, to the model's failures, and to what others may know better; and then knowing what to do with this new information. You will never get bored and never stop learning, and your model will never stop growing.

RALPH: Touché. And wish me luck.

THE ESSENTIAL MESSAGE FOR LEADERS

Donald A. Schön taught all of us—leaders and their coaches, consultants of all breeds—that we do have models that strongly influence how we do our jobs, even when these remain tacit.[9] Many others, most significantly Chris Argyris and colleagues, have taken this idea further,[10] and I have taken it further here. You may not subscribe to the model-building precepts of structural dynamics, but I urge you to do so in these important respects. First, know that you have a model; knowing what it is will help you coach or lead better. Second, leaders who have coaches should find out what their coach's model is. Third, whether you are building a model of coaching or of leading, master the concept of constraint and use it to address the following questions:

1. What are the limits or constraints of your model? What are its questionable assumptions?

2. How must the model (and you, its keeper) respond in the face of likely legitimate constraint?

3. Insofar as the model is represented as serving the public good, does the moral stance inherent in the model hold up under public standards of right and wrong?

From Insight to Action

Remember that there is no clean separation of the practitioner from her practice model. They are not one and the same, but the practitioner's personal model and its representation in her behavioral profile will be seen and heard, especially when she is under great pressure.

Models and Your Behavioral Profile

Think back to the pattern of responses that you and your model had to my theories of the thing, of change, and of practice.

1. Can you see the role that your behavioral profile plays in how your model responds to the models of others?

2. Are your responses and model statements typically in affect, meaning, or power?

3. Does your model yearn for more or less structure and formality?

4. How comfortable are you with parts of others' models that you have difficulty in understanding? ("I lean toward complexity before arriving at simplicity.")

5. What does your model do with ambiguity? ("I am certainly a random, and randoms are gluttons for ambiguity.")

The Model of Models

Constraint indicates a challenge to a model—a gap or failure—but also an opportunity to look deeper into the model to either expand it from within or borrow from others.

Purposefully constraining another model can be an effective way to further articulate your own. Use my meta-model as described in this chapter as inspiration for refining your own theory of leadership and its theories of the thing, of change, and of practice.

The Structural Dynamics Theory of the Thing and Yours

The *thing* elaborated in these pages is the structural dynamics theory of face-to-face communication. It (and I) assert that communicative competency, as defined herein, essentially "defines" the leader.

1. Do you currently have a theory of the thing called leadership? How fully is it articulated?

2. Guided by the questions in this section reflect on which aspects resonate with you and which you call into question. In your mind or on paper, conduct a cross-model conversation, following this format:

   "I am drawn to this aspect of your leadership model because of its similarity with mine."

   "I am called to constrain this aspect of your leadership model because I think mine covers the same territory better, and here is how."

   "I am called on to constrain my own model because this aspect of yours covers the territory better, and here is how."

Theory of Change

Roughly following Darwin, my theory of change in human systems is that it occurs through three mechanisms: gradual or *evolutionary,* in response to environmental needs; rapid or *revolutionary,* in response to unanticipated, apocalyptic events; and *informational,* in response to institutionally deigned rational policy.

Following Norbert Weiner, my theory of change is systemic in its recognition that behavioral change is regulated by positive and negative feedback loops. It is like other systems-oriented approaches in that it sets out to change faulty communication *structures,* but is different in that it conceives of structure in terms of vocal acts that can be observed and measured.

Also, it suggests that most change in human systems, natural and designed, occurs through three very specific stages.

1. Does your model have a change theory? Is it systems oriented?
2. Does it borrow from other sources? Which ones?
3. What does it change? If not structures, what?

Theory of Practice

In my meta-model, a practitioner has a practice model: what she *does* to make change happen. If the practice model is to be fully developed, it is guided by her theory of practice, a theory that, in turn, is conceptually conjoined with her theory of the thing and her theory of change. The practice model and the theory of practice are therefore not one and the same, though they are often confused with each other.

That the change that takes place always occurs in *stages* is core to my theory of practice. This is the case whether the subject of interest is leadership itself, a leader's capacity as a leader, an executive coach's capacity as a coach, that coach's theory of leadership, or that coach's theory of practice and practice model. All go through change in stages.

My theory of practice, in conjunction with my theories of the thing and of change, identifies dysfunctional communication structures and points the way to making them functional. This, too, happens in specific stages of events.

1. Does your model have a stage theory in which different things happen in each stage?

2. Did you take notice of circularity among the three parts of my meta-model? Does it make sense to you?

3. Does your model have its own way of describing circularity among its parts?

4. What parts of my theory of practice does your model embrace? What parts does your model reject? Why?

Models for Coaching

My assertion that one's practice model is a natural extension of one's personal model has implications for training coaches and, of course, for the leaders they coach.

Before moving Ralph Waterman on to building a leadership model, Duncan guided Ralph through his "ten critical junctures for maximal learning." Out of this process of growing functional awareness came Ralph's awareness of his personal model and how, as a leader, that personal model affected his relationships with members of his team (and his wife, Sonia) in easy and hard times.

Coaches should at least examine the relationship between a leader's personal and leadership models, looking for limitations, gaps, and biases in perception and the actions that follow; and leaders should know how the coach's personal model interacts with their own.

Coaches Must Have Their Own Models

Whether a leader must have a model or should build one is to a degree optional or open to question. Not so the coach who coaches leaders who lead teams.

Reflect on the following statement: Such a coach will be called on to have personal access to (1) a theory of leadership with a model for how to get leaders from "here" to "there" as defined by the model, and (2) a theory of teams with a model for how to get the leader and his or her team from "here" to "there" as defined by the model.

1. Does this make sense to you, or does it raise the bar too high?
2. Does Duncan's three-stage Accelerating Team Performance model generally appeal to you?
3. Which parts do and which do not?
4. Would it be fruitful to engage in a virtual cross-model conversation with the fictional Duncan? And do you see where, by constraining his model with yours, you could help him further build his own?
5. Alternately, do you see where, by having your model constrained by his, you could further build your own?

Useful Questions for Reflecting on Your Own Model

1. Does your practice model have a core theory behind it?
2. Did you learn from an original, published practitioner or her model? Whom? Or is the model of your own creation?
3. Is it systems oriented? In what ways specifically?
4. As noted, structural dynamics changes behavioral structures. These can be measured. What do you change?
5. Can what you change be measured?
6. In your model, are you inside or outside the system you "treat"?
7. Does it view intervention as occurring in stages?
8. Is there a specific behavior or behavior change as a goal? What is it?
9. Does your behavioral profile play a part in your practice model? In what ways?

Your Behavioral Profile and Your Client's

Ralph Waterman scores as a mover in random meaning, and Duncan Travis, if he took the BPP, would score as a bystander in open meaning. I deliberately set up this match because many interventionists are good bystanders. Fewer CEOs are random, but those in start-ups tend to be. The "good" match between Duncan and Ralph worked in this particular case. But in general the implications of mismatches have yet to be explored. They are here.

1. Chapters Two through Five provided a format for roughly assessing your own profile.

   - Does it match Ralph's? Duncan's?
   - Could you have coached this CEO as well as Duncan did?
   - Where might tensions have occurred?

2. Does your model for coaching allow for such differences between coaches and the leaders they coach (think cross-model conversation)? Recognize them as natural? Have a way of legitimating and making use of them?

Leaders: Your Coaches and Teams

Most leaders lead teams; sizes vary from two to twenty, but most include between six and ten members. If they have models, the models usually remain tacit. This chapter recommends that you, as a leader, discover your own model and build it, ideally with the help of a coach who has a model of his own and can help you build yours.

1. Does this idea make sense to you, or do you dread it because it adds to an already overtaxed schedule?

2. Consider this statement: A team that lacks diversity as it has been defined here risks the danger of groupthink, and will in the long term be less productive than one with diverse profiles.

3. Consider this statement: Leaders, in the process of developing communicative competency, must develop intervention skills with teams that are on par with those of coaches. Does this make sense, or does it seem preposterous?

Moral Integrity

In keeping with its advice to others, structural dynamics is still evolving, in response to acknowledged constraint. Its response to a recent onslaught of moral lapses in the corporate community led to an attempt, in Chapter Ten, to lay out the parameters of moral decision making. In the chapter you just completed, in a "next step" in model building, it assigned to Ralph the work of showing how moral integrity could be built into a leader's practice model.

1. Do you share my understanding that all future views on leadership will be incomplete at best without some such focus on a person's *capacity for moral action, or his moral sensitivity*?

2. Do you, as leader or coach, currently include moral integrity among the essential capacities of leadership? Is it currently part of your model for leading? Will it be in the future?

chapter THIRTEEN

A Model for Living

Man is born to live, not to prepare for life. Life itself, the phenomenon of life, the gift of life, is so breathtakingly serious!

—Boris Pasternack

On November 27, 2010, the *New York Times* business section ran this story:

> [Last June] when Mr. [Gordon] Murray, a former bond salesman for Goldman Sachs who rose to the managing director level at both Lehman Brothers and Credit Suisse First Boston, decided to cease all treatment . . . for his glioblastoma, a type of brain cancer, his first impulse was not to mourn what he couldn't do anymore or to buy an island or to move to Paris. Instead, he . . . channeled whatever remaining energy [he had into writing a book, *The Investment Answer,* with a friend and financial adviser] to explain investing in a handful of simple steps.

His goal was to puncture the myth that "if you're smart and work hard then you can beat the markets," and to make a statement about Wall Street's moral slide from grace.

When he first landed at Goldman Sachs, the *Times* reported Murray as saying, "our word was our bond, and good ethics was good business. . . . That got replaced by liar loans and 'I hope I'm gone by the time this thing blows up.'" In the wake of the 2008 financial collapse, Murray "testified before [an] open briefing before

315

the House of Representatives, wondering aloud how it was possible that prosecutors had not yet won criminal convictions against anyone in charge at his old firms and their competitors."

In June 2010, when "a brain scan showed a new tumor, Mr. Murray decided to stop all aggressive medical treatment," concluding he had "balance in [his] life." And although the first thing he thought about was his wife and kids, hanging around 24/7 waiting to die was not an option. His friend and coauthor, Dan Goldie, "had a hunch that writing the book would be a life-affirming task for Mr. Murray."

Murray did not expect to reach his sixty-first birthday in March 2011, but still hadn't bothered "memorializing himself with a photograph on his book cover or even mention[ing] his illness inside." He was "willing to do just about anything to make sure that his message is not forgotten, even if he fades from memory himself."

"'This book has increased the quality of his life' [a friend said], 'And it's given him the knowledge and understanding that if, in fact, the end is near, that the end is not the end.'"

Murray's *The Investment Answer* was published in August 2010. He died January 20, 2011.

This chapter concerns a crisis in both life and career that besets many leaders roughly between ages forty-five and fifty-five. It should not be confused with what is commonly called the midlife crisis, though there are similarities and overlaps. I will call it the *breakdown-breakthrough story.* In it, the protagonist experiences a crisis or breakdown, most often beginning with external events, such as the death of a child or spouse, a fall from grace through downsizing, or a life-threatening illness, but sometimes beginning from within, an epiphany, sudden or crawlingly painful, that what was pursued in life has no meaning. Rising from the depths of despair, many leaders then reach a breakthrough and an accompanying change in the course of their lives.

Contracting a fatal form of cancer, Gordon Murray had a revelation. Knowing he was dying, he realized his life as a whole would have greater meaning if he contributed something more to the world—a lesson others needed to hear. For the short time left to him, he designed a life worth living, and left a legacy. He acted greatly when he felt forced to act.

But to act *before* one feels forced to do so is infinitely wiser. That, in brief, is what this chapter is about. In the latter part of it I will describe some of Ralph and Sonia Waterman's efforts to build their models for living, together. To pave the way, I'll discuss why models for living matter and how building them follows the same broad conceptual plan that works for building one's leadership model.

THE MODEL FOR LIVING

Figure 13.1 suggests that for a full life, you do well to see the self as the core of three distinct models, one that covers your personal predilections (the personal model), how you lead (the leadership model), and how you live (the model for living). Think of your model for living as a compass for your life overall, helping you stay true to your beliefs about life, leadership, and love. It is your means of reconciling your life as a leader with the other goals that, for you, are part of living a life of fullness and meaning.

Or think of your model for living as a scale or balance on whose opposite ends you can "weigh," for example, the work side of your life—the product of your leadership model—against the personal side of your life, and decide what might need to be done to keep them in reasonable proportion to each other. If you know your model for living, you are able to make conscious and active trade-offs (and synergies) between competing demands.

However, there are always limits to reason as the sole basis for finding balance. For example, a leader may find herself caught between a personal model that

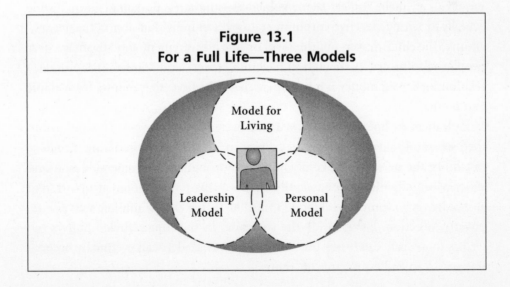

Figure 13.1
For a Full Life—Three Models

places a high value on affect and a leadership model that emphasizes performance and achievement. Or another leader, having recently been warned of stress-related dangers to his health, may vow to ease up at work, but, driven by a childhood story that results in shame if he fails to complete every assignment, continues to put his health at risk. In instances like these, the leader will have to dig deeper than "balance" or pure reason to step into a life worth living.

The Perils of Success

As life centers more and more on work rather than the other way around, successful executives risk overdeveloping their professional selves and forfeiting the rest. Over time, insidious pressure shifts their orientation from their own lives to other things. One shortcut leads to another so that commitments to spouses, to children, and to relationship itself are bent and eventually broken. Life loses sensuality, and they become less and less able to recognize beauty and love. Work becomes the primary source of pleasure, accomplishment, and connections, and they all but forget that there could be time to reflect deeply on the nature of things.

Disturbingly many executives tell themselves that in the current climate "they have no choice." Once this belief takes hold, not only does it become self-reinforcing, but their models start to be built around defending that belief rather than in resistance to it.

At the same time, the natural entitlements of achievement—status, power, and money—can make leaders more vulnerable to simply pursuing "more" while actually forfeiting life. High corporate status sets an individual above "the masses," among "the elite." Power—in the form of role advancement and advantage over people—also grows, particularly in "across" (peer) and "down" (subordinate) relationships. And money is a payoff (perhaps the best) that follows from status and power.

As leaders are bound to agree, status, power, and lots of money are not evil in themselves. However, together they unite in a circularly reinforcing structure much like the ones that make organizations or individuals vulnerable to moral slides. Most individuals are susceptible to the status-power-money structure, and at its edges echo some of childhood's most enduring and painful themes: failure, poverty, rejection. Being inside the structure, in the "inner circle," buffers the terrors those fears can bring, but as that happens, leaders can eventually become trapped in an endless pursuit of "more."

The Time Dilemma and Temporal Anxiety

Extreme time dilemmas make it even easier for many executives to overlook the trade-offs they are making as leadership work swallows the rest of life. I use the term **temporal anxiety** to describe this tortured relationship with time. Many would give an arm and a leg for a few extra hours every day. They are always running from deadline to deadline, crisis to crisis, always short on precious time. They rely on new gadgets to save time and then spend inordinate amounts of their time *saving time.* They go to sleep anxious about what they haven't done and wake up anxious about all they have to do.

Temporal anxiety impels an overworked, rushed executive to forgo the genuine pleasures of love and relationships in favor of more work, more effort, more hurry. Addressing that anxiety becomes a sort of pleasure in itself. He may not even notice what else he is missing because the intoxicating sense of flow, the "high" associated with *measured time,* pushes love, intimacy, and connection off the calendar.

MODELS FOR LIVING AND THE BREAKDOWN-BREAKTHROUGH STORY

Mature and aging individuals are likely to examine their model for living only when it collapses under the weight of many forces. Various crises can bring it on: a spouse falls ill and dies; a fortune is lost through risky investment; a powerful mentor is revealed as corrupt; the company is sold, derailing a fast-track career. Suddenly a lifelong way of doing things makes no sense at all. Work that once energized now begins to enervate. These kinds of natural but unsettling life events cause underlying questions to surface with resounding power:

What have I done with my life? How have I lived?

Am I happy?

Have I been a success or failure?

Through the choices I have made, have I been the best person I can be?

Am I fulfilling my dreams, or is life carrying me along?

For some leaders, these questions and related experiences lead to a breakdown from which recovery is slow. In time, most rebound, often having to claw their way back from the depths of despair and make dramatic changes that alter their lives. For them, this story is one of crisis and redemption—a **breakdown-breakthrough story.** The result is a more complete sense of who they are, what they stand for, and who they want to be.

The leader's midlife story, therefore, has the quality of struggling to come out of the shadows, of dispelling the illusions of childhood and creating a new contract with life and with an organization. It is often a crisis of meaning: "Has my life really meant anything?" But underneath the profound questions about meaning lie the more fundamental questions of love: "Have I given or received love in my life? Am I happy with, do I feel good about [love] the person I have chosen to be?"

Building a model for living can clear your path to "breakthrough" by creating a sense of foundation and purpose. Begun before the worst arrives, it preps you to wrestle with these inevitable questions. Keep in mind that too often an earlier choice of a way of life was actually made after other life activities were in place, like a kind of accessory. Having a model for living means designing a life and a way of life that, in reality, you are starting to live—now!

Leaders, I am saying, must not stop with having a model for leading. At the end of the day, your model for living is an answer to the question I encourage all future leaders to pose for themselves: *How shall I live*? Among all other things, becoming a *beautifully integrated whole* means examining the interaction and causality between that question and *How shall I lead?*

BUILDING A MODEL FOR LIVING

Since the youth-driven revolution in lifestyles that began in the 1960s, countless writers have published often spirituality-coated guides to happier living. Some, like *The Power of Now: A Guide to Spiritual Enlightenment* (1999) and the more recent *Eat, Pray, Love* (2006), have erased all social boundaries and educational levels in their widespread appeal. To build the model for living I am suggesting takes a more systematic approach than these popular varieties. Indeed, designing a life worth living is little different from building a leadership model: it is highly personal; it is done in three phases—*imitation, constraint*, and *autonomy*; it is subject to growth in stages over time; and it, too, is best done under the guidance of a coach.

The Practice of Timefulness: A Must for Leaders

A useful tool in this endeavor is my book and structured diary *Alive in Time,* which redefines the experience of time and presents guidelines for keeping a diary designed to maintain consciousness on a daily basis of time's unsurpassable importance to "having a life."[1] As we shall see, no life has meaning if it fails to grapple with *time*—every entrepreneur and every other consciously aware individual has come up against the fact or terror of mortality and its illusory ties with the experience of time and how to live *in* it. *Alive in Time* began as my own way of dealing with such matters for myself. Not a book about *scheduling* your day to death and not about *time management,* it provides the tools for the development and practice of **timefulness,** an intelligence we can apply to stretch, enrich, and modulate the experience of time. Most of the book is a vehicle for keeping a diary, including quotations, images, and other prompts for freestyle journaling around the central question of whether you may be squandering time when you think you are saving it. You can use *Alive in Time* as is or as a basis for designing your own similar resource. I'll say more about this book later in this chapter.

As in all model building, a model for living also requires some work on the meta-model.

Theories of the Thing, of Change, and of Practice

Your model for living's theory of the thing is an assembly of the principles on which you have built your life, whatever they may be: *One should never compromise that which keeps one whole . . . Never cut short the time for love . . . Be kind . . . Building a legacy is a critical aspect of what we are here to do . . . Hard work is a virtue in and of itself . . . Humanity is defined by its compassion . . . Joy is just as important as hard work . . .*

These principles represent fundamental questions, such as "What is happiness?" and their answers for you. In pursuing the answers, you begin to more actively converse with yourself about happiness than perhaps you have done in the past. The story of the life you want to live is your personal manifesto. That story is a work in progress, but the essentials in your theory of the thing steady the narrative while you continue to write toward the future.

For my theory of the thing, I found these four books most worthy: *Tuesdays with Morrie* (Mitch Albom, 1997), *The Examined Life* (Robert Novick, 1989), *The*

Music of Silence (David Steindl-Rast, 1998), and *The Needs of Strangers* (Michael Ignatieff, 1984).

Your theory of change takes on the challenge of how to maintain commitment to your principles in the face of competing demands. It tackles the difficulties of how to lessen the gaps you see between your theory of the thing and your lived experience. It often includes recognizing patterns in your current theory of practice and facing your fears about doing things differently. These fears frequently originate in the ambitions and sensitivities of your leadership and personal models. Your model for living's theory of change plays in the space between the other two models and deals with how to balance them.

Your theory of practice states those actions you intend to take and be known for that will convey your principles to others in the world. What will you do and, more important, not do, that will truly reflect your model for living? This implies the important step of identifying the gaps between how you are currently living your life and how you would act in the life that you want to live. Conducting this "gap analysis" will focus your efforts at bringing your model for living to fruition.

For my theory of practice, I focused on two phenomena, time and moral decision making and behavior in all aspects of my life. Stephan Rechtschaffen's *Time-shifting* (1996) provided useful bites that led to my book cum structured diary, *Alive in Time*, which conceives of four sorts of time among which one may shift: *measured time*, which is necessary for getting things done; *present time*, for maintaining an awareness of all of my senses; *reflective time*, for keeping all life decisions in line with my narrative purpose; and *contemplative time*, for cultivating and expressing compassion for the less fortunate and for the world in all its troubles. When I keep my diary, I am alive in time. When I do not, I am all but dead.

Rest assured that as I created my model for living, I also made my way through its phases of imitation, constraint, and autonomy. There are limits to how much anyone can further spell out exactly how to go about creating your model for living. In the rest of this chapter, I sketch out some of the dialogues and events that took place between Ralph and Sonia, who recognize that they are creating two separate models for living that will ultimately also feed into a model they can create together.

RALPH, SONIA, AND A LIFE WORTH LIVING

Not every leader has a Sonia in their lives. Sonia is a character but also a symbol of that "other," be he or she lover, friend, parent, sibling, or colleague, someone who has earned your full trust, someone with moral judgment clearer than your own, someone who tells you uncensored truths you do not want to hear. These functions need not even be embodied in one person, but to design a life worth living, you must have these functions available to you.

SONIA: Let's pretend I'm the CEO here. I'll set the agenda for this team today, and I'll be responsible for seeing that disruptive attitudes and private agendas do not get in the way of the work we must do to come up with a three-in-one model for living: ours, yours, and mine. I mention mine last to impress you with the fact that I knowingly made an inequitable deal when we married, a deal I willingly and lovingly signed on to in full compos mentis, a deal I now want to revisit, a deal I must rescind. Until now I've been your sidekick, Tonto to your Lone Ranger. How about you become Caesar and Anthony to my Cleopatra—without the murder and suicides, of course?

RALPH: Ah, Cleo, less "beautiful" than a cunning seductress.

SONIA: True, but a more powerful woman than any woman and most men of her time.

RALPH: Okay, I'm as captivated by you as both those guys were by her. I put myself and this journey entirely in your hands. I *assume* you have a plan?

SONIA: I do, but not so fast. You can't lull me into complacency by what could be feigned compliance. We both know I'm a controlling bitch at times, especially when I think you are out of control and you don't know it. Your words just said one thing, but your voice said another.

RALPH: And it said?

SONIA: It said, "Here she goes; sounds like another *takeover*."

RALPH: And?

SONIA: And it is. *(Both laugh.)* That said, here's my plan and a difficult tag-on condition. My rationale for this "takeover," Ralph, my love, is that you've been brainwashed, a victim of time's depredations, robbed, plundered, ravaged, *and* fooled into thinking you've outfoxed the reaper. No one outfoxes the reaper. Read Duncan's stuff again; read *Alive in Time*. You look awful, not your old self.

RALPH: Thanks. I'm just tired.

SONIA: You're tired from leading an organization, scouring the world for innovative green opportunities, leading two teams, and working on your leadership model like a graduate student meeting a thesis deadline, gassed up on No–Doze or Ritalin. You're not only tired, you're not even only exhausted: you are sleep deprived! Let's face it, when your body fades, and, Zeus willing, we'll both be around when it does, I want all that the serviceable body and that bountiful mind have to offer preserved. You are destroying them.

RALPH: Okay, I'll take the bait; just don't pull too hard on your line. What are you fishing for?

SONIA: Let's begin with our Italy trip. Remember it?

RALPH: Sure, our epiphany.

SONIA: Yes, it was an epiphany because we entered another time space—and I'm not talking about meridian time zones. I loved being there with you, but it was a different you from the busy you. I don't want to circle the globe every time I yearn for slow lovemaking or solitary time with you, the complete you, within reach. I want to look up from a book I'm reading and know where you are. When I read *On the Road* and *Blindness,* two books I could not put down and dreaded to pick up again when I did, and did not have you anywhere near in time or geography to share my dread, I felt lonely and could not bear the waiting.

RALPH: *(Irritated)* You're no sit-at-home, Sonia, not one to die on the vine.

SONIA: *(Picks up a book from a nearby table, extends her arm, and drops it flat onto the wooden floor)* Do I have your attention? This is not about me. We know I am fully capable of taking care of myself. It's about you and *time*. You asked me to read Duncan's "Model for Living" material, and I did. Lapped it up, as you did. What impressed me most was the stuff about time. I'm having this out with you now before we begin, because if we are not on the same page with it, unless we give that feature of this model thing the highest priority, it will all come down to pure posturing, just a lot of (and I do not beg your pardon) bullshit.

RALPH: Are you deliberately picking a fight with me? Why? I'm really with you in this.

SONIA: Well, if it isn't apparent, yes, I am. I took the liberty of speaking with Duncan. Duncan knows you, in that "other" context. I know you better "here," and I've learned a lot about who you are "there." Duncan was a bit suspicious of your unquestioning enthusiasm for this whole project, wanting to do your leadership and life model at the same time, but was taken in; he realized that he had been, after I pointed out how, when you are really, really under the gun, you press harder, race faster, push beyond limits, and take on more, not less, and then compliment yourself for managing to be "the last one standing." If you do not find a better way to "expand your repertoire" as Duncan says, unless you find a way to get done what you absolutely need to get done while at the same time being able to be *with me,* and with yourself, a *whole self,* "alive in time, not dead," as that book [*Alive in Time*] says, all this model building will come to nothing. I would feel more assured that something new and special will come from this exercise if you questioned yourself, your own doubts, not about the wisdom of the program, but about the human possibility of pulling it off.

Now Sonia had Ralph's full attention. He knew how easy it was to forget time journaling, especially with the tricks of the mind that he invented to forget its existence and to surrender to temporal anxiety. These facts were the basis for the "doubts" he reluctantly admitted next.

RALPH: Well, I do have doubts. I have many doubts.

SONIA: Ah, finally, admitting fallibility, admitting you have doubts that you can do it all. Having doubts doesn't forecast failure. It increases the possibility of success.

RALPH: A cheap cliché, but true.

SONIA: *(Relaxing at last)* So, before I present my plan, let me say this. I, too, have doubts, but they could not be assuaged until you admitted yours.

RALPH: Fine.

SONIA: And now for my plan.

Sonia's Plan and a Hard-to-Keep Condition

SONIA: My plan is to do this at a gradual pace, reflecting separately and together, and to stop every so often, go elsewhere, out of work's long-armed reach—let's say, to lovely out-of-the-way inns.

RALPH: Agreed.

SONIA: No computer. No briefcase bulging with unread reports.

RALPH: *(After a very long pause)* Agreed.

SONIA: Sorry, but I'm not quite done. Working together, we'll know when to schedule these three-day retreats—

RALPH: Three days? When will I do my job?

SONIA: Yes, three. I've chosen inns for all seasons, skiing, hiking, swimming, all off the beaten track, and for being alone together.

RALPH: You'll have to teach me how to enjoy solitude. You probably have a long list of books to read.

SONIA: *(Feigning embarrassment)* I do, and you'll find *Intimacy and Solitude* at the top.[2]

RALPH: You must know you're being a stuck mover.

SONIA: Yep, and I hope you're not being courteously compliant *(nervous laughter)*. In effect, we are testing the model's basic premise, which is that you will be more, not less, productive; more, not less, creative.

RALPH: What it doesn't say is how hard it will be. In fact, what we read makes it sound easy. We know better.

Two months later, Ralph and Sonia had arrived for a long, late-summer weekend at Anchorage by the Sea, an oceanfront resort in Ogunquit, Maine. After they had moved through the "easy work," learning how to enjoy activities undistracted by minds full of work obligations, Sonia turned on Ralph with a flat accusation about things that had been going on at home. Sonia's unarticulated fears were validated: Ralph was taking middle of the nighttime breaks from sleep to "catch up."

SONIA: I know what you've been up to.

RALPH: Every moment?

SONIA: You're guilty of purloined time.

RALPH: You mean you caught me in the act?

SONIA: I did. You've been cheating on this "time" stuff, working all day, spending more time at headquarters, pulling back on our time at home.

RALPH: Well, a little.

SONIA: Which is bad enough. You've also been slipping out of bed at night to work on the computer. Three times last week. I'm a light sleeper. When you leave my side, I know it. At first I thought you were snacking or something. By time three, I got up and peeked. You were working.

RALPH: On my leadership model.

SONIA: So it's worse than I thought. First, you broke our agreement about measured time, of doing only what was absolutely necessary.

RALPH: So I slipped. I'm guilty of temporal anxiety.

SONIA: *No,* you *lied* to me, a violation of your moral contract and ours. See the contradiction? Moral leadership my ass.

RALPH: Oh, Sonia, show some compassion. That damned theory part is harder than I thought.

SONIA: I know Duncan is not pushing you on this.

RALPH: No, it's me. I'm sicker than I imagined. I just don't like to fail.

SONIA: Okay. And *(sarcastically)* I reap the benefits.

RALPH: How about if I give you my word right now that I'll take the time diary more seriously?

SONIA: Is that a pledge?

RALPH: It is.

SONIA: For my sake? Ralph, don't you get it? Unless you do, you'll be failing at "time," a required subject, not an elective in this school of life.

Ralph not only made the pledge but kept it, with lapses that became less frequent as he began reaping the benefits of journaling momentum.

Sonia Hits a Wall

It was fall now, and Sonia and Ralph were on their second retreat at the Deerfield Inn in the countryside of western Massachusetts. Sonia was not fully enjoying this traditional country inn, built in 1884. She had been scratchy for the first day and into the second. Ralph concluded it was "women's stuff" or a mild illness that would pass; it didn't.

When they settled in to talk after their walk amid the dazzling spectrum of color in the woods, she declared she was in crisis. She was thinking of *her* narrative and had gotten in touch with the fact that her purpose in life was escaping her. Her adult story had begun with the birth of her first child and had continued through her divorce and deadening routines for a couple of years, followed by her falling in love with Ralph and agreeing to follow him from one job to another. Now that story felt dead in its tracks. When they'd met, she'd been like Jill Clayburgh's Erica in *An Unmarried Woman*: single, having learned that she didn't have to define herself through her relationship with a man.

SONIA: I learned that early, when I was divorced. I have carefully modulated my dependence on you. I have fashioned a life for myself; it has meaning enough, but there is a basic issue that needs looking at and correcting. While I've never put it in these stark terms, in these years, when you have been preoccupied with your world, having my own separate parallel life has worked. I've kept busy by serving the community, and I've been well rewarded.

RALPH: Not as much as you've deserved.

SONIA: Wait. I'm not clear yet how to say this; you and your narrative have been center stage so long that I no longer have a narrative of my own that really suits me. I mean, I was satisfied with our "we"; it seemed intact and strong, but my story, the story of "me," the more I've thought about it lately, the less focus—and less future—it seems to have.

RALPH: You have something new in mind?

SONIA: An adjustment.

RALPH: Spill it.

SONIA: No. I want to work this out by myself and then with you—first what *I* want, and then how that depends on you.

RALPH: My work life, you mean?

SONIA: No, I mean our designed life. I'm a fool if I don't figure out whether I want to continue our present terms of agreement. Will I be content if I do? For how long? Don't get me wrong. I'm not questioning you. I'm questioning myself, and I have no easy answers.

Signs of Change?

Three months later for their next retreat, Ralph and Sonia were at the Three Stallions Inn in Randolph, Vermont—ski country. Sonia preferred downhill; Ralph, cross-country and snowshoeing. But before settling down to some serious skiing as part of the business of rediscovering how to live, Ralph sought Sonia's counsel.

RALPH: I have something to talk about. I'm confused, and need your perspective.

SONIA: I'm listening.

RALPH: Last week, I broke off from work for a fifteen-minute spin along the river. I've been doing that since you caught me at my surreptitious nocturnal affair with my computer. I've been faithful to the diary for many weeks, and the damned thing works. Research on my model, now that I'm not pressing, is coming along fine. But after my walk, I had a strange experience. I felt buoyant, energized; but in the elevator, a feeling of profound despair came over me. It contradicts everything else going on in my life right now, most of it good. All is quiet, relatively speaking anyway, on the ClearFacts home front, and I don't remember when I've loved you more than I have since we took this thing on together.

SONIA: That's good to hear. Go on.

RALPH: Entering our office suite and making my way back to my own office, I passed the others as usual, nodding or waving to each (we tend to keep our office doors open). They were all the same people, but suddenly I didn't recognize them. Who I am in relation to them was out of focus. I wasn't hallucinating, or anything like that, but they were all strangers, and I felt like an alien. Duncan was waiting in my office. I never said a word to him about it. Whatever it was, it had passed. Any ideas?

SONIA: I'm delighted.

This began a long conversation, ending with a simple, accurate insight: this strange experience was a sign that Ralph was undergoing change, nothing more. Such experiences signaling change are fundamental to successfully reaching a goal of one's model for living, that of having it both ways: a meaningful work life and satisfying personal life combined in one. Most successful people are a bit obsessed. This obsession is part of their recipe for success—a clear goal, a harsh self-discipline, and an obsessive drive to succeed. And as *busy* people, many carry additional psychological baggage, heavy enough to sabotage their full commitment to designing a full and integrated life.

Busy leaders, under time's unwavering "mandate" to get what is important to them done and to stamp down what gets in the way, live in (mainly unacknowledged) fear and rock-bottom anxiety. These worrisome emotional states can be stoked by any of the universal or specific themes I cited in Chapter Eight that individuals find—or, rather, make—relevant and thus useful in their campaigns of denial. Two such themes are particularly common: fear of dying prematurely and fear of being a fraud—that is, of not being "who" or "as good as" they say they are. Neither theme finds a comfortable home in a leader's consciousness. It is far easier to keep running. It was for Ralph.

Sonia's Dilemma—Connection Versus Independence

What suffers most in the lives of busy people is real connection outside work. Like the mates of most busy people, Sonia carried a special burden, that of patching together a life beyond work, playing taskmaster and minister of culture as a general rule, and police force when promises were broken. She played all three roles with well-aimed determination. (We saw the couple's dynamics in the earlier dialogue: her stuck mover and his courteous compliance and covert opposition.) Thanks largely to her, the Ralph and Sonia in this story have more than a fair share of domestic connection. And their sex, again largely managed by her "altogether willingly and voluntarily," remained more vital than is true of most post-honeymoon couples.[3]

We must not understate Sonia's immense contribution. The "condition" she initially held out for and which Ralph accepted—that they go off periodically on retreats in beautiful surroundings with opportunities both for play and serious work on their models—was itself a stroke of designed genius, a kind of spring training for the real thing.

But the general ongoing dynamic between the two, it seems safe to say, is not the best formula for them in designing a life worth living, as we define it; this life risks failure unless these roles, both equally subversive, are abandoned. The stuck mover must be relieved of sole responsibility for providing direction, and the covert opposer must undergo correction, wanting to pursue fuller life on his or her own impetus. Until Ralph stepped up to the plate, Sonia's own developmental readiness for an integrated life would remain incomplete and stalled.

When people begin to examine their lives, as they are urged to do here, it is not without cost. In asking questions that must be addressed though not necessarily answered (especially the unanswerable ones that raise what may be the hardest question of all, *Does my life have meaning?*), they often come up against a wall, as Sonia did.

Ralph's Corrections and Sonia's Wall

For their next retreat (and for the first time since courtship), Ralph made the arrangements. Sonia, in a rare state of agitation, had tipped him off. She needed quiet space, with time to work on *her* life and on the problems she was having designing it. To his surprise, he was looking forward to this retreat with a mind swept clean of business-related details; knowing that his enthusiasm was about *him,* he kept his thoughts to himself. This was *her* time.

He made arrangements at Rabbit Hill Inn in Vermont's Northeast Kingdom, a 1795 inn, billed in its brochure as a "tranquil place," "an oasis of unparalleled comfort and a perfect destination for intimate getaways." They took long walks in silence. Her hand felt small in his. He'd rarely felt so protective, and never had that felt not only good but so right. In front of a wood-burning fire, sipping wine, he kept his tongue in check, waiting, proud but not overly so of the changes ("corrections" he called them) in his behaviors (not relying on Sonia to arrange the retreat, relishing rather than tolerating the silences he knew she needed). All signs were that she had come up against a wall.

Each had a book in hand. Occasionally Sonia would look up from hers, indicating that she had something to say, but then return to reading and silence. Then suddenly she spoke of her daughter by her first marriage, who was now away for her first year of college:

SONIA: You must make a new effort to connect with Emily. You used to drive her crazy. She is a very disciplined, straight-thinking young lady. A bit prissy, perhaps, but tolerant generally, and she admires you and what you are trying to do in the world. *(Ralph waits, nods only slightly, says nothing.)* You almost lost her when we started out together, but she came around. You won her heart, but barely.

RALPH: And she won mine.

SONIA: But she doesn't know that.

RALPH: What must I do?

SONIA: Convince her. I leave how to you, but she desperately needs a father. *(More silence)* I think we need a second home, a retreat of our own.

RALPH: I'm a step ahead of you. I have two real estate agents looking, one near the ocean, the other in the country. I think I know what you'd like, modest and removed, and not wired; but let's wait and see.

Their conversation continued a long time. At times she said things with no context. Here is a sample:

"If we choose the ocean, I want you to know it is not about collecting pieces of sea-glass, how many you need to make you happy."

"This model-building exercise is one big deception: it is not about designing a life; it is about questioning the meaning of life, and once you do that you get rained on by a deluge of questions from which no umbrella offers protection."

"Happiness, as most people think of it, is more mythic, like messianic faith, something that is always coming but never arrives, and when it does, it has a short shelf life."

"At first, it seemed so easy, how to balance the euphoria of solitary time and the warm glow of together time. But now it's turned out to be all about questions, about asking big questions that have no answers, and others that you damn well better get answers to."

"I need a sense of location. Stepping back on my life, I'm a bit humbled and humiliated. I've had the leisure to spend time as I please. I've done well enough, served my community, but I've been in a trap, a trap of waiting. A trap of looking forward to 'the time when . . .'"

"In this exercise, you are on your own and feel alone. No wonder 'busy people' don't bother. It is scary. What if there is no meaning to life?"

———————————

As time went on, Sonia's comments grew darker.

SONIA: Thank you for listening. I'm ready to talk now. My trouble is, I know who I was, I think I know who I have become and find myself rejecting it, and I have no clue as to who I want to be for the rest of my life.

(She pulls out a scrap of paper with words from the model-for-living material—a list of the causes of "breakdown.") For me, it is *(reading)* "a lifelong way of doing things suddenly makes no sense at all." "'Work' that once energized begins to enervate." For me, it is worse than that. At times I feel like I'm dying.

RALPH: You are hinting, not quite saying, that there is something wrong with *our* lives.

SONIA: I am, in one sense. You are, in one respect, like your father. He was peripatetic because he left such a bad taste in every parish; he *had* to move. You move because you set goals, reach them, and then get itchy. I don't think you will leave ClearFacts soon, but with you, there is no knowing the future. So where does that leave me? What is my place in this design? My relation to you, my agreement til now, has been to follow you until you found a place where you wanted to be. You appear to have found one. Still, I'm a fool if I don't figure out whether I want to continue our present terms of agreement. Will I be content if I do? For how long? Please do not get me wrong. I'm not questioning you. I made this deal with my eyes open, in fact in rapture of you. I'm not questioning you; I'm questioning myself. And I have no easy answers. *(Wisely, Ralph says nothing. His quiet presence seems to be all Sonia needs. A long silence follows.)*

Thank you again. I do expect that I will come out of my "breakdown" with a "breakthrough." That work is mine alone. I'll ask for help if I need any.

A Shared Narrative Purpose

Two months later:

RALPH: I've learned more about you, me, and us in the months we've been doing this exercise than I have in the eight years of our marriage. You said that you've had a breakthrough.

SONIA: I have. When I became pregnant, I quit law to raise Emily. I never took the bar. I will bone up and do it soon. I would like to join you.

RALPH: If that means we can begin working on our joint narrative purpose, I couldn't be happier. It's lonely up there at the top.

SONIA: And nothing would please me more than converging our parallel lives, and this is tricky, without losing my autonomy. After that sleaze Howard Green was caught making risky investments and cooking the books, you became fixed on the subject of fraud and on moral character, an antidote for this pernicious disease. The law let Howard off the hook. The law has let many on Wall Street who are responsible for the same practices Howard and Jones were into off the hook.

RALPH: At least it gave impetus to my focus on moral action.

SONIA: And since you took up your cause, I have begun to do some reading on the subject. There's this terrific article in the *New Yorker:* "What Good Is Wall Street? Mostly What Investment Bankers Do Is Socially Worthless."[4] The author says that "the history of Wall Street is a series of booms and busts," and that "after each blowup the firms that survive temporarily shy away from risky ventures and cut back on leverage. Over time, the markets recover their losses, memories fade, spirits revive, and the action starts up again, until, eventually, it goes too far. The mere fact that Wall Street poses less of an immediate threat to the rest of us doesn't mean it has permanently mended its ways." It simply made me think. There are hidden but known forms of institutional immorality. I will study all such forms of poorly monitored ethics, some of which are criminal yet enjoy legal sanction. My job will be to find and expose them, perhaps in my own blog. This will bring me closer to your narrative, if you will let me. I promise not to crowd you.

RALPH: I am told that developing a shared narrative purpose is a journey in itself with plenty of pitfalls.

SONIA: There is much more to our narrative purpose than this, I know, but if ours are intertwined as I am suggesting, the rest will more easily fall into place.

Anyone who decides to design a model for living does well to anticipate bumps in the road and even unseen dark holes, as Ralph and Sonia have. If they decide also to tackle their narrative purpose, the pitfalls are even more perilous. Couples I have worked with are instantly drawn to the whole concept, but I have learned not to introduce it until much work has been done and they have the problems they came with well under control. Even then it becomes a difficult journey because it brings into question some basic assumptions they've had about life that they've not seriously faced.

Ralph and a Fear of Dying

This process of self-exploration wasn't easy for Ralph either. When he was well along in his design of a life worth living, and was rolling along smoothly in establishing a relationship between his narrative purpose at work and in his life with Sonia, he came to an uncomfortable realization. It spun off of something Sonia had said at one of their retreats that he later took to deeper level. Sonia had likened his peripatetic career to his despotic father's being driven from one parish to another. Ralph added his own insight: if he kept moving from job to job, he would not have to face his fear of premature death, a theme he cleverly kept from consciousness by his past and current lifestyle.

RALPH: My first surprise was that all this is anxiety inducing; not a fear of dying, but of dying prematurely, before having lived enough to let the Grim Reaper take you by the hand and go with a smile on your face.

Remember that strange experience of sudden despair I had? You were right: it *was* the beginning of change, the start of my course correction, which has held up pretty well since. I am working at a good, steady pace on my leadership model building. Also, I now know better how I can help others not stumble along without ethical or moral responsibility. I have set in place automatic alarms so that we at ClearFacts do not lose our ideals and our commitment to bettering the world. And whether we succeed or fail, I will just be satisfied working to get ClearFacts recognized as one of the hundred best companies to work for.

But I think my "strange experience" was a kind of near-death experience.

SONIA: Let's spend a week living "as if" death, of one or the other, were drawing near. How afraid of dying are you?

RALPH: I'm not afraid of death; it's dying before my time that scares the hell out of me.

SONIA: And that means?

RALPH: That means I've got a lot of work still ahead of me.

SONIA: We both do.

From Insight to Action

This chapter espoused the incredible benefits of becoming a *beautifully integrated whole,* but it did not underestimate the hazards that trying to do so poses for those exposed more to the rewards than to the perils of success.

This stage in a person's journey is more demanding intellectually and emotionally than what comes before because it asks leaders (and coaches) to look at life's most puzzling questions square in the face.

1. On the emotional, existential side:

   - Has my life really meant anything?

   - How much of status, power, and wealth is enough?

   - Have I given and received love?

   - Am I happy with and do I love the person I have chosen to be? If I were to die tomorrow, would I be content that I have lived a life worth living?

2. On the intellectual, model-building side:

   - What implications do my personal and leadership models, with their gaps and shadows, hold for answering the emotional-existential questions?

   - What help do I need in addressing those gaps? What assets will I be able to call on to address those gaps?

Beyond the Behavioral Profile

This chapter is one sort of digest of this book. Chapter Fifteen will be another: a structural dynamics analysis of Barack Obama as a leader, designed to bring the ideas shared in this book into an analysis of the current pressures facing the ultimate executive leader.

Right now, first, I want to briefly revisit six themes that tie in with Level IV of the structural dynamics model. By now I hope you have been convinced of the usefulness of the behavioral profile for reading the room. Yet you may still be skeptical of or reluctant to move yourself and the leaders you coach to the deepest (story) level.

Second, I want to present twenty capacities by which I believe future leaders should be assessed, using members of the ClearFacts management team one final time as examples. In Chapter Fifteen I will use these capacities as part of my analysis of the leader in the Oval Office.

MUST WE REALLY?

Behind any hesitation you may have to incorporate Level IV into your model for coaching and into your coaching itself, or to pass it on to leaders, you may still have doubts about six assertions I have made in this book. Of course, you must draw your own conclusions, so I frame them here in question form. By distilling my own position once more on each, I hope to move you to clarify yours (and, I hope, in this direction).

Must We Really Talk of Love?

Yes, and in our working lives. Although some business leaders persist in saying that their calculations leave no place for love, they themselves feel it manifested in the rewards of status, power, and dollars. A few, like Ralph Waterman, are more conscious of its broader pervasive power in business and are setting out to spread that awareness in the workplace. The culture has changed and will continue to do so, and our future leaders are growing up in this new culture.

Does Empathy Really Matter?

"Only connect!" wrote E. M. Forster in his 1910 novel, *Howard's End*: "That was the whole of her sermon. Only connect the prose and the passion, and both will be exalted, and human love will be seen at its height. Live in fragments no longer."

As I argued in Chapter Ten, empathy is a sine qua non of decision making with regard to moral purpose. It is also central to connecting, identity, love, and leadership. Without empathy, a leader's message of purpose will fall flat or seem false and empty. In hard times, when tough decisions must be made, when in fear or doubt the many look to the few or to the one to guide them to safe landing, the leader's personal connection is what makes others follow.

Empathy is also essential to effective cross-model conversation. If disputants have empathy, or let the "other" exercise it, or, best of all, if as a precondition for engagement they set out to learn about it, they stand a chance of walking away from polar discourse more peacefully and more loved.

This is successful intimacy: succeeding in paying the price of putting one's trust in an "other," giving this other the power to keep our moral failings in check. This ability depends on one's own successful experience of intimacy in some form in one's life. To appreciate the value of this approach, consider the alternatives represented by Arthur and Howard.

Arthur Saunders Connecting Arthur returns to his departmental team, a group of five handpicked types, each an unapologetic opposer, after having a difficult time, mainly with Howard, in a management team meeting. The departmental group is known for its boisterous *sturm und drang*—its means for making creative decisions—but also for its cohesion, its felt sense of warmth and pride, when, following a typical storm, the breaking sun coaxes life back into a wilting stem of an idea.

"Art, you look like you've been to a funeral," one says.

"Right—his own," says another.

"Howard again?" groans a third.

"What's up?" they chant in chorus.

Arthur tries to shuck off their concerns with, "We've work to do."

"Not til we dress your wounds. Just doing what you taught us. You can't tap your best if junk is festering in your mind. Let's get rid of the junk, so we can really get to work."

Howard's Failure to Connect At another moment, Howard is saying "so long" to a fellow traveler, Clyde, with whom he struck up a "down and dirty" conversation on a plane. He's had this kind of conversation only once before, on a fishing trip with Brian Casey, his one close friend at the time, at night by an isolated trout-filled lake in the foothills of the Laurentians. After beating back the swarms of mosquitoes that chased them a harrowing twenty yards from their outboard motorboat to the sanctuary of a cabin, they surrendered to exhaustion. Single-malt scotch went down easy. It greased their tongues. They talked loosely of down-and-dirty sexual adventures both knew were more fantasy than reality.

"Nice meeting you. See ya again some time," Howard and Clyde each say as they walk out of the airport concourse and head off in opposite directions.

Not likely, Howard thinks, shrugging off a perplexingly unwelcome feeling, a blow penetrating somewhere near his heart. It surprises him. *Where's Brian Casey fishing these days? What? Me lonesome? No way. I'm here to haul in my own next big one. Remember how Ian shook my hand when he saw my proposal yesterday and read the client's response? You bet this new sucker—sorry, "client"—has swallowed it, hook, line, and sinker. All I have to do is reel him in. And Ralph embraced me! Unbelievable.*

After days and nights of focused, hard work, Howard is well prepared to do something he knows how to do. Searching for the limo driver who will take him to the hotel, he smiles inwardly, his chest swells. *Let's face it: I am good at what I do.*

But that nagging loneliness bulls its way back into Howard's companionless, unwed, lonely thoughts. *Swat the damn mosquito. Brian. That story I spun him about the sex with Mary Jo.* Howard smiles again. *Well, not quite how it happened.* He remembered Mary Jo's entreaties: "Tie my hands. Not so tight. Stop! It hurts! You're hurting me!" *I didn't stop. I didn't believe her. For me the best sex I ever had. For her, not so. And tomorrow I clinch the deal. Tomorrow night. Sex.*

Why Emphasize the Value of Intimate Partners?

Intimate connectedness is the most obvious source of love. The ideal purpose of this intimacy, true connectedness, is a potential antidote to everything from leader burnout from overwork (Ralph), to maybe being on a wrong career path (Arthur), to disaffecting relationships (Ian), to fraud (Howard and TJ).

Sonia is our exemplar partner in intimacy. By insistently reining in her spouse's inclinations toward self-sacrifice, by her persistent presence and connection with him, and by her insistence on their retreating to intimately communicative time together, over a significant number of years she has enabled him to spend his work time as a healthier, more productive, more moral leader.

Should spouses and partners be saddled with the role that Sonia takes on? Structural dynamics indirectly addresses this question in its insistence that for a leader to be a whole person, work and love must come together in one life, and that designing a life worth living is one way to make this happen. Sonia's strategic move to join Ralph in designing *their* model for living adds an energizing new turn to their relationship.

Can a spouse have too big a role in her partner's career? Could and should Art Saunders have stayed at ClearFacts, or was the influence of his wife, Jane, for the better? The question should be kept in mind.

Should Coaches Elicit Childhood Stories of Love?

Coaches who have trained in structural dynamics see a clear connection between communication styles and all four levels of the structural dynamics model. Childhood and later stories shape how the leader reads the room (sees, hears, and names what he perceives) and what actions he takes. Like the rest of us, leaders have deeply personal childhood and hero stories that can arouse strong feelings driven by shadows.

Are coaches equipped to elicit such connections in a productive and safe way? Or can they be? The question is not trivial, but in fact many times I have successfully elicited such stories and witnessed their transformational power, and have coached other consultants to do the same. In light of this, in my own training of coaches I have introduced methods that help the practitioner develop the capacity to deal at the level of childhood stories. None report anything but success.

Why So Much Emphasis on Models?

Any leader who must function under pressure should build and articulate a practice model under the guidance of a rigorously trained coach. And under my own watch, the coach's training *is* rigorous, including developing a practice model of her own and submitting to supervision of her work in the field by another, more senior and already qualified consultant.

You or your leaders may assume that time spent building a model will distract and burden them. To the contrary, my experience is that having a model raises the quality of both a leader's work and his life.

Why So Much Focus on Fraud?

If we define fraud broadly as setting out to "beat the system" for personal gain, fraud is now pandemic and viral in our culture's financial, political, and other institutions. I have argued that people in positions of power are particularly vulnerable.[1]

On an individual level, what can be done to turn the pandemic around? Leaders can begin to build self-correcting leadership models with well-trained coaches as their guides, themselves fully equipped to speak truth to power. Members of such leaders' teams can be afforded similar options to grow personally and professionally in creating a life of meaning, a sure immunization against fraud.

RAISING THE BAR: TWENTY LEADER CAPACITIES

The list here collects and briefly summarizes twenty capacities that structural dynamics suggests are essential for outstanding leaders. It is useful as a more or less complete structural dynamics framework for assessing where a given leader's practice stands. Think in terms of a rating for each—for example, a scale from 1 (low) to 7 (high). Together, they can raise the bar for future leaders, converging in what structural dynamics considers the ultimate capacity: leader *communicative competency* that moves outward from reading the conference room to reading and narrating the story of an even larger one.

Twenty Leader Capacities

1. **Knowing the self.** Leaders must be aware of their personal stories; how these lead to patterned behavioral propensities; and in particular, how their shadows, those darker parts of stories, impact others.

2. **Soliciting feedback.** Leaders must know how to ask for and accept critiques, criticisms, and hard truths in up, down, and across relationships, without penalizing the informant. When models are in contention, leaders must know how to allow and manage constraint, a key form of feedback.

3. **Managing teams.** To manage teams and working groups, leaders must know how small, face-to-face groups work as systems. To promote the team's ultimate goal of communicative competency, they must be able to diagnose structures and intervene in real time.

4. **Tolerating language differences.** In its framework of speech acts, domains, and preferred operating systems, structural dynamics describes the different languages that individuals prefer and use to achieve their communicational goals. Tolerant leaders recognize the value that each language system brings to the table and can help team members bend each language system toward shared goals.

5. **Connecting with others.** Leaders must be able to connect with those within their inner circle as well as those outside it. Loosely speaking, sympathy and emotional connection are shared inside the inner circle; empathy, including compassion for strangers, extends to those outside the circle.

6. **Compromising with others.** In situations dominated by polarizing stances or fears, leaders must be able and often willing to credit, take into account, and accept positions, stances, and interests other than their own. This allows vital issues to move toward resolution, after reasonable debate. In structural dynamic terms, most "difference" is fueled by normal model differences that can harden into model clashes. Effective cross-model conversation often charts a path to compromise.

7. **Building a practice model.** Models are ubiquitous among mechanics, surgeons, and others. Leaders should have a model. Knowing oneself is equivalent to knowing one's personal model and its impacts on one's own leadership practice model. The leader's practice model comprises guidelines for ways of performing—of acting, interpreting and responding to acts of others, and correcting his or her own model's flaws.

8. **Balancing arrogance and humility.** Arrogance and humility represent two ends of a continuum. Extreme arrogance is seen as evidence of overgrown self-importance; extreme humility is seen as evidence of a leader's low

opinion of his worth. In moderation, both add value. Self-knowledge and the ability to read the room help leaders maintain balance.

9. **Operating under pressure.** In high-stakes situations, leaders must be able to stay focused and under self-regulated control in order to see present dangers and make decisions that guide others toward best solutions. One's own shadow tends to surface uninvited in high-stakes situations and crises. High-stakes leaders must take responsibility for their own shadows and be prepared to help others manage theirs.

10. **Taking risks.** Risk is necessary, but the justification for risk should always be the common welfare rather than personal interest. Taking on proper risk is courageous without being reckless. It requires vision, but also judgment as to when to "buck the crowd." It may require putting one's job at risk for the sake of unacknowledged truths—a strength of exit leaders.[2]

11. **Recognizing patterns.** In observing face-to-face relations—and relations in larger contexts—leaders must be able to recognize repeating patterns in sequences of verbal and nonverbal exchange. Reading the room, leaders can discern constructive and destructive communication patterns and know how to manage both.

12. **Understanding systems.** Systems thinking, recognizing an organization's complexities and ambiguities, avoids the trappings of simple but misleading explanations. In systems thinking, cause and effect are circular. Circularity sheds a more neutral explanatory light than do one-sided blame and moral judgment.

13. **Managing organizations.** As managers of large organizations, leaders know their own and their leadership team members' strong and weak capacities and their own and team members' edges of growth. Their own model includes leading team members toward personal growth and leading the team collectively toward effective communication. Leaders also know how large organizations work *as systems* and are able to navigate unruliness and competition between subsystems. They can also direct a large membership that looks to them for meaning in work and a clear purpose toward which to strive.

14. **Acting morally.** A moral act here is a decision to sacrifice personal material gain. An organization without a moral purpose will eventually collapse. External controls play a necessary role in preventing immoral acts, but final

responsibility rests with individual leaders. Leaders recognize that most critical decisions have moral repercussions that affect the lives of others, and include this recognition in decision making.

15. **Storytelling.** Leaders are able to create, refine, and communicate effective narratives to relevant audiences. They know the distinction between a *structural story* and a *moral story*. A moral story blames, whereas a structural story describes in morally neutral terms. In high-stakes situations, structural dynamic thinking puts a damper on moral storytelling. Storytelling ability includes a will to know and, when appropriate, tell one's own stories, and the ability to imagine and/or take in others' behavior-explaining stories.

16. **Imagining possibilities.** Organizations tend to ripen and then go stale. Leaders who have or are open to visionary foresight are needed for steady growth in the future, but they must also gather an inner circle capable of constraint; that is, they must welcome diverse profiles into the group.

17. **Mobilizing energy and morale.** Accomplishing existing goals and setting new ones call for a leader who can mobilize energy and morale from coleaders and lieutenants, from the organization's membership, and from external agencies and communities whose confidence matters.

18. **Optimizing.** Optimization is the path to functioning at the highest level. Leaders who optimize recognize limits that are imposed on them and are realistic about what is possible, but do not allow pessimism to stifle their ambitions and goals. They don't doze at the helm and are prepared for the unexpected. With leadership team diversity in place (not only followers but an ample crew of strong opposers and bystanders as well), leaders understand how high stakes affect even the best performers, including themselves.

19. **Maintaining confidence.** When belief and faith plunge, leaders are on deck as their organization's prime mover, its voice—whether they issue a call to act unilaterally with conviction, to patiently wait, or to bridge and compromise. On the arrogance-humility continuum, they know where to stand firm, casting an image of confidence others will follow.

20. **Articulating narrative purpose.** Leaders must have a "big story" of their organization's larger purpose, including a model for carrying out that purpose, and both the story and the model are buttressed by an underlying

moral premise. They and their top teams must encourage but integrate their differences into a coherent message that is effectively conveyed to the organization and the world at large.

For the following section, I rated, using the 1–7 scale I mentioned earlier, each of the ClearFacts team members in terms of their strengths in each of these twenty capacities of leaders. I used a rough method with no pretense of science. At the end of the chapter, I will ask you to do some ratings of your own.

To rate, I established with two research assistants a set of criteria for high, medium, and low ratings. My assistants then rated the ClearFacts team members independently of each other, reconciled their differences, and shared their perspectives with me. I will report our judgments in terms of high, low, and growing-edge capacities. An average of 6–7 was considered high; 4 or less, low; and 2 or 1, growing edge.

THE CLEARFACTS TEAM: INDIVIDUAL CAPACITIES AND CONTRIBUTIONS

You probably possess a strong sense now of who the ClearFacts characters are as people and as leaders, and of the personal and professional challenges they have faced from a structural dynamics perspective. You've seen them engaging in interpersonal clashes and responding to unexpected external events. You've heard rising up in them, often surprisingly, major parts of their childhood histories and how those histories affected them as they have faced certain tests of worth, moral character, and performance in rocky times.

Here, to demonstrate the applicability of the twenty criteria in efforts to raise the bar for future leaders, I will summarize what we've learned about the strengths and weaknesses of each of the ClearFacts people as leaders. I will also suggest some implications for other leaders with similar profiles.

Ralph Waterman

I will assess Ralph as he was before his year of executive coaching with Duncan. Because in previous chapters I have documented Ralph's growth during that year, I will also say a few words about his future.

A bystander in random meaning, Ralph was, as we know, a rare choice of CEO for an established organization. At the outset Ralph had a model of his own, though it was not fully articulated or developed at the time. Central to it was the idea of making the management team more diverse, and he did so in these respects: bringing in a female, Martha, open in affect, to balance the team's closed power dominance; and bringing in Ron, open in meaning, to bolster support for Ralph's green energy goals.

Ralph made one other important decision later: seeking strategic reform after the high-stakes firestorm, he decided to increase the size of his team. Again, his goal was ever-richer diversity, which comes more naturally to leaders such as he (with open and random profiles) than it does to closed leaders.

In this sense, as well as in terms of other criteria for assessing a leader (in the structural dynamics model, at least), Ralph showed himself as a leader whose decisions support systemic rather than personal goals.

Ralph brings much else to our understanding of what an ideal future leader could look like. He empowered his coach to

- Help him become a skilled team leader
- Challenge and check his (random) tendency to decide things impetuously
- Look closely at whom he favored or disfavored (including his nemesis) and why
- Come to terms with his hurt-child view of his history
- Push back on his suspect stand on transparency
- Look more deeply into his self for traces of shadow behaviors, and take responsibility for them
- Up-end his self-deluding conviction that busy people know how to master the experience of time (see Chapter Thirteen)
- Help him commit himself to the difficult work of model building
- Help him unify his two core worlds, work and intimacy, and the two selves that reside there, into one integrated whole

Ralph exemplifies what one can achieve through disciplined learning, first with a guide and subsequently on one's own. Table 14.1 sums up his salient capacities.

Ralph is a natural for model building. His appetite for learning about himself and about models (natural to someone high in meaning) suggests that he can improve weak capacities with coaching, and probably on his own.

Table 14.1
Ralph's Highs, Lows, and Growing Edge

Highs	Lows	Growing Edge
Soliciting feedback	Managing teams	Balancing arrogance and humility
Tolerating language differences	Balancing arrogance and humility	Managing organizations
Connecting with others	Managing organizations	
Building a practice model		
Articulating narrative purpose		
Imagining possibilities		

What else does Ralph's example suggest about the random type? Randoms do better at imagining the future than dealing with current realities; that is, they are better vision leaders than performance leaders. But they can be good to great leaders if they choose their team with an eye toward balance, and work with others who love managing, as Ralph deployed Ian. If Ralph ever moves on to another organization, he will again need a closed-type second in command like Ian. We'd advise him to hold out for one who is also interested in developing his own model.

Ian Maxwell

Ian Maxwell, ClearFacts's CFO, COO, and Ralph's second in command, was too stern for some and a problem for Martha, with whom he often clashed. Still, he ran his unit well, consistently achieved desired results, and, to his credit, presented as a man who kept his word. With his eye fixed on the bottom line, he held in check his CEO's tendencies toward expansiveness, which Ian often thought were reckless.

Ian showed more capacity for change than one would have expected at the beginning of our story. This was due in large part to coach Duncan, who broke through Ian's off-putting boundedness. Approaching him through meaning, Duncan made a rare connection with a man who kept himself at a distance by choice.

A few months earlier, Ian had, in an uncharacteristic move, approached Duncan with a personal problem. In Ian's mind, Duncan was still a newcomer, but Ian was distressed by a massive breakdown in communication with his son, Hector, and by fear for the boy's life. Unable to engage in cross-model conversation with a young man strong in affect, Ian feared his son was threatening suicide when he received a cryptic phone message. Duncan was able to walk Ian through his response, and as a result, Ian came to respect Duncan's methods and view Duncan as more of a part of the team. This episode also played a part in his awakening to the necessity of human connection, a behavioral dimension leaders of this type must add to their repertoires.

The fraud crisis helped put Ian's integrity on display. When others sought punitive retribution, Ian, to their surprise, insisted on treating Howard and Template Jones fairly, in the mode of the adjudicator. Table 14.2 sums up Ian's salient capacities.

Movers in closed power like Ian call for special attention. The business world recognizes their value. They are heavily recruited and generally helped up the career ladder with promotions; they occupy the top notches in our most powerful

Table 14.2
Ian's Highs, Lows, and Growing Edge

Highs	Lows	Growing Edge
Managing teams	Knowing the self	Connecting with others
Operating under pressure	Soliciting feedback	Building a practice model
Acting morally	Tolerating language differences	
Maintaining confidence	Connecting with others	
	Storytelling	

organizations. Unfortunately, some organizations encourage the type to circle around regulations in search of new routes to profit.

Leaders with Ian's profile tend to turn down the opportunity to build their models, but I think this does an injustice to the business world and to themselves. It's good that Duncan is on a campaign to bring Ian along, preparing him to join his colleagues in model building with a coach's guidance.

Howard Green

Howard's is a cautionary tale. Hard working and highly productive, he is a mover and opposer in closed power. Howard is unlike closed mover Ian in that Howard's absorption in *analytic* meaning all but totally eclipses any sight of *philosophical* meaning. Howard fanatically applies mathematical analysis to demonstrate his ability to generate profits, for which he was dutifully rewarded at ClearFacts. His views about affect, connection, and intimacy are clouded at least in part by skepticism, and markedly distorted by his history as to what love is about.

Unlike Ian, Howard is weighted down by dark shadows that render anything that gets in the way of his achieving his goals a nuisance he must get rid of or destroy. Given room to make deals, he hires an accomplice in moral turpitude, and together they conspire to commit fraud that strikes at his firm's raison d'être. Table 14.3 sums up Howard's capacities. He received many other low scores, too, but the ones I show are the most relevant to our model of a future leader.

Table 14.3
Howard's Highs, Lows, and Growing Edge

Highs	Lows	Growing Edge
Operating under pressure	Connecting with others	Connecting with others
Maintaining confidence	Operating under pressure	Operating under pressure
	Taking risks	Taking risks
	Acting morally	Acting morally

My assistants and I were struck by how hard it was to find many high scores for Howard. Of course, I had portrayed him as the team's villain. Nevertheless, I hold that his low ratings have very real implications for the ongoing discourse about what leadership is and how to help develop it. Business schools, clearly the most influential institutions responsible for training business leaders, should take notice by asking the following questions:

- Should we consider moral intelligence and emotional intelligence, along with business intelligence, in selecting students?

- What would a course on morals—one that actually inspires moral decision making—look like?

- Is it possible to induce leaders to monitor their own behavior as they evolve as leaders?

Martha Curtis

Martha is an exemplary proponent of the open system. Her signature speech act, mover in open affect, is backed by her wide behavioral repertoire: she moves, follows, and opposes effectively in all three communication domains and is the team's best bystander, except when she is triggered by certain closed-power people.

For Martha, as for many leaders who profess a preference for an open system, shadow forces from childhood can at times prove the lie; they lead Martha to look more closed than she is. Leading her own team, she can maintain her open-system stance, tolerating difference, making and supporting compromise, and connecting. And in the management team, led by a random with whom she has bonded and whom she trusts, these capacities and her strong opposer are appreciated.

But in a training assignment with Ian, an unrepentant closed type, Martha's protector hero frequently erupted in defense "of the innocent," the young, the promising "potentials being put through the wringer under Ian's deliberately military style."

In other words, in high stakes she becomes a protector who can be provoked to slide into her gray zone—that is, when toxic themes she's carried with her from her childhood are triggered. Her overwrought clash of profiles with Howard, who triggered her most toxic themes, threw her off balance. When she clears up this

Table 14.4

Martha's Highs, Lows, and Growing Edge

Highs	Lows	Growing Edge
Soliciting feedback	Compromising with others	Knowing the self (especially the shadow and its impact on others)
Managing teams	Operating under pressure	
Connecting with others		Tolerating language differences
Taking risks		Building a practice model
Recognizing patterns		

glitch, she will become the leader she is meant to be. By the end of our story, she is in fact prepared to do so in therapy or coaching and by getting on with building her model, as she enthusiastically plans to do. Table 14.4 sums up her capacities.

Martha's scores were almost universally in the high middle to high range; her lows, usually the downsides of highs rather than truly shadowed behavior, made it difficult to find low lows, without unduly forcing choices.

As more and more women make their way into positions of power, this question stands out: Must they bury or disguise their natural behavioral tendencies in order to "make it"? In the current sociocultural climate, the question itself has an inescapable taint of stereotype. Yet it must be addressed. As this trend continues, women who score high in affect will have to contend with men who are closed in power and indisposed to emotional expression.

Ian's profile and style remain *the* branded leader prototype, the one that is coveted by our current corporate mind-set. His attitude toward women and their place in this world is still alive and kicking back, as Martha discovered. Attempting to break free of stereotype, I deliberately supplied her with scars and warts to match Ian's. My presenting Ian as a leader undergoing real change was also a deliberate attempt to break free of stereotype.

Martha is a high performer in her specialty. We trust that her readiness for self-knowledge and her genuine eagerness to be coached in developing her model will pay off.

Ron Stuart

On the Behavioral Propensities Profile, Ron would rate as a mover in open meaning. In his language domain propensities, power would rank behind meaning and affect. In high stakes, he would prosecute some and strongly advocate for others. In crisis, he is a level-headed survivor, dedicated to the firm's purpose and strong moral foundation—perhaps *too* committed, putting his intimate relationship at risk.

Made sensitive by racial insult, Ron reveals a complicated profile, his "act" before coming to ClearFacts contradicting his real profile, which was more varied than was reputed. As a black, he had decided at the start of his rise as a leader to wear a mask of aggression; he would play "the man's" game. "I'm no Uncle Tom," he told Ralph in confidence, and "I'm no Angry Black either. (Not even at racists; we're all racist. I only get angry at extreme racists who deny their bigotry, like Howard.) I just gave them what they wanted: a smart, hard-driving, profit-making power guy. But it got me to you."

Ralph had quickly swept race off the table and reached Ron's more authentic self. The two connected from the start. Both were committed to alternative energy. Both were prescient and entrepreneurial in their view of electric cars as an important wave of the future. Both were convinced that this meant longer-lasting batteries would be crucial.

But the two connected even more deeply on a personal level. A little psychologizing would suggest that Ron was the son Ralph would never have, and that Ralph represented the father Ron wished he'd had. It is safe to say that bonds like these—bonds of love—do occur in the workplace. Their implications for leadership must be named, and their positive and negative aspects explored. Table 14.5 shows Ron's capacities.

Ron is a leader whose performance will not peak until he deals with his childhood story and how it limits his functional awareness. Easy as it is to support his attitude toward people like Howard, as a leader Ron will have to deal with such individuals. Building a strong leadership model with a coach capable of eliciting his story of imperfect love and that story's structural impacts will help. At our story's end, he is on that path.

Table 14.5
Ron's Highs, Lows, and Growing Edge

Highs	Lows	Growing Edge
Soliciting feedback	Tolerating language differences	Knowing the self
Recognizing patterns		
Acting morally	Compromising with others	
Articulating narrative purpose		
Imagining possibilities	Optimizing	

Ron presents a problem for leaders like Ralph, whose own random tendencies lead Ralph to secretly support Ron's attitudes toward the darkly tainted authoritarian ways of some closed people.

Ralph is not alone as a leader whose ego is fanned by a talented young protégé. He does Ron no favors, however, if he goes too far in treating him as a favorite son who shares his dreams for the firm, and fails to treat his protégé's personal life and need to evolve as a leader as equal in priority to his contribution to the firm.

When Ron arrived at ClearFacts, he did so wearing a mask. People who don masks feel compelled to hide out or to go underground with who they really are for fear that they will be mismatched with the organization in which they find themselves. In time, in part because of his relationship with Ralph, and also because the team culture permitted him to find his voice, Ron showed his true rich range of behavior. A naturally good bystander, he developed the ability to oppose and a strong voice to move convincingly, and was able to follow as a matter of choice on issues he could support.

However, his relationship with Ralph raises an easily ignored leader-follower issue. Ron opposes his boss with ease and makes strong moves as well. However, a meta-level look at their dynamics reveals that over time Ron overly follows, sharing Ralph's narrative burdens and, like Ralph, sacrificing his personal life, but without a Sonia to rein him in.

In heroic terms, Ron is a survivor with a strong commitment to a shared cause. Ron could, out of loyalty and devotion to Ralph, slip easily into his type's gray zone where abandonment of self for cause effectively leads to abandoning those closest to him, and the possibility of their having a life worth living. Fortunately, Duncan has identified the issue as one Ron must deal with in his evolving practice model. There are many leaders in similar situations who do not acknowledge this kind of problem.

Arthur Saunders

Art has risen to the position of director of advertising and marketing in Clear-Facts's products division, heads a team dominated by creative random types, and holds a place on the management team, where, despite being the much valued and adored "voice and image" of the firm, he doesn't really belong.

Arthur's profile, like Martha's, extends across various types. He is primarily a mover in open meaning. In low stakes, Art is a good follower and bystander, but a weak opposer. A poet at heart, he has enough random propensity to connect with Ralph, his random CEO, and with most other people in the firm, excepting Howard Green, who sees him as a competitor to be struck down; also, Howard has picked him out for a fight because Art's qualities and behaviors resemble those of Howard's brother, whom Howard has since childhood made an object of aggression.

Howard's appetite for combat and his competitor's aversion for it hastens Art's eventual exit from the company, an exit that had long been inflexibly championed by Art's wife, Jane. Well aware of her husband's story of a father whose own image is enhanced by his son's success in the world and who puts psychological pressure on the son to pursue a business career at which the father failed, Jane applies her own pressure on Art to leave the combative, commercial world of business for a place better suited to Art's nature: a sanctum where ideas, aesthetics, and beauty are valued for their own sake. See Table 14.6.

What makes Art a figure of special interest for discourse on leadership is that on his own merits he could succeed in leadership's major leagues, though not as a number-four clean-up slugger, not as a franchise player, but as a solid number six or seven in the batting order: a player who's "got the right stuff," solid and dependable in the arts of the game.

The business world is home to more Arts than is known because they do not show up as vividly as our protagonist has here. Often they live in misery, pretend-

Table 14.6
Art's Highs, Lows, and Growing Edge

Highs	Lows	Growing Edge
Connecting with others	Operating under pressure	Maintaining confidence
Recognizing patterns	Taking risks	
Acting morally	Maintaining confidence	
Storytelling	Managing organizations	
Imagining possibilities		

ing more than really wanting to be there; hiding out, at cost to themselves and to their firms.

Here are some remedies that could help correct this wasteful problem of profile mismatches that lead to questionably premature departures:

- *Spot the issue early.* This means developing more precise and predictive tools for selecting promising as well as established leaders. Smart candidates size up an organization's preferred profile, then cover up to get the job. Organizations of the future, understanding the value of diversity (strategic use of different profiles), will develop procedures aimed at making a proper place and role for those who belong but do not fit the dominant model.

- *Develop mentors who understand the need for diversity.* Such leader mentors would keep an eye not on shaping recruits in their own or the organization's pursuit of "profits now" but on a longer view. For example, they would advocate assignments that are geared to a long-term view of the mentee's development as a leader.

- *Allow changes in role.* I look forward to a time when people like Art, who, having served time as performance leader, are given the opportunity to stay on but in a different role that accommodates their life circumstances and their own proclivities. In the ideal future organization, Art would stay with his team but step down as its director, give up his place on the management team, and serve ClearFacts in the role of wisdom leader or citizen leader.

From Insight to Action

In Table 14.7, rate yourself, Ralph, your boss or a colleague, and President Obama on a 1–7 scale, with 1 being low and 7 high.

Table 14.7
Twenty Leader Capacities

Capacity	Myself	Ralph	My Boss (or My Colleague)	President Obama
1. Knowing the self				
2. Soliciting feedback				
3. Managing teams				
4. Tolerating language differences				
5. Connecting with others				
6. Compromising with others				
7. Building a practice model				
8. Balancing arrogance and humility				
9. Operating under pressure				
10. Taking risks				
11. Recognizing patterns				

Capacity	Myself	Ralph	My Boss (or My Colleague)	President Obama
12. Understanding systems				
13. Managing organizations				
14. Acting morally				
15. Storytelling				
16. Imagining possibilities				
17. Mobilizing energy and morale				
18. Optimizing				
19. Maintaining confidence				
20. Articulating narrative purpose				

chapter FIFTEEN

A Structural Dynamics Analysis of Barack Obama

Immediately after the 2008 presidential election, journalists John Heilemann and Mark Halperin interviewed scores of campaign participants from both major parties, collecting their first-person, behind-the-scenes accounts of the performance of the candidates' teams in the primary and general campaigns. Their 2010 book, *Game Change*, captured the workings (sometimes spectacular, sometimes awful) inside the leadership teams of contenders Clinton, Obama, Edwards, McCain, and others. In doing so, it illustrated the main concern of this book: the grim extent to which a high-stakes leader's success or failure hangs on his or her skills in creating and leading not far-flung networks of supporters but his or her own close, face-to-face team. Along the way, *Game Change* rawly displays a second major theme of *Reading the Room*: that, for better and worse, the personal lives of people on teams will either promote or hamper effective work within the team. By *personal lives* I mean team members' histories and the nature and quality of their relationships with spouses, lovers, family, and closest companions outside work.

The same cultural shift of the 1960s that enlarged leaders' possibilities beyond the John Wayne stereotype and ushered women into widespread leadership in the workplace also profoundly changed our premises about leadership in politics. Politics is about competing ideologies, and its traditional focus has been power, but politics is also "the art of the possible," with reasoning and compromise as necessary secondary resorts for "getting something done" and "getting my bill passed." Yet because ideologies and willingness to follow a champion are both heavily imbued with passion, politics is also fundamentally influenced by the same structural dynamics themes of *love* that Chapter Fourteen reemphasized in the world of business.

Fifteen years different in age, but both having "grown up" in and since the 1960s, Presidents Clinton and Obama have been changing the nature and possibilities of the office in line with that cultural shift, and there is reason to expect that other presidents to come will continue along their lines. One of many aspects of the change is that the spouses of presidents are now able to play very different roles in their tenure at the White House than most chose or were able to play in the past, and U.S. citizens want to and feel entitled to know far more about the private lives of presidents than they ever did in the past. As Sonia Waterman is altering the terms and resources of Ralph Waterman's role as CEO, so Hillary Clinton and Michelle Obama have altered and continue to alter their spouses' political lives (as Bill also does Hillary's).

This chapter shows how structural dynamics thinking can illuminate our understanding of political leaders in general and help us speculate usefully about what they are likely to do in office. The chapter also provides some speculations about Obama's growing edge and future.

I read Obama as a remarkable figure in numerous ways, only one of which is his being the first African American to occupy the White House. For example, he is one of those rare leaders who, without a coach like Duncan Travis, set out consciously to build his own theory and practice model for how he would act as a leader.

This chapter describes Obama's behavioral profile, his formative stories, his quest for identity, and his ultimate settling on a moral mode and hero type. It explores his past and likely future behaviors under high-stakes conditions.

In the past it has always been difficult for those outside an administration to fathom a president's political actions, and inevitably the later parts of this chapter will speculate. But in Obama's case we have unusual resources, beginning with his own extensive writings and *Game Change*. As I proceed, I'll mention other sources that have allowed perhaps a more candid and complete view of a president still in office than has been possible before.

OBAMA'S BEHAVIORAL PROFILE

In low-stakes settings, structural dynamics would describe Obama as a bystander in open meaning.

Obama the Bystander

Obama's dominant mode is that of mover from the bystander stance. He is a classically strong bystander who takes information in, internally assesses what he experiences, and interprets before taking overt action; in other words, he chooses to remain silent before making a statement that either adds perspective or bridges other actors. The action he takes can be a move of his own, a follow to a previous action, or an oppose to a previous action, but in a neutral voice. Obama is skillful in this strategy, and the bystander stance gives him a greater range than classically strong movers, followers, and opposers.

Obama's status as a bystander likely stems from a childhood that defined him as a citizen of the world rather than as a citizen of a homogeneous community. Born of a mother from Kansas and a father from Kenya; growing up in Indonesia and Hawaii, and raised by white grandparents; being a black man who, by circumstance if not by choice, found himself always on the outside looking in—all of these factors probably contributed to his tendencies to play the bystander.

In his now famous speech on race on March 18, 2009, Obama demonstrated his fluency as an interpreter. Being a good bystander, like being a good interpreter, requires fluency in more than one language. "As a biracial person," according to Cassandra Butts, a fellow law student at Harvard, "[Obama] . . . has had to come to an understanding of the two worlds he's lived in. . . . Living in those worlds, he functions as an interpreter to others. He has seen people in both worlds at their most intimate moments, when their humanity and imperfections shone through. His role is as an interpreter, in explaining one side to the other." At Harvard, "[almost] from the start, Obama attracted attention . . . for the confidence of his bearing and his way of absorbing and synthesizing the arguments of others in a way that made even the most strident opponent feel understood."[1]

Obama has great skill in bridging people who speak the different structural dynamics languages of affect, power, and meaning.

Obama's Language Preference of Meaning

Obama certainly prefers the domain of meaning. What led him to it? For one thing, his grandparents and mother (and stories about his absent father) instilled in him a strong faith in the value of ideas. Obama was clearly inspired by his father's Harvard pedigree, going so far as to reference him directly in his autobiography. Obama's mother, according to David Remnick's *The Bridge*, would wake him at 4:30 in the morning to tutor him. Furthermore, Obama's time at the elite institutions he attended—Occidental College, Columbia University, and Harvard Law School—unquestionably shaped the special value he places on meaning.

Obama's career choices also reflect a preference for meaning. He writes of his first postcollege job, at Business International Corporation, that although his time there was comfortable and perhaps the start of a profitable career in business (power) befitting his academic pedigree, he derived little sense of meaning out of this job. He then left to do community organizing in Chicago; after a number of years, he realized that his education must continue if he wanted to make a *true* difference, and headed off to Harvard Law.[2]

In a little understood nuance, Obama also speaks well at the interface of meaning and power (what I call *meaning as power*). His well-known ability to absorb, digest, and analyze large amounts of complex information and then to display his understanding in words both spoken and written takes the communicative act of meaning as power to new heights. By infusing power with meaning, he artfully connects with a skeptical audience hungry for leadership.

In making connection with others, Obama also infuses meaning with affect (*meaning as affect*). Excepting occasional moments, as in his Tucson speech on January 12, 2011 after the shooting of Rep. Giffords, he is not known for the expression of feelings in public, apart from passion for his cause of change. He does not connect, as former president Bill Clinton is capable of doing, on an emotional level. But he does connect through the affect-meaning blend of *empathy*. In other words, whereas Clinton *expresses* emotions, Obama conveys that he *understands* the feelings and thoughts of others.

No one would expect to hear Obama echo anything like Clinton's famous "I feel your pain." When people find themselves in a room with Clinton, they feel embraced, their feelings not only recognized but *felt* by him. In a room with Obama, they feel understood, known. This may account for his ability to bridge people of different persuasions. Other observers note Obama's distinctive proneness to empathy. Kloppenberg, for example, says, "Obama himself saw empathy as an essential piece of organizing. He wanted to know what made people tick."[3]

Similarly, here's how Kenneth W. Mack, Obama's colleague on the *Harvard Law Review*, saw Obama: "Barack Obama was catapulted into national prominence, in part, because of his skill at building bonds of empathy with supporters from a seemingly impossibly broad political base. Conservatives marveled at his use of language and metaphors that resonated with their core beliefs. Liberals and progressives believed that [his] rise to prominence . . . represented a triumph for their own core agenda. People of a wide variety of viewpoints saw something of themselves in Barack."[4]

That Obama is an instinctive maker of empathic meaning is also evident in what follows from his autobiography. Leaving the company of colleagues late one night, he sensed danger. Four black youths, who, given the time and place, could only be up to no good, were looking him over, as prey perhaps. This excerpt from his story captures a depth of knowing, of empathy, that is difficult to match: these boys, he muses, have no "margin for error." They face "a truth . . . that has forced them, or others like them, eventually to shut off access to any empathy *they* may once have felt" (emphasis mine). He goes on to speculate, more as an empathic philosopher than as a community organizer cum lawyer, that "these boys will have to search long and hard for . . . any order that includes them as more than objects of fear or derision."[5]

Obama's Preference for Open Systems

Obama is a clear proponent—in principle, policy, behavior, and speech—of the open system, which, on one hand, encourages its members to express their different views even in the extreme (positive loop), but when all voices are heard, on the other hand, requires that they reach some agreement, even if it is provisional, by consensus (negative loop).

Obama's culturally sensitive mother, an anthropologist, and his uniquely adaptive, racially tolerant, affectionately "underbearing" grandparents seem to have succeeded in cultivating in him a tolerance for difference, a core human value that the open system uses, through a balancing of positive and negative feedback loops, to regulate the boundaries of the system and, within those boundaries, the behaviors, including speech behaviors, of its members.

His open-system preferences are reflected in every context in which both Obama and others have tried to describe and explain him: his gregarious bearing, his pluralistic perspectives, his stances, his commitment to debate and compromise on fanatically defended issues, and the ways in which he tends to handle others, even those whose positions conflict with his own.

Remnick's book offers evidence from various informants: "His talent, that habit of mind, was . . . evident in his openness in engaging people with whom he disagrees . . . You come to the problem [of complexity] with your own compass, your opinions and principles, but you have to be open. That was Barack."[6]

Bipartisanship in politics goes hand in hand with open systems. Obama's proclivities for this system and worldview can be seen early when, as newly elected president of the *Harvard Law Review*, he had to assemble his editorial team, a process "made more complicated by ego, politics, and race. Obama could have loaded the masthead with liberals and African-Americans. Instead he followed the traditional system of selection, and the result was that three of the four editors were conservative."[7]

Further evidence of Obama's predilection for the open system, with its firm commitment both to the uninhibited expression of individual differences and the rule that these must be settled in consensus, is his reliance on bipartisan debate that is expected to result in compromise. I will argue later in this chapter that this expectation is a feature of his practice model, and that this in turn is guided by a theory of practice (Chapter Thirteen)—deliberative, or participatory, democracy, to which he was exposed at Harvard Law. Whether his model, as evidenced in a stubborn call for bipartisan debate on vital issues, has or can succeed in the viciously polarized Congress he encountered in his first term remains to be seen.

OBAMA'S FORMATIVE STORIES

Obama's gripping formative stories have already been told by the man himself in *Dreams from My Father* (2005) and by three marksman interpreters: David Remnick (*The Bridge*, 2010), Jonathan Alter (*The Promise*, 2010), and James Kloppenberg (*Reading Obama*, 2010).

I begin here with my own attempt to capture Obama's childhood story in the style he himself might have felt and rehearsed in early years. The voice I use to tell his and other stories is deliberately fantasmagoric. I do this to capture what is in the room when adults reexperience the felt dramas of childhood deprivation. Here I tell it as if Obama were in the room with me.

Childhood Story

Obama's childhood story is that of a boy determined to find his "roots."

———————————

Wanting more sleep, the boy strains, pressing tight his still tired eyes, his dream starting to slip away, his mind trying to hold it back. He calls out. *Wait! Who are you?* he asks the mysterious, fast-fading dream figure. But it is too late. It is gone. *Where do dreams go?* he wonders. *Where do they come from?*

Come, come, my love, rise up. We've much work to do. It is his mother, barely visible in the predawn darkness. Awake now, but not happy about it, he asks, *Can* one's mind write its own dreams? I mean writing them to order—not just any dream, but a mind-shaped dream? Ann sighs; she's been here before. *Do not woo me with your clever philosophical distractions. We can talk about such things when you've learned the basics, and you've got miles to go. Hup to; I'll get the books.* Like most children too quick to judgment over small slights ballooned large, he thinks, *She doesn't love me*, then wishes he could erase the thought from his mind.

I'm tired too, he thinks he hears her mumble, which makes him feel even worse. He's willed himself to bury the kinds of thoughts he has begun having lately about his mother. *I'm like her luggage, packed and ready for another of her dreamy adventures.* Or *The world isn't as she imagines it to be.* Or *I see things about my father she doesn't see.* Or *She's my teacher, my "moral muse"* [a term he's read somewhere], *but I know things she doesn't know, about being black.*

His being black is, for his mother, almost a source of pride, something she can show off to the world. But it isn't so easy for him: *I am different from other kids at school. You kiss my head, smell it lovingly, caress my hair lovingly. They look at me strangely. When Sasha, a girl at school, asked if she could touch it, I wanted to hide. You want me to be as proud as you are about my black father, of my own blackness. I am confused now, but I will figure all this out. I will.*

One day his mother blushes with excitement: *Your father is coming to visit.* Barry thinks, *At last the mystery of who he is, and therefore who I am, will be solved.* He resists the urge to ask her if his father the prince has become a king. Instead he waits, fired by anticipation.

From the day of his father's arrival, his boy world is turned upside down. *This is no king; this is not even a prince. He is but a man, and not much of a man.* Barry watches, as is his way, his anticipation reduced to embers. As he watches, a small war unfolds over territory, between a weakened, naked would-be king and Barry's grandparents. It seems that the war forces his mother to take sides over Barry in a territory of love or of control—he can't tell which. Afterward he tells himself, *When my father left, I did not feel loved; I felt lost, lost in a dark jungle, a tangle of confusion.* A basketball, a gift from his father, the one sure comfort. (See Figure 15.1.)

Come away with me, his mother says, *to my new country, my new home, where there are cultural riches beyond imagination . . .* Barry looks at his mother, mutely, tuning it out. Like his father, she now seems smaller. Or in some strange way, he has magically grown taller. Looking "down" at her for the first time, he feels ashamed, not of *her*, but of what *he* sees: *My beloved mother—tutor, muse,*

Figure 15.1
Obama, the Boy Left Behind

protector—is simply an innocent; yes, the most just and tolerant person he has ever known is no more than that. Trying to sweep away such tainted thoughts, he finally speaks: *No, this is my home, a place where the ground does not move under my feet.* But to himself he says, *I am homeless. My father's home is Africa; my mother's home is Asia. But I am rootless.*

Post-Childhood Stories in Search of an Adult Identity

In Obama's early adolescence, his search for adult identity began at the privileged Punahou School in Hawaii, with critical stops at Occidental College in California, Columbia University in New York, and Chicago's black communities and churches. After an important interlude at Harvard Law School and following study there, he ended his search with his return to Chicago to teach at the university, to establish his black roots in community service, and ultimately to rise rapidly in the political sphere.

Harvard Law opened windows of opportunity, decision, and choice. From the start, he was a star among both students and faculty as his intellectual prowess bloomed. Election as president of the law review earned him a contract to tell his story in *Dreams*. Connecting in unique style, he impressed and formed close, sometimes all but equal relationships with faculty.

Obama's African American origins were a major issue for him in his search for identity throughout his adolescence and early adulthood. In their search for a kind of hero to serve as a model for heroic behavior in hard times, black youth face a compound question: not just *Who am I?* but *Who am I as a black person?* And then, *What kind of hero meets my standards and matches my heroic inclinations?*

Obama had to come to terms with his racial identity and, like so many black youth, a father who abandoned him. Further, he was primed for confusion by a white mother who idealized blackness and her African husband, thereby inadvertently denying her son's right to ordinary feelings of loss and anger. At the same time, her love and that of his almost "color-blind" white grandparents were another factor in his confusion and intense search, and certainly a major factor in the astonishing success of that search.

From his early years, Obama seemed to know that he'd have to settle a psychological score with his father. His image of his father—an image made more powerful by geographical and cultural distance—was magnetically attractive. "Not knowing" him made him evocatively elusive. It follows that if Obama were to find himself, he'd have to find his father and bury the image.

Perhaps the following captures something of the hero story Obama was inwardly working out. One might call it "Yes I can."

———————————

My father, a great man I was told, won my mother's heart, gathered her in his strong arms, and entered her, leaving his seed both in her heart and in her soul, and then left. I was the seed he left behind. When he came a second time, he left his shadowed mark on me, but left before I got to know him. He remains a mystery I must solve.

When he came to America to fill his head with new knowledge, he won great acclaim. The keepers of that knowledge opened their vaults, filling his mind with what he needed to make his country strong like him.

My mother wept but shed no tears. *You have his name*, she said. *His race is your race; you must honor both.* She did not say this in so many words, but in the stories she told me to keep his memory alive. *You must grow your mind so that he will be proud of you. He is black, and you are black. Be proud of that. Do not be angry at him for turning his back; he does what he must do; that is what makes him what he is.*

Influenced by her stories, I wasn't angry at my father for leaving us, but I was confused. I tried to believe, to trust, but still, in my secret heart, I wondered, *Who am I? What does it mean to be black?* Later, I would experiment, find out. For now, I would just keep an eye on things, think for myself, wait and see. As for my mother's leaving me with strangers I hardly knew, I told myself she was making me strong enough to go it alone. And when I found myself, and when I was really loved, I would give something important to the world.

———————

Before leaving Harvard, Obama made a crucial decision to go to Kenya to learn who his father really was and to connect with his African family. After Harvard and a short stint in corporate law, he famously chose community organizing as a first step toward a "larger purpose." As a uniquely equipped African American, he was determined to serve both his race and his country. Harvard confirmed what America's purer purposes were about. The country's blemished history on racial policy focused his future on doing something about it.

Ongoing Triggering Themes

Chapter Six established the relationship between the childhood story and the behavior-triggering themes it gives birth to. As I suggested earlier, Obama's stories reveal a strong sense of *abandonment* by both his parents, along with its tepid cousin, the sense of being *alone*. Another theme, *need to belong*, is a psychological roommate to abandonment, and Obama did set out to search for community, in Chicago's streets and in church, and then for family, at Michelle's behest.

Abandonment always leaves psychological traces; but though his mother "left him behind" to pursue her life and career without him, his stories show little or no direct anger toward her (though he may have shown it indirectly by his down-grading of her). This absence of anger is notable in recent behaviors as well and seems unnatural to him, though it is consistent with his general behavioral profile. For example, when Joe Wilson (R-South Carolina) shouted "You lie!" during Obama's first inaugural address, he kept his cool, and did so again when criticized by the media for not being more forceful, for not entering the ring to take his naysayer adversaries to the mat. Perhaps one could find an answer to this in his behavioral profile (bystander in open meaning), which lends itself to restraint.

Every human has a dark side, and it is safe to say that Obama is not exempt. But although his anger is mentioned from time to time, nowhere do we find extremes, such as rage, ugly threats, or verbal assaults on the character of others. In pursuit of his dark side, one could speculate that, in light of his avowed higher purpose of addressing black grievances, he consciously suppresses extreme anger to avoid being viewed as an "angry black man." In addition, one could look to his childhood story and to his ambivalent relationship with his father, who was, in a sense, let off the hook. Arguably, Obama should be angry at a father who so thoroughly abandoned him. I take up the absence of anger as a shadow of this relationship later in this chapter.

Another, even more speculative dark-side element—which structural dynamics suggests Michelle would be most likely to experience—is that, in some form or other, he may psychologically abandon those he loves (Chapter Nine).

OBAMA'S IDENTITY QUEST

Like all of us, Obama arrived at his postures of moral justice and his heroic type through self-selected stories that I will follow along with in describing four paths he took in reaching his overall identity as a hero leader with a cause larger than himself.

- Finding his racial identity
- Establishing a theory of justice in which to frame his cause
- Cultivating his scholarly bent
- Forming his models of practice

Finding His Racial Identity

Much has been said on this subject by Obama and others. I wish only to call attention to those aspects that follow his trail out of confusion toward his ultimate role as leader.

At various points along the way—Punahou, Columbia and Harlem, Chicago, Harvard, Chicago again, Kenya, and in the presence of Michelle and family—

Obama engaged in several activities typical of someone with his profile. He singled out people to talk to about race; he observed, as bystanders are prone to do; and he reflected on what he observed, alone and with others. Overlapping with these attempts to find meaning in discourse, he made a move in line with the bystander's tendency to observe and reflect before acting.

Becoming a community organizer was a move to discover himself by getting to know inner-city African Americans in their often neglected urban environment, and was typical of Obama's behavioral profile. Also crucial to his identity journey, as I will describe, he took active notice of a long list of heroic black figures, models from whom to pick and choose those who best fit his own emerging tendencies.

Two further decisions brought closure to his identity search. One was discovering and choosing a mate who would love him for who he was, including his heroic self.

Michelle Robinson—smarter than he, some say, a Harvard-trained lawyer as determined as he was to commit to some larger cause, less smitten than most with predictions that he would be the first black president, and thus able to rein in his alleged arrogance—got him all he needed in a mate and, more, the family he yearned for.

The second decision was to write the final chapter of his two formative stories by tracking his real father, putting the myth in perspective, and proving himself a match for both.

What we see now is a man who has chosen public service over the seductions of a corporate career sure to hand him the usual rewards; a man distinct for his instinct to create a life worth living, to use our terms; a self-directed man who, far sooner than most who do it all, took the path of responsible self-evolution, also our terms. In our framework, he's left only one stone unturned in his childhood story: his mother. Recall that with a coach's help, Ralph Waterman revisited the view he had of his mother. Obama may someday want to do the same.

Establishing a Theory of Justice in Which to Frame His Cause

It is rare for leaders in the corporate world to conscientiously build a model, and probably as rare among politicians. But my "reading" of Obama suggests that this is what he began to do during his time at Columbia. Recall our meta-model (Chapter Twelve), which says that a model requires three theories: of *the thing*, of *change*, and of *practice*. Although Obama himself has not publicly mentioned

John Rawls's *A Theory of Justice* (1971) as an influence, I suspect it is a source of his theory of the thing. Kloppenberg reports that Rawls's arguments played a decisive role in debates about justice when Obama was studying political science at Columbia and law at Harvard, and when he was teaching at the University of Chicago. In brief, Rawls's book argues for a principled reconciliation of liberty and equality, based on principles of justice, and Obama's speeches reflect these ideas when he talks about justice as fairness and about the role of justice in social cooperation.

Cultivating His Scholarly Bent

Obama refers to the period of transferring from Occidental to Columbia as his "ascetic" phase. Living deliberately "like a monk" in a sparse Harlem apartment, he began to write, journal, and read as if starving to know (see Figure 15.2).

Obama's identity as a scholar took shape in the course of a dazzling amount of subsequent reading, including William James, W.E.B. Du Bois, Adam Smith, Ralph Ellison, John Dewey, Franz Fanon, Saul Alinsky, Richard Wright, Langston Hughes, Lawrence Tribe, Malcolm X, Alexis de Tocqueville, Frederick Arthur, John Rawls, and others.

Framing His Models of Practice

I believe that between Chicago's streets and Ivy libraries, Obama has mindfully crafted a practice model without actually naming it as such. My hunch is that his theory and model of practice come from two sources: deliberative democracy and the work of Saul Alinsky.

Deliberative democracy is a turn that democratic theory took in the later twentieth century. It is a system of political decision making that relies on popular consultation to make policy, very similar to the kind of decision making that takes place in high-level executive teams. Both emphasize the importance of the process of discussion. It is this discourse that gives validity to decisions, even though the populace does not necessarily make the actual decision. In theories of deliberative democracy, within the moral framework of society, citizens "must reason beyond their narrow-self interest and consider what can be justified to people who reasonably disagree with them."[8]

At Harvard, Obama immersed himself in fine-point theoretical discussions on the subject. According to Kloppenberg's *Reading Obama*, "What we need, [Obama]

Figure 15.2
Obama, a Young Adult on a Quest

suggests, is a 'shift in metaphors,' a willingness to see 'our democracy not as a house to be built, but as a conversation to be had' . . . [the Constitution] not a 'fixed blueprint' [but rather] . . . a framework that cannot resolve all our differences but offers . . . 'a way by which we argue about our future.'"[9]

As noted earlier, Obama echoes deliberative democracy in his speeches. His stubborn insistence on bipartisan debate, often in defiance of his advisers, is another demonstration of it in his practice.

Obama used the work of the radical American community organizer, Saul Alinsky (1909–1972)—whom William F. Buckley Jr. described as "very close to being an organizational genius"—to fashion his practice model "on the ground." (Obama also taught Alinsky's method at the University of Chicago.) Obama's signature trait of empathy was also characteristic of Alinsky.

Alinsky was famously confrontational in his profile and tactics, in sharp contrast to Obama's profile-consistent, famous bystander aversion to confrontation. This difference between them was part of what Obama had to contend with in the second, *constraint* stage of model building (Chapter Twelve).

OBAMA'S HIGH-STAKES TENDENCIES

Even before the 2008 campaign, Obama had acted in high-stakes political situations. At a White House meeting at the height of the financial crisis, it was Obama rather than then President Bush or Republican nominee John McCain, who was in charge, according to Jonathan Alter in *The Promise*, physically preventing a fight between Congressman Barney Frank and Hank Paulsen, treasury secretary.

Since his inauguration, high stakes have been the rule. On the domestic front: a crippling recession; record-high unemployment; united opposition from Senate Republicans; the rising antigovernment Tea Party movement; questions about his identity and citizenship from the so-called Birthers; a liberal base whose high expectations were bound to be disappointed by the realities of the presidency; more unexpectedly, an attempted terrorist attack over Christmas 2009 and a Gulf Coast oil spill that is the worst environmental disaster in American history. On the foreign policy front: inherited wars in Afghanistan and Iraq, an increasingly aggressive North Korea and Iran, and the Wikileaks leaking of military and diplomatic cables. Obama's status as the first black U.S. president, the Muslim religious strand in his heritage, and his formative years spent in a foreign country further raise the stakes and dangers related to the fact that so many Americans view him as a hostile "other" despite his completely unhostile manner. (Daily threats on his life are reported at four times the number aimed at his predecessor.[10])

Moral Posture and Hero Choice

In high-stakes situations, Obama's profile suggests a moral tendency toward the adjudicator in his handling of events and the "other." But this is balanced somewhat by an advocate strain, which, again, he keeps under wraps both for political and personal reasons (Chapter Nine).

Earlier I mentioned Obama's theme of abandonment, which is associated with the hero choice of survivor in very high stakes; and Obama is primarily a survivor. As I also mentioned earlier, the dark side here is that as survivors tend to abandon themselves to a larger cause, in the process of extrapolation, they abandon, through psychological or physical distancing, those they love and those who love them most. But at the same time, I suspect that Obama reserves and maintains a protector side for personal relations, a side that does not typically get expressed in public. I mentioned one striking exception to this—his behavior before and during his 2011 speech after the shooting in Tucson. In his desire to hear and publicly share people's stories, he visited victims in the hospital and spoke with their families. What made his speech that night one of his best and most moving was his display of empathy, which is how he exhibits his protector self.

How did Obama come to choose the survivor and protector modes? For one thing, his mother was most likely a survivor (with random tendencies in meaning). Ann in no way resembles the fixer hero, and whatever protector inclinations she harbored were undermined by her tendencies to drift in a sea of possibilities far from home and hearth. She found meaning and worthy causes to get excited about where others saw only the ordinary. In one of the random's frequent contradictions, she could knuckle down and get things done. Her thousand-page dissertation, which developed a model of microfinance that is now Indonesia's standard, and the seven years she spent as consultant and research coordinator for Indonesia's oldest bank are examples.[11]

Some of this must have rubbed off on the young Obama. Ann's no-nonsense, predawn homeschooling instilled endurance, stoic self-discipline, and an explorer's appetite for the adventure of learning, a perfect recipe for the survivor type.

Survivors are very good bystanders, and most bystanders get their start early, from seeing their own families "from the balcony," so to speak. Obama began practicing at Punahou. His good fortune at attending there notwithstanding, being one of four blacks among thirty-five hundred mostly white and privileged students drove him to a social space where survivors hang out and thrive—at the margin. On one hand, perhaps more in his own mind than in reality, his blackness set him apart. On the other hand, defining himself as an outsider looking in was great boot-camp training for a neophyte survivor.

Survivors have a tolerance for physical and mental challenge (one could even say they have a need to define themselves in terms of such challenges); and for some, the harsher the conditions, the better. Obama's first ascetic experiences came in his boyhood, with his mother as his guide. Later as a young man, concluding that life at Occidental College was seductively easy and soft, he chose the cold, harsh Northeast, where, again ascetically stripping down to essentials, he could explore, under more challenging conditions, his identity and his destiny.

Obama's reading at Columbia included writings by and about a long list of past and present black and nonblack accomplished heroes. From those giants he apparently singled out a few, according to two criteria: they were models of heroic character by *his measures*, principally that they contributed to uncensored recognition of the shame and fully neglected rights of blacks; and they matched his own emerging heroic behavioral propensities. They had great minds (Lincoln), took heroic stands in crises that put them at risk (Martin Luther King Jr.), represented great causes that benefited those shortchanged in man's universal right to justice and fairness (both Lincoln and King), had testable strategies designed to realize such a noble cause (Alinsky and Mandela), and expressed a strong "I can" personal mantra. All these men were or are, by our definition and not coincidentally, also survivor types.

"I've Never Seen a Meeting Like That"

Earlier I noted Obama's high-stakes moral tendency toward the adjudicator and briefly mentioned his role in one Bush-era White House meeting. Here is a fuller account of that incident, in which dramatically outsized behaviors of other leaders shocked the aggression-averse Obama. The account is based largely on evidence from Alter's *The Promise*, which is remarkably balanced and free of moral certitude.[12]

In this scene, Obama is the mover; McCain is a disabled follower, then a silent or disabled bystander; when Cheney lapses into silence, he becomes an intimidating bystander as covert opposer; Bush throughout is an ineffectual mover who concedes the meeting to Obama; Barney Frank is gearing up for a high-stakes battle in his mover-opposer stance. Here's what happened:

When the 2008 recession hit, just before the presidential debates were about to begin, Senator McCain called for a meeting in the cabinet room. The group was to vote on Treasury Secretary Henry Paulson's three-page bailout plan. Obama "was the only one of the big dogs who seemed to know what he was talking about. Obama was taking charge of the meeting—and the crisis— peppering the others with detailed questions."

Barney Frank and Spencer Bachus were ready for a brawl. The two men started squabbling over whether the Democrats had been blindsided that morning.

"Now Paulson was down on one knee, pleading with the Democrats not to 'blow up' the deal. It was hard to know how serious he was, but others in the room found it scary to see the treasury secretary pathetically praying in the middle of a crisis."

Barney Frank "started yelling, 'Fuck you, Hank! Fuck you! Blow up this deal? We didn't blow up this deal! Your guys blew up the deal. You better tell Bachus and the rest of them to get their shit together!' When Paulson tried to equivocate, Frank threw in another 'Fuck you, Hank!'—his third of the day." (Moving from escalation to noise, Frank is almost out of control—and behaving typically for the mover-opposer in extreme high-stakes situations.)

"The only person standing between Frank and Paulson was Barack Obama, who bent his arms and spread his palms to keep the two men apart. 'Okay, guys,' Obama said, like a teacher preventing a playground brawl."

"Obama took control of the conversation, cool as usual. 'Calm down, Barney. Let's sort this out,' he said. 'Hank, you've got to go back and talk to Spencer and put this thing back together.'"

Obama was cool from start to finish: at the start, fully prepared from having read Paulson's document (typical bystander in meaning), but ready to facilitate— that is, to invite others to speak, or move—with rapid-fire questions (moving from the bystander stance), and remaining "cool" (preserving his power as a bystander). When Barney Frank, likely after something or someone triggered a toxic theme, raised the stakes for all when his anger almost turned physical, Obama, still cool and rational, put out the fire. For him the external stakes were as high as they were for Frank, Pelosi, and others, but his bystander capacity carried the day.

This brawl, enacted in behind-the-scenes politics, exactly captures the tone and intensity of the ClearFacts team's escalation described in Chapter Eight.

President Obama has been on a microscope slide of acute political observation since he stepped on the national stage to deliver his party's keynote in 2004. He remains so to this day and, I suspect, will continue to be scrupulously studied until his place in history is firmly established. Obama is *liked* well enough, but the 2012 election will test his mettle. As the world watches, the right batters him over the head with a debt ceiling, and the left accuses him of hamstringing government programs. More than ever, in his bid for a second term it is important that he fight.

The media, across the political spectrum, have had surprisingly similar, and mostly critical, things to say about Obama's performance as a leader to date. In contrast, historians and biographers have seen this same leader in a mostly positive light. I have attempted to put both perspectives through our own allegedly objective prism, but also praised him for what I believe all leaders must do, the hard work of developing a model.

Now I take another step, daring to write a memo to the president, about how his role as a leader in the future affects his constituents, all Americans, and indeed the world at large.

EXIT MEMORANDUM

TO: President Obama

FROM: Duncan Travis (aka Dr. David Kantor)

RE: FAREWELL, AND MOVING FORWARD

President Obama: I will present my thoughts on your story and behavioral profile and how it affects your leadership. I will also provide you with a road map for your future as president. You should know by now that the deliverer of change is inseparable from what is being changed, so read this with my behavioral profile in mind.

I firmly believe that most manifestations of a leader's patterned behaviors emerge from what I call the childhood story of imperfect love; that this story in turn leads to the gathering of another set of structural stories that determine the leader's behavioral preferences; and finally that these stories create themes from mild to toxic that affect his or her behavior in high stakes.

Mr. President, the monarch's (that is, your father's) role in your childhood stories is quite clear. The missing act of love by the mother is less clear. It would be of great benefit to explore both of these relationships (and stories) further.

Until you put your mother's contribution to your success in the world in better perspective than you express in *Dreams from My Father*, you may leave unfilled gaps in your capacity to love (and perhaps, come across as cold and aloof). Failure to take into account your father's effects on you can similarly handicap your potential. You operate in the volatile and oppositional world of politics. Although your trip to Kenya, described in *Dreams from My Father*, resulted positively in dissipation rather than liberation of legitimate anger, this very anger is needed to confront those rivals whose hostility threatens you, your policies, and the nation. Your capacity as a leader can be inhibited by the calm you've learned.

You also could be putting excessive pressure on the First Lady to compensate for your mother's alleged lapses in love. The way I read your story, abandonment (though you might call it loneliness) is a leftover toxic theme. Mrs. Obama has revealed enough of her story to make clear that she feels at least slightly burdened by your unfinished family business.

Judging from your young-adult hero myth, you are a survivor hero. For some insight into your relationships with Mrs. Obama, look to the survivor's gray zone (Chapter Nine) and how the hero's psychological self-abandonment leaves his lover in the shadow of the scaffold as he chooses his cause over life and love (a reference to Arthur Miller's *The Crucible*). Mr. President, the First Lady seems to tighten the reins (such as when you were deliberating whether to enter the campaign).

The role you play in life as a survivor requires immense input and commitment and self-sacrifice. Fortunately, your wife is savvy enough to avoid being eclipsed by the demands on you by focusing on fighting childhood obesity.

Mr. President, your survivor hero tendencies have been in quiet but abundant display from the day you assumed office. Your campaign slogan, "Yes We Can," is the survivor's mantra (Chapter Nine). Your ability to endure has seen you through great pressure, and it is clear that it will continue to serve you as you mature as a leader.

Now I will focus on your behavioral profile.

I have assessed you primarily as a *bystander in open meaning*. In the media, you have taken considerable flack. It is common for the media—especially opinion makers—to speak in moral language (Chapter Eight). Structural dynamics and the behavioral profile attempt to describe the same behavior in "structural" terms, a studiously nonjudgmental language.

The media have leveled criticism on you. What we see and hear criticized is a leader with a *model*, what I think is deliberative democracy. Few political leaders have models that go beyond ideology. What the media has been referring to in moral tones and that I have been translating into the neutral language of structural dynamics is your behavioral profile in action under relentlessly high-stakes conditions. (Chapters Eight and Nine show how our profiles change when subjected to high stakes.)

One addition: the media, and even your most ardent supporters, have said you have failed to deliver a coherent narrative. Considering your well-received books and inspiring presidential campaign in 2008, your failure at storytelling a la Roosevelt and Reagan is puzzling. Please refer to my chapter on narrative purpose (Chapter Seven) and get to work on creating your own.

The twenty leader capacities are discussed in Chapter Fourteen. Here is how I believe you score:

Obama's Highs, Lows, and Growing Edge

Highs	Lows	Growing Edge
Empathizing with others	Showing humility	Balancing arrogance and humility
Operating under pressure	Articulating narrative purpose	Articulating narrative purpose
Knowing the self (with the exception of knowing when to show legitimate anger)	Knowing when to show legitimate anger	Knowing when to show legitimate anger
Managing teams	Taking risks	
Acting morally		
Tolerating difference		
Compromising with others		

First, the sugar; then, the medicine. And then . . . the doctor is out!

The Highs

You showed incredible empathy in your speech at the funeral of Christina Taylor Green in January 2011. You were even criticized by political foes for suggesting that empathy was a quality you would look for in a Supreme Court justice.

Politics aside, you have amassed impressive accomplishments in your short time as president, including health care reform, financial reform, the repeal of "Don't Ask, Don't Tell," and the killing of Osama bin Laden.

You have performed admirably under tremendous pressure—two wars in the Middle East, the worst financial crisis since the Great Depression, and a fractured populace—and this is because you put together a competent, bipartisan cabinet; were willing to tolerate debate; and sought compromise when you could.

Your eloquent books and speeches show that you are remarkably reflective on yourself and introspective and have a firm set of core moral values. These qualities will be of use to you as you and your staff read *Reading the Room* (I can only hope) and continue to develop your model.

The Lows and the Growing Edge

A man of so many successes—the presidency of the *Harvard Law Review*; a best-selling, well-acclaimed book; a mesmerizing and winning campaign for the presidency; and the Nobel Peace Prize, for that matter—understandably thinks well of himself.

But Mr. President, it is widely believed that you are not a humble man. I have spoken with friends and colleagues of yours, over dinner-table conversations in Cambridge, and this has been their primary criticism. Furthermore, you infamously said, "You're likeable enough, Hillary" during the 2008 campaign, a comment that made even your staffers gasp in disappointment. Ms. Clinton handled herself gracefully, but this embarrassing put-down made you seem arrogant and vain. However, the "shellacking" you took in the 2010 elections since changed your tone, and your announcement of the death of Osama bin Laden—an obvious occasion for puffing your chest feathers—was instead short, somber, and serious. Here, you have a growing edge.

I must make one final point about your low and growing-edge scores. I have said this before: you must fight, and, in order to succeed, you must break through the calm you have developed. There is a delicate line you walk as perhaps the most watched and listened to black man in the world. You look to the fallout over Reverend Wright's explosion as a warning, but *you* hold a different position and set of responsibilities. Your duty to the country commands you to fight; I encourage you to look to the unfinished business with your father and find the spirit to do so.

As I previously mentioned, articulating a grand, inspiring vision for the country is a challenge with which every president struggles. Reading Chapter Seven, Narrative Purpose, will help. So, too, will the 2012 presidential campaign. You have shown an ability to connect—such as in your speeches at the 2004 Democratic National Convention on race and in Tucson—and you must find a way to translate this ability to address the gigantic sum of peoples, places, and problems that is America.

The only low score you receive where I do not see a growing edge is in taking risks. Democrats and liberals remain frustrated that you did not seek a public option in your health care bill. Your predecessor, known as "the Decider," would have scored high here. (Due to the nature of risks, though, this is not always the best quality.) My advice: you have a high capacity for acting morally. When you believe something is morally important and right (for example, the assassination of Osama bin Laden) and has a good chance of success, the hazard of risk taking becomes the *necessity* of risk taking—an audacious suggestion; however, I believe you are quite familiar with audacity.

It has been a true pleasure working with you. Good luck, and God Bless America.

David Kantor, Ph.D.

AFTERWORD
WHERE STRUCTURAL DYNAMICS GOES
FROM HERE

Structural dynamics theory began in the 1970s in the course of my studying face-to-face communication in families. In the 1990s, it extended to the study of couples in therapy. Between 2000 and 2008, I began to expand the theory and to apply it to corporations and their teams. Going forward, structural dynamics will focus primarily on teams, team behavior in low and high stakes, and the ability to measure change using computerized instruments with the capacity to code and capture structural dynamics' basic unit of measurement, the speech act.

Over time, the speech act became the theory's basic unit for coding and measuring what happens in human vocal discourse in social networks like families, couples, and teams. Within the speech act, with the development of the first Behavioral Propensities Profile, I was able to statistically establish high levels of validity and reliability for structural dynamics' thirty-six speech acts.[1] Few issues are more important than how leaders lead in high-stakes situations, but very few instruments currently in use address such situations. Although structural dynamics and its tools are still in early stages of development, they are already in use and capable of putting leaders in touch with damaging impacts they have on others and getting them on a sounder developmental path.

The leadership capacities, and the assignment of ratings in each capacity as described in this chapter, is still in a very early stage of development. The long-term goal in developing this tool is to move it toward a more formal, reliable method of measurement.

Understanding the relationship between the structural nature of human discourse and the performance of teams is one of the exciting research goals of those who work in structural dynamics. We seek to do this through empirical studies of change from a valid baseline measure of behavior, the Behavioral Propensities

Profile. Because top-level leaders are willing to put themselves and their teams under the confines of research-based scrutiny, we foresee additional, potentially breakthrough learning in the near future.

Future empirical testing will include analyzing the following:

- The influence of meeting format (formal, structured, informal, leaderless) on discourse and its outcome
- Typologies of stakes-raising themes and circumstances
- How the formal status of the team leader (the presence of "power") affects discourse patterns
- Subversive communication as a covert response to power
- Assumptions about "the voice of gender" in high-level teams
- The relationship between turn taking and interaction order and communicational productivity
- "Language differences" in supposed homogeneous cultures
- Intrateam trends
- Interteam comparisons
- Team interfaces
- Mixed cultural teams

NOTES

PREFACE

1. Before launching the family study, these two questions were raised: Would you be able to recruit families that would allow researchers to observe their most protected private lives? Would they hide their scars and scabs? Although the establishment of trust was pivotal in getting through the door, we were surprised by what we heard on the tapes once in. Some couples, in the midst of their ritual fights, seemed to address the microphones. It was as if they were saying (and one couple indeed did), "Listen to this, David; this is how it is." We were witnessing reality TV being born.

2. My choice of participant observers was of more than administrative interest. Concerned that professionally trained observers would look for and find support, conscious or not, for theories they knew, I recruited "naïve" observers: undergraduate students on school breaks. Free of family constraints, they could live in; and ostensibly free of professional bias, they could report strictly what they saw and heard.

3. To pay the families back for their immense contribution to the field, we constructed, as promised at the study's outset, a two-hour tape for each family, patching together excerpts from their raw data. We, Kantor and Lehr, met with the family for four to six hours to discuss "the story you have told us about your family and how it was contributing to science." They loved it, as you might imagine. Sharing the results of the study was scientifically rewarding to an unexpected degree. It was, in effect, a test of validity. "Yes, that's us! And how you describe us hits home, but you should know why we behave and communicate that way."

4. The Friedmans, three months' pregnant when we moved the cameras in, were eager to put themselves on display. Open about "serious communication problems" that were spoiling the anticipated joys of child bearing and child rearing, they wanted to be among the first couples to have the birthing filmed in-hospital and to get help in knowing what their fights were about. They were a perfect match for addressing our own research question.

5. Kantor, D. "Critical Identity Image: A Concept Linking Individual, Couple, and Family Development." In J. K. Pearce and L. J. Friedman (eds.), *Family Therapy: Combining Psychodynamic and Family Systems Approaches* (pp. 137–167). New York: Grune & Stratton, 1980.

6. For two years in the early 1990s, along with Argyris, Schön, Schein, and Senge, I was part of an informal eight-member learning group that met monthly at MIT to share our different perspectives on systems and their structures, and how these applied in the world of business consulting. It only occurs to me at this writing that herein was sown the seed of a structural dynamics idea, the meta-model (the model of models), a missing link in the chain of concepts that holds my theory together.

7. There is no end to my thanking Innovation Associates, Interaction Associates, and Dialogos—especially their directors, Charlie Kiefer, Thomas Rice, and Bill Isaacs, respectively—for providing already enriched soil for growing new ideas, many of them spreading willy-nilly throughout *Reading the Room* without credit to those I worked with in developing them.

8. Isaacs, W. *Dialogue and the Art of Thinking Together*. New York: Doubleday, 1999.

9. Monitor Group is a strategy consulting company with a penchant, spurred by its chairman, Mark Fuller, for breaking new ground while preserving its core practice. Before others saw the wisdom of and critical need for integrating strategy with systems-oriented behavioral theories, Fuller did, bringing Chris Argyris, who was still at Harvard, aboard. Business school geniuses who spat out numbers were asked to swallow and digest what they instinctively had little taste for. Argyris's ideas, summed up as Action Science and implemented by him and protégés like Diana Smith, intended to change not only individuals put through the rigors of change but their culture as well. To my benefit, ground was broken for the arrival a few years later of another complementary set of ideas—structural dynamics.

CHAPTER 1

1. The program was conducted at the Kantor Institute. Programs of this kind are cropping up across the country. In Cambridge there is Action Design, a program led by Diana Smith, Robert Putnam, and Phil McArthur, and one at Dialogos. Both of these adapt concepts developed at the Kantor Institute.

2. While working at Monitor Group, I developed with colleagues a computerized assessment instrument that codifies with high inter-item scores for reliability and validity, and a computer program that facilitates the work of an observer "in the room" who codes the team's speeches. For more information on the Observation Deck project, please visit the Kantor Institute Web site: (www.kantorinstitute.com).

3. Kilburg, R. *Executive Wisdom: Coaching and the Emergence of Virtuous Leaders.* Washington, D.C.: American Psychological Association, 2006.

CHAPTER 2

1. For a more detailed description of this basic theory, see Kantor, D., and Lehr, W. *Inside the Family.* San Francisco: Jossey-Bass, 1975.

CHAPTER 3

1. Goleman, D. *Emotional Intelligence: Why It Can Matter More Than IQ.* New York: Bantam Dell, 2006. N/A.

2. Goleman, D. *Social Intelligence: The New Science of Human Relationships.* New York: Bantam Dell, 1995, p. 4.

3. Kantor, D., and Lehr, W. *Inside the Family.* San Francisco: Jossey-Bass, 1975.

CHAPTER 4

1. If you are not already familiar with systems thinking or would like to read more about how structural dynamics fits in with other systems approaches, see my book *Systems Theory for Executive Coaches*, 2004 (available through the Kantor Institute Web site, www.kantorinstitute.com, or through Meredith Winter Press, www.meredithwinterpress.com).

2. Important contributions to this field have come from Chris Argyris's extensive work on organizational learning and routines that disable learning, and from Peter Senge's system archetypes. Argyris, C., and Schön, D. A. *Organizational Learning: A Theory of Action Perspective.* Reading, Mass.: Addison-Wesley, 1978; Senge, P. M. *The Fifth Discipline.* New York: Doubleday, 1990.

3. What Norbert Weiner called "feedback of a complex kind." Weiner, N. *Cybernetics: Or Control and Communication in the Animal and the Machine.* Cambridge, Mass.: MIT Press, 1948.

4. Senge, P. M., Kleiner, A., Roberts, C., Ross, R., and Smith, B. *The Fifth Discipline Fieldbook: Strategies and Tools for Building a Learning Organization.* New York: Doubleday, 1990, p. 7.

5. Gawande, A. *Complications: A Surgeon's Notes on an Imperfect Science.* New York: Metropolitan Books, 2002, p. 63.

CHAPTER 6

1. The research, now beyond a long period of gestation, is in process. It assumes for now that a working theory that drives moral behavior and its lapses can be tracked to the kinds of stories that appear in these pages. It addresses the following questions: How is adult moral character formed? Is it based on stories? If so, are they structural in nature? And under what conditions are moral behaviors fixed or malleable? But it seemed intellectually remiss in a book on leadership, especially in this era, not to address the moral issues it does—albeit with an incomplete theoretical backup—without stories behind them that are crucial to character, identity, and behavior.

2. Kantor, D. *My Lover, Myself: Self-Discovery Through Relationship.* New York: Riverhead Books, 1999.

3. Kilburg, R. *Executive Wisdom: Coaching and the Emergence of Virtuous Leaders.* Washington, D.C.: American Psychological Association, 2006, pp. 249, 266.

4. Kantor, D. "The Structural-Analytic Approach to the Treatment of Family Developmental Crisis." In H. A. Liddle (vol. ed.) and J. C. Hansen (ed.), *Clinical Implications of the Family Life Cycle.* Rockville, Md.: Aspen, 1983.

5. For more information, see my "Couples Therapy, Crisis Induction, and Change." In A. Gunnan (ed.), *Casebook of Marital Therapy*. New York: Guilford Press, 1985; and *My Lover, Myself*. New York: Riverhead Books, 1999.

6. In particular, see Diana Smith's *Divide or Conquer: How Great Teams Turn Conflict into Strength*. New York: Penguin, 2008.

CHAPTER 7

1. Tkaczyk, C. "World's Most Admired Companies" [snapshot of Apple]. *Fortune*, Mar. 22, 2010, CNNMoney. http://money.cnn.com/magazines /fortune/mostadmired/2010/snapshots/670.html.

2. Collins, J., and Porras, J. I. *Built to Last*. New York: HarperCollins, 1994, p. 78.

3. Ferguson, N. *The Ascent of Money: A Financial History of the World*. New York: Penguin, 2008.

4. Risen, C. "How the South Was Won." *Boston Globe*, Mar 5, 2006. www .boston.com/news/globe/ideas/articles/2006/03/05/how_the_south _was_won/.

5. Greenberg, A. C., with Singer, M. *The Rise and Fall of Bear Stearns*. New York: Simon & Schuster, 2010. N/A.

6. De Pree, M. *Leadership Is an Art*. New York: Doubleday, 2004.

7. Ward, V. *The Devil's Casino: Friendship, Betrayal, and the High-Stakes Games Played Inside Lehman Brothers*. Hoboken, NJ: Wiley, 2010.

8. Thomas J. Watson Jr., quoted in Collins and Porras, *Built to Last*, p. 73.

9. Hastings, M. "The Runaway General." *Rolling Stone*, June 22, 2010. www .rollingstone.com/politics/news/the-runaway-general-20100622.

10. Kilburg, R. *Executive Wisdom: Coaching and the Emergence of Virtuous Leaders*. Washington, D.C.: American Psychological Association, 2006, p. 212.

11. Ibid., p. 191.

12. Ibid., p. 194.

13. Ibid.

14. Tkaczyk, C. "World's Most Admired Companies" [snapshot of Coca-Cola]. *Fortune,* Mar. 22, 2010, CNNMoney. http://money.cnn.com/magazines/fortune/mostadmired/2010/snapshots/100.html.

15. Christensen, C. "How Will You Measure Your Life?" *Harvard Business Review,* July-Aug. 2010. http://hbr.org/2010/07/how-will-you-measure-your-life/ar/1.

CHAPTER 8

1. Hirshfield, J. *Nine Gates: Entering the Mind of Poetry.* New York: Harper Perennial, 1998, p. 29.

2. See Diana Smith's *Divide or Conquer: How Great Teams Turn Conflict into Strength.* New York: Penguin, 2008.

3. Many problems in teams are so entrenched that it takes a multistep intervention to effect change. To address this issue, a book by the author tentatively called *Making Change Happen* is in progress, which is a detailed description of the structural dynamics practice model. *Making Change Happen* relies on *Reading the Room* for its theory of the thing, a concept described in Chapter Twelve of this book.

CHAPTER 9

1. Elkind, P. "Epiphany to Disgrace." *Albany Times Union,* Apr. 25, 2010, p. A1.

2. See Ernest Freeberg's *Democracy's Prisoner: Eugene Debs, the Great War, and the Right to Dissent.* Cambridge, Mass.: Harvard University Press, 2008.

3. Jung, C. *The Archetypes and the Collective Unconscious* (R.F.C. Hull, trans.). (*Collected Works of C. G. Jung,* Vol. 9, Part 1). Princeton, N.J.: Princeton University Press, 1969.

4. Campbell, J. *The Hero with a Thousand Faces.* New York: Pantheon Books, 1949.

5. *My Lover, Myself* elaborates on the role of this myth in partnership and long-term love relationships. Kantor, D. *My Lover, Myself.* New York: Riverhead Books, 1999.

6. Chipp, H. B. *Theories of Modern Art.* Berkeley: University of California Press, 1968, p. 487.

7. Philip Gourevitch, quoted in Mackey, R. "March 18 Updates on Libya and Arab Uprisings." The Lede: Blogging the News with Robert Mackey, Mar. 18, 2011. *New York Times,* http://thelede.blogs.nytimes.com/2011/03/18/latest-updates-on-libya-and-arab-uprisings/.

8. Hemingway, E. *The Old Man and the Sea.* New York: Simon & Schuster, 2002, p. 65. (Originally published 1952.)

9. Perhaps this partly explains creative writers' proneness to suicide. Being overly sentimental teams up with the shadows of childhood stories, followed by "learned pessimism." If gene-based tendencies toward clinical depression are added, there is a powerful incentive to commit suicide.

10. I highlight gender here for a reason. Although the culture is redressing the issue, it has not completed the job. Men, especially in violent contexts like American football and the military, are not free to acknowledge vulnerability; but in fact they do not do so well with the thunder of war, the need to kill, and having to watch their buddies die. Posttraumatic stress disorder, I propose, may be the protector breaking down while still in the closet, but also after he is released. His breakdown is then but a more dramatic form of an overwhelming sense of vulnerability, the psychological gateway to the dark zone.

11. Carroll, J. *Constantine's Sword: The Church and the Jews.* New York: First Mariner Books, 2001. N/A.

12. Allow me to mention here again that most people are a mix of the three heroic types. Franklin Delano Roosevelt stands out among political examples. A recent, highly praised biography cracks the surface of Roosevelt the man, his behavioral profile in our terms, and his mixed heroic modes. See Black, C. *Franklin Delano Roosevelt: Champion of Freedom.* New York: Public Affairs, 2003.

CHAPTER 10

1. U.S. Attorney, Southern District of New York. "Bernard L. Madoff Pleads Guilty to Eleven-Count Criminal Information and Is Remanded into Custody" [Press release], Mar. 12, 2009. www.usdoj.gov/usao/nys/press releases/March09/madoffbernardpleapr.pdf; Frank, R. "Madoff Jailed After Admitting Epic Scam." *Wall Street Journal,* Mar. 13, 2009. http://online.wsj.com/article/SB123685693449906551.html?mod=djemalertNEWS;

Zambito, T. "Bye Bye Bernie: Ponzi King Madoff Sentenced to 150 Years." *New York Daily News*, June 29, 2009. www.nydailynews.com/money /2009/06/29/2009–06–29_madoff_gets_max.html; Tse, T. M. "Madoff Sentenced to 150 Years." *Washington Post*, June 30, 2009. www .washingtonpost.com/wp-dyn/content/article/2009/06/29/ AR2009062902015.html.

2. "The Madoff Case: A Timeline," Mar. 12, 2009. http://online.wsj.com /article/SB112966954231272304.html?.

3. Ackerman, M. "The Psychology Behind Bernie Madoff." *Huffington Post*, Dec. 18, 2008. www.huffingtonpost.com/mona-ackerman/the-psychology -behind-ber_b_151966.html.

4. Paulson, M. "Cardinal Begs Abuse Victims' Forgiveness." *Boston Globe*, Nov. 4, 2002, p. A1.

5. Jack, I. "Ireland: The Rise and the Crash." *New York Review of Books*, Nov. 11, 2010, *57*(17). www.nybooks.com/articles/archives/2010/nov/11/ireland -rise-crash/.

6. Goldman, L., and Blakeley, K. "The 20 Richest Women in Entertainment." *Forbes.com*, Jan. 17, 2007. www.forbes.com/2007/01/17/richest-women -entertainment-tech-media-cz_lg_richwomen07_0118womenstars _lander.html.

7. "Stewart Sentenced to Five Months in Prison." Reuters, July 17, 2004. www .smh.com.au/articles/2004/07/17/1089694573700.html.

8. Scannell, K., and Cohen, L. P. "Martha Stewart Pleads Not Guilty to Charges." *Wall Street Journal Online*, June 5, 2003. http://online.wsj.com/article/0 ,SB105473045227104600,00.html.

CHAPTER 11

1. Between 2001 and 2004, our research team at Monitor Group developed two tools to substantiate and strengthen my theoretical hypotheses. A sample of the first, the Behavioral Propensities Profile, is available as Premium Web Content at www.josseybass.com/go/davidkantor. The second, the Observation Deck, is a computerized assessment instrument that codifies with high inter-item scores for reliability and validity, and a computer program that facilitates the work of an observer "in the room" who codes the team's

speeches. For more information on the Observation Deck project, please visit the Kantor Institute Web site: www.kantorinstitute.com.

2. As part of the process of writing this book, I took the Behavioral Propensities Profile instrument for Ralph and each team member, standing proxy, as it were. I ask readers to allow this with the justification that, having created the characters, I "knew them" as well as they knew themselves. You can find Ralph's full report as Premium Web Content at www.josseybass .com/go/davidkantor.

3. All that is required in the short route is evidence of a pattern of damaging behavior (in example here, by an obsessively, harshly controlling project director) seen as such by those affected (his team); a trusting relationship between the perpetrator and the interventionist (the CEO I am coaching); and an appropriate, private context, such as a woodsy walk at the CEO's country home. On my advice to "find your own way to get the story behind the behavior," at a chosen moment, in a voice of blameless inquiry, the CEO said, "You seem so driven, so much more like a bulldozer than the leader you're trying to be. It scares the bejeezus out of your team. Somebody from your childhood is slashing a whip at your back, or something. What's the story?" He got one gush of emotion.

4. We can act in different ways under pressure. Which path we take depends on the spread in our low-stakes repertoire, as seen in our behavioral profile. For example, if Person A is 80 percent closed power, she will tend toward more strongly closed-power behaviors in high stakes—let's say from harsh to brutal power stances—and is unlikely to tend toward open affect. If Person B is a 40 percent opposer and 50 percent mover in low stakes, we are unlikely to see much following behavior in high stakes. In contrast, if Person C scores 25 percent in all four action stances, with equal spread across the other two dimensions in low stakes, her options to act differently in high stakes are greater than A's or B's. For more information on the Behavioral Propensities Profile, or to arrange for you or your team to take it, please visit the Kantor Institute Web site (www.kantorinstitute.com).

CHAPTER 12

1. The term *leadership model building* was suggested by Alan Daignault, then at Sprint, in the first course on model building conducted in 1999–2000

under the auspices of the Kantor Family Institute. The course was co-led with B. C. Huselton. I thank Alan for the idea, which has stuck.

2. Peale, N. V. *My Favorite Quotations*. New York: HarperOne, 1990.

3. I created the concept of the meta-model—the model of models—at the Kantor Family Institute sometime during its fifteen-year history, which ended in 1995. It was first introduced to organizational consulting in a seminar offered to consultants in 1990, co-led with Diana Smith.

4. For a more complete description, see my paper "Five Leadership Pathways," available through the Kantor Institute (www.kantorinstitute.com).

5. Kantor, D. "Couples Therapy, Crisis Induction, and Change." In A. Gunnan (ed.), *Casebook of Marital Therapy*. New York: Guilford Press, 1985.

6. In this book, Coles looks at what moral leadership is and the varieties in which it comes. Using Robert Kennedy and Dorothy Day as prime exemplars, it reveals the ways in which a range of individuals can bring us all up morally and can become part of a nation's moral fiber. Coles, R. *Lives of Moral Leadership*. New York: Random House, 2001.

7. Kilburg, R. *Executive Wisdom: Coaching and the Emergence of Virtuous Leaders*. Washington, D.C.: American Psychological Association, 2006. Kilburg insists that the wise leader wears moral awareness on his sleeve (pp. 141–143), gives vivid examples of a business entity that steered off course (p. 212), and poses eight provocative questions that will help leaders develop moral awareness (pp. 221–222). Ralph liked these ideas but thought he could improve on them by translating Sharma's audience concept (see note 8) into ongoing action.

8. Sharma, D. "The Importance of Audience Effect to Family/Human Communication and Development" (n.d.). www.psychoscience.net /importance_of_audience_effect.htm. Drawing on a literature review of audience effect and social facilitation, Sharma's paper refers to Chris VerWys's "Mere Presence of Others," noting how the presence of others affects how human beings and animals behave. Ralph makes the connection between this literature and bystanding, opining that consciously drawing on the bystander's "presence" would help individuals sustain moral behavior.

9. Schön, D. A. *The Reflective Practitioner: How Professionals Think in Action*. New York: Basic Books, 1984.

10. Argyris, C., Putnam, R., and Smith, D. M. *Action Science: Concepts, Methods and Skills for Research and Intervention*. San Francisco: Jossey-Bass, 1985.

CHAPTER 13

1. Kantor, D. *Alive in Time*. Cambridge, Mass.: Meredith Winter Press, 2002. Available through the Kantor Institute (www.kantorinstitute.com), or through Meredith Winter Press (www.meredithwinterpress.com).

2. Dowrick, S. *Intimacy and Solitude: Balancing Closeness and Independence*. New York: Norton, 1991.

3. Kantor, D. *My Lover, Myself: Self-Discovery Through Relationship*. New York: Riverhead Books, 1999. Available at www.meredithwinterpress.com.

4. Cassidy, J. "What Good Is Wall Street? Mostly What Investment Bankers Do Is Socially Worthless." *New Yorker*, Nov. 19, 2010. N/A.

CHAPTER 14

1. Kantor, D. "Sex and the CEO." Unpublished paper, 2010.

2. The exit leader is the organization's "sanctioned iconoclast." This leader's unique contribution rests in his ability to recognize and call out aspects of the organization and its performance that others lack the courage to challenge. His focus is not to critique but to improve by constantly seeking higher and higher levels of performance and by engaging in candid self- and organizational reflection. The exit leader is a critical but too often absent role in a well-functioning leadership system.

CHAPTER 15

1. Cassandra Butts, quoted in Remnick, D. *The Bridge: The Life and Rise of Barack Obama*. New York: Knopf, 2010. N/A.

2. As Harvard historian James T. Kloppenberg observes, Obama's "books manifest his serious engagement with the life of the mind" and that "[m]uch as he might need to mask it on the campaign trail . . . his books make clear that Barack Obama is also very much an intellectual."

Kloppenberg, J. T. *Reading Obama: Dreams, Hope, and the American Political Tradition.* Princeton, N.J.: Princeton University Press, 2010.

3. Kloppenberg, *Reading Obama.*

4. Mack, K. W. "Barack Obama Before He Was a Rising Political Star." *Journal of Blacks in Higher Education,* Autumn 2004, pp. 98–101.

5. Obama, B. *Dreams from My Father.* New York: Three Rivers Press, 1995.

6. Christopher Edley Jr., quoted in Remnick, *The Bridge: The Life and Rise of Barack Obama.* N/A.

7. Remnick, *The Bridge: The Life and Rise of Barack Obama,* p. 208.

8. Reykowski, J. "Deliberative Democracy and 'Human Nature': An Empirical Approach." *Political Psychology,* 2006, *27*(3), 325.

9. Kloppenberg, *Reading Obama.*

10. Harnden, T. "Barack Obama Faces 30 Death Threats a Day, Stretching US Secret Service." *Telegraph,* Aug. 3, 2009. www.telegraph.co.uk/news /worldnews/barackobama/5967942/Barack-Obama-faces-30-death -threats-a-day-stretching-US-Secret-Service.html.

11. Scott, J. *A Singular Woman: The Untold Story of Barack Obama's Mother.* New York: Riverhead Books, 2011.

12. All quotations in this account are from Alter, J. *The Promise.* New York: Simon & Schuster, 2010, pp. 11–13.

AFTERWORD

1. The reliability of the Behavioral Propensities Profile (BPP) was assessed by analyzing its internal consistency, which evaluates individual questions in comparison with one another for their ability to give consistent results. The analysis was conducted on a sample of over two hundred respondents and resulted in a robust Cronbach's alpha (α) of .96 for the overall scale. For more information on the BPP or to arrange for you or your team to take it, please visit the Kantor Institute Web site (www.kantorinstitute.com).

ACKNOWLEDGMENTS

The birth of *Reading the Room* was preceded by decades of loving collaborations with colleagues who helped or stood by ready to assist as the foundation, walls, and roof of the theory of structural dynamics were being built. I mention them briefly here: Will Lehr, Carter Umbarger, Barry Dym, Uli Detling, Chris Argyris, Don Schön, Ed Schein, Peter Senge, Charlie Kiefer, Thomas Rice, Bill Isaacs, Mark Fuller, B. C. Huselton, Robert Hanig, and Lisa Stefanac.

I thank Kathe Sweeney, who fulfills every writer's dream of how a publisher should manage an author. Kathe's quiet patience and enthusiastic support, never more than a click away, coaxed, steered, and ushered this book to shore with impeccable finesse.

Editors: The contributions of Shani Harmon, Nancy Lonstein, and Alan Venable cannot be overestimated. This book bears the distinct imprint of their skills.

Artists: Working with the design studio at Monitor Group was a "trip," a creative high, and a six-year journey with a crew of graphic artists who never failed in brilliantly transforming ideas into pictorial representations. When I entered their space I was a kid in a candy shop.

Special mention to Kelly Alder, an illustrator whose skill in bringing concepts and stories to life is hardly comparable to any I have seen anywhere else. The many illustrations he did in my Monitor midyears make a book by themselves. His last two pieces, the Obama drawings, bring the president's storied history into the present with verve and meaning.

Administrative assistants: Allison Mikita, Laura Delano, Michael Dubois, and Caitria O'Neill made those blasted machines work, acting as skilled organizers,

399

typists, and wizards. Thank you for your editing, substantive research, and no hesitation in saying "Why don't you try to say it this way . . . ?"

Friends: Dinners with Sally Jackson and Paul Nace, Sib and Judy Wright, and Dick and Polly La Brie, taking place with embarrassing frequency in their homes, never failed to circle back to progress on the book. This wonderful group, with careers and backgrounds different from my own, never failed to lead me in new and interesting directions, for which I thank them.

Family: To my seven children, five biological—Matthew, Marcia, Richard, Jessica, and Pamela—and two step, Melissa and Sam, I offer my infinite gratitude for helping me keep "growing up." Raised to develop their own spirits, who they've each become never ceases to amaze me.

ABOUT THE AUTHOR

Over the past fifty years, **David Kantor, Ph.D.,** has been instrumental in bringing his unique model and counseling expertise to families, couples, organizations, leaders, and interventionists as they work to achieve success through generative relationships with others.

David began his career as a clinical psychologist and lecturer in Harvard University's Department of Social Relations. From 1965 to 1975, he was an assistant professor of clinical psychiatry at Tufts University School of Medicine and served as the director of psychological research and later as chief psychologist at Boston State Hospital. He also founded and became director of the Boston Family Institute, the first systems training program in Massachusetts; the Kantor Family Institute; and the Center for Training in Family Therapy at Boston State Hospital.

David has also served as a charter member of the American Family Therapy Association; an approved supervisor, clinical member, and fellow of the American Association of Marriage and Family Therapy; a diplomate of the American Board of Family Psychology; and an editor and referee for the *Journal of Family Process*. In the 1980s and 1990s, David began introducing his models to businesses, top-level executives, and organizational consultants, among them Arthur D. Little, Innovation Associates, MIT's Dialogue Project, Origins, and Dialogos. From 2000 to 2009, David served as a thought leader and partner at Monitor Group, where he developed innovative products, such as Leadership Model Building, a leadership development program; Observation Deck, speech-coding software; and the Kantor Profiles, a suite of assessment instruments.

During his career, David has trained over a thousand systems interventionists and has written dozens of articles and several books, including research-based *Inside the Family* (coauthored with William Lehr; Jossey-Bass, 1975, and Meredith Winter Press, 2003) and *My Lover, Myself* (Riverhead Books, 1999), producing a rich breadth of work that grounds his communication theories and practices today. David feels that his most important contributions to organizational theory and practice spring from two sources: his meta-model (model of models) and his trainees themselves.

INDEX

Page references followed by *fig* indicate an illustrated figure; followed by *t* indicate a table.

A

The abandoner, 217

Abandonment trigger, 370–371, 376

Absence of empathy, 245–246

Accelerating Team Performance (ATP): ClearFacts's adoption of, 296; description of, 265; Duncan's version of, 301–303; how leader's profile constrains, 303–304; Ralph's application for model-building, 297–307. *See also* Leadership model

Accenture, 160

Ackerman, Mona, 235

Acting in the room, definition of, 121

Action archetypes: compliance archetypes, 40; courteous compliance, 40, 238–239, 254; covert opposition, 40; description of, 39; point-counterpoint, 39

Action sequences: Art's unexpected outburst and, 34–38; description of, 35; evolution and context of, 36*fig*; move-oppose-move-follow example of, 35

Action stance examples: of speech acts, affect domain, and, 53; of speech acts and Level I, 24–32, 35–38; of speech acts, Level II communication domains, and, 49–50, 53–57; of speech acts, meaning domain, and, 57; of speech acts, power domain, and, 56

Action stance insights: on knowing your most used action stances, 44–45; on outbursts at ClearFacts, 43–44; on reading the room, 46–47; on structures of action stances in different contexts, 45

Action stances: during Art's unexpected outburst, 27–34; bystanding to read the room for, 40–43; of ClearFacts meeting in Ralph's absence, 110–119; ClearFacts team domains and, 59–62; description of, 9; the four-player model of, 9, 23–47; high-stakes structural dynamics and, 176; from insights to action regarding, 44–47; intro to bystand, 9, 25; intro to follow, 9, 24, 25; intro to move, 9, 23–24, 25; intro to oppose, 9, 24, 25; intro to pure, compound, and mixed, 26–27; required for effective communication, 43; structures, sequences, and patterns of, 34–40. *See also specific action stance*; Speech acts

Action structures: Art's unexpected outburst and, 34–38; evolution and context of, 36*fig*; structural pattern, 35

Adjudicator moral posture, 202–206

Advocate moral posture, 202–206

Affect domain: behavioral profiles in, 120–122; characteristics of, 52–53*fig*, 54; description of, 9, 49; examples of speech act, stance, and, 53; mismatched closed versus open, 186*fig*; Obama's talent for infusing meaning with, 364; private voices and, 171*t*, 172*t*, 173*t*; productive communication interface between Martha and Ralph using, 65; strengths and weaknesses of, 58–59*fig*

The Age of Turbulence (Greenspan), 258

Albom, Mitch, 321

Alinsky, Saul, 373, 374–375

Alive in Time (Kantor), 321, 322

Alter, Jonathan, 366, 375, 377

Andersen, Arthur, 158, 160

Animal Farm (Orwell), 241

Apple, 95, 152

Archetypal structural patterns: compliance archetypes, 40; courteous compliance, 40, 238–239, 254; covert opposition, 40; point-counterpoint, 39

Argyris, Chris, 308

Arrogance-humility balance: leader capacity for, 344–345; maintaining confidence while maintaining, 346

Arthur Andersen, LLP, 158, 160, 246

Arthur, Frederick, 373

Arthur (or Art): behavioral profile of, 120–122; ClearFacts meeting in Ralph's absence and role of, 110–122; connecting accomplished by, 340–341; introduction to ClearFacts's director of marketing, 4, 23; latest ClearFacts

weekly meeting and role of, 50–52, 60; leader capacities and contributions of, 356–357*t*; mismatched communication between ClearFacts team members and, 186*fig*; moves, follows, opposes, and bystander roles taken by, 33–34, 41*fig*; preference for open systems by, 84, 88; Ralph's behavioral impact on, 269; resignation of, 294–295; response to Ralph's Bomb by, 81, 101; speech acts and stances by, 24–25; stances and domains preference of, 59–62; unexpected outburst at ClearFacts by, 27–38, 41*fig*, 43–44; at work and at home, 19*fig*

Articulating narrative purpose, 346–347

Art's unexpected outburst: action structures, action sequences, and structural patterns of, 34–38; Art at home with Jane after, 44; behavioral tendencies during, 32–34; bystanding to read the room during, 40–43; first sequence ("business plus strategy") of, 29–30; a prior moment between Art and Howard, 43; second sequence ("business plus strategy" transition to "culture plus people") of, 30–31; speech act and description of, 27–29; third sequence ("culture plus people") of, 31–32

The Ascent of Money: A Financial History of the World (Ferguson), 153

Attitudes toward difference, 177

Audience effect, 306

Authors Guild, 237

Autonomy stage of model building, 290*fig*–291, 306–307

B

Bachus, Spencer, 378

Bear Stearns, 154, 158

Behavioral profiles: acting in the room ability and, 121; of Barack Obama, 362–366; of the coach and their clients, 312–313; consciously expanding your repertoire, 267–268; how childhood stories impact, 11–12, 130–149; how communication is impacted by, 11; how Ian's behavior is impacted by his, 109–110; how the ATP model handles leader's, 303–304; importance of understanding your, 109–110; insights into model-building process and your, 308–309; insights into using, 123–124; private voices and, 171t–173t; relevance to high-stakes structural dynamics, 176–177; remedies for correcting mismatched, 357; revealed during ClearFacts meeting in Ralph's absence, 119–121; stories behind a, 131; tendency toward fraud, 253–257. *See also* Heroic leaders; The shadow behaviors; *specific level of structural dynamics*

Behavioral Propensities Profile (BPP), 267, 298, 302, 385–386

Behavioral tendencies (Level I): Art's unexpected outburst, 32–34; for fraud, 253–257; strong behavioral tendency, 32; stuck behavioral tendency, 32; weak behavioral tendency, 32

Bell System, 91, 95

Berardino, Joe, 160

bin Laden, Osama, 382, 383, 384

Birthers, 375

Born, Brooksley, 258, 292

Boundaries: closed system, 90; open system, 86

Brandeis, Louis D., 205

Breakdown-breakthrough story: Gordon Murray's, 316–317; models for living and, 319–320

The Bridge (Remnick), 363, 366

Buckley, William F., Jr., 374–375

Bush, George, 375

Business mismatches: closed affect versus open affect, 186*fig*; closed meaning versus open/random meaning, 186*fig*; closed power versus random power, 185*fig*; description and famous examples of, 184; remedies for correcting, 357

Butts, Cassandra, 363

Bystander action stance: Barack Obama's, 362–363, 377–378, 381; description of, 9, 25; meaning domain and, 11; speech act, affect domain, and, 53; speech act, meaning domain, and, 57; speech act, power domain, and, 56. *See also* Action stances; Reading the room

C

Capacity for responsible self-evolution, 17

Carroll, James, 221

Casebook of Marital Therapy, 130

Cassandra of Troy, 220

Catholic Church, 157

Cayne, James, 154

Chad (Ralph's roommate), 272–273

Change: narrative purpose impacted by, 157–158; rise and fall of Arthur Andersen through leadership, 158, 160; theory of, 287–288, 301, 310, 322, 372; theory of practice applied to, 288, 310–311, 322, 372

Cheney, Dick, 377

Childhood stories: Barack Obama's formative, 366–367*fig*; description and behavioral impact of, 11–12, 130–149; disclosing your, 271; insight into behavioral profile of Ian, 122; insight into choice of domains by Ian, 67–69;

Childhood stories *(continued)*
   insight into Ralph's system preference,
   98–99; insights on importance of, 149–
   150; issues regarding coaches' eliciting,
   342; knowing the self through
   personal, 343; linking structure-
   forming stories and, 271–273; of
   Martha and Lance's marital
   relationship, 134–145; narrative
   purpose of, 151–166; narrative
   structure of, 133; of perfect love and
   imperfect love, 131–134, 137–140,
   248–249; Ralph's relationship with
   women and men based on his, 272–
   273; on Ron's shadow, 146–149; seven
   features of mythically toned, 133–134;
   understanding Howard's fraud
   through adult and, 247–253; young-
   adult hero myth ("When I Grow Up"),
   134, 145, 207, 208. *See also* Level IV
   (identity and structured behavior);
   Narrative structure; Stories
Christensen, Clayton, 163
Circular causal reasoning, 82
Civil Rights Act (1964), 153
ClearFacts crisis: background on TJ's
   character relevant to the, 196–197;
   events following return from Asia,
   199–200; events leading into the, 193–
   196; Ian and Duncan's experience in
   Asia, 197–199; insider-outsider
   complex during, 194, 200–202; moral
   postures and heroic modes during,
   224t; structural dynamics on enemy
   "other" during, 200–202
ClearFacts latest weekly meeting:
   examining the stances and domains of,
   50–52, 59–62; surprise at the end of
   the, 69–73
ClearFacts leadership model: adoption of
   moral, 232–233; model building

process for, 292–307; move from
   personal model to, 265–278
ClearFacts meeting in Ralph's absence:
   behavioral profiles revealed during,
   119–121; speech acts, stance, domain,
   and system of, 110–119
ClearFacts story: Art's departure from
   ClearFacts, 294–295; Art's unexpected
   outburst, 27–39, 41*fig*, 43–44;
   capacities of individual leadership
   team members, 347–357; ClearFacts's
   narrative purpose, 161–164; closed-
   system preferences at, 92–93; the crisis
   mounts at ClearFacts, 193–202;
   Howard's fraud, 231, 247–257;
   introduction to main characters of the,
   1–6; latest weekly meeting, 50–52,
   59–62, 69–73; Martha's eruption, 168–
   170, 201–202; mismatches and
   resulting high-stakes situation in,
   185*fig*–186*fig*; moral postures and
   heroic modes of, 224t; moving from
   personal to leadership model, 265–278;
   open-system preferences at, 88; Ralph's
   Bomb, 79–83, 88, 92–93, 96–101;
   stances and domains across the
   ClearFacts team, 59–62; team members
   at work and at home, 19*fig*
ClearFacts team capacities: Arthur
   Saunders, 356–357; Howard Green,
   351t–352; Ian Maxwell, 349–351;
   Martha Curtis, 352–354; Ralph
   Waterman, 347–349t; Ron Stuart,
   354–356. *See also* Twenty leader
   capacities
Clinton, Bill, 241, 362, 364
Clinton, Hillary, 362, 383
Closed systems: characteristics of, 88–92;
   definition of, 10; domain of power
   preference for, 11; Ian and Howard's
   general preference for, 84, 88, 92–93;

preferences at ClearFacts for, 92–93; private voices and, 171t; story opener suggesting, 132

Co-opting the inner circle, 239–241

Coaches: behavioral profiles of clients and their, 312–313; eliciting childhood stories of love, 342; getting stuck in Level II (communication domains), 75–76; having their own models, 311–312; insights on developing a leadership model, 279; narrative purpose suggestions for, 166; operating systems issues for, 106–107; reading the room for high-stakes situations, 192

Coaching: connectedness/connecting encouraged through, 340–341; emphasizing the value the intimate partners, 342; models used for, 311–312, 343; overcoming hesitation to incorporate Level IV into your, 339–343; personal stories used in, 129–130; role of love and empathy in, 339–340; why empathy matters in, 340; why so much focus on fraud in, 343

Coaching structural dynamics: stage 1: functional awareness, 16, 266–278; stage 2: system awareness, 16, 345; stage 3: moral awareness, 16–17, 305–306, 345–346; stage 4: responsible self-evolution, 17

Coca-Cola, 161

Coles, R., 305

Collective intelligence, 296

Communication: all four action stances required for effective, 43; behavioral profiles and effective, 11; collective intelligence competency for effective, 296; how models drive, 12; Level I: action stances, 9, 23–47; Level II: communication domains, 9–10, 49–78;

Level III: operating systems, 10–11, 79–107; Level IV: childhood stories, 11–12; structural levels of, 8fig–12. See also Cross-model conversations; Language

Communication domains: of ClearFacts meeting in Ralph's absence, 110–119; of the ClearFacts team, 59–62; ClearFacts weekly meeting and use of, 50–52, 59–62, 69–73; description of, 9–10, 49–50; examples of speech act, stance and, 49–50; high-stakes structural dynamics and, 177; insights into effective use of, 76–78; intro to affect domain, 9, 49; intro to meaning domain, 9, 50; intro to power domain, 9, 50; propensities toward different, 62; strengths and weaknesses of each, 58–59fig; trilingual use of, 65–67; where coaches can get stuck using, 75–76. See also specific domain

Communication interface: becoming trilingual, 66–67; description of, 62–63; example of positive Martha and Ralph, 65; between trilingual leaders, 65–66fig; between two individuals, 63–65

Communication problems: of attitudes toward difference in cross-model conversation, 177; between Martha and Ian, 64fig; mismatched language and resulting high-stakes situations, 185fig–186fig; unseen influence of structural dynamics as causing, 7

Communicative competency, definition of, 13

Compliance archetypes, 40

Compound action stance, 26–27

Compromising with others, 344

Confidence, 346

Confucius, 233

Connectedness/connecting: Arthur's experience his team and, 340–341; Howard's failure to, 341; leader capacity for, 344; Sonia's dilemma between independence versus, 330–331; as source of love and intimacy, 342; systematically developed through stories, 131. *See also* Love

Constraint stage of model building, 289–290*fig*

Constraints: definition of, 286; how Ralph's moral integrity functions as model-building, 305–306; model building and definition of, 286; Ralph's model-building phase of, 303

Contemplative time, 322

Corporate culture: ATP on establishing learning as part of, 302; Bell System, 91; evolution of change in, 102; influence of celebrity culture on, 207; memories making up, 242, 259; model-building and role of, 284*fig*; moral corruption of, 239, 256; structural pattern of group's, 35; transition from business plus strategy to people plus, 30–31. *See also* Organizations

Courteous compliance archetype, 40, 238–239, 254

Cover-ups, 245

Covert opposition archetype, 40

Crises: ClearFacts moral postures and heroic modes during, 224*t*; examining structural dynamics of, 200–202; the fixer heroic type during, 194*fig*, 206, 209*fig*–213; heroic square-offs in times of, 221–224*t*; insights on dealing with, 226–229; knowing your behavior during, 273–274; leader capacity for operating under pressure during, 345; mounting ClearFacts, 193–200;

postures of moral justice during, 202–206; the protector heroic type during, 194*fig*, 206, 217–221; shadow work and why it is needed for, 224–227; the survivor heroic type during, 194*fig*, 206, 213–217; three heroic types in, 194*fig*. *See also* High-stakes situations

Cross-model conversations: constraints and practice of, 286; description and issues related to, 12, 177; social models and, 282; uses of, 283. *See also* Communication

The Crucible (Miller), 217, 380

Culture. *See* Corporate culture

Curtis, Lance. *See* Lance

Curtis, Martha. *See* Martha

D

Dark sides: functional awareness of, 16; Jung's concept of the shadow and, 207. *See also* The shadow

Darrow, Clarence, 206

"Davos" (World Economic Forum), 161

De Pree, Max, 154

Debs, Eugene, 205, 213

Deception story theme, 134, 142–144

Defender-advocates, 218

Deliberative democracy, 373

Democratic National Convention (2004), 384

Deviation: closed system ways of managing, 90–91; open system ways of managing, 87–88; random system ways of managing, 95

Dewey, John, 373

Different "other." *See* "Other" structural dynamics

Disfavor story theme, 134, 142–144

Displayed model, 283–284*fig*

Domains. *See* Communication domains

Dominant heroic mode, 208

Dreams from My Father (Obama), 366, 369, 380

Du Bois, W.E.B., 373

Duncan: Accelerating Team Performance (ATP) version used by, 301–303; Art's unexpected outburst and role of, 27–38; asked to help create a leadership model, 265–278; ClearFacts crisis and role of, 193–202; as ClearFacts team member, 19fig; ClearFacts weekly meeting and role of, 50–52, 60–62, 71–73; helping to interpret Martha's childhood stories, 137–145; introduction to ClearFacts's coach, 2, 3, 4–5; on Martha's eruption, 170; model-building with Ralph, 292–294, 297–307; perspective of Duncan-Ralph relationship by, 15; Ralph's Bomb debrief by, 81–82, 96–100; shift in role from observer to facilitator, 232–233; on stance and domain preference of ClearFacts team, 59–62; as survivor hero, 219; working on Ralph's awareness to improve high-stakes situations, 179–181

Dysfunctional closed system, 91–92

Dysfunctional open system, 88

Dysfunctional random systems, 95–96

E

Eat, Pray, Love (Gilbert), 320

Edwards, Elizabeth, 240–241

Edwards, John, 240, 241, 255

Ellison, Ralph, 373

Empathy: absence of, 245–246; as critical to good moral judgment, 245; Obama's ability to express, 364, 382; tendency toward fraud and absence of, 254–255; why it matters, 340

Empowerment paradox, 238

Enemy and "other": how empathy impacts perception of, 246; structural dynamics of the, 200–202

Enron scandal (2001), 246

Escalations: drivers of, 183–184; noise and impact on, 184

Euripides, 221

The Examined Life (Novick), 321

Excessive ambition, 256

Executive Wisdom (Kilburg), 158, 305

F

Family insider-outsider shifts, 201–202

Fanon, Franz, 373

Fastow, Andrew, 246

Fear of dying, 335–336

Feedback loops: closed and open system mechanisms of, 87, 90; control devices in, 83; increasing output with positive, 82–83; leader solicitation of feedback through, 344; as protecting moral integrity, 234–235; reduced output with negative, 83

Feedback mechanisms: closed system, 90; open system, 87

Ferguson, Niall, 153

Final Accounting (Toffler), 305

Five Leadership Pathways, 295

The fixer hero: characteristics and behaviors of, 209fig–213; fixer-protector pairing, 222; fixer-survivor pairing, 223–224; overview of heroic leader modes including, 206–209

Follow action stance: during Art's unexpected outburst, 27–34; description of, 9, 24; speech act, affect domain, and, 53; speech act, meaning domain, and, 57; speech act, power domain, and, 56. *See also* Action stances

Forgetting history, 241–242

Forster, E. M., 340

Fortune magazine's 2010 list of best managed companies, 154

Fortune magazine's 2010 list of most admired companies, 152

Four-player model. *See* Level I (four-player model of action stances)

Frank, Barney, 375, 377, 378

Frank (Howard's uncle), 249–250, 254

Frankl, Victor, 215

Fraud: characteristics showing tendency toward, 253–257; ClearFacts story on Howard's, 231, 247–257; coaching focus on, 343; "fraudster" character of TJ's, 196–197; Howard's childhood stories for understanding his, 247–253; Madoff's ponzi, 235–236. *See also* Moral corruption

French Revolution (1789), 241

Friedman, Milton, 291

From insight to action: on behavioral profiles, 123–124; on childhood stories, 149–150; on dealing with crisis, 226–229; on Level I: action stances, 44–47; on Level II: communication domains, 76–78; on Level III: operating systems, 104–107; on model-building, 308–314; on models for living, 336–337; on moral leadership and corruption, 259–261; on narrative purpose, 164–166; on personal and leadership model building, 278–279; on twenty leader capacities, 358–359

Functional awareness: applying to your relationships, 277–278; Ralph's current personal model and, 266–277; what happens during stage of, 16

Functional closed systems, 91–92

Functional open system, 88

Functional random systems, 95–96

G

Gaddafi, Muammar, 213

Game Change (Heilemann and Halperin), 361, 362

Gawande, Atul, 102

Giffords, Rep., 364

Giffords speech, shooting at (2011), 364, 376, 382, 384

Giuliani, Rudolph, 253

Goldie, Dan, 316

Goldman Sachs, 315

Google, 157

Google Books, 237

Gould, Jay, 213

Gourevitch, Philip, 213

Great Recession (2008), 157, 256, 315, 383

Green, Christina Taylor, 382

Green, Howard. *See* Howard

Greenberg, Alan C., 154, 291–292

Greenspan, Alan, 258

Guilt story theme, 134, 142–144

H

Halperin, Mark, 361

Hart, Gary, 241

Harvard Business Review, 74, 163, 383

Harvard Law Review, 205, 364

Hayward, "Big Bill," 213

Heilemann, John, 361

Hemingway, Ernest, 215

Herman Miller, 154

Heroic leaders: ClearFacts crisis and emergence of, 193–200; fixer-protector pairing, 222; fixer, survivor, and protector modes taken by, 206–221; fixer-survivor pairing, 223–224; insights into, 226–229; moral justice postures taken by, 202–206; Obama's moral posture and choice of, 375–377; showing tendency toward fraud by choice of, 253–254; square-offs modes taken in times of crisis by, 221–224*t*; structural dynamics on enemy "other" by, 200–202; survivor-protector pairing, 222–223; why shadow work is needed by, 224–226. *See also* Behavioral profiles; Leaders

Heroic modes of leaders: ClearFacts moral postures and, 224*t*; dominant heroic mode of, 208; the fixer, 206, 209*fig*–213; light, gray, and dark zones of, 208–209; overview of the three, 206–209; the protector, 206, 217–221, 376; the survivor, 206, 213–217, 376

Heroic self, 134, 145

High-stakes behaviors: Barack Obama's tendencies and, 375–379; insights into your own, 189–191; six phenomena of, 178–179; system in crisis due to, 178, 179*fig*; working on Ralph's awareness to improve, 179–181

High-stakes situations: ATP used for deepening skills in, 302–303; Barack Obama's tendencies during, 375–379; description of, 167; getting in touch with triggers for, 167–168; insights into, 189–192; knowing your behavior during, 273–274; leader capacity for operating under pressure during, 345; Martha's eruption, 168–170, 201–202; three types of moral posture in, 202–206; working on Ralph's awareness to prevent, 179–181. *See also* Crises; Organizations

High-stakes structural dynamics: between Martha and Howard, 187, 189; competing themes and their shadows impacting, 177–178; escalation of,

183–184; illustrated diagram of rising, 188*fig*; learning to listen to voices, 181–182; mismatches in a business setting, 184–187; noise impact on, 184; relevance of behavioral profiles to, 176–177; sender voices, receiver reactions, 182–183; six phenomena of, 178–179; stress and behaviors of, 178, 179*fig*; voices, themes, and triggers of, 170–178; watching shadows, 183; what makes them personal, 175–176

Hiring guidelines, 295–297

Hitler, Adolf, 213

Holmes, Oliver Wendell, Jr., 205

Holocaust, 201

Howard: Art's unexpected outburst and role of, 27–38, 41*fig*, 43; behavior under pressure, 251–252; behavioral profile of, 120–122; behind closed doors with TJ, 189, 257; choice of hero by, 249–250; ClearFacts crisis enemy role of, 193–202; ClearFacts meeting in Ralph's absence and role of, 110–122; failure to connect by, 341; high-stakes structural dynamics between Martha and, 187, 189; introduction to ClearFacts's director of sales, 4, 23; lack of empathy by, 254–255; leader capacities and contributions of, 351*t*–352; Martha's eruption at, 168–170, 201–202; mismatched communication between ClearFacts team members and, 186*fig*; preference for closed systems by, 84, 93; prosecutor moral posture taken by, 206; Ralph's behavioral impact on, 269–270; relationship between Vera and, 250–251; response to Ralph's Bomb by, 80–81, 101; sex and power in adult life of, 250–251; speech acts and stances preference of, 24–25; stances and

Howard *(continued)*
domains preference of, 59–62; as strong mover, follower, and opposer in different contexts, 33; understanding moral corruption of fraud by, 231, 247–257; weekly ClearFacts meeting and role of, 59–60, 69–73; at work and at home, 19*fig*

Howard's End (Forster), 340

Huffington Post, 235

Hughes, Langston, 373

Humility-arrogance balance: leader capacity for, 344–345; maintaining confidence while maintaining, 346

Hunter, Rielle, 240

The hurtful monarch story, 133, 141–142

Hussein, Saddam, 213

I

Ian: Art's unexpected outburst and role of, 27–38; blended prosecutor and adjudicator moral postures taken by, 206; as branded leader prototype, 353; childhood story insight into behavioral profile, 122; childhood story insight into choice of domains by, 67–69; ClearFacts crisis and role of, 193–202; ClearFacts meeting in Ralph's absence and role of, 110–122; communication interface between Martha and, 63–65; communication problems between Martha and, 64*fig*; failed marriage of, 122; how his behavioral profile impacts his behavior, 109–110, 120–121, 122; insider-outsider shift on TJ's status by, 202; introduction to ClearFacts's CFO and COO, 3–4, 23; leader capacities and contributions of, 349–351; mismatched communication between ClearFacts team members and, 185*fig*, 186*fig*; preference for closed systems by, 84, 92; Ralph's behavioral impact on, 270; response to Ralph's Bomb by, 80–81, 101; speech acts and stances by, 24–25; as strong mover, 33; weekly ClearFacts meeting and role of, 50–52, 59–62, 69–73; at work and at home, 19*fig*

IBM, 155

Ideal mate story, 134, 145

Identity: Barack Obama's quest for, 368–375; high-stakes situations and role of, 175–176; insights on childhood stories and, 149–150; Ron's childhood story on awakening of an, 148–149; understanding how love is linked to, 128–129; the "When I Grow Up" hero and emerging sense of, 145. *See also* Level IV (identity and structured behavior)

Ignatieff, Michael, 322

Imagining possibilities, 346

Imitation stage of model building, 289, 290*fig*

Imperfect love story: childhood stories on sexual abuse and/or, 248–249; description of, 131–134; Martha's childhood story revealing, 137–140

Information access: closed system, 90; open system, 86

Insider-outsider shifts, 194, 200–202

Intimate partners, 342, 342

The Investment Answer (Murray and Goldie), 315, 316

J

Jane: following Art's outburst and at home with, 44; as Ian's wife, 19*fig*

Jobs, Steve, 184

Johns Hopkins University, 129

Johnson & Johnson Tylenol crisis (1982), 153–154

Johnson, Lyndon B., 153
Jung, Carl, 207

K

Kent, Muhtar, 161
Kilburg, Richard, 17, 129, 130, 158, 305
King, Martin Luther, Jr., 213, 217, 377
Kloppenberg, James, 364, 366, 373–374
Knowing the self, 343

L

Lance: as husband of Martha, 2, 101; insider-outsider shift of Martha and, 202; past and present stories of, 136–137; ritual impasse of relationship of Martha and, 38–39, 176; stories of relationship with wife Martha, 134–145
Language: Barack Obama's preference for meaning domain, 363–365; effective communication requiring common, 158; leader ability to tolerate differences in, 344; mismatches and resulting high-stakes situation, 185*fig*–186*fig*. *See also* Communication
Lani (Ron's Fiancée), 187
Law, Cardinal Bernard, 242–243
Leaders: as being great in face-to-face talk, 20; capacity for responsible self-evolution by, 17; communicative competency by, 13; cultural shift in ideologies regarding, 361–362; expectations demanded of, 13; in high-stakes situations, 167–192; how systems thinking benefits, 101–103; insights on developing a leadership model, 279; insights on model-building for, 308–314; moral corruption in, 231–261; narrative purpose suggestions for, 165; operating systems and leadership issues for, 107;

self-assessment of your moral and heroic choices, 227–228; self-assessment of your shadows, 229; structural dynamics of Barack Obama as a, 339; trilingual capacity of, 65–67; twenty leader capacities of, 343–347, 358–359, 382–384; unifying the love and work schism of today's, 14; why shadow work is necessary for, 224–226. *See also* Heroic leaders
Leadership: moral, 153–154, 232–233, 345–346; moral challenges and means of correction, 233–236; rise and fall of Arthur Andersen through, 158, 160
Leadership Is an Art (De Pree), 154
Leadership model: building ClearFacts 292–307; ClearFacts's model-building process, 292–307; ClearFacts's move from personal to, 265–278; insights on establishing and using, 278–279; personal, model for living, and, 317*fig*. *See also* Accelerating Team Performance (ATP); Models; Personal model
Leadership system, 102
Leadership teams: Art's departure from ClearFacts, 294–295; capabilities of individual ClearFacts team members, 349–357; guidelines for hiring onto a, 295–297; insights on model-building for your, 313; leader abilities for managing, 346; structural dynamics on performance of, 385–386
Legitimate constraint, 258
Lehman Brothers, 155
Level I (four-player model of action stances): bystanding to read the room using, 40–43; of ClearFacts meeting in Ralph's absence, 110–119; description of, 9, 23; examining action structures, action sequences, and structural

Level I *(continued)*
patterns using, 34–40; examining Art's unexpected outburst at ClearFacts using, 27–39, 43–44; examining behavioral tendencies at Level I using, 32–34; high-stakes structural dynamics and, 176; insights from using the, 44–47; on move, follow, oppose, bystand action stances, 23–25; on pure, compound, and mixed actions, 26–27; on voice of a speech act, 25–26. *See also* Behavioral profiles; Models

Level II (communication domains): affect domain, 9, 49, 52–54, 58–59*fig*; of ClearFacts meeting in Ralph's absence, 110–119; ClearFacts weekly meeting and use of, 50–52, 59–62, 69–73; description of, 9–10, 49–50; high-stakes structural dynamics and, 177; insights into effective use of, 76–78; meaning domain, 9, 50, 54–58*fig*; power domain, 9, 50, 54–56, 58–59*fig*; propensities toward different domains, 62; value of all three domains of, 58–59*fig*; where coaches can get stuck, 75–76. *See also* Behavioral profiles

Level III (operating systems): of ClearFacts meeting in Ralph's absence, 110–119; during ClearFacts meeting in Ralph's absence, 110–119; closed system, 10, 11, 83–84, 88–93; description of, 10–11, 79; high-stakes structural dynamics and, 177; how leaders benefit from understanding, 101–103; insights into, 104–107; open system, 10, 11, 83–84, 85*fig*–88, 92; Ralph's Bomb, 79–83, 88, 92–93, 96–101; random system, 10, 83–84, 93*fig*–100; recognizing preferences for systems, 84–85; three types of system, 10, 83–84; understanding systems approaches in general, 82–83. *See also* Behavioral profiles

Level IV (identity and structured behavior): childhood stories of love, 131–134; childhood story's narrative structure, 140–145; description of, 127–128; how identity is linked to love, 128–129; insights into using childhood stories, 149–150; overcoming hesitation to incorporate into model of coaching, 339–343; ritual fight of Martha and Lance, 134–140; shadows, 145–149, 177–178, 183; stories component of, 11, 129–131. *See also* Childhood stories; Identity; Stories

Limits on speech: closed system, 90; open system, 86–87; random system, 94

Lives of Moral Leadership (Cole), 305

Longing for ideal mate story, 134, 145

Love: childhood stories on sexual abuse and/or imperfect, 248–249; connectedness as source of intimacy and, 342; high-stakes situations and role of, 176; imperfect love story, 131–134, 137–140, 248–249; importance of discussing, 339–340; insights on childhood stories of, 149–150; perfect love story, 131–134; relationship between identity and, 128–129; schism between work and, 14; "shadow" putting you in touch with disappointment in, 145–149; survivor hero choosing the cause over, 216. *See also* Connectedness/connecting

M

Mack, Kenneth W., 364

Madoff, Bernard L., 235, 254–255

Madoff's ponzi fraud, 235–236

Making Change Happen (Kantor), 15

Malcolm X, 373

Mandela, Nelson, 214

Man's Search for Meaning (Frankl), 215

Martha: Art's unexpected outburst and role of, 27–38; "Cassandra syndrome" of, 220; ClearFacts crisis and role of, 193–202; ClearFacts meeting in Ralph's absence and role of, 110–122; ClearFacts weekly meeting and role of, 50–52, 69–73; communication interface between Ian and, 63–65; communication problems between Ian and, 64*fig*; eruption by, 168–170, 201–202; high-stakes structural dynamics between Howard and, 187, 189; insider-outsider shift of Lance and, 202; introduction to ClearFacts's HR director, 2, 23; leader capacities and contributions of, 352–354; mismatched communication between Ian, Howard, and, 186*fig*; as mover with an opposing edge, 33; open affect behavioral profile of, 110, 120–122; positive communication interface between Ralph and, 65; preference for open systems by, 84, 88, 92, 93; prosecutor moral posture taken by, 206; Ralph's behavioral impact on, 269; response to Ralph's Bomb by, 80–81, 101; ritual impasse of relationship of Lance and, 38–39, 176; speech acts and stances by, 24–25; stances and domains preference of, 59–62; stories of relationship with husband Lance, 134–145; at work and at home, 19*fig*

Martha's stories: childhood Stories and features, 137–145; Lance's Past and Present, 136–137; The Quarrel, 134–136

Martyr (survivor hero), 213, 217

Maura (Ian's ex-wife), 122

Maxwell, Ian. *See* Ian

McCain, John, 375, 377

McNamara, Robert, 256

Meaning domain: Barack Obama's preference for, 363–365, 381; behavioral profiles in, 120–122; characteristics of, 56–57*fig*, 58; description of, 9, 50; example of speech act, stance, and, 57; mismatched closed versus open/random, 186*fig*; Obama on interface of meaning and power in, 364; private voices and, 171*t*, 172*t*, 173*t*; productive communication interface between Martha and Ralph using, 65; strengths and weaknesses of, 58–59*fig*

Measured time, 322

Medea story, 221

Melancholic disappointment story, 134, 144

Melville, Herman, 246

Mentors, 357

Meta-model (model of models), 286, 300–301, 372–373

Mideast uprisings (2010-11), 157

Miller, Arthur, 217, 380

Mismatches. *See* Business mismatches

Mixed action stance, 26–27

Moby-Dick (Melville), 246

Model building: defining constraints for, 286; description of, 283, 285; essential message for leaders on, 308; failure of Greenspan's, 291–292; insights into, 308–314; leader capability for, 344; of personal models, 267–279; by Ralph and Duncan, 292–294, 297–307; three stages of, 289–291

Model-building process: Duncan's version of ATP for, 301–303; how a leader's profile constrains, 303–304; how clients or team constrain leader's,

Model-building process (continued) 304–305; how Ralph's moral integrity functions as constraint, 305–306; learning by doing, 297–299; overview of the, 284fig, 285–286; Ralph's constraint phase of, 303; Ralph's meta-models used for, 300–301

Model-building stages: autonomy, 290fig–291, 306–307; constraint, 289–290fig; imitation, 289, 290fig

Models: clashes between, 12; coaching, 311–312, 343; cross-model conversations and social, 12, 282; definition of, 12, 281; displayed, 283–284fig; functions of, 281–282; leadership, personal, and model for living, 317fig; meta-model (model of models), 286, 300–301, 372–373; practice, 155. See also Leadership model; Level I (four-player model); Personal model; Theories

Models for living: breakdown-breakthrough story and, 316–317, 319–320; building a, 320–322; description of the, 317fig–319; insights into building, 337; perils of success to, 318; Ralph and Sonia's building a life worth living through, 322–336; temporal anxiety and, 319; theories of the thing, of change, and of practice, 321–322; timefulness practice for, 321

Moral awareness: leader capacity for, 345–346; Ralph's moral integrity as model-building constraint, 305–306; what happens during stage of, 16–17

Moral compromise, 255

Moral corruption: examining Howard's fraud and, 231, 247–257; good models that go bad and end in, 257–258; hourglass of moral corruptors and, 236fig–247; importance of recognizing, 231–232; insights on how to avoid, 259–261; ten dimensions or indicators tending toward fraud and, 253–257. See also Fraud

Moral corruption indicators: absence of empathy, 254–255; behavioral profile, 253; choice of hero, 253–254; evidence of moral compromise, 255; excessive ambition and aggressive striving, 256; narcissism, 255; not knowing and admitting no error, 242–244, 255–256; proneness to insidious forms of courteous compliance, 254; weak intimate ties, 257

Moral corruptors: absence of empathy, 245–246; co-opting the inner circle, 239–241; courteous compliance, 40, 238–239, 254; empowerment paradox, 238; external events, 237; face-to-face structures, 237; forgetting history, 241–242; hourglass diagram of verbal interaction, 236fig; individual structures, 242; not admitting error, 245, 255–256; "not knowing," 242–244, 255–256; recklessness, 246–247; reverence for power, 245; silencing the witnesses, 241, 256; unquestioning loyalty to the chief, 244–245

Moral integrity: insights on model-building and, 313–314; leader capacity for, 345–346; model-building constraint of Ralph's, 305–306

Moral intelligence, 261

Moral justice postures: Barack Obama's hero choice and, 375–377; ClearFacts heroic modes and, 224t; overview of the three, 202–206; three types in high stakes situations, 203t–204t

Moral leadership: capacity for, 345–346; challenges and means of correction, 233–236; ClearFacts's adoption of, 232–233, 258–259; Duncan's focus on creating ClearFacts, 232–233; feedback loops used to protect, 234–235; insights on, 259–261; Johnson & Johnson's example of, 153–154; models of, 257–258; need to increase understanding of, 257

Moral story, 346

Moral voice, 184

Morgan, J. P., 213

Move action stance: during Art's unexpected outburst, 27–34, 41*fig*; description of, 9, 23–24; Obama's Bush-era White House meeting adoption of, 377–378; speech act, affect domain, and, 53; speech act, meaning domain, and, 57; speech act, power domain, and, 56. *See also* Action stances

Muir, John, 218

Murray, Gordon, 315–316

The Music of Silence (Steindl-Rast), 321–322

My Lover, Myself (Kantor), 129, 130

Myers-Briggs Type Indicator, 207

N

Narcissism, 255

Narrative purpose: broken, 159*fig*; clarity of purpose aspect of, 152–153; description of, 151–152; how to build and secure a, 160–161; illustrated diagram of broken, 159*fig*; insights into, 164–166; leader ability to articulate, 346–347; a moral, social dimension aspect of, 153–154; obstacles without and within that impact, 157–158; presence or absence of, 155–160; Ralph's and ClearFacts,' 161–164; a shareable big picture aspect of, 154; an underlying practice model aspect of, 155

Narrative structure: description of, 133; of Martha's childhood story, 140–145; seven recurring features of, 133–134. *See also* Childhood stories; Stories

National Right to Life Committee, 157

The Needs of Strangers (Ignatieff), 322

Nemesis, 175, 182

New Deal policies, 239

New York Times, 300, 315

New Yorker blog, 213

New Yorker magazine, 334

9/11, 200

Nixon, Richard, 212

Noise, 184

Not admitting error, 245, 255–256

"Not knowing," 242–244, 255–256

Novick, Robert, 321

O

Obama administration: in-fighting over the Afghanistan war (2010) by, 158; U.S. foreign policies of, 157

Obama, Barack: behavioral profile of, 362–366; challenges facing, 378–379, 384; empathy expressed by, 364, 382; exit memo from Duncan (aka David Kantor) to, 379–384; formative stories and behavior-triggering themes of, 366–371; Giffords shooting speech (2011) by, 364, 376, 382, 384; high-stakes tendencies of, 375–379; identity quest by, 368–375; structural dynamics analysis as a leader, 17, 339, 361–384; twenty leader capacities rating of, 358–359, 382–384

Obama, Michelle, 362, 371

Obama's behavioral profile: bystander stance, 362–363; language preference of meaning, 363–365; preference for open systems, 365–366, 381

Obama's formative stories: books which retell, 366; childhood story, 366–368*fig*; ongoing triggering themes of, 370–371; post-childhood stories in search of an adult identity, 368–370; the shadow in, 371

Obama's high-stakes tendencies: abandonment trigger and, 370–371, 376; Bush-era White House meeting and, 377–378; choosing between survivor and protector modes, 376; moral posture and hero choice, 375–377; political and personal attacks on Obama, 375

Obama's identity quest: cultivating his scholarly bent, 373; establishing theory of justice to frame his cause, 372–373; finding his racial identity, 371–372; framing his models of practice, 373–375; post-childhood stories in search of an adult identity, 368–370

The Old Man and the Sea (Hemingway), 215

Open systems: Art and Martha's general preference for, 84, 88, 92; Barack Obama's preference for, 365–366, 381; characteristics of, 85*fig*–88; definition of, 10; opposer domain preference for, 11; private voices and, 172*t*; story opener suggesting, 132

Operating systems: during ClearFacts meeting in Ralph's absence, 110–119; description and functions of, 10–11, 79; general understanding of systems approaches, 82–83; high-stakes structural dynamics and, 177; how leaders benefit from understanding, 101–103; how Ralph's Bomb disrupts the, 79–83, 88, 92–93, 96–101; insights into, 104–107; intro to closed, 10, 11, 83–84; intro to open, 10, 11, 83–84; intro to random, 10, 83–84; recognizing preferences for different types of, 84–85; story openers and suggested, 132; three types of, 10, 83–84. *See also specific type of operating system*; Systems thinking

Oppose action stance: during Art's unexpected outburst, 27–34, 41*fig*; courteous compliance ostracizing, 40, 238–239, 254; description of, 9, 24; speech act, affect domain, and, 53; speech act, meaning domain, and, 57; speech act, power domain, and, 56. *See also* Action stances

Optimizing ability, 346

Organization stories: building and securing narrative purpose for, 160–161; clarity of purpose aspect of, 152–153; moral and social dimension of, 153–154; practice model underlying the, 155; presence or absence of narrative purpose in, 155–160; shareable big picture aspect of, 154; understanding narrative purpose of, 151–152

Organizations: broken narrative purpose of, 159*fig*; common language of, 158; leader capacity for managing, 345; leader vision for, 346; narrative purpose of stories of, 152–160, 346–347. *See also* Corporate culture; High-stakes situations

Orientation: closed system, 89; open system, 85*fig*, 86; random system, 94

Orwell, George, 241

"Other" structural dynamics: description of, 194, 200–202; expanding your tolerance for difference, 275; how empathy impacts, 246; of successful intimacy, 340

O'Toole, Fintan, 243

P

Partner intimacy, 342

Pasternack, Boris, 315

Patterns: definition of, 7, 11; leader capacity for recognizing, 345; recognizing model clashes and their repetitive, 270–271; team speech act, 11

Patton, George S., 222, 253

Paulsen, Hank, 375, 378

Paulson, Henry, 377

Pelosi, Nancy, 378

People access: closed system, 90; open system, 86

Perfect love story, 131–134

Personal model: ClearFacts's move to leadership model from, 265–278; description of, 12; leadership, model for living, and, 317*fig*; legitimate constraint to, 258; Madoff's fraud as product of his, 235–236; moral corruption when good models go bad, 257–258; Ralph's current functional awareness and, 266–277. *See also* Leadership model; Models

Personal model building: consciously expanding your behavioral profile repertoire, 267–268; disclosing your childhood stories and themes, 271; expanding your tolerance for difference, 275; identifying and taking responsibility for your shadow, 274–275; insights on, 278–279; knowing your behavior in high stakes and crises, 273–274; linking childhood story and structure-forming stories, 271–273; linking work and personal relationships, 275–277; recognizing and taking responsibility for your impacts on others, 268–270; recognizing model clashes and their repetitive patterns, 270–271; taking Behavioral Propensities Profile (BPP), 267, 298, 302

Planned Parenthood, 157

Point-counterpoint escalation, 39

Point-counterpoint structural pattern, 39–40

The Politician (Young), 240

"Ponderosa Boys" (Lehman Brothers), 155

Ponzi, Charles, 235

Power: Obama on interface of meaning and, 364; reverence for, 245; self-assessing your relationship to, 259–260

Power domain: behavioral profiles in, 120–122; characteristics of, 54–56; description of, 9, 49; example of speech act, stance, and, 56; mismatched closed versus random, 185*fig*; private voices and, 171*t*, 172*t*, 173*t*; productive communication interface between Martha and Ralph using, 65; strengths and weaknesses of, 58–59*fig*

The Power of Now: A Guide to Spiritual Enlightenment (Tolle), 320

Practice model: description of, 155; leader capability for building, 344; Obama's framing of his, 373–375; theory of practice and, 288, 310–311, 322, 372

Present time, 322

Primary mover, 303

Private voices: behavioral profiles and, 171*t*–173*t*; our high-stakes, 170–171, 174

Problematic tendencies, 242

The Promise (Alter), 366, 375, 377

Prosecutor moral posture, 202–206

The protector hero: characteristics and behavior of, 217–221; fixer-protector pairing, 222; Obama's choice of survivor and, 376; overview of heroic leader modes including, 206–209; survivor-protector pairing, 222–223

Pure action stance, 26–27

R

Rabbit Hill Inn (Vermont), 331

Ralph: Art's resignation meeting with, 294–295; Art's unexpected outburst and role of, 27–38; brought in as ClearFacts's CEO, 18, 23; "Building a Green Economy Is the Most Alluring Challenge of the 21st Century" article written by, 74; building a model for living with Sonia, 322–336; childhood stories impacting relationship with men and women, 272–273; childhood story roots of random system preference by, 98–99; ClearFacts crisis debriefing by Duncan for, 195; ClearFacts meeting in Ralph's absence and role of, 110–119; as ClearFacts team member at work and home, 19fig; ClearFacts weekly meeting and role of, 50–52, 60–62, 69–73; coaching perspective of Duncan-Ralph relationship, 15; current functional awareness and personal model, 266–277; first meeting with Ron, 73–75; on his fear of dying, 335–336; introduction to ClearFacts's CEO, 1–6, 11; leader capacities and contributions of, 347–349t; leadership model for ClearFacts instituted by, 232–233, 258–259, 292–307; Martha's eruption and role of, 168–170; mismatched communication between Ian and, 185fig; model-building by, 292–294, 297–307; moving ClearFacts from personal to leadership model, 265–278; narrative purpose of, 161–164; positive communication interface between Martha and, 65; preference for random systems by, 84, 96–99; preventing high-stakes situations by working on awareness, 179–181; Ralph's Bomb role by, 79–82, 96–101; random meaning profile of, 110; relationship between Sonia and, 2, 62; Sonia reining in, 232–233, 273; Sonia's warning about Ron to, 75; speech acts and stances by, 24–25; stance and domain preference of, 59–62; as strong mover, 33; as survivor hero, 213, 216. See also Sonia

Ralph's Bomb: debriefing by Duncan on impact of, 81–82, 96–100; how Ron fared after, 101; responses to, 80–81; on Ron Stuart's demands, 79

Rand, Ayn, 291–292

Random systems: characteristics of, 93fig–96; description of, 10, 83–84; private voices and, 173t; Ralph's preference for, 84, 96–99; story opener suggesting, 132

Rawls, John, 373

Reading Obama (Kloppenberg), 366, 373–374

Reading the room: ClearFacts story on, 1–6; coaching perspective of, 15–17; insights into high-stakes situations and, 191–192; insights on behavioral profiles for, 124; insights on childhood stories for, 150; insights on communication domains for, 77–78; insights on four action stances for, 46–47; insights on operating systems used for, 106; for structural patterns of interaction as a bystander, 40–43. *See also* Bystander action stance; Structural dynamics

Realities: addressing social interaction, 13–14; damage of life, 14

Recession (2008), 157, 256, 315, 383

Rechtschaffen, Stephen, 322

Recklessness, 246–247

Reflective time, 322

Remnick, David, 363, 365, 366

Resonant themes: description of, 134; of Martha's childhood stories, 142–144; shades of anger and resulting, 143*fig*

Responsible self-evolution: leader capacity for, 17; what happens during stage of, 17

Reverence for power, 145

The Rise and Fall of Bear Stearns (Greenberg), 154

Risk-taking capacity, 345

Ritual impasse, 38–39, 176

Robinson, Michelle, 372

Rockefeller, John D., 213

Ron: childhood shadow story of, 146–149; ClearFacts meeting in Ralph's absence and role of, 110–119; first meeting with Ralph, 73–75; introduction to, 18, 73; leader capacities and contributions of, 354–356; Ralph's behavioral impact on, 269; Ralph's Bomb on demands by, 79–83, 88, 92–93, 96–101; role in high-stakes structural dynamics between Martha and Howard, 187, 189

Roosevelt, F. D., 239

Rubin, Robert, 258

S

Sadness story theme, 134, 142–144

Sam (Howard's brother), 248, 249, 250, 251, 252, 257

Saunders, Arthur. *See* Arthur (or Art)

Saunders, Jane. *See* Jane

Schön, Donald A., 308

Sculley, John, 184

September 11th, 200

Sequences, definition of, 7, 11

The shadow: Barack Obama and, 371; being aware of, 183; as buried memory of betrayed child, 145–146; of competing themes impacting high-stakes situation, 177–178; identifying and taking responsibility for your, 274–275; Jung's concept of, 207; Ron's story on, 146–149; why we need to understand, 224–226. *See also* Dark sides

The shadow behaviors: of fixer hero, 212–213; functional awareness of, 16; of protector hero, 221; self-assessment of your, 229; of survivor hero, 216–217. *See also* Behavioral profiles

Shadow dance, 222

Silencing witnesses, 241, 256

The silent conspirator story, 133, 142

Smith, Adam, 373

Soliciting feedback, 344

Sonia: building a model for living with Ralph, 322–336; her connection versus independence dilemma, 330–331; reining in Ralph, 216, 273; relationship between Ralph and, 2, 62; taking Ralph on needed vacation, 232–233; warning to Ralph about Ron, 75; working on high-stakes situations between Ralph and, 179–180. *See also* Ralph

Spacek, Leonard, 160

Speech act examples: of affect domain, stance, and, 53; during Art's unexpected outburst, 27–38;

Speech act examples (continued)
of Level I action stances and,
24–32, 35–38; of Level II
communication domains and, 49–50,
53, 57; of meaning domain, stance,
and, 57; of power domain, stance,
and, 56; of productive communication
interface between Martha and
Ralph, 65
Speech act structure: illustrated diagram
showing levels of, 8fig; Level I: action
stances, 9, 23–27; Level II:
communication domains, 9–10; Level
III: operating systems, 10–11; Level IV:
childhood stories, 11–12
Speech acts: acting in the room ability
to execute the right, 121; of ClearFacts
meeting in Ralph's absence,
110–119; description of, 7; four
levels of structure, 8fig–12; sequences
and patterns of, 7, 11, 270–271,
345; team patterns of, 11; the voice
of a, 25–26. See also Action
stances
Spitzer, Eliot, 205, 206, 253
Spousal intimacy, 342
Stalin, Joseph, 213
Stances. See Action stances
Steindl-Rast, David, 322
Stewart, Martha, 243
Stories: Barack Obama's post-childhood
search of adult identity, 368–370;
behind behavioral profiles, 131;
breakdown-breakthrough, 316–317,
319–320; coaching role of personal,
129–130; knowing the self through
personal, 343; leader ability to tell, 346;
linking childhood stories and
structure-forming, 271–272; making
sense of the world through, 130; of
Martha and Lance's marital
relationship, 134–145; narrative
purpose of, 151–166, 346–347;
operating systems indicated by openers
of, 132; organization, 151–166; the
power of, 11; seven features of
mythically toned, 133–134; structure
versus moral, 346; systematic
development through connections,
131; understanding Howard's fraud
through his, 247–253. See also
Childhood stories; Level IV (identity
and structured behavior); Narrative
structure
Storytelling ability, 346
Structural dynamics: analysis of Barack
Obama as a leader, 17, 339, 361–384;
coaching perspective of teaching,
15–17; for discerning universal
structures of conversations, 6–7; leader
behavior in high-stakes situations,
167–192; on leader crisis response to
enemy "other," 200–202; linking work
and personal relationships, 276–277;
origins and description of, 6; "other,"
194, 200–202, 246, 275, 340; on speech
as an act, 7–12; on team performance,
385–386; on three postures of moral
justice, 202–206. See also Reading the
room
Structural dynamics analysis: examining
Barack Obama's leadership using, 17,
339, 361; exit memo from Duncan
(aka David Kantor) to Obama, 379–
384; Obama's behavioral profile, 362–
366; Obama's formative stories, 366–
371; Obama's high-stakes tendencies,
375–379; Obama's identity quest,
371–375
Structural dynamics model: behavioral
profiles of, 11–12, 109–110, 119–124,
131; Level I: four-player model, 9,

23–47, 110–119; Level II: communication domains, 9–10, 49–78, 110–119; Level III: operating systems, 10–11, 79–103, 110–119; Level IV: identity and structured behavior, 11, 127–150, 339–343

Structural dynamics theory: future empirical testing of the, 386; origins of, 385; value of understanding and using the, 385–386. *See also* Theories

Structural patterns: archetypal, 39–40; bystanding to read the room for, 40–43; description of, 35; evolution and context of, 36*fig*; how behaviors are molded by, 38–39; ritual impasse of, 38–39

Structure story, 346

Stuart, Ron. *See* Ron

Summers, Larry, 258

The survivor hero: characteristics and behavior of, 213–217; fixer-survivor pairing, 223–224; Obama's choice of protector and, 376; overview of heroic leader modes including, 206–209; survivor-protector pairing, 222–223

System awareness: leader capacity for, 345; what happens during stage of, 16

System thinking benefits: guiding development and change, 102; "having a life," 103; improved problem solving and decision making, 102–103; increasing capacity to communicate with multiple audience, 103; leadership system development, 102

Systems thinking: circular causal reasoning role in, 82; control devices in feedback loops, 83; description of, 10; how leaders benefit from, 101–103; negative feedback loops that reduce output of, 83; positive feedback loops impacting output of, 82–83. *See also* Operating systems

T

Team profiles: of ClearFacts leadership team, 349–357; insights into, 124

Teams. *See* Leadership teams

Template Jones. *See* TJ (Template Jones)

Temporal anxiety, 319

Terry (TJ and Howard's assistant), 198

Themes: Barack Obama's ongoing triggering, 370–371; definition of, 174; disclosing your childhood stories and their, 271; high-stake situations and competing, 177–178; resonant story, 134, 142–144; ten universal, 174–175; toxic, 175; triggering receiver reactions, 182–183

Theories: constraints generated by, 286; theory of change, 287–288, 301, 310, 322, 372; theory of justice, 372, 372–373; theory of practice, 288, 310–311, 322, 372; theory of the thing, 286–287, 309, 321–322, 372–373. *See also* Models; Structural dynamics theory

Teresa, Mother, 218

Three Stallions Inn (Vermont), 329

Time: four conceptions of, 322; timefulness practice for experiencing, 321

Time-shifting (Rechtschaffen), 322

Timefulness practice, 321
TJ (Template Jones): background on "fraudster" character of, 196–197; behind closed doors with Howard, 189, 257; ClearFacts crisis enemy role of, 193–202; corruption of power by, 212; insider-outsider shift of, 202; introduction to, 70
Tkaczyk, Christopher, 152
Tocqueville, Alexis de, 373
Toffler, Barbara Ley, 305
Tononi, Giulio, 300, 301
Tough Choices (Toffler), 305
Toxic themes, 175
Travis, Duncan. *See* Duncan
Tribe, Lawrence, 373
Trilingual communication domains: leaders with the ability for, 65–66; process of becoming competent in, 66–67
The truant hero story, 134, 144–145
Tuesdays with Morrie (Albom), 321
Twenty leader capacities: acting morally, 345–346; articulating narrative purpose, 346–347; balancing arrogance and humility, 344–345; Barack Obama's rating in, 358–359, 382–384; building a practice model, 344; compromising with others, 344; connecting with others, 344; imaging possibilities, 346; insights into, 358–359; knowing the self, 343; maintaining confidence, 346; managing organizations, 345; managing teams, 344; mobilizing energy and morale, 346; operating under pressure, 345; optimizing, 346; recognizing patterns, 345; soliciting feedback, 344; storytelling, 346; taking risks, 345; tolerating language differences, 344; understanding systems, 345. *See also* ClearFacts team capacities
"Tyranny of process," 93
"Tyranny of the monarch," 92

U

An Unmarried Woman (film), 328
Unquestioning loyalty, 244–245

V

Values: closed system, 89–90; open system, 86; random system, 94
Vanderbilt, Cornelius, 213
Vera (relationship with Howard), 250–251, 257
Victimization, 221
Vietnam War, 256
Vision: articulating narrative purpose and, 346–347; leader capacity for imagining possibilities and, 346
Voices: behavioral profiles and private, 171t–173t; escalation driven by one's moral, 184; high-stakes situations and receiver reactions to sender, 182–183; improving high-stakes situations by listening to, 181–182; our high-stakes private, 170–171, 174

W

The Warning (PBS Frontline documentary), 258
Waterman, Ralph. *See* Ralph
Waterman, Sonia, 2, 62.

Watson, Thomas J., Jr., 155

Weak intimate ties, 257

"What Good Is Wall Street? Mostly What Investment Bankers Do Is Socially Worthless" (*New Yorker*), 334

The "When I Grow Up" (young-adult) hero myth, 134, 145, 207, 208

William, James, 373

Wilson, Joe, 370

Work: linking personal relationships and, 275–276; schism between love and, 14

Wright, Frank Lloyd, 281

Wright, Reverend, 384

Wright, Richard, 373

Y

Young-adult hero myth, 134, 145, 207, 208

Young, Andrew, 240